Microsoft Exchange 2010 PowerShell Cookbook

Manage and maintain your Microsoft Exchange 2010 environment with Windows PowerShell 2.0 and the Exchange Management Shell

Mike Pfeiffer

[PACKT] enterprise 🞲
PUBLISHING
professional expertise distilled

BIRMINGHAM - MUMBAI

Microsoft Exchange 2010 PowerShell Cookbook

First published: July 2011

Production Reference: 1150711

Published by Packt Publishing Ltd.
32 Lincoln Road
Olton
Birmingham, B27 6PA, UK.

ISBN 978-1-849682-46-6

www.packtpub.com

Cover Image by Artie Ng (artherng@yahoo.com.au)

Credits

Author
Mike Pfeiffer

Reviewers
Jason Helmick
Shay Levy
Robert Martin
Anderson Patricio

Acquisition Editor
Kerry George

Development Editor
Gaurav Mehta

Technical Editors
Neha Damle
Joyslita D'Souza
Aditi Suvarna

Project Coordinator
Zainab Bagasrawala

Proofreader
Lucy Henson

Indexer
Monica Ajmera Mehta

Production Coordinator
Melwyn D'sa

Cover Work
Melwyn D'sa

About the Author

Mike Pfeiffer has been in the IT field for over 13 years, spending most of his time as an enterprise consultant focused on Active Directory and Exchange implementation and migration projects. He is a Microsoft Certified Master on Exchange 2010, and a Microsoft Exchange MVP. You can find his writings online at `mikepfeiffer.net`, where he blogs regularly about Exchange Server and PowerShell-related topics.

I'd like to thank my wife Abby and my daughter Isabel for their love, support, and patience with me while I was locked away in my office writing this book. I'd also like to thank the technical reviewers, Jason Helmick, Shay Levy, Anderson Patricio, and Robert Martin for their hard work, dedication, and contributions to the technical community.

About the Reviewers

Jason Helmick is an instructor at Interface Technical Training and has spent 19 years as an IT professional including experience with enterprise-level infrastructure and systems deployment, e-commerce, and n-tier software development and management.

Jason specializes in PowerShell and Exchange. He and Mike Pfeiffer are the founders and hosts of the Arizona PowerShell User Group (http://www.azposh.com).

You can check out Jason's blog at http://www.jasonhelmick.com or you can catch him on twitter at @thejasonhelmick.

> To my loving wife and daughter, thanks for making the work easy. To Mike Pfeiffer, thanks for making an awesome book! To Jeffrey Snover, thanks for creating PowerShell.

Shay Levy is a Windows PowerShell MVP and System Administrator for a government institute in Israel. He has worked with Microsoft platforms for more than 20 years, focusing on Microsoft Exchange and Active Directory.

As a long time PowerShell community supporter, he has become a moderator of multiple forums and a co-director of the PowerShellCommunity.org website.

He is the creator of the popular PowerShell Community browser toolbar, a one-stop shop for various PowerShell resources such as downloads, webcasts, videos, podcasts, and more. He often covers PowerShell-related topics on his blog http://PowerShay.com. You can also follow him on Twitter at http://twitter.com/ShayLevy.

Robert Martin has been in the IT Industry for over 15 years and is a senior consultant specializing in VMware and Exchange. Robert has achieved several certifications over the years, demonstrating his commitment to the industry. Among others, his certifications include VCP3, VCP4, MCSA, CCNA, CNA, CCA, A+, and HP Accredited Platform Specialist. Robert dedicates much of his time to automating daily tasks and tasks of his peers in PowerShell and C#. In addition, Robert maintains a VMware, Exchange, and PowerShell blog as his way of sharing solutions to daily tasks with other administrators.

Robert currently works for Choice Hotels International in Phoenix, AZ. For more information about Robert Martin or the scripts he contributes, visit his blog at http://robertwmartin.com.

Anderson Patricio is an Exchange MVP and works as a messaging consultant for clients located in the South and North America. He has been working with Exchange since version 5 of the product and he has had the opportunity to use PowerShell since the beta release (code name Monad at that time).

Anderson is a TechEd presenter in South America and he has an exchange resource site in Portuguese with several articles about Exchange, PowerShell, and Active Directory and he also publishes monthly articles at MSExchange.org in English.

He is the reviewer of *Windows PowerShell in Action* by Bruce Payette and *PowerShell in Practice* by Richard Siddaway.

www.PacktPub.com

Support files, eBooks, discount offers and more

You might want to visit www.PacktPub.com for support files and downloads related to your book.

Did you know that Packt offers eBook versions of every book published, with PDF and ePub files available? You can upgrade to the eBook version at www.PacktPub.com and, as a print book customer, you are entitled to a discount on the eBook copy. Get in touch with us at service@packtpub.com for more details.

At www.PacktPub.com, you can also read a collection of free technical articles, sign up for a range of free newsletters, and receive exclusive discounts and offers on Packt books and eBooks.

http://PacktLib.PacktPub.com

Do you need instant solutions to your IT questions? PacktLib is Packt's online digital book library. Here, you can access, read, and search across Packt's entire library of books.

Why subscribe?

- ▸ Fully searchable across every book published by Packt
- ▸ Copy and paste, print, and bookmark content
- ▸ On demand and accessible via web browser

Free access for Packt account holders

If you have an account with Packt at www.PacktPub.com, you can use this to access PacktLib today and view nine entirely free books. Simply use your login credentials for immediate access.

Instant updates on new Packt books

Get notified! Find out when new books are published by following @PacktEnterprise on Twitter, or the *Packt Enterprise* Facebook page.

Table of Contents

Preface

The book is full of immediately-usable task-based recipes for managing and maintaining your Microsoft Exchange 2010 environment with Windows PowerShell 2.0 and the Exchange Management Shell. The focus of this book is to show you how to automate routine tasks and solve common problems. While the Exchange Management Shell provides hundreds of cmdlets, we will not cover every single one of them individually. Instead, we'll focus on common, real-world scenarios. You'll be able to use these recipes right away, allowing you to get the job done quickly, and the techniques that you'll learn will allow you to write your own amazing one-liners and scripts with ease.

What this book covers

Chapter 1, *PowerShell Key Concepts*, introduces several PowerShell core concepts such as command syntax and parameters, working with the pipeline, and flow control with loops and conditional logic. The topics covered in this chapter lay the foundation for the code samples in the following chapters.

Chapter 2, *Exchange Management Shell Common Tasks*, covers day-to-day tasks and general techniques for managing Exchange from the command line. Topics include configuring manual remote shell connections, exporting reports to external files, sending e-mail messages from scripts, and scheduling scripts to run with the Task Scheduler.

Chapter 3, *Managing Recipients*, demonstrates some of the most common recipient-related management tasks, such as creating mailboxes, distribution groups, and contacts. You'll also learn how to manage server side inbox rules, Out of Office settings, and import user photos into Active Directory.

Chapter 4, *Managing Mailboxes*, shows how to perform various mailbox management tasks that include moving mailboxes, importing and exporting mailbox data, and detecting and repairing corrupt mailboxes. In addition, you'll learn how to delete and restore items from a mailbox and generate some basic reports.

Chapter 5, Distribution Groups and Address Lists, takes you deeper into distribution group management. Topics include distribution group reporting, distribution group naming policies, and allowing end users to manage distribution group membership. You'll also learn how to create Address Lists and Hierarchal Address Books.

Chapter 6, Mailbox and Public Folder Databases, shows how to set database settings and limits and configure Public Folder replication. Report generation for mailbox database size, average mailbox size per database, and backup status are also covered in this chapter.

Chapter 7, Managing Client Access, introduces the concept of Client Access Arrays and covers the creation and configuration of this key component in Exchange 2010. We'll also take a look at controlling connections from various clients, including ActiveSync devices.

Chapter 8, Managing Transport Servers, explains various methods used to control mail flow within your Exchange organization. You'll learn how to create send and receive connectors, allow application servers to relay mail, and manage transport queues.

Chapter 9, High Availability, covers the implementation and management tasks related to Database Availability Groups (DAGs). Topics include creating DAGs, adding mailbox database copies, and performing maintenance on DAG members.

Chapter 10, Exchange Security, introduces the new Role Based Access Control (RBAC) permissions model. You'll learn how to create custom RBAC roles for administrators and end-users, and also how to manage mailbox permissions and implement SSL certificates.

Chapter 11, Compliance and Audit Logging, covers the new compliance and auditing features included in Exchange 2010. Archive mailboxes and Discovery Search are covered here, as well as administrator and mailbox audit logging.

Chapter 12, Server Monitoring and Troubleshooting, shows you how to monitor and report on service availability and resource utilization using PowerShell core cmdlets and WMI. Event log monitoring and Exchange server role troubleshooting tactics are also covered.

Chapter 13, Scripting with the Exchange Web Services Managed API, introduces advanced scripting topics that leverage Exchange Web Services. In this chapter, you'll learn how to write scripts and functions that go beyond the capabilities of the Exchange Management Shell cmdlets.

Appendix A, provides a list of commonly-used automatic shell variables and type accelerators, along with a listing of scripts that are installed with Exchange 2010.

Appendix B, includes additional information about Advanced Query Syntax (AQS), which is used to perform queries when performing discovery searches, item restores, and item removal.

What you need for this book

To complete the recipes in this book, you'll need the following:

- ▶ PowerShell v2, which is already installed by default on Windows 7 and Windows Server 2008 R2.

- ▶ A fully operational lab environment with an Active Directory forest and Exchange organization.

- ▶ Ideally, your Exchange Servers will run Windows Server 2008 R2, but they can run Windows Server 2008 SP2, if needed.

- ▶ You'll need to have at least one Microsoft Exchange 2010 SP1 server.

- ▶ To work with the recipes in this book, you should be logged on with an account that is a member the Organization Management role group. The user account used to install Exchange 2010 SP1 is automatically added to this group.

- ▶ If possible, you'll want to run the commands, scripts, and functions in this book from a client machine. The 64-bit version of Windows 7 with the Exchange 2010 SP1 Management Tools installed is a good choice. You can also run the tools on Windows Vista. Each client will need some additional prerequisites in order to run the tools; see Microsoft's TechNet documentation for full details.

- ▶ If you don't have a client machine, you can run the management shell from an Exchange 2010 SP1 server.

- ▶ Chapter 13 requires the Exchange Web Services Managed API version 1.1, which can be downloaded from the following URL:
  `http://www.microsoft.com/download/en/details.aspx?id=13480`

The code samples in this book should be run in a lab environment and should be fully tested before deployed into production. If you don't have a lab environment set up, you can download a pre-configured Hyper-V virtual hard disk (VHD) from Microsoft. It includes a fully-functioning virtual environment with Exchange 2010 SP1 that can be evaluated for 180 days. You can download the files from the following URL:

`http://www.microsoft.com/download/en/details.aspx?id=5002`

Who this book is for

This book is for messaging professionals who want to learn how to build real-world scripts with Windows PowerShell 2.0 and the Exchange Management Shell. If you are a network or systems administrator responsible for managing and maintaining the on-premise version of Exchange Server 2010, then this book is for you.

The recipes in this cookbook touch on each of the core Exchange 2010 server roles and require a working knowledge of the supporting technologies, such as Windows Server 2008 or 2008 R2, Active Directory, and DNS.

All of the topics in the book are focused on the on-premise version of Exchange 2010 SP1, and we will not cover Microsoft's hosted version of Exchange Online through Office 365. However, the concepts you'll learn in this book will allow you to hit the ground running with that platform since it will give you an understanding of PowerShell's command syntax and object-based nature.

Conventions

In this book, you will find a number of styles of text that distinguish between different kinds of information. Here are some examples of these styles and an explanation of their meanings.

Code words in text are shown as follows: "We can read the content of an external file into the shell using the Get-Content cmdlet."

Commands and blocks of code are set as follows:

```
Get-Mailbox -ResultSize Unlimited | Out-File C:\report.txt
```

Commands like this can be invoked interactively in the shell, or from within a script or function.

Most of the commands you'll be working with will be very long. In order for them to fit into the pages of this book, we'll need to use line continuation. For example, here is a command that creates a mailbox-enabled Active Directory user account:

```
New-Mailbox -UserPrincipalName jsmith@contoso.com `
-FirstName John `
-LastName Smith `
-Alias jsmith `
-Database DB1 `
-Password $password
```

Notice that the last character on each line is the backtick (`` ` ``) symbol, also referred to as the grave accent. This is PowerShell's line continuation character. You can run this command as is, but make sure there aren't any trailing spaces at the end of each line. You can also remove the backtick and carriage returns and run the command on one line. Just ensure the spaces between the parameters and arguments are maintained.

You'll also see long pipeline commands formatted like the following example:

```
Get-Mailbox -ResultSize Unlimited |
  Select-Object DisplayName,ServerName,Database |
    Export-Csv c:\mbreport.csv -NoTypeInformation
```

PowerShell uses the pipe character (|) to send objects output from a command down the pipeline so it can be used as input by another command. The pipe character does not need to be escaped. You can enter the previous command as is, or you can format the command so that everything is on one line.

Any command-line input or output that must be done interactively at the shell console is written as follows:

```
[PS] C:\>Get-Mailbox administrator | ft ServerName,Database -Auto


ServerName Database
---------- --------
mbx1       DB01
```

New terms and **important words** are shown in bold. Words that you see on the screen, in menus or dialog boxes for example, appear in the text like this: "Open the Exchange Management Shell by clicking on **Start | All Programs | Exchange Server 2010.**"

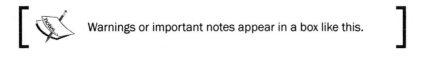

Warnings or important notes appear in a box like this.

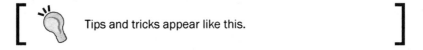

Tips and tricks appear like this.

Reader feedback

Feedback from our readers is always welcome. Let us know what you think about this book—what you liked or may have disliked. Reader feedback is important for us to develop titles that you really get the most out of.

To send us general feedback, simply send an e-mail to feedback@packtpub.com, and mention the book title via the subject of your message.

If there is a book that you need and would like to see us publish, please send us a note in the **SUGGEST A TITLE** form on www.packtpub.com or e-mail suggest@packtpub.com.

If there is a topic that you have expertise in and you are interested in either writing or contributing to a book, see our author guide on www.packtpub.com/authors.

Customer support

Now that you are the proud owner of a Packt book, we have a number of things to help you to get the most from your purchase.

Downloading the example code

You can download the example code files for all Packt books you have purchased from your account at `http://www.PacktPub.com`. If you purchased this book elsewhere, you can visit `http://www.PacktPub.com/support` and register to have the files e-mailed directly to you.

Errata

Although we have taken every care to ensure the accuracy of our content, mistakes do happen. If you find a mistake in one of our books—maybe a mistake in the text or the code—we would be grateful if you would report this to us. By doing so, you can save other readers from frustration and help us improve subsequent versions of this book. If you find any errata, please report them by visiting `http://www.packtpub.com/support`, selecting your book, clicking on the **errata submission form** link, and entering the details of your errata. Once your errata are verified, your submission will be accepted and the errata will be uploaded on our website, or added to any list of existing errata, under the Errata section of that title. Any existing errata can be viewed by selecting your title from `http://www.packtpub.com/support`.

Piracy

Piracy of copyright material on the Internet is an ongoing problem across all media. At Packt, we take the protection of our copyright and licenses very seriously. If you come across any illegal copies of our works in any form on the Internet, please provide us with the location address or website name immediately so that we can pursue a remedy.

Please contact us at `copyright@packtpub.com` with a link to the suspected pirated material.

We appreciate your help in protecting our authors, and our ability to bring you valuable content.

Questions

You can contact us at `questions@packtpub.com` if you are having a problem with any aspect of the book, and we will do our best to address it.

1
PowerShell Key Concepts

In this chapter, we will cover the following:

- ▶ Understanding command syntax and parameters
- ▶ Using the help system
- ▶ Understanding the pipeline
- ▶ Working with variables and objects
- ▶ Formatting output
- ▶ Working with arrays and hash tables
- ▶ Looping through items
- ▶ Using flow control statements
- ▶ Creating custom objects
- ▶ Creating PowerShell functions
- ▶ Creating and running scripts
- ▶ Setting up a profile

Introduction

So, your organization has decided to move to Exchange Server 2010 to take advantage of the many exciting new features such as integrated e-mail archiving, discovery capabilities, and high availability functionality. Like it or not, you've realized that PowerShell is now an integral part of Exchange Server management and you need to learn the basics and have a point of reference for building your own scripts. That's what this book is all about. In this chapter, we'll cover some core PowerShell concepts that will provide you with a foundation of knowledge for using the remaining examples in this book. If you are already familiar with PowerShell, you may want to use this chapter as a review or as a reference for later after you've started writing scripts.

If you're completely new to PowerShell, the concept may be familiar if you've worked with UNIX command shells. Like UNIX-based shells, PowerShell allows you to string multiple commands together on one line using a technique called pipelining. This means that the output of one command becomes the input for another. But, unlike UNIX shells that pass text output from one command to another, PowerShell uses an object model based on the .NET Framework, and objects are passed between commands in a pipeline, as opposed to plain text. From an Exchange perspective, working with objects gives us the ability to access very detailed information about servers, mailboxes, databases, and more. For example, every mailbox you manage within the shell is an object with multiple properties, such as an e-mail address, database location, or send and receive limits. The ability to access this type of information through simple commands means that we can build powerful scripts that generate reports, make configuration changes, and perform maintenance tasks with ease.

Performing some basic steps

To work with the code samples in this chapter, follow these steps to launch the Exchange Management Shell:

1. Log onto a workstation or server with the Exchange Management Tools installed.
2. Open the Exchange Management Shell by clicking on **Start | All Programs | Exchange Server 2010**.
3. Click on the **Exchange Management Shell** shortcut.

Understanding command syntax and parameters

Windows PowerShell provides a large number of built-in cmdlets (pronounced *command-lets*) that perform specific operations. The Exchange Management Shell adds an additional set of PowerShell cmdlets used specifically for managing Exchange. The Exchange Management Console, which is the graphical management tool for Exchange 2010, is built completely on top of these cmdlets and any operations performed within this tool are translated into PowerShell commands. We can also run these cmdlets interactively in the shell, or through automated scripts. When executing a cmdlet, parameters can be used to provide information, such as which mailbox or server to work with, or which attribute of those objects should be modified. In this recipe, we'll take a look at basic PowerShell command syntax and how parameters are used with cmdlets.

How to do it...

When running a PowerShell command, you type the cmdlet name, followed by any parameters required. Parameter names are preceded by a hyphen (-) followed by the value of the parameter. Let's start with a basic example. To get mailbox information for a user named `testuser`, use the following command syntax:

```
Get-Mailbox -Identity testuser
```

Downloading the example code

You can download the example code fles for all Packt books you have purchased from your account at `http://www.PacktPub.com`. If you purchased this book elsewhere, you can visit `http://www.PacktPub.com/support` and register to have the fles e-mailed directly to you.

Alternatively, the following syntax also works and provides the same output, because the `-Identity` parameter is a positional parameter:

```
Get-Mailbox testuser
```

Most cmdlets support a number of parameters that can be used within a single command. We can use the following command to modify two separate settings on the *testuser* mailbox:

```
Set-Mailbox testuser -MaxSendSize 5mb -MaxReceiveSize 5mb
```

How it works...

All cmdlets follow a standard verb-noun naming convention. For example, to get a list of mailboxes you use the `Get-Mailbox` cmdlet. You can change the configuration of a mailbox using the `Set-Mailbox` cmdlet. In both examples, the verb (Get or Set) is the action you want to take on the noun (Mailbox). The verb is always separated from the noun using the hyphen (-) character. With the exception of a few Exchange Management Shell cmdlets, the noun is always singular.

Cmdlet names and parameters are not case sensitive. You can use a combination of upper and lowercase letters to improve the readability of your scripts, but it is not required.

Parameter input is either optional or required, depending on the parameter and cmdlet you are working with. You don't have to assign a value to the `-Identity` parameter since it is not required when running the `Get-Mailbox` cmdlet. If you simply run `Get-Mailbox` without any arguments, the first 1,000 mailboxes in the organization will be returned.

 If you are working in a large environment with more than 1,000 mailboxes, you can run the `Get-Mailbox` cmdlet setting the `-ResultSize` parameter to `Unlimited` to retrieve all of the mailboxes in your organization.

Notice that in the first two examples we ran `Get-Mailbox` for a single user. In the first example, we used the `-Identity` parameter, but in the second example we did not. The reason we don't need to explicitly use the `-Identity` parameter in the second example is because it is a positional parameter. In this case, `-Identity` is in position 1, so the first argument received by the cmdlet is automatically bound to this parameter. There can be a number of positional parameters supported by a cmdlet, and they are numbered starting from one. Other parameters that are not positional are known as named parameters, meaning we need to use the parameter name to provide input for the value.

The `-Identity` parameter is included with most of the Exchange Management Shell cmdlets, and it allows you to classify the object you want to take an action on.

 The `-Identity` parameter used with the Exchange Management Shell cmdlets can accept different value types. In addition to the alias, the following values can be used: ADObjectID, Distinguished name, Domain\ Username, GUID, LegacyExchangeDN, SmtpAddress, and User principal name (UPN).

Unlike the `Get-Mailbox` cmdlet, the `-Identity` parameter is required when you are modifying objects, and we saw an example of this when running the `Set-Mailbox` cmdlet. This is because the cmdlet needs to know which mailbox it should modify when the command is executed. When you run a cmdlet without providing input for a required parameter, you will be prompted to enter the information before execution.

 In order to determine whether a parameter is required, named or positional, supports wildcards, or accepts input from the pipeline, you can use the `Get-Help` cmdlet which is covered in the next recipe in this chapter.

Multiple data types are used for input depending on the parameter you are working with. Some parameters accept string values, while others accept integers or Boolean values. Boolean parameters are used when you need to set a parameter value to either true or false. PowerShell provides built-in shell variables for each of these values using the $true and $false automatic variables.

> For a complete list of PowerShell v2 automatic variables, run Get-Help about_automatic_variables. Also see Appendix A for a list of automatic variables added by the Exchange Management Shell.

For example, you can enable or disable a send connector using the Set-SendConnector cmdlet with the -Enabled parameter:

```
Set-SendConnector Internet -Enabled $false
```

Switch parameters don't require a value. Instead they are used to turn something on or off, or to either enable or disable a feature or setting. One common example of when you might use a switch parameter is when creating an archive mailbox for a user:

```
Enable-Mailbox testuser -Archive
```

PowerShell also provides a set of common parameters that can be used with every cmdlet. Some of the common parameters, such as the risk mitigation parameters (-Confirm and -Whatif), only work with cmdlets that make changes.

> For a complete list of common parameters, run Get-Help about_CommonParameters.

Risk mitigation parameters allow you to preview a change or confirm a change that may be destructive. If you want to see what will happen when executing a command without actually executing it, use the -WhatIf parameter:

```
[PS] C:\>Get-Mailbox -Database DB1 | Remove-Mailbox -WhatIf
What if: Removing mailbox "uss.local/Users/Test User" will remove the Active
 Directory user object and mark the mailbox and the archive (if present) in
the database for removal.
[PS] C:\>_
```

When making a change, such as removing a mailbox, you'll be prompted for confirmation, as shown in the following screenshot:

```
Machine: MBX1.CONTOSO.COM                                          _ □ ×
[PS] C:\>Remove-Mailbox -Identity testuser

Confirm
Are you sure you want to perform this action?
Removing mailbox "testuser" will remove the Active Directory user object
and mark the mailbox and the archive (if present) in the database for
removal.
[Y] Yes  [A] Yes to All  [N] No  [L] No to All  [?] Help (default is "Y"):
```

To suppress this confirmation set the `-Confirm` parameter to `false`:

```
Remove-Mailbox testuser -Confirm:$false
```

Notice here that when assigning the `$false` variable to the `-Confirm` parameter that we had to use a colon immediately after the parameter name and then the Boolean value. This is different to how we assigned this value earlier with the `-Enabled` parameter when using the `Set-SendConnector` cmdlet. Remember that the `-Confirm` parameter always requires this special syntax, and while most parameters that accept a Boolean value generally do not require this, it depends on the cmdlet with which you are working. Fortunately, PowerShell has a great built-in help system that we can use when we run into these inconsistencies. When in doubt, use the help system, which is covered in detail in the next recipe.

Cmdlets and parameters support tab completion. You can start typing the first few characters of a cmdlet or a parameter name and hit the tab key to automatically complete the name or tab through a list of available names. This is very helpful in terms of discovery and can serve as a bit of a time saver.

In addition, you only need to type enough characters of a parameter name to differentiate it from another parameter name. The following command using a partial parameter name is completely valid:

```
Set-Mailbox -id testuser –Office Sales
```

Here we've used `id` as a shortcut for the `-Identity` parameter. The cmdlet does not provide any other parameters that start with `id`, so it automatically assumes you want to use the `-Identity` parameter.

Another helpful feature that some parameters support is the use of wildcards. When running the `Get-Mailbox` cmdlet, the `-Identity` parameter can be used with wildcards to return multiple mailboxes that match a certain pattern:

```
Get-Mailbox -id t*
```

In this example, all mailboxes starting with the letter `t` will be returned. Although this is fairly straightforward, you can reference the help system for details on using wildcard characters in PowerShell by running `Get-Help about_Wildcards`.

There's more...

Parameter values containing a space need to be enclosed in either single or double quotation marks. The following command would retrieve all of the mailboxes in the *Sales Users* OU in Active Directory. Notice that since the OU name contains a space, it is enclosed in single quotes:

```
Get-Mailbox -OrganizationalUnit 'contoso.com/Sales Users/Phoenix'
```

Use double quotes when you need to expand a variable within a string:

```
$City = 'Phoenix'
Get-Mailbox -OrganizationalUnit "contoso.com/Sales Users/$City"
```

You can see here that we first create a variable containing the name of the city, which represents a sub OU under *Sales Users*. Next, we include the variable inside the string used for the organizational unit when running the Get-Mailbox cmdlet. PowerShell automatically expands the variable name inside the double quoted string where the value should appear and all mailboxes inside the *Phoenix* OU are returned by the command.

 Quoting rules are documented in detail in the PowerShell help system. Run Get-Help about_Quoting_Rules for more information.

See also

- ▶ *Using the help system*
- ▶ *Working with variables and objects*

Using the help system

The Exchange Management Shell includes over 600 cmdlets, each with a set of multiple parameters. For instance, the New-Mailbox cmdlet accepts up to 50 parameters, and the Set-Mailbox cmdlet has over 120 available parameters. It's safe to say that even the most experienced PowerShell expert would be at a disadvantage without a good help system. In this recipe, we'll take a look at how to get help in the Exchange Management Shell.

How to do it...

To get help information for a cmdlet, type Get-Help, followed by the cmdlet name. For example, to get help information about the Get-Mailbox cmdlet, run the following command:

```
Get-Help Get-Mailbox -full
```

How it works...

When running `Get-Help` for a cmdlet, a synopsis and description for the cmdlet will be displayed in the shell. The `Get-Help` cmdlet is one of the best discovery tools to use in PowerShell. You can use it when you're not quite sure how a cmdlet works or what parameters it provides.

You can use the following switch parameters to get specific information using the `Get-Help` cmdlet:

- ▶ **Detailed**: The detailed view provides parameter descriptions and examples and uses the following syntax:

  ```
  Get-Help <cmdlet name> -Detailed
  ```

- ▶ **Examples**: You can view multiple examples of how to use a cmdlet by running the following syntax::

  ```
  Get-Help <cmdlet name> -Examples
  ```

- ▶ **Full**: Use the following syntax to view the complete contents of the help file for a cmdlet:

  ```
  Get-Help <cmdlet name> -Full
  ```

Some parameters accept simple strings as input, while others require an actual object. When creating a mailbox using the `New-Mailbox` cmdlet, you'll need to provide a secure string object for the `-Password` parameter. You can determine the data type required for a parameter using `Get-Help`:

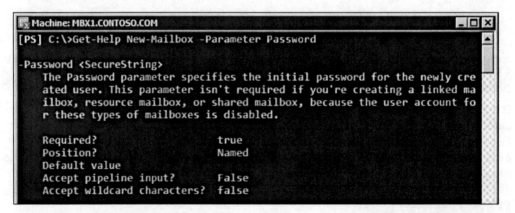

You can see from the command output that we get several pieces of key information about the `-Password` parameter. In addition to the required data type of `<SecureString>`, we can see that this is a named parameter. It is required when running the `New-Mailbox` cmdlet and it does not accept wildcard characters. You can use `Get-Help` when examining the parameters for any cmdlet to determine whether or not they support these settings.

You could run Get-Help New-Mailbox -Examples to determine the syntax required to create a secure string password object and how to use it to create a mailbox. This is also covered in detail in the recipe titled *Adding, modifying, and removing mailboxes* in *Chapter 3, Managing Recipients*.

There's more...

There will be times when you'll need to search for a cmdlet without knowing its full name. In this case, there are a couple of commands you can use to find the cmdlets you are looking for.

To find all cmdlets that contain the word "mailbox", you can use a wildcard, as shown in the following command:

```
Get-Command *Mailbox*
```

You can use the -Verb parameter to find all cmdlets starting with a particular verb:

```
Get-Command -Verb Set
```

To search for commands that use a particular noun, specify the name with the -Noun parameter:

```
Get-Command -Noun Mailbox
```

The Get-Command cmdlet is a built-in PowerShell core cmdlet, and it will return commands from both Windows PowerShell as well as the Exchange Management Shell. The Exchange Management Shell also adds a special function called Get-Ex command that will return only Exchange specific commands.

In addition to getting cmdlet help for cmdlets, you can use Get-Help to view supplemental help files that explain general PowerShell concepts that focus primarily on scripting. To display the help file for a particular concept, type Get-Help about_ followed by the concept name. For example, to view the help for the core PowerShell commands type the following:

```
Get-Help about_Core_Commands
```

You can view the entire list of conceptual help files using the following command:

```
Get-Help about_*
```

Don't worry about trying to memorize all the Exchange or PowerShell cmdlet names. As long as you can remember Get-Command and Get-Help, you can search for commands and figure out the syntax to do just about anything.

Getting help with cmdlets and functions

One of the things that can be confusing at first is the distinction between cmdlets and functions. When you launch the Exchange Management Shell, a remote PowerShell session is initiated to an Exchange server and specific commands, called proxy functions, are imported into your shell session. These proxy functions are essentially just blocks of code that have a name, such as `Get-Mailbox`, and that correspond to the compiled cmdlets installed on the server. This is true even if you have a single server and when you are running the shell locally on a server.

When you run the `Get-Mailbox` function from the shell, data is passed between your machine and the Exchange server through a remote PowerShell session. The `Get-Mailbox` cmdlet is actually executing on the remote Exchange server, and the results are being passed back to your machine. One of the benefits of this is that it allows you to run the cmdlets remotely regardless of whether your servers are on-premise or in the cloud. In addition, this core change in the tool set is what allows Exchange 2010 to implement its new security model by allowing and restricting which cmdlets administrators and end-users can actually use through the shell, the management console, or the web-based control panel.

We'll get into the details of all this throughout the remaining chapters in the book. The bottom line is that, for now, you need to understand that, when you are working with the help system, the Exchange 2010 cmdlets will show up as functions and not as cmdlets.

Consider the following command and output:

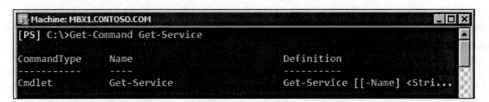

Here we are running `Get-Command` against a PowerShell v2 core cmdlet. Notice that the `CmdletType` shows that this is a `Cmdlet`.

Now try the same thing for the `Get-Mailbox` cmdlet:

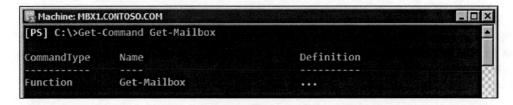

And as you can see, the `CommandType` for the `Get-Mailbox` cmdlet shows that it is actually a `Function`. So, there are a couple of key points to take away from this. First, throughout the course of this book, we will refer to the Exchange 2010 cmdlets as cmdlets, even though they will show up as functions when running Get-Command. Second, keep in mind that you can run Get-Help against any function name, such as Get-Mailbox, and you'll still get the help file for that cmdlet. But if you are unsure of the exact name of a cmdlet, use Get-Command to perform a wildcard search as an aid in the discovery process. Once you've determined the name of the cmdlet you are looking for, you can run Get-Help against that cmdlet for complete details on how to use it.

Try using the help system before going to the internet to find answers. You'll find that the answers to most of your questions are already documented within the built-in cmdlet help.

See also

▶ *Understanding command syntax and parameters*

▶ *Manually configuring remote PowerShell connections* in *Chapter 2, Exchange Management Shell Common Tasks*

▶ *Working with Role Based Access Control* in *Chapter 10, Exchange Security*

Understanding the pipeline

The single most import ant concept in PowerShell is the use of its flexible, object-based pipeline. You may have used pipelines in UNIX-based shells, or when working with the cmd.exe command prompt. The concept of pipelines is similar in that you are sending the output from one command to another. But, instead of passing plain text, PowerShell works with objects, and we can accomplish some very complex tasks in just a single line of code. In this recipe, you'll learn how to use pipelines to string together multiple commands and build powerful one-liners.

How to do it...

The following pipeline command would set the office location for every mailbox in the DB1 database:

```
Get-Mailbox -Database DB1 | Set-Mailbox -Office Headquarters
```

How it works...

In a pipeline, you separate a series of commands using the pipe (|) character. In the previous example, the Get-Mailbox cmdlet returns a collection of mailbox objects. Each mailbox object contains several properties that contain information such as the name of the mailbox, the location of the associated user account in Active Directory, and more. The Set-Mailbox cmdlet is designed to accept input from the Get-Mailbox cmdlet in a pipeline, and with one simple command we can pass along an entire collection of mailboxes that can be modified in one operation.

You can also pipe output to filtering commands, such as the `Where-Object` cmdlet. In this example, the command retrieves only the mailboxes with a `MaxSendSize` equal to 10 megabytes:

```
Get-Mailbox | Where-Object{$_.MaxSendSize -eq 10mb}
```

The code that the `Where-Object` cmdlet uses to perform the filtering is enclosed in curly braces ({ }). This is called a script block, and the code within this script block is evaluated for each object that comes across the pipeline. If the result of the expression is evaluated as true, the object is returned, otherwise, it is ignored. In this example, we access the `MaxSendSize` property of each mailbox using the `$_` object, which is an automatic variable that refers to the current object in the pipeline. We use the equals (`-eq`) comparison operator to check that the `MaxSendSize` property of each mailbox is equal to 10 megabytes. If so, only those mailboxes are returned by the command.

Comparison operators allow you to compare results and find values that match a pattern. For a complete list of comparison operators, run `Get-Help about_Comparison_Operators`.

When running this command, which can also be referred to as a one-liner, each mailbox object is processed one at a time using stream processing. This means that as soon as a match is found, the mailbox information is displayed on the screen. Without this behaviour, you would have to wait for every mailbox to be found before seeing any results. This may not matter if you are working in a very small environment, but without this functionality in a large organization with tens of thousands of mailboxes, you would have to wait a long time for the entire result set to be collected and returned.

One other interesting thing to note about the comparison being done inside our `Where-Object` filter is the use of the `mb` multiplier suffix. PowerShell natively supports these multipliers and they make it a lot easier for us to work with large numbers. In this example, we've used `10mb`, which is the equivalent of entering the value in bytes because behind the scenes, PowerShell is doing the math for us by replacing this value with `1024*1024*10`. PowerShell provides support for the following multipliers: `kb`, `mb`, `gb`, `tb`, and `pb`.

There's more...

You can use advanced pipelining techniques to send objects across the pipeline to other cmdlets that do not support direct pipeline input. For example, the following one-liner adds a list of users to a group:

```
Get-User |
    Where-Object{$_.title -eq "Exchange Admin"} | Foreach-Object{
        Add-RoleGroupMember -Identity "Organization Management" `
        -Member $_.name
    }
```

This pipeline command starts off with a simple filter that returns only the users that have their `Title` set to "Exchange Admin". The output from that command is then piped to the `ForEach-Object` cmdlet that processes each object in the collection. Similar to the `Where-Object` cmdlet, the `ForEach-Object` cmdlet processes each item from the pipeline using a script block. Instead of filtering, this time we are running a command for each user object returned in the collection and adding them to the "Organization Management" role group.

Using aliases in pipelines can be helpful because it reduces the amount of characters you need to type. Take a look at the previous command, modified to use aliases:

```
Get-User |
  ?{$_.title -eq "Exchange Admin"} | %{
    Add-RoleGroupMember -Identity "Organization Management" `
    -Member $_.name
  }
```

Notice the use of the question mark (?) and the percent sign (%) characters. The ? character is an alias for the `Where-Object` cmdlet, and the % character is an alias for the `ForEach-Object` cmdlet. These cmdlets are used heavily, and you'll often see them used with these aliases because it makes the commands easier to type.

 You can use the `Get-Alias` cmdlet to find all of the aliases currently defined in your shell session and the `New-Alias` cmdlet to create custom aliases.

The `Where-Object` and `ForEach-Object` cmdlets have additional aliases. Here's another way you could run the previous command:

```
Get-User |
  where{$_.title -eq "Exchange Admin"} | foreach{
    Add-RoleGroupMember -Identity "Organization Management" `
    -Member $_.name
  }
```

Use aliases when you're working interactively in the shell to speed up your work and keep your commands concise. You may want to consider using the full cmdlet names in production scripts to avoid confusing others who may read your code.

See also

- ▶ _Looping through items_
- ▶ _Creating custom objects_
- ▶ _Dealing with concurrent pipelines in remote PowerShell in_ Chapter 2, _Exchange Management Shell Common Tasks_

Working with variables and objects

Every scripting language makes use of variables as placeholders for data, and PowerShell is no exception. You'll need to work with variables often to save temporary data to an object so you can work with it later. PowerShell is very different from other command shells in that everything you touch is, in fact, a rich object with properties and methods. In PowerShell, a variable is simply an instance of an object just like everything else. The properties of an object contain various bits of information depending on the type of object you're working with. In this recipe we'll learn to create user-defined variables and work with objects in the Exchange Management Shell.

How to do it...

To create a variable that stores an instance of the *testuser* mailbox, use the following command:

```
$mailbox = Get-Mailbox testuser
```

How it works...

To create a variable, or an instance of an object, you prefix the variable name with the dollar sign ($). To the right of the variable name, use the equals (=) assignment operator, followed by the value or object that should be assigned to the variable. Keep in mind that the variables you create are only available during your current shell session and will be destroyed when you close the shell.

Let's look at another example. To create a string variable that contains an e-mail address, use the following command:

```
$email = "testuser@contoso.com"
```

 In addition to user-defined variables, PowerShell also includes automatic and preference variables. To learn more, run Get-Help about_Automatic_Variables and Get-Help about_Preference_Variables.

Even a simple string variable is an object with properties and methods. For instance, every string has a Length property that will return the number of characters that are in the string:

```
[PS] C:\>$email.length
20
```

When accessing the properties of an object, you can use dot notation to reference the property with which you want to work. This is done by typing the object name, then a period, followed by the property name, as shown in the previous example. You access methods in the same way, except that method names always end with parenthesis ().

The string data type supports several methods, such as Substring, Replace, and Split. The following example shows how the Split method can be used to split a string:

```
[PS] C:\>$email.Split("@")
testuser
contoso.com
```

You can see here that the Split method uses the "@" portion of the string as a delimiter and returns two substrings as a result.

> PowerShell also provides a -Split operator that can split a string into or more substrings. Run Get-Help about_Split for details.

There's more...

At this point, you know how to access the properties and methods of an object, but you need to be able to discover and work with these members. To determine which properties and methods are accessible on a given object, you can use the Get-Member cmdlet, which is one of the key discovery tools in PowerShell along with Get-Help and Get-Command.

To retrieve the members of an object, pipe the object to the Get-Member cmdlet. The following command will retrieve all of the instance members of the $mailbox object we created earlier:

```
$mailbox | Get-Member
```

> To filter the results returned by Get-Member, use the -MemberType parameter to specify whether the type should be a Property or a Method.

Let's take a look at a practical example of how we could use Get-Member to discover the methods of an object. Imagine that each mailbox in our environment has had a custom MaxSendSize restriction set and we need to record the value for reporting purposes. When accessing the MaxSendSize property, the following information is returned:

```
[PS] C:\>$mailbox.MaxSendSize
IsUnlimited Value
----------- -----
False       10 MB (10,485,760 bytes)
```

We can see here that the `MaxSendSize` property actually contains an object with two properties: `IsUnlimited` and `Value`. Based on what we've learned, we should be able to access the information for the `Value` property using dot notation:

```
[PS] C:\>$mailbox.MaxSendSize.Value

10 MB (10,485,760 bytes)
```

That works, but the information returned contains not only the value in megabytes, but also the total bytes for the `MaxSendSize` value. For the purpose of what we are trying to accomplish, we only need the total megabytes. Let's see if this object provides any methods that can help us out with this using `Get-Member`:

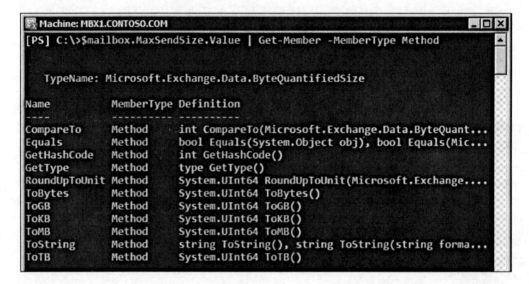

```
Machine: MBX1.CONTOSO.COM                                          _ □ X
[PS] C:\>$mailbox.MaxSendSize.Value | Get-Member -MemberType Method


    TypeName: Microsoft.Exchange.Data.ByteQuantifiedSize

Name          MemberType Definition
----          ---------- ----------
CompareTo     Method     int CompareTo(Microsoft.Exchange.Data.ByteQuant...
Equals        Method     bool Equals(System.Object obj), bool Equals(Mic...
GetHashCode   Method     int GetHashCode()
GetType       Method     type GetType()
RoundUpToUnit Method     System.UInt64 RoundUpToUnit(Microsoft.Exchange....
ToBytes       Method     System.UInt64 ToBytes()
ToGB          Method     System.UInt64 ToGB()
ToKB          Method     System.UInt64 ToKB()
ToMB          Method     System.UInt64 ToMB()
ToString      Method     string ToString(), string ToString(string forma...
ToTB          Method     System.UInt64 ToTB()
```

From the output shown in the previous screenshot, we can see this object supports several methods that can be used convert the value. To obtain the `MaxSendSize` value in megabytes, we can call the `ToMB` method:

```
[PS] C:\>$mailbox.MaxSendSize.Value.ToMB()

10
```

In a traditional shell, you would have to perform complex string parsing to extract this type of information, but PowerShell and the .NET Framework make this much easier. As you'll see over time, this is one of the reasons why PowerShell's object-based nature really outshines a typical text-based command shell.

An important thing to point about this last example is that it would not work if the mailbox had not had a custom `MaxSendSize` limitation configured. Nevertheless, this provides a good illustration of the process you'll want to use when you're trying to learn about an object's properties or methods.

Variable expansion in strings

As mentioned in the first recipe in this chapter, PowerShell uses quoting rules to determine how variables should be handled inside a quoted string. When enclosing a simple variable inside a double-quoted string, PowerShell will expand that variable and replace the variable with the value of the string. Let's take a look at how this works by starting off with a simple example:

```
[PS] C:\>$name = "Bob"
[PS] C:\> "The user name is $name"
The user name is Bob
```

This is pretty straightforward. We stored the string value of "Bob" inside the $name variable. We then include the $name variable inside a double-quoted string that contains a message. When we hit return, the $name variable is expanded and we get back the message we expect to see on the screen.

Now let's try this with a more complex object. Let's say that we want to store an instance of a mailbox object in a variable and access the PrimarySmtpAddress property inside the quoted string:

```
[PS] C:\>$mailbox = Get-Mailbox testuser
[PS] C:\>"The email address is $mailbox.PrimarySmtpAddress"
The email address is test user.PrimarySmtpAddress
```

Notice here that when we try to access the PrimarySmtpAddress property of our mailbox object inside the double-quoted string, we're not getting back the information that we'd expect. This is a very common stumbling block when it comes to working with objects and properties inside strings. We can get around this using sub expression notation. This requires that you enclose the entire object within $() characters inside the string:

```
[PS] C:\>"The email address is $($mailbox.PrimarySmtpAddress)"
The email address is testuser@contoso.com
```

Using this syntax, the PrimarySmtpAddress property of the $mailbox object is properly expanded and the correct information is returned. This technique will be useful later when extracting data from objects and generating reports or log files.

Strongly typed variables

PowerShell will automatically try to select the correct data type for a variable based on the value being assigned to it. You don't have to worry about doing this yourself, but we do have the ability to explicitly assign a type to a variable if needed. This is done by specifying the data type in square brackets before the variable name:

```
[string]$a = 32
```

Here we've assigned the value of 32 to the $a variable. Had we not strongly typed the variable using the [string] type shortcut, $a would have been created using the Int32 data type, since the value we assigned was a number that was not enclosed in single or double quotes. Take a look at the following screenshot:

```
Machine: MBX1.CONTOSO.COM                                          _ □ ×
[PS] C:\>$var1 = 32
[PS] C:\>$var1.gettype()

IsPublic IsSerial Name                                    BaseType
-------- -------- ----                                    --------
True     True     Int32                                   System.ValueType


[PS] C:\>[string]$var2 = 32
[PS] C:\>$var2.GetType()

IsPublic IsSerial Name                                    BaseType
-------- -------- ----                                    --------
True     True     String                                  System.Object
```

As you can see here, the $var1 variable is initially created without any explicit typing. We use the GetType() method, which can be used on any object in the shell, to determine the data type of $var1. Since the value assigned was a number not enclosed in quotes, it was created using the Int32 data type. When using the [string] type shortcut to create $var2 with the same value, you can see that it has now been created as a string.

It is good to have an understanding of data types because when building scripts that return objects, you may need to have some control over this. For example, you may want to report on the amount of free disk space on an Exchange server. If we store this value in the property of a custom object as a string, we lose the ability to sort on that value. There are several examples throughout the book that use this technique.

See *Appendix A* for a listing of commonly-used type shortcuts.

Formatting output

One of the most common PowerShell questions is how to get information returned from commands in the desired output on the screen. In this recipe, we'll take a look at how you can output data from commands and format that information for viewing on the screen.

How to do it...

To change the default output and view the properties of an object in list format, pipe the command to the `Format-List` cmdlet:

```
Get-Mailbox testuser | Format-List
```

To view specific properties in table format, supply a comma-separated list of property names as parameters, as shown next when using `Format-Table`:

```
Get-Mailbox testuser | Format-Table name,alias
```

How it works...

When you run the `Get-Mailbox` cmdlet, you only see the `Name`, `Alias`, `ServerName`, and `ProhibitSendQuota` properties of each mailbox in a table format. This is because the `Get-Mailbox` cmdlet receives its formatting instructions from the `exchange.format.ps1xml` file located in the Exchange server bin directory.

PowerShell cmdlets use a variety of formatting files that usually include a default view with only a small subset of predefined properties. When you need to override the default view, you can use `Format-List` and `Format-Table` cmdlets.

You can also select specific properties with `Format-List`, just as we saw when using the `Format-Table` cmdlet. The difference is, of course, that the output will be displayed in list format.

Let's take a look at the output from the `Format-Table` cmdlet, as shown previously:

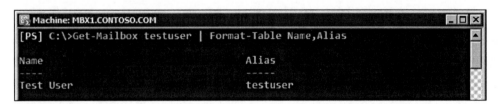

As you can see here, we get both properties of the mailbox formatted as a table.

When using `Format-Table` cmdlet, you may find it useful to use the `-Autosize` parameter to organize the columns based on the width of the data:

```
Machine: MBX1.CONTOSO.COM
[PS] C:\>Get-Mailbox testuser | Format-Table Name,Alias -AutoSize

Name      Alias
----      -----
Test User testuser
```

This command selects the same properties as our previous example, but this time we are using the -Autosize parameter and the columns are adjusted to use only as much space on the screen as is needed. Remember, you can use the ft alias instead of typing the entire Format-Table cmdlet name. You can also use the fl alias for the Format-List cmdlet. Both of these aliases can keep your commands concise and are very convenient when working interactively in the shell.

There's more...

One thing to keep in mind is that you never want to use the Format-*cmdlets in the middle of a pipeline since most other cmdlets will not understand what to do with the output. The Format-*cmdlets should normally be the last thing you do in a command unless you are sending the output to a printer or a text file.

To send formatted output to a text file, you can use the Out-File cmdlet. In the following command, the Format-List cmdlet uses the asterisk (*) character as a wildcard and exports all of the property values for the mailbox to a text file:

```
Get-Mailbox testuser | fl * | Out-File c:\mb.txt
```

To add data to the end of an existing file, use the -Append parameter with the Out-File cmdlet. Even though we're using the Out-File cmdlet here, the traditional cmd output redirection operators such as > and >> can still be used. The difference is that the cmdlet gives you a little more control over the output method and provides parameters for tasks including setting the encoding of the file.

You can sort the output of a command using the Sort-Object cmdlet. For example, this command will display all mailbox databases in alphabetical order:

```
Get-MailboxDatabase | sort name | ft name
```

We are using the sort alias for the Sort-Object cmdlet specifying name as the property we want to sort. To reverse the sort order, use the descending switch parameter:

```
Get-MailboxDatabase | sort name -desc | ft name
```

See also

- ▶ *Understanding the pipeline*
- ▶ *Exporting reports to text and CSV files* in *Chapter 2, Exchange Management Shell Common Tasks*

Working with arrays and hash tables

Like many other scripting and programming languages, Windows PowerShell allows you to work with arrays and hash tables. An array is a collection of values that can be stored in a single object. A hash table is also known as an associative array, and is a dictionary that stores a set of key-value pairs. You'll need to have a good grasp of arrays so that you can effectively manage objects in bulk and gain maximum efficiency in the shell. In this recipe, we'll take a look at how we can use both types of arrays to store and retrieve data.

How to do it...

You can initialize an array that stores a set of items by assigning multiple values to a variable. All you need to do is separate each value with a comma. The following command would create an array of server names:

```
$servers = "EX1","EX2","EX3"
```

To create an empty hash table, use the following syntax:

```
$hashtable = @{}
```

Now that we have an empty hash table, we can add key-value pairs:

```
$hashtable["server1"] = 1
$hashtable["server2"] = 2
$hashtable["server3"] = 3
```

Notice in this example that we can assign a value based on a key name, not using an index number as we saw with a regular array. Alternatively, we can create this same object using a single command using the following syntax:

```
$hashtable = @{server1 = 1; server2 = 2; server3 = 3}
```

You can see here that we used a semicolon (;) to separate each key-value pair. This is only required if the entire hash table is created in one line.

You can break this up into multiple lines to make it easier to read:

```
$hashtable = @{
   server1 = 1
   server2 = 2
   server3 = 3
}
```

How it works...

Let's start off by looking at how arrays work in PowerShell. When working with arrays, you can access specific items and add or remove elements. In our first example, we assigned a list of server names to the $servers array. To view all of the items in the array, simply type the variable name and hit return:

```
[PS] C:\>$servers

EX1

EX2

EX3
```

Array indexing allows you to access a specific element of an array using its index number inside square brackets ([ ]). PowerShell arrays are zero-based, meaning that the first item in the array starts at index zero. For example, use the second index to access third element of the array, as shown next:

```
[PS] C:\>$servers[2]

EX3
```

To assign a value to a specific element of the array, use the equals (=) assignment operator. We can change the value from the last example using following syntax:

```
[PS] C:\>$servers[2] = "EX4"

[PS] C:\>$servers[2]

EX4
```

Let's add another server to this array. To append a value, use the plus equals (+=) assignment operator as shown here:

```
[PS] C:\>$servers += "EX5"

[PS] C:\>$servers

EX1

EX2

EX4

EX5
```

To determine how many items are in an array, we can access the Count property to retrieve the total number of array elements:

```
[PS] C:\>$servers.Count

4
```

We can loop through each element in the array with the `ForEach-Object` cmdlet and display the value in a string:

```
$servers | ForEach-Object {"Server Name: $_"}
```

We can also check for a value in an array using the `-Contains` or `-NotContains` conditional operators:

[PS] C:\>$servers -contains "EX1"

True

In this example, we are working with a one-dimensional array, which is what you'll commonly be dealing with in the Exchange Management Shell. PowerShell supports more complex array types such as jagged and multidimensional arrays, but these are beyond the scope of what you'll need to know for the examples in this book.

Now that we've figured out how arrays work, let's take a closer look at hash tables. When viewing the output for a hash table, the items are returned in no particular order. You'll notice this when viewing the hash table we created earlier:

[PS] C:\>$hashtable

Name	Value
server2	2
server1	1
server3	3

If you want to sort the hash table, you can call the `GetEnumerator` method and sort by the `Value` property:

[PS] C:\>$hashtable.GetEnumerator() | sort value

Name	Value
server1	1
server2	2
server3	3

Hash tables can be used when creating custom objects, or to provide a set of parameter names and values using parameter splatting. Instead of specifying parameter names one by one with a cmdlet, you can use a hash table with keys that match the parameter's names and their associated values will automatically be used for input:

```
$parameters = @{
  Title = "Manager"
  Department = "Sales"
```

```
    Office = "Headquarters"
}
Set-User testuser @parameters
```

This command automatically populates the parameter values for `Title`, `Department`, and `Office` when running the `Set-User` cmdlet for the *testuser* mailbox.

For more details and examples for working with hash tables, run `Get-Help about_Hash_Tables`.

There's more...

You can think of a collection as an array created from the output of a command. For example, the `Get-Mailbox` cmdlet can be used to create an object that stores a collection of mailboxes, and we can work with this object just as we would with any other array. You'll notice that, when working with collections, such as a set of mailboxes, you can access each mailbox instance as an array element. Consider the following example:

First, we retrieve a list of mailboxes that start with the letter `t` and assign that to the `$mailboxes` variable. From looking at the items in the `$mailboxes` object, we can see that the *testuser* mailbox is the second mailbox in the collection.

Since arrays are zero-based, we can access that item using the first index, as shown next:

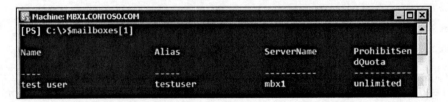

If your command only returns one item, then the output can no longer be accessed using array notation. In the following example, the `$mailboxes` object contains only one mailbox and will display an error when trying to access an item using array notation:

```
Machine: MBX1.CONTOSO.COM                                          _ □ ✕
[PS] C:\>$mailboxes = Get-Mailbox testuser
[PS] C:\>$mailboxes[0]
Unable to index into an object of type Microsoft.Exchange.Data.Directory.Ma
nagement.Mailbox.
At line:1 char:12
+ $mailboxes[ <<<< 0]
    + CategoryInfo          : InvalidOperation: (0:Int32) [], RuntimeExcep
   tion
    + FullyQualifiedErrorId : CannotIndex
```

Even though it will only store one item, you can initialize this object as an array, using the following syntax:

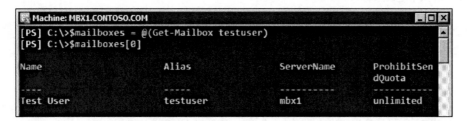

You can see here that we've wrapped the command inside the @() characters to ensure that PowerShell will always interpret the $mailboxes object as an array. This can be useful when you're building a script that always needs to work with an object as an array, regardless of the number of items returned from the command that created the object. Since the $mailboxes object has been initialized as an array, you can add and remove elements as needed.

We can also add and remove items to multi-valued properties, just as we would with a normal array. To add an e-mail address to the *testuser* mailbox, we can use the following commands:

```
$mailbox = Get-Mailbox testuser
$mailbox.EmailAddresses += "testuser@contoso.com"
Set-Mailbox testuser -EmailAddresses $mailbox.EmailAddresses
```

In this example, we created an instance of the *testuser* mailbox by assigning the command to the $mailbox object. We can then work with the EmailAddresses property to view, add, and remove e-mail addresses from this mailbox. You can see here that the plus equals (+=) operator was used to append a value to the EmailAddresses property.

We can also remove that value using the minus equals (-=) operator:

```
$mailbox.EmailAddresses -= "testuser@contoso.com"
Set-Mailbox testuser -EmailAddresses $mailbox.EmailAddresses
```

There is actually an easier way to add and remove e-mail addresses on recipient objects. See *Adding and removing recipient e-mail addresses* in *Chapter 3* for details.

We've covered the core concepts in this section that you'll need to know when working with arrays. For more details run `Get-Help about_arrays`.

See also

▶ *Working with variables and objects*

▶ *Creating custom objects*

Looping through items

Loop processing is a concept that you will need to master in order to write scripts and one-liners with efficiency. You'll need to use loops to iterate over each item in an array or a collection of items, and then run one or more commands within a script block against each of those objects. In this recipe, we'll take a look at how you can use foreach loops and the `ForEach-Object` cmdlet to process items in a collection.

How to do it...

The `foreach` statement is a language construct used to iterate through values in a collection of items. The following example shows the syntax used to loop through a collection of mailboxes, returning only the name of each mailbox:

```
foreach($mailbox in Get-Mailbox) {$mailbox.Name}
```

In addition, you can take advantage of the PowerShell pipeline and perform loop processing using the `ForEach-Object` cmdlet. This example produces the same result as the one shown previously:

```
Get-Mailbox | ForEach-Object {$_.Name}
```

You will often see the given command written using an alias of the `ForEach-Object` cmdlet, such as the percent sign (%):

```
Get-Mailbox | %{$_.Name}
```

How it works...

The first part of a `foreach` statement is enclosed in parenthesis and represents a variable and a collection. In the previous example, the collection is the list of mailboxes returned from the `Get-Mailbox` cmdlet. The script block contains the commands that will be run for every item in the collection of mailboxes. Inside the script block, the `$mailbox` object is assigned the value of the current item being processed in the loop. This allows you to access each mailbox one at a time using the `$mailbox` variable.

When you need to perform loop processing within a pipeline, you can use the `ForEach-Object` cmdlet. The concept is similar, but the syntax is different because objects in the collection are coming across the pipeline.

The `ForEach-Object` cmdlet allows you to process each item in a collection using the `$_` automatic variable, which represents the current object in the pipeline. The `ForEach-Object` cmdlet is probably one of the most commonly-used cmdlets in PowerShell, and we'll rely on it heavily in many examples throughout the book.

The code inside the script block used with both looping methods can be more complex than just a simple expression. The script block can contain a series of commands or an entire script. Consider the following code:

```
Get-MailboxDatabase -Status | %{
  $DBName = $_.Name
  $whiteSpace = $_.AvailableNewMailboxSpace.ToMb()
  "The $DBName database has $whiteSpace MB of total white space"
}
```

In this example, we're looping through each mailbox database in the organization using the `ForEach-Object` cmdlet. Inside the script block, we've created multiple variables, calculated the total megabytes of whitespace in each database, and returned a custom message that includes the database name and corresponding whitespace value. This is a simple example, but keep in mind that inside the script block you can run other cmdlets, work with variables, create custom objects, and more.

PowerShell also supports other language constructs for processing items such as `for`, `while`, and `do` loops. Although these can be useful in some cases, we won't rely on them much for the remaining examples in this book. You can read more about them and view examples using the `get-help about_for`, `get-help about_while`, and `get-help about_do` commands in the shell.

There's more...

There are some key differences about the `foreach` statement and the `ForEach-Object` cmdlet that you'll want to be aware of when you need to work with loops. First, the `ForEach-Object` cmdlet can process one object at a time as it comes across the pipeline. When you process a collection using the `foreach` statement, this is the exact opposite. The `foreach` statement requires that all of the objects that need to be processed within a loop are collected and stored in memory before processing begins. We'll want to take advantage of the PowerShell pipeline and its streaming behaviour whenever possible since it is much more efficient.

The other thing to make note of is that in PowerShell, `foreach` is not only a keyword, but also an alias. This can be a little counterintuitive, especially when you are new to PowerShell and you run into a code sample that uses the following syntax:

```
Get-Mailbox | foreach {$_.Name}
```

At first glance, this might seem like we're using the `foreach` keyword, but we're actually using an alias for the `ForEach-Object` cmdlet. The easiest way to remember this distinction is that the `foreach` language construct is always used before a pipeline. If you use `foreach` after a pipeline, PowerShell will use the `foreach` alias which corresponds to the `ForEach-Object` cmdlet.

See also

- ▶ *Working with arrays and hash tables*
- ▶ *Understanding the pipeline*
- ▶ *Creating custom objects*

Using flow control statements

Flow control statements are used in the shell to run one or more commands based on the result of a conditional test. You can use the `If` statement to test one or more conditional statements, and you can also use `switch` statements when multiple `If` statements would otherwise be required. This recipe will show you how to control the flow of execution that your scripts will use in the shell.

How to do it...

Let's store the status of a database called `DB1` in a variable that can be used to perform some conditional checks:

```
$DB1 = Get-MailboxDatabase DB1 -Status
```

When using an `If` statement, you use the `If` keyword followed by an expression enclosed in parenthesis that performs a conditional check. If the expression is evaluated as true, any commands in the proceeding script block will be executed:

```
if($DB1.DatabaseSize -gt 5gb) {
  "The Database is larger than 5gb"
}
```

You can use the `ElseIf` keyword to add another conditional check:

```
if($DB1.DatabaseSize -gt 5gb) {
  "The Database is larger than 5gb"
}
elseif($DB1.DatabaseSize -gt 10gb) {
  "The Database is larger than 10gb"
}
```

You can also add the `Else` statement to run commands if none of the conditions evaluate as true:

```
if($DB1.DatabaseSize -gt 5gb) {
  "The Database is larger than 5gb"
}
elseif($DB1.DatabaseSize -gt 10gb) {
  "The Database is larger than 10gb"
}
else {
  "The Database is not larger than 5gb or 10gb"
}
```

If you need to check more than a few conditions, you may want to consider using a switch statement instead of series of `If` and `ElseIf` statements:

```
switch($DB1.DatabaseSize) {
  {$_ -gt 5gb}  {"Larger than 5gb"; break}
  {$_ -gt 10gb} {"Larger than 10gb"; break}
  {$_ -gt 15gb} {"Larger than 15gb"; break}
  {$_ -gt 20gb} {"Larger than 20gb"; break}
  Default       {"Smaller than 5gb"}
}
```

How it works...

To control the flow and execution of commands in your scripts, you can use the `If`, `Elseif`, and `Else` conditional statements. The syntax of an `If` statement is pretty straightforward. Let's break it down in simple terms. In the first example, we're simply asking PowerShell if the database size of `DB1` is greater than five gigabytes, and, if it is, to output a string with the message "The database is larger than 5gb".

In the second example, we extend this logic by simply asking another question: if the database size of `DB1` is greater than 10 Gigabytes, output a string with the message "The database is larger than 10gb".

Next, we use an `Else` statement that will only run commands if either the `If` or `ElseIf` statements do not evaluate to true. If that's the case we simply output a string with the message "The database is not larger than 5gb or 10gb".

One interesting thing to point out here is that the code within parenthesis is like any other expression we might type into the shell. There's no requirement to first create a variable, as shown previously. We could just do something like this:

```
if((Get-MailboxDatabase DB1 -Status).DatabaseSize -gt 5gb) {
   "The database is larger than 5gb"
}
```

Since we know that the `Get-MailboxDatabase` cmdlet can return an object with a `DatabaseSize` property, we can simply wrap the command in parenthesis and access the property directly using dot notation. This is a technique that can cut down on the amount of code you write and greatly speed up your work when you are typing commands interactively into the shell.

It's possible to use multiple `ElseIf` statements to run a series of multiple conditional checks, but the `switch` statement is much better suited for this task. The `switch` statement syntax may be a little harder to understand. After using the `switch` keyword, you specify the object that you want to perform multiple conditional checks against. Each line within the body of the switch can evaluate an expression or check for a precise value. If an expression evaluates to true or a match is found, any commands in the associated script block will run.

In our previous example, we evaluated a number of expressions to determine if the size of the database was greater than a specific value. Notice that in each script block we used the `break` keyword. This means that we exit the switch statement immediately after an expression has been evaluated as true and any following checks will be skipped. Finally, the last item in the switch uses the `Default` keyword which will only run if the previous expressions are false.

You can also use a switch statement that will run commands when matching a specific value. Take a look at the following code:

```
$number = 3

switch ($number) {
  1 {"One"  ; break}
  2 {"Two"  ; break}
  3 {"Three"  ; break}
  4 {"Four"  ; break}
  5 {"Five"  ; break}
  Default {"No matches found"}
}
```

In this example, the `$number` variable is set to 3. When the switch statement runs, the word `Three` will be returned. If `$number` had been set to a value that was not defined, such as `42`, the `Default` script block would run and output the string "No Matches Found".

`Switch` statements can also be used to perform complex matches with regular expressions, wildcards, exact matches, case sensitive values, and data read in from external files. For more details, run `Get-Help About_Switch`.

There's more...

Let's take a look at a more practical example of how you might use flow control statements in a real script. Here we'll loop through each mailbox in the organization to configure some of the mailbox quota settings:

```
foreach ($mailbox in Get-Mailbox) {
  if($mailbox.office -eq "Sales") {
   Set-Mailbox $mailbox -ProhibitSendReceiveQuota 5gb `
   -UseDatabaseQuotaDefaults $false
  }
  elseif($mailbox.office -eq "Accounting") {
   Set-Mailbox $mailbox -ProhibitSendReceiveQuota 2gb `
   -UseDatabaseQuotaDefaults $false
  }
  else {
   Set-Mailbox $mailbox -UseDatabaseQuotaDefaults $true
  }
}
```

In this example we are checking to see if the `Office` setting for each mailbox is set to "Sales" using the `If` statement. If so, the `ProhibitSendReceiveQuota` is set to five gigabytes. If not, the `ElseIf` statement will check that the `Office` setting is set to "Accounting", and, if it is, the `ProhibitSendReceiveQuota` is set to two gigabytes. If the `Office` setting is not set to either of these values, we can configure the mailbox to use database quota defaults.

> Notice the use of the back tick (`` ` ``) character used in the previous example with the `Set-Mailbox` cmdlet. This can be used as a line continuation character to break up long commands into multiple lines.

See also

▶ *Looping through items*

Creating custom objects

The fact that PowerShell is an object-based shell gives us a great deal of flexibility when it comes to writing one-liners, scripts, and functions. When generating detailed reports, we need to be able to customize the data output from our code so it can be formatted or piped to other commands that can export the data in a clean, structured format. We also need to be able to control and customize the output from our code so that we can merge data from multiple sources into a single object. In this recipe, you'll learn a few techniques used to build custom objects.

How to do it...

The first thing we'll do is create a collection of mailbox objects that will be used as the data source for a new set of custom objects:

```
$mailboxes = Get-Mailbox
```

You can add custom properties to any object coming across the pipeline using calculated properties. This can be done using either the `Select-Object` or `Format-Table` cmdlets:

```
$mailboxes |
  Select-Object Name,
    Database,
    @{name="Title";expression={(Get-User $_.Name).Title}},
    @{name="Dept";expression={(Get-User $_.Name).Department}}
```

Another easy way to do this is by assigning a hash table to the `-Property` parameter of the `New-Object` cmdlet:

```
$mailboxes | %{
  New-Object PSObject -Property @{
    Name = $_.Name
    Database = $_.Database
    Title = (Get-User $_.Name).Title
    Dept = (Get-User $_.Name).Department
  }
}
```

You can also use the `New-Object` cmdlet to create an empty custom object, and then use the `Add-Member` cmdlet to tack on any custom properties that are required:

```
$mailboxes | %{
  $obj = New-Object PSObject
  $obj | Add-Member NoteProperty Name $_.Name
  $obj | Add-Member NoteProperty Database $_.Database
  $obj | Add-Member NoteProperty Title (Get-User $_.Name).Title
  $obj | Add-Member NotePropertyDept (Get-User $_.Name).Department
  Write-Output $obj
}
```

Each of these three code samples will output the same custom objects that combine data retrieved from both the `Get-Mailbox` and `Get-User` cmdlets. Assuming that the `Title` and `Department` fields have been defined for each user, the output would look similar to the following:

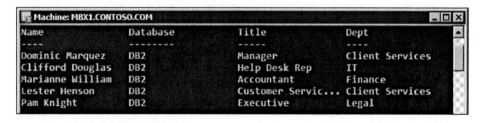

How it works...

The reason we're building a custom object here is because we want to merge data from multiple sources into a single object. The `Get-Mailbox` cmdlet does not return the `Title` or `Department` properties that are tied to a user account: the `Get-User` cmdlet needs to be used to retrieve that information. Since we may want to generate a report that includes information from both the `Get-Mailbox` and `Get-User` cmdlets for each individual user, it makes sense to build a custom object that contains all of the required information. We can then pipe these objects to other cmdlets that can be used to export this information to a file.

We can modify one of our previous code samples and pipe the output to a CSV file used to document this information for the current user population:

```
$mailboxes |
  Select-Object Name,
    Database,
    @{n="Title";e={(Get-User $_.Name).Title}},
    @{n="Dept";e={(Get-User $_.Name).Department}} |
      Export-CSV -Path C:\report.csv -NoType
```

Keep in mind that even though you can also create calculated properties using the `Format-Table` cmdlet, you'll want to use `Select-Object`, as shown previously, when converting these objects to CSV or HTML reports. These conversion cmdlets do not understand the formatting information returned by the `Format-Table` cmdlet, and you'll end up with a lot of useless data if you try to do this.

When building custom objects with the `Select-Object` cmdlet, we can select existing properties from objects coming across the pipeline and also add one or more calculated properties. This is done using a hash table that defines a custom property name in the hash table key and a script block within the hash table value. The script block is an expression where you can run one or more commands to define the custom property value. In our previous example, you can see that we've called the `Get-User` cmdlet to retrieve both the `Title` and `Department` properties for a user that will be assigned to calculated properties on a new object.

The syntax for creating a calculated property looks a little strange at first glance since it uses `name` and `expression` keywords to create a hash table that defines the calculated property. You can abbreviate these keywords as shown next:

```
$mailboxes |
  Select-Object Name,
    Database,
    @{n="Title";e={(Get-User $_.Name).Title}},
    @{n="Dept";e={(Get-User $_.Name).Department}}
```

The property name uses the string value assigned to n, and the property value is assigned to e using a script block. Abbreviating these keywords with n and e just makes it easier to type. You can also use label or l to provide the calculated property name.

Using the New-Object cmdlet and assigning a hash table to the -Property parameter is a quick and easy way to create a custom object. The only issue with this technique is that the properties can be returned in a random order. This is due to how the .NET Framework assigns random numeric values to hash table keys behind the scenes, and the properties are sorted based on those values, not in the order that you've defined them. The only way to get the properties back in the order you wants to continue to pipe the command to Select-Object and select the property names in order, or use one of the other techniques shown in this recipe.

Creating an empty custom object and manually adding note properties with the Add-Member cmdlet can require a lot of extra typing, so generally this syntax is not widely used. This technique becomes useful when you want to add script methods or script properties to a custom object, but this is an advanced technique that we won't need to utilize for the recipes in the remainder of this book.

There's more...

There is another useful technique for creating custom objects which utilizes the Select-Object cmdlet. Take a look at the following code:

```
$mailboxes | %{
   $obj = "" | Select-Object Name,Database,Title,Dept
   $obj.Name = $_.Name
   $obj.Database = $_.Database
   $obj.Title = (Get-User $_.Name).Title
   $obj.Dept = (Get-User $_.Name).Department
   Write-Output $obj
}
```

You can create a custom object by piping an empty string variable to the Select-Object cmdlet, specifying the property names that should be included. The next step is to simply assign values to the properties of the object using the property names that you've defined. This code loops through the items in our $mailboxes object and returns a custom object for each one. The output from this code returns the same exact objects as all of the previous examples.

Watch out for concurrent pipeline errors

One of the reasons we first stored the collection of mailboxes in the $mailbox variable is due to the way PowerShell deals with multiple cmdlets executing through a remote session. Ideally, we would just do the following:

```
Get-Mailbox | %{
  New-Object PSObject -Property @{
    Name = $_.Name
    Database = $_.Database
    Title = (Get-User $_.Name).Title
    Dept = (Get-User $_.Name).Department
  }
}
```

Unfortunately, even though this is syntax is completely valid, it will not work consistently in the Exchange Management Shell. This is because, as the Get-Mailbox cmdlet is sending objects down the pipeline to ForEach-Object, we're also trying to run the Get-User cmdlet to build our custom object, and PowerShell remoting does not support more than one pipeline executing at a time. To get around this, use the technique shown previously to save the results of the first command to a variable, and then pipe that variable to ForEach-Object. For more details on this, refer to out the recipe titled *Dealing with concurrent pipelines in remote PowerShell*.

See also

- ▶ *Looping through items*
- ▶ *Working with variables and objects*
- ▶ *Exporting reports to text and CSV files* in *Chapter 2, Exchange Management Shell Common Tasks*
- ▶ *Dealing with concurrent pipelines in remote PowerShell* in *Chapter 2, Exchange Management Shell Common Tasks*

Creating PowerShell functions

Functions are used to combine a series of commands into a reusable block of code that can be called using a single command. Functions can make a configuration change or return one or more objects that can either be displayed in the console or exported to an external file. You can assign the output of functions to a variable, or pipe a function to another cmdlet. In this recipe, you'll learn how to create a PowerShell function.

How to do it...

To create a function, you need to use the `function` keyword, followed by the name of the function, and then the function code enclosed within curly braces { }. For example, this very basic function displays three properties of a mailbox in list format:

```
function Get-MailboxList {
  param($name)
  Get-Mailbox $name | fl Name,Alias,ServerName
}
```

When running the function, you must supply the identity of the mailbox as a parameter. The mailbox `Name`, `Alias`, and `ServerName` are displayed in a list.

How it works...

PowerShell functions give us the ability to run a sequence of commands that can be called using a single function name. We can add input parameters to our own functions and also process pipeline input. This gives us the ability to write our own reusable functions that can behave just like a cmdlet.

There are a few ways you can add functions into your shell session. First, you can save your functions inside a `.ps1` script. To make them available in the shell, your script just needs to be "dotted", or dot sourced. You do this by typing a period, a space, and then the path to the file. There has to be a space between the dot and the file name, otherwise it won't work. See the recipe *Creating and Running Scripts* for an example.

Another convenient method for adding functions to your shell session is to use a profile. PowerShell profiles are actually just a `.ps1` script that gets executed when you start the shell. If you don't have a profile set up, check out the recipe titled *Setting up a Profile*.

If you're working interactively, you may find it convenient to simply copy and paste the function code straight into the shell. Keep in mind that, if you do this, the function will only be available during the current session. If you close the shell and open a new instance, the function will no longer be available.

There's more...

The best way to provide input to a function is to declare formal parameters. We did this with the previous example, and the `$name` parameter was added to the function using the `param` keyword. We can add a list of parameters using this syntax by separating each parameter name with a comma.

We can access informal function parameters inside the body of a function using the automatic $args variable, which is an array that contains an element for each unbound argument passed to a function. While this can be useful in some cases, formal parameters provide much more flexibility. Formal parameters with descriptive names are easier to understand; they can be initialized with default values and support several attributes such as the position ID, whether or not they accept pipeline input, and whether they are required or optional.

In other scripting or programming languages, it is sometimes required to use a keyword to return a value from a function, but we don't have to do this in PowerShell. Let's say we've called the Get-Mailbox cmdlet inside the body of a function, without capturing the output in a variable. In this case, the return value for the function will be the data returned by the cmdlet. You can explicitly return an object using the Write-Output cmdlet and, although it makes for good readability when viewing the code, it is not required.

PowerShell functions can be written to accept and process pipeline input using three stages of execution by utilizing Begin, Process, and End blocks, each of which Is described next:

▶ **Begin**: The begin block runs only once, at the beginning of the function. Any customization or initialization can happen here.

▶ **Process**: The process block runs once for each object in the pipeline. Each object that comes through the pipeline can be accessed using the $_ automatic variable.

▶ **End**: The end block runs after all of the objects in the pipeline have been processed.

We can create a simple pipeline function using only the Process block. The Begin and End blocks are optional. For example, the following function will return the name for each mailbox sent across the pipeline:

```
function Get-MailboxName {
  process {
    "Mailbox Name: $($_.Name)"
  }
}
```

We can pipe the Get-Mailbox command to this function and each mailbox name will be returned:

```
Machine: MBX1.CONTOSO.COM
[PS] C:\>Get-Mailbox -Database DB1 | Get-MailboxName
Mailbox Name: Ruben Macias
Mailbox Name: Nicholas Shannon
Mailbox Name: Sheila Winters
Mailbox Name: Test User
[PS] C:\>
```

Taking it a step further

Let's take a look at a practical example that combines the `Get-MailboxStatistics` and `Set-Mailbox` cmdlets into a function used to automate a task and demonstrate the capabilities of PowerShell functions. The following function will set the `ProhibitSendReceiveQuota` limit for a mailbox, given values for the mailbox name and desired quota size. The function will only modify a mailbox if the total mailbox size does not already exceed the value provided for the quota setting:

```
function Set-SendReceiveQuota {
  param(
    [Parameter(Mandatory=$true,ValueFromPipelineByPropertyName =
      $true)]
    $name,
    [Parameter(Mandatory=$true)]
    $quota
  )
  begin {
    $count = 0
    Write-Output "Started: $(Get-Date -format T)"
  }
  process {
    $count += 1
    $mailboxstatistics = Get-MailboxStatistics $name
    $total = $mailboxstatistics.TotalItemSize.Value.ToMB()
    if($total -lt $quota) {
      Set-Mailbox $name -ProhibitSendReceiveQuota $quota `
      -UseDatabaseQuotaDefaults $false
    }
  }
  end {
    Write-Output "Ended: $(Get-Date -format T)"
    Write-Output "Mailboxes Processed: $count"
  }
}
```

You can see in this example that we've added the `[Parameter ()]` attribute in order to define characteristics for each parameter. In this case, both parameters are mandatory and the `$name` parameter will accept its value from the pipeline by property name.

> Parameters can use a number of arguments and attributes. For a complete list, run `Get-Help about_Functions_Advanced_Parameters`.

Like a cmdlet, this function can process pipeline input and it can also be run against one object at a time. Let's start off by running the function for a single mailbox:

The `Begin` block runs only once, immediately at the beginning, and the start time is returned as soon as the function is called. Within the `Process` block, the code is run once and we increment the `$count` variable to keep track of how many objects have been processed. The `End` block is run last, reporting the total number of items that have been processed. We can see from the output in the previous screenshot that the function processed one mailbox and the operation only took one second to complete.

Now let's run the function for a collection of mailboxes:

```
Machine: MBX1.CONTOSO.COM                                    _ □ X
[PS] C:\>$mailboxes = Get-Mailbox t*
[PS] C:\>$mailboxes | Set-SendReceiveQuota -quota 300mb
Started: 12:01:28 AM
Ended: 12:01:29 AM
Mailboxes Processed: 3
[PS] C:\>_
```

The syntax of the command is very different this time. We pipe all of the mailboxes starting with the letter t to the `Set-SendReceiveQuota` function. Notice that we've only specified the `-quota` parameter. This is because the `$name` parameter will automatically receive a value from each mailbox objects `Name` property as it comes across the pipeline. Looking at the output again, you can see that the operation took one second to complete, and we modified three mailboxes in the process.

PowerShell functions are a very broad topic and could easily be the focus of an entire chapter. We've covered some key points about functions here, but to learn more, run `Get-Help about_functions` and `Get-Help about_functions_advanced`.

See also

► *Understanding the pipeline*
► *Creating and running scripts*
► *Setting up a profile*

Creating and running scripts

You can accomplish many tasks by executing individual cmdlets or running multiple commands in a pipeline, but there may be times where you want to create a script that performs a series of operations or that loads a library of functions and predefined variables and aliases into the shell. In this recipe, we'll take a look at how you can create and run scripts in the shell.

How to do it...

1. Let's start off by creating a basic script that automates a multi-step process. We'll start up a text editor, such as Notepad, and enter the following code:

```
param(
    $name,
    $maxsendsize,
    $maxreceivesize,
    $city,
    $state,
    $title,
    $department
)

Set-Mailbox -Identity $name `
-MaxSendSize $maxsendsize `
-MaxReceiveSize $maxreceivesize

Set-User -Identity $name `
-City $city `
-StateOrProvince $state `
-Title $title `
-Department $department

Add-DistributionGroupMember -Identity DL_Sales `
-Member $name
```

2. Next, we'll save the file on the `C:\` drive using the name `Update-SalesMailbox.ps1`.

3. We can then run this script and provide input using parameters that have been declared using the `param` keyword:

```
C:\Update-SalesMailbox.ps1 -name testuser `
-maxsendsize 25mb `
-maxreceivesize 25mb `
-city Phoenix `
```

```
-state AZ `
-title Manager `
-department Sales
```

4. When the script runs, the specified mailbox will be updated with the settings provided.

How it works...

The concept of a PowerShell script is similar to batch files used with `cmd.exe`, but, instead of a `.bat` extension, PowerShell scripts use a `.ps1` extension. To create a script, you can use a basic text editor such as Notepad or you can use the Windows PowerShell **Integrated Scripting Environment (ISE)**.

Just like a function, our script accepts a number of parameters. As you can see from the code, we're using this script to automate a task that modifies several properties of a mailbox and add it to a distribution group. Since this requires the use of three separate cmdlets, it makes sense to use a script to automate this task.

If we wanted to run this script against a collection of mailboxes, we could use a `foreach` loop, as shown:

```
foreach($i in Get-Mailbox -OrganizationalUnit contoso.com/sales) {
  c:\Update-SalesMailbox.ps1 -name $i.name `
  -maxsendsize 100mb `
  -maxreceivesize 100mb `
  -city Phoenix `
  -state AZ `
  -title 'Sales Rep' `
  -department Sales
}
```

Here you can see we're simply looping through each mailbox in the *Sales* OU and running the script against each one. You can modify the script to run any number of cmdlets. Also, keep in mind that, although we're using parameters with our script, they are not required.

 Comments can be added to a script using the pound (#) character.

Think of a script as the body of a function. We can use the same three phases of execution such as `Begin`, `Process`, and `End` blocks, and add as many parameters as required. You may find it easier to create all of your code in the form of functions as opposed to scripts, although one of the nice things about scripts is that they can easily be scheduled to run as a task using the task scheduler.

There's more...

Here's something that seems a little strange at first and might take a little getting used to. When you want to execute a PowerShell script in the current directory, you need to prefix the command with a dot slash (. \) as shown:

```
[PS] C:\>.\New-SalesMailbox.ps1
```

We can use either the forward or backslash characters; it doesn't matter which. This is just a security mechanism which prevents you from executing a script in an unknown location. As you might expect, you can still run a script using its full path, just as you would with an executable or batch file.

Another thing to be aware of is the concept of dot-sourcing a script. This gives us the ability to execute commands in a script and also load any custom aliases, functions, or variables that are present within the script into your PowerShell session. To dot-source a script, use the dot operator: type a period, followed by a space, and then the path to the script as shown next:

```
[PS] C:\>. .\functions.ps1
```

This technique can be used to load functions, modules, variables, and aliases from within other scripts.

Execution policy

Windows PowerShell implements script security to keep unwanted scripts from running in your environment. You have the option of signing your scripts with a digital signature to ensure that scripts that are run are from a trusted source. In order to implement this functionality, PowerShell provides four script execution modes that can be enabled:

1. **Restricted**: Scripts will not run even if they are digitally signed

2. **AllSigned:** All scripts must be digitally signed

3. **RemoteSigned**: You can run local scripts, but scripts downloaded from the internet will not run

4. **Unrestricted**: All scripts will run whether they are signed or not, or have been downloaded from an internet site

The default execution policy on a machine is `Restricted`. When you install Exchange 2010 on a server, or the Exchange Management Tools on a workstation, the execution policy is automatically set to `RemoteSigned`. This is required by Exchange in order to implement the remote shell functionality.

It is possible to manage Exchange 2010 through PowerShell remoting on a workstation or server without the Exchange Tools installed. In this case, you'll need to make sure your script execution policy is set to either `RemoteSigned` or `Unrestricted`. To set the execution policy, use the following command:

```
Set-ExecutionPolicy RemoteSigned
```

Make sure you do not change the execution policy to `AllSigned` on machines where you'll be using the Exchange cmdlets. This will interfere with importing the commands through a remote PowerShell connection which is required for the Exchange Management Shell cmdlets to run properly.

You can reference the help system on this topic by running `Get-Help about_Execution_Policies`.

See also

▶ *Setting up a profile*

Setting up a profile

You can use a PowerShell profile to customize your shell environment and to load functions, modules, aliases, and variables into the environment when you start your Exchange Management Shell session. In this recipe, we'll take a look at how you can create a profile.

How to do it...

Profiles are not created by default, but you may want to verify one has not already been created. Start off by running the `Test-Path` cmdlet:

```
Test-Path $profile
```

If the `Test-Path` cmdlet returns `$true`, then a profile has already been created for the current user. You can open an existing profile by invoking `notepad.exe` from the shell:

```
notepad $profile
```

If the `Test-Path` cmdlet returns `$false`, you can create a new profile for the current user by running the following command:

```
New-Item -type file -path $profile -force
```

How it works...

A PowerShell profile is a just a script with a `.ps1` extension that is run every time you start the shell. You can think of a profile as a logon script for your PowerShell or Exchange Management Shell session. Inside your profile you can add custom aliases, define variables, load modules, or add your own functions so that they will be available every time you start the shell. In the previous example, we used the automatic shell `$profile` variable to create a profile script for the current user, which in this case would create the profile in the `$env:UserProfile\Documents\WindowsPowerShell\`directory.

Since PowerShell is simply executing a `.ps1` script to load your profile, your execution policy must allow the execution of scripts on your machine. If it does not, your profile will not be loaded when starting the shell and you'll receive an error.

There are four types of profiles that can be used with PowerShell:

1. `$Profile.AllUsersAllHosts`: This profile applies to all users and all shells and is located in `$env:Windir\system32\WindowsPowerShell\v1.0\profile.ps1`

2. `$Profile.AllUsersCurrentHost`: This profile applies to all users but only the PowerShell.exe host and is located in `$env:Windir\system32\WindowsPowerShell\v1.0\ Microsoft.PowerShell_profile.ps1`

3. `$Profile.CurrentUserAllHosts`: This profile applies to the current user and all shells and is located in `$env:UserProfile\Documents\WindowsPowerShell\profile.ps1`

4. `$Profile.CurrentUserCurrentHost`: This profile applies to the current user and only to the PowerShell.exe host and is located in `$env:UserProfile\Documents\WindowsPowerShell\Microsoft.PowerShell_profile.ps1`

Using the `$profile` variable alone to create the profile will default to the `CurrentUserCurrentHost` location and is probably the most commonly-used profile type. If you need to create a profile for all the users on a machine, use one of the *AllUsers* profile types.

You may be wondering at this point what the difference is between the "Current Host" and "All Hosts" profile types. The PowerShell runtime can be hosted within third-party applications, so the "All Hosts" profile types apply to those instances of PowerShell. The "Current Host" profile types can be used with `PowerShell.exe` and when you are running the Exchange Management Shell.

In addition to defining custom aliases or functions in a profile, you may want to consider loading any other modules that may be useful. For example, you may want to load the Active Directory module for PowerShell so that those cmdlets are also available to you whenever you start the shell.

When you're done making changes to your profile, save and close the file. In order for the changes to take effect, you can either restart the shell, or you can dot-source the script to reload the profile:

```
. $profile
```

You can create multiple `.ps1` scripts that include aliases, functions, and variables and then dot-source these scripts within your profile to have them loaded every time you start your PowerShell session.

You can reference the help system on this topic by running `Get-Help about_profiles`.

There's more...

Trying to remember all of the profile types and their associated script paths can be a little tough. There's actually a pretty neat trick that you can use with the `$profile` variable to view all of the profile types and file paths in the shell. To do this, access the `psextended` property of the `$profile` object:

```
$profile.psextended | Format-List
```

This will give you a list of each profile type and the path of the `.ps1` script that should be used to create the profile.

See also

▶   *Creating and running scripts*

2
Exchange Management Shell Common Tasks

In this chapter, we will cover:

- ▸ Using command discovery through the Exchange Management Console
- ▸ Manually configuring remote PowerShell connections
- ▸ Transferring files through remote shell connections
- ▸ Dealing with concurrent pipelines in remote PowerShell
- ▸ Managing domains or an entire forest using recipient scope
- ▸ Using explicit credentials with PowerShell cmdlets
- ▸ Exporting reports to text and CSV files
- ▸ Sending SMTP e-mails through PowerShell
- ▸ Scheduling scripts to run at a later time
- ▸ Logging shell sessions to a transcript
- ▸ Automating tasks with the scripting agent
- ▸ Scripting an exchange server installation

Introduction

Microsoft introduced some radical architectural changes in Exchange 2007, including a brand new set of management tools. PowerShell v1, along with an additional set of exchange specific cmdlets, finally gave administrators an interface that could be used to manage the entire product from a command line shell. This was an interesting move, as was the fact that the entire graphical management console was built on top of this technology. Any tasks performed from the graphical interface, known as the **Exchange Management Console**, were translated into PowerShell commands that were carried out in the background. This meant that for the first time, administrators could completely automate anything that could be done from the graphical console using this new command line interface called the **Exchange Management Shell**. This was a total departure from how the management tools worked in previous versions of Exchange, but it finally provided the automation capabilities that had been desired by many people for several years.

This same architecture still exists with this latest version of Exchange, and PowerShell is even more tightly integrated with the product. Of course, there are many new cmdlets and core functionality changes. Exchange 2010 uses PowerShell v2, and relies heavily on its new remoting infrastructure. This provides seamless administrative capabilities from a single seat with the Exchange Management Tools, whether your servers are on premise or in the cloud.

Even if you've worked with the Exchange Management Shell previously, the syntax used with some of the existing cmdlets has changed in Exchange 2010, and the new remoting functionality has introduced some changes that you'll want to be aware of.

In this chapter, we'll cover these topics, as well as common tasks that will allow you to effectively write scripts with this latest release. We'll also take a look at some general tasks such as scheduling scripts, sending e-mails, generating reports, and more.

Performing some basic steps

To make use of all the examples in this chapter, we'll need to use the Exchange Management Shell, the Exchange Management console, and a standard PowerShell v2 console.

You can launch the Exchange Management Shell or the Exchange Management Console by using the following steps:

1. Log onto a workstation or server with the Exchange Management Tools installed

2. Open the Exchange Management Shell by clicking on **Start | All Programs | Exchange Server 2010**

3. Click on the **Exchange Management Shell** or the **Exchange ManagementConsole** shortcut

To launch a standard PowerShell console, use the following steps:

1. On Windows Vista, Windows 7, or Windows Server 2008, open a standard PowerShell console by clicking on **Start | All Programs | Accessories,** click on the **Windows PowerShell** folder, and then click the **Windows PowerShell** shortcut.

2. On Windows XP and Windows Server 2003, click on **Start | Programs | Accessories**, click on the **Windows PowerShell** folder, and then click the **Windows PowerShell** shortcut.

 Unless specified otherwise in the *Getting ready* section, all of the recipes in this chapter will require the use of the Exchange Management Shell.

Using command discovery through the Exchange Management Console

The Exchange Management Console simply carries out PowerShell commands in the background as you add, remove, and modify objects. One of the nice features is that most of these commands are exposed through the console, and you can use it as a tool to learn PowerShell. In this recipe, we'll look at a few ways in which you can discover which PowerShell commands are being executed when making changes in the console.

Getting ready

To use the examples in this recipe, you will need to launch the Exchange Management Console.

How to do it...

In the Exchange Management Console, highlight an item in the console tree, click on the **View** menu, and select **View Exchange Management Console Command Log**, as shown in the following screenshot:

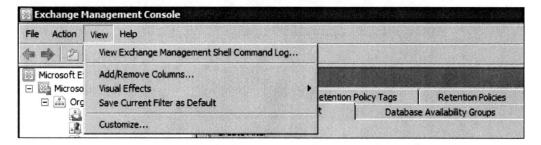

This will bring up the Exchange Management Shell Log window, as shown in the following screenshot:

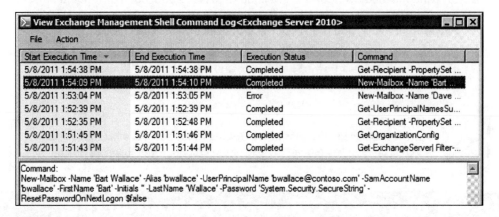

In addition to command logging, you can use the PowerShell command button when modifying the settings of an object. For example, after modifying the `Office` setting for a mailbox, the PowerShell command button located at the lower-left hand corner of the properties window will be enabled:

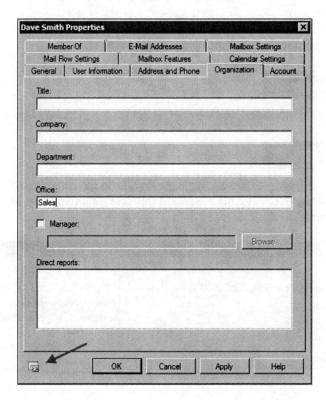

After clicking the PowerShell command button, you'll be able to view the cmdlet and the parameters that will be used to carry out the change:

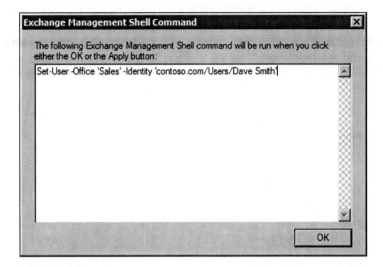

How it works...

PowerShell command logging is enabled by default and will record the last 2,048 commands generated by Exchange. Each logged command shows the start and end of execution time, along with the status. You can highlight the log entry to view the command and any parameters used in the bottom window. You can go to the **Action** menu and modify several properties, such as stopping or starting command logging, increasing the number of commands the system should keep track of, or copying any previously run commands.

Using the PowerShell command button is also a good way to figure out the syntax for the commands being used to change a setting. Imagine that you needed to know how to write a script that would enable a custom storage quota at the mailbox level for a group of users. You could go into the properties of one mailbox and modify the storage quota setting. Before clicking **Apply** and **OK**, you can click the PowerShell command button to figure out the syntax for the command. You could then write a script based on this information that could be run against one or more mailboxes.

There's more...

In addition to PowerShell Command Logging and the PowerShell command button, the Exchange Management Console will also provide the commands used to perform a task. For example, when creating a mailbox in the console, you are taken through a wizard that allows you to configure the required settings for the mailbox. At the end of the wizard, you'll see a screen that will give you the exact command carried out by Exchange to create the mailbox, like the following:

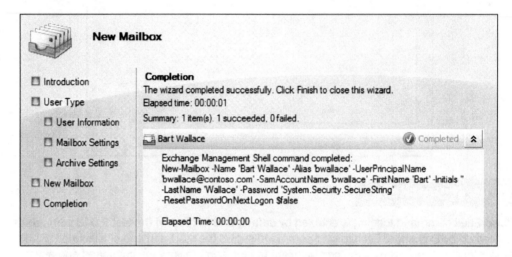

As you can see, the final screen at the end of the **New Mailbox** wizard provides the command used to create the mailbox using the New-Mailbox cmdlet. All of the values entered into the previous screens have been converted to parameter values. You can click *ctrl + c* on this screen to copy the command used to create the mailbox.

See also

▸ *Understanding command syntax and parameters* in *Chapter 1, PowerShell Key Concepts*

▸ *Using the help system* in *Chapter 1, PowerShell Key Concepts*

Manually configuring remote PowerShell connections

One of the major changes in Exchange 2010 is the toolset and its reliance on PowerShell remoting. When you double-click the Exchange Management Shell shortcut on a server or workstation with the Exchange Management Tools installed, you are connected to an Exchange server using a remote PowerShell session.

PowerShell remoting also allows you to remotely manage your Exchange servers from a workstation or a server even when the Exchange Management Tools are not installed. In this recipe, we'll create a manual remote shell connection to an Exchange server using a standard PowerShell console.

Getting ready

To complete the steps in this recipe, you'll need to log on to a workstation or a server and launch Windows PowerShell.

How to do it...

1. First, create a credential object using the `Get-Credential` cmdlet. When running this command, you'll be prompted with a Windows authentication dialog box. Enter a username and password for an account that has administrative access to your Exchange organization. Make sure you enter your user name in DOMAIN\USERNAME or UPN format:

   ```
   $credential = Get-Credential
   ```

2. Next, create a new session object and store it in a variable. In this example, the Exchange server we are connecting to is specified using the `-ConnectionUri` parameter. Replace the server FQDN in the following example with one of your own Exchange servers:

   ```
   $session = New-PSSession -ConfigurationName Microsoft.Exchange `
   -ConnectionUri http://mail.contoso.com/PowerShell/ `
   -Credential $credential
   ```

3. Finally, import the session object:

   ```
   Import-PSSession $session
   ```

4. After you execute the preceding command, the Exchange Management Shell cmdlets will be imported into your current PowerShell session, as shown in the following screenshot:

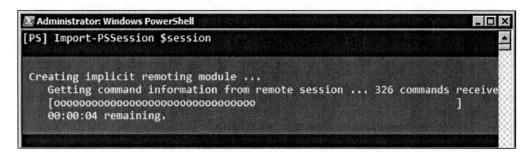

How it works...

Every Exchange 2010 server role, with the exception of the Edge server role, utilizes PowerShell remoting. Each server runs IIS and supports remote PowerShell sessions via HTTP. Exchange Servers host a PowerShell virtual directory in IIS. This contains several modules that perform authentication checks and determine which cmdlets and parameters are assigned to the user making the connection. This happens both when running the Exchange Management Shell with the tools installed, and when creating a manual remote connection.

Remote PowerShell connections to Exchange 2010 servers use a special feature called implicit remoting that allows us to import remote commands into the local shell session. With this feature, we can use the Exchange PowerShell snap-in installed on the server in our local PowerShell session without installing the Exchange tools.

 You'll need to allow the execution of scripts in order to create a manual remote shell connection on a machine that does not have the Exchange tools installed. For more details, refer to the *Creating and running scripts* recipe in *Chapter 1, PowerShell Key Concepts*.

You may be curious as to why Exchange uses remote PowerShell even when the tools are installed and when running the shell from the server. There are a couple of reasons for this, but some of the main factors are permissions. The Exchange 2010 permissions model has been completely transformed in this latest version and uses a new feature called **Role Based Access Control** (**RBAC**) which defines what administrators can and cannot do. When you make a remote PowerShell connection to an Exchange 2010 server, the RBAC authorization module in IIS determines which cmdlets and parameters you have access to. Once this information is obtained, only the cmdlets and parameters that have been assigned to your account via an RBAC role are loaded into your PowerShell session using implicit remoting.

The Exchange 2010 Management Tools can only be installed on 64-bit systems and there are no 32-bit tools available. If you need the ability to manage Exchange from a 32-bit workstation, you can use a manual remote shell session to load the cmdlets into your local PowerShell session, as long as you have the Windows Management Framework Core installed.

There's more...

In the previous example, we explicitly set the credentials used to create the remote shell connection. This is optional and not required if the account you are currently logged on with has the appropriate Exchange permissions assigned. To create a remote shell session using your currently logged on credentials, use the following syntax to create the session object:

```
$session = New-PSSession -ConfigurationName Microsoft.Exchange `
-ConnectionUri http://mail.contoso.com/PowerShell/
```

Once again, import the session:

```
Import-PSSession $session
```

You can see here that the commands are almost identical to the previous example, except this time we've removed the -Credential parameter and the assigned credential object. After this is done, you can simply import the session and the commands will be imported into your current session using implicit remoting.

 Although you can manually load the Exchange snap-in within a standard PowerShell console on a machine with the Exchange tools installed, this is not supported. You may also have mixed results when doing this, since this method bypasses remoting and, therefore, the RBAC system which may be required to give you the appropriate rights.

In addition to implicit remoting, Exchange 2010 servers running PowerShell v2 can also be managed using fan-out remoting. This is accomplished using the Invoke-Command cmdlet and it allows you to execute a script block on multiple computers in parallel. For more details, run Get-Help Invoke-Command and Get-Help about_remoting.

You may also want to check out the *Administrator's Guide to Windows PowerShell Remoting*. It is a great resource that covers PowerShell remoting in depth and it can be downloaded from the following URL:

```
http://powershell.com/cs/media/p/4908.aspx
```

See also

> ▸ *Using explicit credentials with PowerShell commands*

Transferring files through remote shell connections

Since the Exchange 2010 Management Shell commands are executed through a remote PowerShell session, importing and exporting files requires a new special syntax. There are a handful of shell cmdlets that require this, and in this recipe we'll take a look at the syntax that needs to be used to transfer files through a remote shell connection.

How to do it...

Let's say that you are creating an Edge subscription to the hub transport servers in the default Active Directory site. After generating your XML subscription file on the Edge server, you can import the file using the `New-EdgeSubscription` cmdlet, using syntax similar to the following:

```
[byte[]]$data = Get-Content -Path "C:\Edge.xml" `
-Encoding Byte `
-ReadCount 0

New-EdgeSubscription -FileData $data -Site Default-First-Site
```

In this example, the file data is first read into a variable called `$data`. The subscription is then created using the `New-EdgeSubscription` cmdlet by assigning the `$data` variable as a value to the `-FileData` parameter.

How it works...

When you launch the Exchange 2010 Management Shell, special commands called proxy functions are imported into your local shell session. These proxy functions represent the compiled cmdlets that are actually installed on your Exchange server. When you run these commands, any data required for input through parameters are transferred through a remote connection from your machine to the server and the command is then executed. Since the commands are actually running on the server and not on your machine, we cannot use a local path for files that need to be imported.

In the previous example, you can see that we first stored the file data in a variable. What we are doing here is reading the file content into the variable using the `Get-Content` cmdlet in order to create a byte-encoded object. This variable is then assigned to the cmdlet's `-FileData` parameter, which requires a byte-encoded value.

There are a number of Exchange Management Shell cmdlets that include a `-FileData` parameter used to provide external files as input:

 ▶ `Import-ExchangeCertificate`: Used for importing certificates

 ▶ `Import-JournalRuleCollection`: Imports a collection of journal rules

 ▶ `Import-RecipientDataProperty`: Used for importing photos into Active Directory

 ▶ `Import-TransportRuleCollection`: Allows you to import a collection of transport rules

 ▶ `New-EdgeSubscription`: Imports an Edge subscription file

This is a good example of how remote PowerShell sessions have changed things in Exchange 2010. For example, if you have worked with the shell in Exchange 2007, you may remember the `Import-ExchangeCertificate` cmdlet. This cmdlet used to accept a local file path when importing a certificate into a server, but, due to the new remoting functionality, the commands used to perform this task have changed, even though the cmdlet name is still the same.

There's more...

We also have to take remote shell connections into consideration when exporting data. For example, let's say that we need to export the user photo associated with a mailbox from Active Directory. The command would look something like this:

```
Export-RecipientDataProperty -Identity dsmith -Picture | %{
  $_.FileData | Add-Content C:\pics\dsmith.jpg -Encoding Byte
}
```

When using the `Export-RecipientDataProperty` cmdlet with the `-Picture` switch parameter, the photo can be retrieved from the `FileData` property of the object returned. The photo data is stored in this property as a byte array. In order to export the data, we need to loop through each element stored in this property and use the `Add-Content` cmdlet to re-construct the image to an external file.

When dealing with cmdlets that import or export data, make sure you utilize the help system. Remember, you can run `Get-Help <cmdlet name> -Examples` with any of these cmdlets to determine the correct syntax.

See also

- *Using the Help System* in *Chapter 1*, *PowerShell Key Concepts*
- *Manually Configuring Remote PowerShell Connections*

Dealing with concurrent pipelines in remote PowerShell

One of the issues you are bound to run into, sooner or later, is a concurrent pipeline error when working in a remote PowerShell session. This is a common stumbling block for most administrators, since all Exchange Management Shell tasks are done through PowerShell remoting. Concurrent pipeline errors can often be counter-intuitive because the same command syntax works fine in a standard PowerShell session. In this recipe, we'll take a look at why this happens and what you can do to get around it.

How to do it...

PowerShell remoting does not support more than one pipeline running at a time. When executing multiple cmdlets within a pipeline, you may need to store the output of one or more commands in an object that can be then be passed down the pipeline to other commands. For example, to pipe a collection of mailboxes to the `New-InboxRule` command, use the following syntax to avoid a concurrent pipeline operation:

```
$mailboxes = Get-Mailbox -Database DB1
$mailboxes | %{
  New-InboxRule -Name Attach `
  -Mailbox $_ `
  -HasAttachment $true `
  -MarkImportance High
}
```

How it works...

In this example, we first create a collection of all the mailboxes in the `DB1` database by storing them in the `$mailboxes` variable. We then loop through each mailbox object by piping `$mailboxes` to the `ForEach-Object` cmdlet (using the `%` alias), and, for each item in the collection, we create an inbox rule that marks any message with an attachment as of high importance.

Some Exchange Management Shell cmdlets are designed specifically to accept input from other cmdlets. One good example of this is how the `Get-Mailbox` and `Set-Mailbox` cmdlets work together. You can simply pipe the `Get-Mailbox` cmdlet directly to the `Set-Mailbox` cmdlet, and the parameter binding is automatic. As you can see from the example, when dealing with cmdlets that are not designed to work together such as the `Get-Mailbox` and `New-InboxRule` cmdlets, you need to use the `ForEach-Object` cmdlet or a `foreach` loop statement so you can explicitly identify the object that needs to be modified.

In a typical PowerShell session, you can pipe one command to another in this way without any problems, but this is not the case when working in a remote PowerShell session. PowerShell remoting does not support multiple pipelines executing at the same time.

Had we tried to pipe the results from `Get-Mailbox` directly to `ForEach-Object`, we would have gotten the following error:

```
Machine: MBX1.CONTOSO.COM                                          _ □ ×
[PS] C:\>Get-Mailbox | %{New-InboxRule -Name Attach -Mailbox $_ -HasAttachme
nt $true -MarkImportance High}
Pipeline not executed because a pipeline is already executing. Pipelines ca
nnot be executed concurrently.
```

There's more...

In the first example, we used the `ForEach-Object` cmdlet to process each mailbox in the `$mailboxes` collection to avoid executing concurrent pipelines. You can also use a `foreach` statement to accomplish the same thing. This code is an alternative to the previous example but will achieve the same end result:

```
foreach($i in Get-Mailbox -Database DB1) {
    New-InboxRule -Name Attach `
    -Mailbox $i `
    -HasAttachment $true `
    -MarkImportance High
}
```

Notice that we're still working with the same set of mailboxes, but since we are using the `foreach` construct, we identify the mailbox object that the `New-InboxRule` cmdlet needs to work with, using the `$i` variable as opposed to the `$_` pipeline variable used with the `ForEach-Object` cmdlet.

See also

- ▶ *Understanding the pipeline* in *Chapter 1, PowerShell Key Concepts*
- ▶ *Looping through items* in *Chapter 1, PowerShell Key Concepts*
- ▶ *Adding, modifying, and removing sever-side inbox rules* in *Chapter 3, Managing Recipients*

Managing domains or an entire forest using recipient scope

The Exchange Management Tools can be configured to use specific portions of your Active Directory hierarchy using a specific recipient scope. When you set the recipient scope to a location in the Active Directory, such as a domain or a an organizational unit, the Exchange Management Shell will only allow you to view the recipients that are stored in that location and any containers beneath it. In this recipe, we'll look at how to set the recipient scope when working with the Exchange Management Shell.

How to do it...

1. We can set the recipient scope in the Exchange Management Shell using the `Set-AdServerSettings` cmdlet. For example, to set the recipient scope to the *Sales* OU in the `contoso.com` domain, use the following command:

   ```
   Set-AdServerSettings -RecipientViewRoot contoso.com/sales
   ```

2. We can also specify the value using the distinguished name of the OU:

```
Set-AdServerSettings -RecipientViewRoot `
"OU=sales,DC=contoso,DC=com"
```

How it works...

In Exchange 2007, recipient scope was set using the `AdminSessionADSettings` global session variable. With Exchange 2010, we use the `Set-AdServerSettings` cmdlet. When you first start the Exchange Management Shell, the default recipient scope is set to the domain of the computer that is running the shell. If you change the recipient scope, the setting will not be retained when you restart the shell. The default domain scope will always be used when you launch the shell. You can override this by adding these commands to your PowerShell profile to ensure that the setting is always initially configured as needed.

In the previous example, we set the recipient scope to a specific OU in the domain. If you are working in a multi-domain forest, you can use the `-ViewEntireForest` parameter so that all recipient objects in the forest can be managed from your shell session. Use the following command to view the entire forest:

```
Set-AdServerSettings -ViewEntireForest $true
```

To change the recipient scope to a specific domain, set the `-RecipientViewRoot` to the full qualified domain name of the Active Directory domain:

```
Set-AdServerSettings -RecipientViewRoot corp.contoso.com
```

There's more...

If you're working in a large environment with multiple domains and OUs, setting the recipient scope can improve the speed of the Exchange Management Shell, since it will limit the total number of recipients returned by your commands.

If you have Exchange recipients in multiple Active Directory domains or sites, you may have to take replication latency into account when working with a broad recipient scope. To handle this, you can use the `Set-AdServerSettings` cmdlet to specify domain controllers and global catalog servers that you want to work with.

To set the preferred domain controllers and global catalog that should be used with your recipient scope, use the `-SetPreferredDomainControllers` and `-PreferredGlobalCatalog` paramters to specify the FQDN of the servers:

```
Set-AdServerSettings -ViewEntireForest $true `
-SetPreferredDomainControllers dc1.contoso.com `
-PreferredGlobalCatalog dc1.contoso.com
```

Setting the preferred domain controller can be useful to ensure your commands will read the latest list of recipients in Active Directory. If you have a provisioning process that uses a specific domain controller when creating recipients, it may take some time to replicate this information throughout the forest. Setting the preferred domain controllers can be used to ensure that you are working with the latest set of recipients available, even if they haven't been replicated throughout the forest.

Using explicit credentials with PowerShell cmdlets

There are several PowerShell and Exchange Management Shell cmdlets that provide a credential parameter that allows you to use an alternate set of credentials when running a command. You may need to use alternate credentials when making manual remote shell connections, sending e-mail messages, working in cross-forest scenarios, and more. In this recipe, we'll take a look at how you can create a credential object that can be used with commands that support the -Credential parameter.

How to do it...

To create a credential object, we can use the Get-Credential cmdlet. In this example, we store the credential object in a variable that can be used by the Get-Mailbox cmdlet:

```
$credential = Get-Credential
Get-Mailbox -Credential $credential
```

How it works...

When you run the Get-Credential cmdlet, you are presented with a Windows authentication dialog box requesting your username and password. In the previous example, we assigned the Get-Credential cmdlet to the $credential variable. After typing your username and password into the authentication dialog box, the credentials are saved as an object that can then be assigned to the -Credential parameter of a cmdlet. The cmdlet that utilizes the credential object will then run using the credentials of the specified user.

Supplying credentials to a command doesn't have to be an interactive process. You can programmatically create a credential object within your script without using the Get-Credential cmdlet:

```
$user = "contoso\administrator"
$pass = ConvertTo-SecureString -AsPlainText P@ssw0rd01 -Force
$credential = New-Object System.Management.Automation.PSCredential `
-ArgumentList $user,$pass
```

You can see here that we've created a credential object from scratch without using the `Get-Credential` cmdlet. In order to create a credential object, we need to supply the password as a secure string type. The `ConvertTo-SecureString` cmdlet can be used to create a secure string object. We then use the `New-Object` cmdlet to create a credential object specifying the desired user name and password as arguments.

If you need to prompt a user for their credentials but you do not want to invoke the Windows authentication dialog box, you can use this alternative syntax to prompt the user in the shell for their credentials:

```
$user = Read-Host "Please enter your username"
$pass = Read-Host "Please enter your password" -AsSecureString
$credential = New-Object System.Management.Automation.PSCredential `
-ArgumentList $user,$pass
```

This syntax uses the `Read-Host` cmdlet to prompt the user for both their username and password. Notice that when creating the `$pass` object we use `Read-Host` with the `-AsSecureString` parameter to ensure that the object is stored as a secure string.

There's more...

After you've created a credential object, you may need to access the properties of that object to retrieve the username and password. We can access the username and password properties of the `$credential` object created previously using the following commands:

```
Machine: MBX1.CONTOSO.COM
[PS] C:\>$credential.UserName
contoso\administrator
[PS] C:\>$credential.GetNetworkCredential().Password
P@ssw0rd01
[PS] C:\>
```

You can see here that we can simply grab the username stored in the object by accessing the `UserName` property of the credential object. Since the `Password` property is stored as a secure string, we need to use the `GetNetworkCredential` method to convert the credential to a `NetworkCredential` object that exposes the `Password` property as a simple string.

Exporting reports to text and CSV files

One of the added benefits of the Exchange Management Shell is the ability to run very detailed and customizable reports. With the hundreds of `Get-*` cmdlets provided between Windows PowerShell and the Exchange Management Shell, the reporting capabilities are almost endless. In this recipe, we'll cover exporting command output to plain text and CSV files that can be used to report on various resources throughout your Exchange environment.

How to do it...

To export command output to a text file, use the `Out-File` cmdlet. To generate a report of mailboxes in a specific mailbox database that can be stored in a text file, use the following command:

```
Get-Mailbox | Select-Object Name,Alias | Out-File c:\report.txt
```

You can also save the output of the previous command as a CSV file that can then be opened and formatted in Microsoft Excel:

```
Get-Mailbox | Select-Object Name,Alias |
    Export-CSV c:\report.csv –NoType
```

How it works...

The `Out-File` cmdlet is simply a redirection command that will export the output of your command to a plain text file. Perhaps one of the most useful features of this cmdlet is the ability to add data to the end of an existing file using the `-Append` parameter. This allows you to continuously update a text file when processing multiple objects or creating persistent log files or reports.

 You can also use the `Add-Content`, `Set-Content`, and `Clear-Content` cmdlets to add, replace, or remove data from files.

The `Export-CSV` cmdlet converts the object's output, by your command, into a collection of comma-separated values and stores them in a CSV file. When we ran the `Get-Mailbox` cmdlet in the previous example, we filtered the output, selecting only the `Name` and `Alias` properties. When exporting this output using `Export-CSV`, these property names are used for the column headers. Each object returned by the command will be represented in the CSV file as an individual row, therefore populating the `Name` and `Alias` columns with the associated data.

You may have noticed in the `Export-CSV` example that we used the `-NoType` switch parameter. This is commonly-used and is shorthand notation for the full parameter name `-NoTypeInformation`. If you do not specify this switch parameter, the first line of the CSV file will contain a header specifying the .NET Framework type of the object that was exported. This is rarely useful. If you end up with a strange-looking header in one of your reports, remember to run the command again using the `-NoTypeInformation` switch parameter.

There's more...

One of the most common problems that Exchange administrators run into with `Export-CSV` is when exporting objects with multi-valued properties. Let's say we need to run a report that lists each mailbox and its associated e-mail addresses. The command would look something like the following:

```
Get-Mailbox |
    Select-Object Name,EmailAddresses |
        Export-CSV c:\report.csv -NoType
```

The problem here is that each mailbox can contain multiple e-mail addresses. When we select the `EmailAddresses` property, a multi-valued object is returned. The `Export-CSV` cmdlet does not understand how to handle this, and when you open the CSV file in Excel, you'll end up with a report that looks like the following:

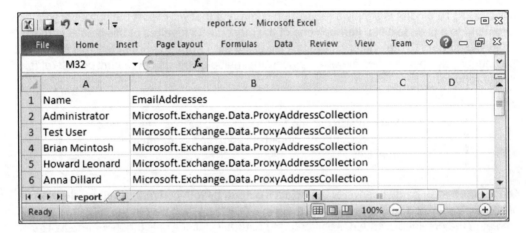

From looking at the this screenshot, you can see that on the first line, we have our header names that match the properties selected during the export. In the first column, the `Name` property for each mailbox has been recorded correctly, but, as you can see, the values listed in the `EmailAddresses` column have a problem. Instead of the e-mail addresses, we get the .NET Framework type name of the multi-valued property. To get around this, we need to help the `Export-CSV` cmdlet understand what we are trying to do and specifically reference the data that needs to be exported.

One of the best ways to handle this is to use a calculated property and join each value of the multi-valued property as a single string:

```
Get-Mailbox |
  Select-Object Name,@{n="Email";e={$_.EmailAddresses -Join ";"}} |
    Export-CSV c:\report.csv -NoType
```

In this example, we've modified the previous command by creating a calculated property that will contain each e-mail address for the associated mailbox. Since we need to consolidate the `EmailAddresses` property data into a single item that can be exported, we use the `-Join` operator to create a string containing a list, separated by semi-colons, of every e-mail address associated with each mailbox. The command is then piped to the `Export-CSV` cmdlet, and the report is generated in a readable format that can be viewed in Excel:

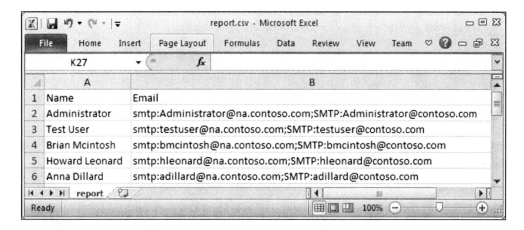

As you can see in this screenshot, each e-mail address for a mailbox is now listed in the `Email` column and is separated using a semi-colon. Each address has an SMTP prefix associated with it. An SMTP prefix in all capital letters indicates that the address is the primary SMTP address for the mailbox. Any remaining secondary addresses use an SMTP prefix in lower case characters. If you do not want to export the prefixes we can modify our code even further:

```
Get-Mailbox |
  select-Object Name,
    @{n="Email";
      e={($_.EmailAddresses | %{$_.SmtpAddress}) -Join ";"}
    } | Export-CSV c:\report.csv -NoType
```

Here you can see that, within the expression of the calculated property, we're looping through the `EmailAddresses` collection and retrieving only the `SmtpAddress`, which does not include the SMTP prefix and returns only the e-mail addresses. Once the data is exported to a CSV file we can review it in Excel:

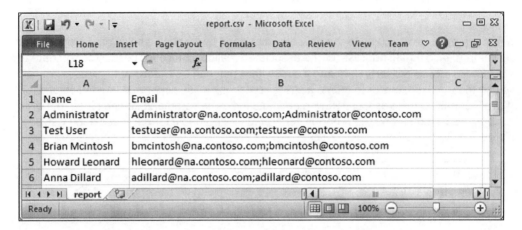

As you can see here, we now get each e-mail address associated with each mailbox without the SMTP prefix within the `Email` column of our CSV file.

See also

▸ *Formatting output* in *Chapter 1, PowerShell Key Concepts*

▸ *Creating custom objects* in *Chapter 1, PowerShell Key Concepts*

Sending SMTP e-mails through PowerShell

As an Exchange administrator, will probably need an automated solution for sending e-mails from your PowerShell scripts. Whether it's for sending notifications to users in a specific database or e-mailing the output of your scripts to a reporting mailbox, the transmission of messages like these will prove very useful in performing common day-to-day administrative scripting tasks. In this recipe, we'll take a look at how you can send SMTP e-mail messages from PowerShell to the recipients in your Exchange organization.

How to do it...

PowerShell v2 includes a core cmdlet that can be used to send e-mail messages via SMTP to one or more recipients. Use the following syntax to send an e-mail message:

```
Send-MailMessage -To user1@contoso.com `
-From administrator@contoso.com `
```

```
-Subject "Test E-mail" `
-Body "This is just a test" `
-SmtpServer ex01.contoso.com
```

How it works...

In PowerShell v1, the `Send-MailMessage` cmdlet didn't exist. In the early days before Exchange 2007 SP2 and PowerShell v2 support, we had to use the classes in the `System.Net.Mail` namespace in the .NET Framework to send SMTP e-mail messages. This was difficult for some administrators because working with .NET classes can be confusing without prior programming experience. The good news is that the `Send-MailMessage` cmdlet utilizes these same .NET classes that allow you to create rich e-mail messages that can contain one or more attachments, using an HTML formatted message body, support message priority, and more. Here are some of the more useful parameters that can be used with the `Send-MailMessage` cmdlet:

- `Attachments`: This specifies the path to the file that should be attached. It separates multiple attachments with a comma.
- `Bcc`: This allows you to specify a blind-copy recipient. It separates multiple recipients using a comma.
- `Body`: This specifies the content of a message.
- `BodyAsHtml`: This is a switch parameter that ensures the message will use an HTML-formatted message body.
- `Cc`: This allows you to specify a carbon-copy recipient. It separates multiple recipients using a comma.
- `Credential`: You can provide a `PSCredential` object created by the `Get-Credential` cmdlet to send the message using the credentials of another user.
- `DeliveryNotificationOption`: This specifies the delivery notification options for the message. The default value is **None**, but other valid options are **OnSuccess**, **OnFailure**, **Delay**, and **Never**.
- `From`: This is the e-mail address of the sender. You can define a display name using the following format: `Dave <dave@contoso.com>`.
- `Priority`: This specifies the importance of the message. The default value is **Normal**. The remaining valid values are **High** and **Low**.
- `SmtpServer`: This needs to be the name or IP address of your SMTP server. When working in an Exchange environment, this will be set to one of your Hub Transport servers.
- `Subject`: This is the subject of the e-mail message.
- `To`: This allows you to specify an e-mail recipient. It separates multiple recipients with a comma.

There's more...

When using this cmdlet, you'll need to specify an SMTP server in order to submit the message. Unless you are already using some type of mail relay system within your environment, you'll want to use a Hub Transport server in your Exchange organization. Out of the box, Exchange servers will not allow workstations or untrusted servers to relay e-mail messages. Depending on where you are sending the message from, you may need to allow the machine running your scripts to relay e-mail.

PowerShell v2 includes a preference variable called `$PSEmailServer` that can be assigned the name or IP address of an SMTP server. When this variable is defined, you can omit the `-SmtpServer` parameter when using the `Send-MailMessage` cmdlet. You can add this variable assignment to your PowerShell profile so that the setting will persist across all of your shell sessions.

Sending messages with attachments

You may want to write a script that generates a report to a text or CSV file and then e-mail that data to an administrator mailbox. The `-Attachment` parameter can be used with the `Send-MailMessage` cmdlet to do this. For example, let's say you've generated a CSV report file for the top 10 largest mailboxes in your environment and it needs to be e-mailed to your staff. The following command syntax could be used in this scenario:

```
Send-MailMessage -To support@contoso.com `
-From powershell@contoso.com `
-Subject "Mailbox Report for $((Get-Date).ToShortDateString())" `
-Body "Please review the attached mailbox report." `
-Attachments c:\report.csv `
-SmtpServer ex01.contoso.com
```

Notice that all we need to do here is provide the path and file name to the `-Attachment` parameter. You can send multiple message attachments this way by providing a comma-separated list of files.

Sending command output in the body of a message

Instead of exporting command data to an external file and sending it as an attachment, you may want to add this information to the body of an e-mail. In this example, we'll send a message that displays the top 10 largest mailboxes in the organization in the body of an HTML-formatted message:

```
[string]$report = Get-MailboxDatabase |
  Get-MailboxStatistics| ?{!$_.DisconnectDate} |
    Sort-Object TotalItemSize -Desc |
      Select-Object DisplayName,Database,TotalItemSize -First 10 |
      ConvertTo-Html
```

```
Send-MailMessage -To support@contoso.com `
-From powershell@contoso.com `
-Subject "Mailbox Report for $((Get-Date).ToShortDateString())" `
-Body $report `
-BodyAsHtml `
-SmtpServer ex01.contoso.com
```

Here you can see that the report data is generated with a fairly sophisticated one-liner and the output is saved in a string variable called `$report`. We need to strongly type the `$report` variable as `string` because that is the data type required by the `-Body` parameter of the `Send-MailMessage` cmdlet. Notice that we're using the `ConvertTo-Html` cmdlet at the end of the one-liner to convert the objects to an HTML document. Since the `$report` variable will simply contain raw HTML, we can assign this value to the `–Body` parameter and use the `-BodyAsHtml` switch parameter to send the report data in the body of an HTML-formatted message.

See also

▸ *Allowing application servers to relay mail* in *Chapter 8, Managing Transport Servers*

▸ *Sending e-mail messages with EWS* in *Chapter 13, Scripting with the Exchange Web Services Managed API*

▸ *Setting up a profile* in *Chapter 1, PowerShell Key Concepts*

▸ *Reporting on mailbox size* in *Chapter 4, Managing Mailboxes*

Scheduling scripts to run at a later time

One of the most common tasks that Exchange administrators perform is scheduling scripts to run at a later time. This can be useful when performing maintenance after hours or running monitoring scripts on a regular basis. In this recipe, you'll learn how to schedule your PowerShell scripts to run with the Windows Task Scheduler.

How to do it...

To create a scheduled task that runs from one of your Exchange servers use the following steps:

1. Open the Windows Task Scheduler by clicking on **Start | All Programs | Accessories**, click on the **System Tools** folder, and then click the **Task Scheduler** shortcut.

2. From the **Action** menu, click **Create Basic Task**.

3. Give your task a name and description, and click **Next**.

4. On the Trigger screen, select the how often you'd like the script to run (Daily, Weekly, Monthly, and so on).

5. When asked what action you want the task to perform, select **Start a Program**.

6. Use the following syntax in the Program/Script field and click on **Next**:
   `C:\Windows\System32\WindowsPowerShell\v1.0\powershell.exe -command ". 'C:\Program Files\Microsoft\Exchange Server\V14\bin\RemoteExchange.ps1'; Connect-ExchangeServer -auto; c:\Scripts\MoveMailboxes.ps1".`

7. You will receive a prompt that says **It appears as though arguments have been included in the program text box. Do you want to run the following program?** Click **Yes**.

8. This will bring you to a summary screen where you can click **Finish**.

How it works...

The syntax used in this example may look a little strange at first. What we are actually doing here is scheduling `PowerShell.exe` and using the `-Command` parameter to execute multiple statements. This allows us to pass the contents of a PowerShell script to `PowerShell.exe`. In this case, our script has multiple lines and each statement is separated by a semi-colon.

The first thing we do is dot-source the `RemoteExchange.ps1` script located in the Exchange Server Bin directory. This file initializes some Exchange shell variables and imports several Exchange specific functions.

The next line of the script calls the `Connect-ExchangeServer` function using the `-Auto` parameter, allowing the Exchange Management Shell environment to load automatically from the best Exchange Server in the local AD site.

Finally, we provide the path to our `.ps1` script that utilizes any required Exchange Management Shell cmdlets and the script is executed, carrying out whatever it is that we need to be done.

It's worth mentioning here that you do not have to use a `.ps1` script file with this syntax. You can replace the call to the `MoveMailboxes.ps1` file with any valid PowerShell commands. If you have a script that contains multiple lines, you can continue to separate each line using a semi-colon.

When using this method, make sure that you configure the scheduled task to run as a user that has administrative access to your Exchange organization. Also, if you have **User Account Control** (**UAC**) enabled, you may need to enable the option to **Run with highest privileges** in the properties of the scheduled task. Additionally, you will probably want to enable the option to **Run whether user is logged on or not** in the properties of the scheduled task.

There's more...

The previous example demonstrated scheduling a task from an Exchange server using the installed Exchange Management Shell tools. Since all of the Exchange Management Shell connections utilize PowerShell remoting, it is possible to schedule a script to run from a workstation or server without the Exchange tools installed. The only requirement is that the machine must be running PowerShell v2.

To schedule a task from a machine without the Exchange tools installed, use the steps from the previous example, but use the following syntax for the program action:

```
C:\Windows\System32\WindowsPowerShell\v1.0\powershell.exe -command "$s
= New-PSSession -ConfigurationNameMicrosoft.Exchange -ConnectionUri
http://ex01.contoso.com/PowerShell/; Import-PSSession $s ; c:\Scripts\
MoveMailboxes.ps1"
```

You can see here again we are scheduling the `PowerShell.exe` program and specifying the script using the `-Command` parameter. The difference is that this time we are not using the locally installed Exchange tools. Instead we are creating a manual implicit remoting connection to a particular Exchange server. The length of the command line wrapping makes it difficult to read, but keep in mind that this is all done on one line.

When using this method, you can configure the scheduled task to run as a user that has administrative access to your Exchange organization, or you can provide explicit credentials used to create the session object and run the script as another user.

See also

▶ *Manually configuring remote PowerShell connections*

▶ *Using explicit credentials with PowerShell cmdlets*

▶ *Creating and running scripts* in *Chapter 1, PowerShell Key Concepts*

Logging shell sessions to a transcript

You may find it useful at times to record the output of your shell sessions in a log file. This can help you save the history of all the commands you've executed and determine the success or failure of automated scripts. In this recipe, you'll learn how to create a PowerShell transcript.

How to do it...

1. To create a transcript, execute the `Start-Transcript` cmdlet:

   ```
   Start-Transcript -Path c:\logfile.txt
   ```

2. You can stop recording the session using the `Stop-Transcript` cmdlet:

```
Stop-Transcript
```

How it works...

When starting a PowerShell transcript, you can specify a path and a file name that will be used to record your commands and their output. The use of the `-Path` parameter is optional; if you do not provide a file path, the cmdlet will create a transcript file with a random name in the default documents folder in your profile path, as shown in the following screenshot:

When you are done, you can run the `Stop-Transcript` cmdlet or simply exit the shell. You can use the `-Append` parameter with the `Start-Transcript` cmdlet to add a new transcript to an existing log file. When doing so, you'll need to specify the name of the file you want to append to using the `-Path` parameter.

You can record your entire session every time you start the Exchange Management Shell by adding the `Start-Transcript` cmdlet to your user profile. If you choose to do this, make sure you specify the same log file to use every time the shell starts and use the `-Append` parameter so that each session is added to the log file every time.

There's more...

By default, only the output from PowerShell cmdlets will be recorded in your transcript. If you execute an external program, such as the Exchange `eseutil.exe` utility, the output from this command will not be saved in your transcript file, even though it was run within the current shell session. You can pipe external programs to the `Out-Default` cmdlet and this will force the output to be stored in your transcript.

See also

▶ *Setting up a Profile* in *Chapter 1, PowerShell Key Concepts*

Automating tasks with the scripting agent

Exchange 2010 introduced the concept of cmdlet extension agents to extend the functionality of the Exchange Management Tools. The scripting extension agent can be used to trigger custom commands as changes are being made by administrators from the management console or the shell. In this recipe, we'll take a look at how to use the scripting agent to automate a task in the Exchange Management Shell.

Getting ready

To complete the steps in the recipe, you'll need to create an XML file. You can simply use Notepad or any XML editor of your choice.

How to do it...

1. Let's say that you need to enable single item recovery for every mailbox that gets created in your organization. By default, single item recovery is disabled when you create a mailbox. To automatically enable single item recovery for each mailbox as it is created, add the following code to a new file:

```
<?xml version="1.0" encoding="utf-8" ?>
<Configuration version="1.0">
  <Feature Name="MailboxProvisioning" Cmdlets="New-Mailbox">
    <ApiCall Name="OnComplete">
      if($succeeded) {
        $mailbox =
          $provisioningHandler.UserSpecifiedParameters["Name"]
        Set-Mailbox $mailbox -SingleItemRecoveryEnabled $true
      }
    </ApiCall>
  </Feature>
</Configuration>
```

2. Next, save the file as `ScriptingAgentConfig.xml` on the Exchange server in the `<install path>\V14\Bin\CmdletExtensionAgents` directory.

3. Finally, you need to enable the scripting agent using the following command:

```
Enable-CmdletExtensionAgent "Scripting Agent"
```

If you have multiple Exchange servers in your environment, copy the `ScriptingAgentConfig.xml` file to each server into the `CmdletExtentionAgents` directory as described previously.

How it works...

When the scripting agent is enabled, it is called every time a cmdlet is run in your Exchange environment. This includes cmdlets run from within the shell or any of the graphical management tools.

You can see from the code that, in this example, we're using the `OnComplete` API, which runs immediately after the cmdlet has been completed. Using the `Feature` tag, we've specified that this block of code should only be executed upon completion of the `New-Mailbox` cmdlet.

After the `New-Mailbox` cmdlet has completed, we check the built-in `$succedded` variable to ensure the command was successful. If so, we retrieve the value that was used with the `-Name` parameter and store the result in the `$mailbox` variable. This value is then used to specify the identity when running the `Set-Mailbox` cmdlet to enable single item recovery.

There's more...

You can add multiple scripts to the XML file if needed by defining multiple `Feature` tags under the configuration tag. Each block of code within the `Feature` tag should have an `ApiCall` tag as shown in the previous example.

The state of the scripting agent is an organization-wide setting. If you enable the scripting agent, it is important that the `ScriptingAgentConfig.xml` is copied to every Exchange server in your organization.

Using multiple cmdlets with the OnComplete API

Let's take a look at another example. Imagine that, in addition to enabling single-item recovery for all newly-created mailboxes, we also want to disable the ActiveSync protocol for each mailbox. This means that, in addition to calling the `Set-Mailbox` cmdlet to enable single item recovery, we'll also need to call the `Set-CASMailbox` cmdlet to disable ActiveSync. Also, mailboxes can be created using both the `New-Mailbox` and `Enable-Mailbox` cmdlets. Since we'd like our custom settings to be applied regardless of how the mailbox is created, we can use the following code in our XML file:

```
<?xml version="1.0" encoding="utf-8" ?>
<Configuration version="1.0">
  <Feature Name="Mailboxes" Cmdlets="new-mailbox,enable-mailbox">
    <ApiCall Name="OnComplete">
      if($succeeded) {
        $id = $provisioningHandler.UserSpecifiedParameters["Alias"]
        Set-Mailbox $id -SingleItemRecoveryEnabled $true
        Set-CASMailbox $id -ActiveSyncEnabled $false
      }
    </ApiCall>
```

```
  </Feature>
</Configuration>
```

This code is similar to our previous example, except in this version we've specified that our custom code will be called when both the `New-Mailbox` and `Enable-Mailbox` cmdlets are used. The code in the `ApiCall` tag captures the `Alias` of the mailbox and then uses the `Set-Mailbox` and `Set-CASMailbox` to modify the settings as required.

There are multiple scripting agent APIs that can be used to extend the Exchange Management Shell functionality even further. For examples on how to use these APIs, reference the `ScriptingAgentConfig.xml.sample` file in the `<install path>\V14\Bin\ CmdletExtensionAgents` folder.

See also

- ▸ *Adding, modifying, and removing mailboxes* in *Chapter 3, Managing Recipients*
- ▸ *Managing ActiveSync, OWA, POP3, and IMAP4 mailbox settings* in *Chapter 7, Managing Client Access*

Scripting an Exchange server Installation

If you are performing mass deployment of Exchange servers in a large environment, automating the installation process can minimize administrator error and speed up the overall process. The `setup.com` utility can be used to perform an unattended installation of Exchange, and, when combined with PowerShell and just a little bit of scripting logic, create a fairly sophisticated installation script. This recipe will provide a couple of examples that can be used to script the installation of an Exchange server.

Getting ready

You can use a standard PowerShell console from the server to run the scripts in this recipe.

How to do it...

1. In this example, we'll create an automated installation script that installs Exchange based on the host name of the server. Using Notepad or your favourite scripting editor, add the following code to a new file:

```
if(Test-Path $Path) {
    switch -wildcard ($env:computername) {
        "*-HCM-*"  {$role = "HT,CA,MB" ; break}
        "*-MB-*"   {$role = "MB" ; break}
        "*-CA-*"   {$role = "CA" ; break}
        "*-HT-*"   {$role = "HT" ; break}
```

```
        "*-ET-*"  {$role = "ET" ; break}
        "*-UM-*"  {$role = "UM" ; break}
    }
    $setup = Join-Path $Path "setup.com"
    Invoke-Expression "$setup /InstallWindowsComponents /r:$role"
}
else {
    Write-Host "Invalid Media Path!"
}
```

2. Save the file as `InstallExchange.ps1`.

3. Execute the script from a server where you want to install Exchange using the following syntax:

```
InstallExchange.ps1 -Path D:
```

The value provided for the `-Path` parameter should reference the Exchange 2010 SP1 media, either on DVD or extracted to a folder.

How it works...

One of the most common methods for automating an Exchange installation is determining the required roles based on the hostname of the server. In the previous example, we assume that your organization uses a standard server naming convention. When executing the script, the switch statement will evaluate the hostname of the server and determine the required roles. For example, if your mailbox servers use a server name such as `CONTOSO-MB-01`, the mailbox server role will be installed. If your CAS servers use a server name such as `CONTOSO-CA-02`, the CAS role will be installed, and so on.

It's important to note that Exchange 2010 SP1 requires several Windows operating system hotfixes. Windows Server 2008 R2 SP1 includes these operating system hotfixes required by Exchange 2010 SP1. You'll also want the .NET Framework 3.5.1 installed prior to running this script, which can also be automated using the `ServerManager` PowerShell module that is included in Windows Server 2008 R2.

When calling the `Setup.com` installation program within the script, we use the `/InstallWindowsComponents` switch, which is a new `Setup.com` feature in Exchange Server 2010 SP1. This will allow the setup program to load any prerequisite Windows roles and features, such as IIS, and so on, before starting the Exchange installation.

There's more...

Scripting the installation of Exchange based on the server names may not be an option for you. Fortunately, PowerShell gives us plenty of flexibility. The following script uses similar logic, but performs the installation based on different criteria.

Let's say that your core Exchange infrastructure has already been deployed. Your corporate headquarters already has the required CAS and Hub Transport server infrastructure in place and therefore you only need to deploy mailbox servers in the main Active Directory site. All remaining remote sites will contain multi-role Exchange servers. Replace the code in the `InstallExchange.ps1` script with the following:

```
param($Path)
$site = [DirectoryServices.ActiveDirectory.ActiveDirectorySite]

if(Test-Path $Path) {
  switch ($site::GetComputerSite().Name) {
    "Headquarters" {$role = "MB"}
    Default {$role = "HT,CA,MB"}
  }
  $setup = Join-Path $Path "setup.com"
  Invoke-Expression "$setup /InstallWindowsComponents /r:$role"
}
else {
  Write-Host "Invalid Media Path!"
}
```

This alternate version of the script determines the current Active Directory site of the computer executing the script. If the computer is in the *Headquarters* site, only the Mailbox role is installed. If it is located at any of the other remaining Active Directory sites, the Hub Transport, Client Access, and Mailbox server roles are installed.

As you can see, combining the `Setup.com` utility with a PowerShell script can give you many more options when performing an automated installation.

See also

- ▸ *Looping through items* in *Chapter 1*, *PowerShell Key Concepts*
- ▸ *Using flow control statements* in *Chapter 1*, *PowerShell Key Concepts*

3

Managing Recipients

In this chapter, we will cover the following:

- ▸ Adding, modifying, and removing mailboxes
- ▸ Working with contacts
- ▸ Managing distribution groups
- ▸ Managing resource mailboxes
- ▸ Creating recipients in bulk using a CSV file
- ▸ Working with recipient filters
- ▸ Adding and removing recipient e-mail addresses
- ▸ Hiding recipients from address lists
- ▸ Configuring recipient moderation
- ▸ Configuring message delivery restrictions
- ▸ Managing automatic replies and out of office settings for a user
- ▸ Adding, modifying, and removing server-side inbox rules
- ▸ Managing mailbox folder permissions
- ▸ Importing user photos into Active Directory

Introduction

If you are like many other administrators, you probably spend the majority of your time performing recipient-related management tasks when dealing with Exchange. If you work in a large environment with thousands of recipients, using the Exchange Management Console to create, update, and delete recipients will probably be a cumbersome and time consuming process. Of course, the obvious solution to this is to use the Exchange Management Shell. Utilizing the Exchange Management Shell, you can automate all of your recipient management tasks and drastically speed up your work.

The concept of an Exchange recipient is more than just a user with a mailbox. An Exchange recipient is any Active Directory object that has been mail-enabled and can receive messages within the Exchange organization. This can be a distribution group, a contact, a mail-enabled public folder, and more. These object types include individual sets of cmdlets that can be used to completely automate the administration of the Exchange recipients in your environment.

The goal of this chapter is to show you some common solutions that can be used when performing day-to-day recipient management from within the shell. Quite often, Exchange recipients are provisioned or updated in bulk through an automated process driven by a PowerShell script. The recipes in this chapter will provide solutions for these types of scripts that you can use right away. You can also use these concepts as a guide to build your own scripts from scratch to automate recipient related tasks in your environment.

Performing some basic steps

To work with the code samples in this chapter, we'll need to launch the Exchange Management Shell using the following steps:

1. Log onto a workstation or server with the Exchange Management Tools installed
2. Open the Exchange Management Shell by clicking on **Start | All Programs | Exchange Server 2010**
3. Click on the **Exchange Management Shell** shortcut

If any additional steps are required they will be listed at the beginning of the recipe in the *Getting ready* section.

Adding, modifying, and removing mailboxes

One of the most common tasks performed within the Exchange Management Shell is mailbox management. In this recipe, we'll take a look at the command syntax required to create, update, and remove mailboxes from your Exchange organization. The concepts outlined in this recipe can be used to perform basic day-to-day tasks and will be useful for more advanced scenarios such as creating mailboxes in bulk.

How to do it...

1. Let's start off by creating a mailbox-enabled Active Directory user account. To do this, we can use the `New-Mailbox` cmdlet as shown in the following example:

```
$password = ConvertTo-SecureString -AsPlainText P@ssw0rd -Force

New-Mailbox -UserPrincipalName dave@contoso.com `
-Alias dave `
-Database DAGDB1 `
```

```
-Name DaveJones `
-OrganizationalUnit Sales `
-Password $password `
-FirstName Dave `
-LastName Jones `
-DisplayName 'Dave Jones'
```

2. Once the mailbox has been created we can modify it using the `Set-Mailbox` cmdlet:

```
Set-Mailbox -Identity dave `
-UseDatabaseQuotaDefaults $false `
-ProhibitSendReceiveQuota 5GB `
-IssueWarningQuota 4gb
```

3. To remove the Exchange attributes from the Active Directory user account and mark the mailbox in the database for removal, use the `Disable-Mailbox` cmdlet:

```
Disable-Mailbox -Identity dave -Confirm:$false
```

How it works...

When running the `New-Mailbox` cmdlet, the `-Password` parameter is required and you need to provide a value for it using a secure string object. As you can see from the code, we've used the `ConvertTo-SecureString` cmdlet to create a `$password` variable that stores a specified value as an encrypted string. This `$password` variable is then assigned to the `-Password` parameter when running the cmdlet. There's no requirement to first store this object in a variable; we could have done it inline, as shown next:

```
New-Mailbox -UserPrincipalName dave@contoso.com `
-Alias dave `
-Database DAGDB1 `
-Name DaveJones `
-OrganizationalUnit Sales `
-Password (ConvertTo-SecureString -AsPlainText P@ssw0rd -Force) `
-FirstName Dave `
-LastName Jones `
-DisplayName 'Dave Jones'
```

Keep in mind that the password used here needs to comply with your Active Directory password policies, which may enforce a minimum password length and have requirements for complexity.

Only a few parameters are actually required when running `New-Mailbox`, but the cmdlet itself supports several useful parameters that can be used to set certain properties when creating the mailbox. You can run `Get-Help New-Mailbox -Detailed` to determine which additional parameters are supported.

The `New-Mailbox` cmdlet creates a new Active Directory user and then mailbox-enables that account. We can also create mailboxes for existing users with the `Enable-Mailbox` cmdlet, using syntax similar to the following:

```
Enable-Mailbox steve -Database DAGDB1
```

The only requirement when running the `Enable-Mailbox` cmdlet is that you provide the identity of the Active Directory user that should be mailbox-enabled. In the previous example, we've specified the database in which the mailbox should be created, but this is optional. The `Enable-Mailbox` cmdlet supports a number of other parameters that you can use to control the initial settings for the mailbox.

You can use a simple one-liner to create mailboxes in bulk for existing Active Directory users:

```
Get-User -RecipientTypeDetails User |
    Enable-Mailbox -Database DAGDB1
```

Notice that we've run the `Get-User` cmdlet specifying `User` as the value for the `-RecipientTypeDetails` parameter. This will retrieve only the accounts in Active Directory that have not been mailbox-enabled. We then pipe those objects down to the `Enable-Mailbox` cmdlet and mailboxes are created for each of those users in one simple operation.

Once mailboxes have been created, they can be modified with the `Set-Mailbox` cmdlet. As you may recall from our original example, we used the `Set-Mailbox` cmdlet to configure custom storage quota settings after creating a mailbox for *Dave Jones*. Keep in mind that the `Set-Mailbox` cmdlet supports over 100 parameters, so anything that can be done to modify a mailbox can be scripted.

Bulk modifications to mailboxes can be done easily by taking advantage of the pipeline and the `Set-Mailbox` cmdlet. Instead of configuring storage quotas on a single mailbox, we can do it for multiple users at once:

```
Get-Mailbox -OrganizationalUnit contoso.com/sales |
    Set-Mailbox -UseDatabaseQuotaDefaults $false `
    -ProhibitSendReceiveQuota 5GB `
    -IssueWarningQuota 4gb
```

Here we are simply retrieving every mailbox in the *Sales* OU using the `Get-Mailbox` cmdlet. The objects returned from that command are piped down to `Set-Mailbox` which modifies the quota settings for each mailbox in one shot.

The `Disable-Mailbox` cmdlet will strip the Exchange attributes from an Active Directory user and will disconnect the associated mailbox. By default, disconnected mailboxes are retained for 30 days. You can modify this setting on the database that holds the mailbox. In addition to this, you can also use the `Remove-Mailbox` cmdlet to delete both the Active Directory account and the mailbox at once:

```
Remove-Mailbox -Identity dave -Confirm:$false
```

After running this command, the mailbox will be purged once it exceeds the deleted mailbox retention setting on the database. One common mistake is when administrators use the `Remove-Mailbox` cmdlet when the `Disable-Mailbox` cmdlet should have been used. It's important to remember that the `Remove-Mailbox` cmdlet will delete the Active Directory user account.

There's more...

When we ran the `New-Mailbox` cmdlet in the previous examples, we assigned a secure string object to the `-Password` parameter using the `ConvertTo-SecureString` cmdlet. This is a great technique to use when your scripts need complete automation, but you can also allow an operator to enter this information interactively. For example, you might build a script that prompts an operator for a password when creating one or more mailboxes. There are a couple of ways you can do this. First, you can use the `Read-Host` cmdlet to prompt the user running the script to enter a password:

```
$pass = Read-Host "enter password" -AsSecureString
```

Once a value has been entered into the shell, your script can assign the `$pass` variable to the `-Password` parameter of the `New-Mailbox` cmdlet.

Alternatively, you can supply a value for the `-Password` parameter using the `Get-Credential` cmdlet:

```
New-Mailbox -Name Dave -UserPrincipalName dave@contoso.com `
-Password (Get-Credential).password
```

You can see that the value we are assigning to the `-Password` parameter in this example is actually the `password` property of the object returned by the `Get-Credential` cmdlet. Executing this command will first launch a Windows authentication dialog box where the caller can enter a username and password. Once the credential object has been created, the `New-Mailbox` cmdlet will run. Even though a username and password must be entered into the authentication dialog box, only the password value will be used when the command executes.

Setting active directory attributes

Some of the Active Directory attributes that you may want to set when creating a mailbox might not be available using the `New-Mailbox` cmdlet. Good examples of this are a user's city, state, company, and department attributes. In order to set these attributes, you'll need to call the `Set-User` cmdlet after the mailbox has been created:

```
Set-User –Identity dave –Office IT –City Seattle –State Washington
```

You can run `Get-Help Set-User -Detailed` to view all of the available parameters supported by this cmdlet.

See also

▶ *Using the help system* in *Chapter 1, PowerShell Key Concepts*

▶ *Creating recipients in bulk using a CSV file*

▶ *Managing distribution groups*

Working with contacts

Once you've started managing mailboxes using the Exchange Management Shell, you'll probably notice that the concepts and command syntax used to manage contacts are very similar. The difference of course is that we need to use an different set of cmdlets. In addition, we also have two types of contacts to deal with in Exchange. We'll take a look at how you can manage both of them in this recipe.

How to do it...

1. To create a mail-enabled contact, use the `New-MailContact` cmdlet:

   ```
   New-MailContact -Alias rjones `
   -Name "Rob Jones" `
   -ExternalEmailAddress rob@fabrikam.com `
   -OrganizationalUnit sales
   ```

2. Mail-enabled users can be created with the `New-MailUser` cmdlet:

   ```
   New-MailUser -Name 'John Davis' `
   -Alias jdavis `
   -UserPrincipalName jdavis@contoso.com `
   -FirstName John `
   -LastName Davis `
   -Password (ConvertTo-SecureString -AsPlainText P@ssw0rd -Force) `
   -ResetPasswordOnNextLogon $false `
   -ExternalEmailAddress jdavis@fabrikam.com
   ```

How it works...

Mail contacts are useful when you have external e-mail recipients that need to show up in your global address list. When you use the `New-MailContact` cmdlet, an Active Directory contact object is created and mail-enabled with the external e-mail address assigned. You can mail-enable an existing Active Directory contact using the `Enable-MailContact` cmdlet.

Mail users are similar to mail contacts in that they have an associated external e-mail address. The difference is that these objects are mail-enabled Active Directory users, and that explains why we needed to assign a password when creating the object. You might use a mail user for a contractor who works onsite in your organization and needs to be able to logon to your domain. When users in your organization need to e-mail this person, they can select them from the global address list and messages sent to these recipients will be delivered to the external address configured for the account.

Just as when dealing with mailboxes, there are a couple of considerations that should be taken when it comes to removing contacts and mail users. You can remove the Exchange attributes from a contact using the `Disable-MailContact` cmdlet. The `Remove-MailContact` cmdlet will remove the contact object from Active Directory and Exchange. Similarly, the `Disable-MailUser` and `Remove-MailUser` cmdlets work in the same fashion.

There's more...

Like mailboxes, mail contacts, and mail-enabled user accounts have several Active Directory attributes that can be set such as job title, company, department, and more. To update these attributes you can use the `Set-*` cmdlets available for each respective type. For example, to update our mail contact we could use the `Set-Contact` cmdlet with the following syntax:

```
Set-Contact -Identity rjones `
-Title 'Sales Contractor' `
-Company Fabrikam `
-Department Sales
```

To modify the same settings for a mail-enabled user, use the `Set-User` cmdlet:

```
Set-User -Identity jdavis `
-Title 'Sales Contractor' `
-Company Fabrikam `
-Department Sales
```

Both cmdlets can be used to modify a number of different settings. Use the help system to view all of the available parameters.

See also

▸ *Using the help system* in *Chapter 1, PowerShell Key Concepts*

▸ *Adding, modifying, and removing mailboxes*

Managing distribution groups

In many Exchange environments, distribution groups are relied upon heavily and require frequent changes. This recipe will cover the creation of distribution groups and how to add members to groups, which might be useful when performing these tasks interactively in the shell or through automated scripts.

How to do it...

1. To create a distribution group use the `New-DistributionGroup` cmdlet:

   ```
   New-DistributionGroup -Name Sales
   ```

2. Once the group has been created, adding multiple members can be done easily using a one-liner:

   ```
   Get-Mailbox -OrganizationalUnit Sales |
       Add-DistributionGroupMember -Identity Sales
   ```

3. We can also create distribution groups whose memberships are set dynamically:

   ```
   New-DynamicDistributionGroup -Name Accounting `
   -Alias Accounting `
   -IncludedRecipients MailboxUsers,MailContacts `
   -OrganizationalUnit Accounting `
   -ConditionalDepartment accounting,finance `
   -RecipientContainer contoso.com
   ```

How it works...

There are two types of distribution groups that can be created with Exchange. First, there are regular distribution groups, which contain a distinct list of users. Secondly, there are dynamic distribution groups, whose members are determined at the time a message is sent based on a number of conditions or filters that have been defined. Both types have a set of cmdlets that can be used to add, remove, update, enable, or disable these groups.

By default, when creating a standard distribution group, the group scope will be set to `Universal`. You can create a mail-enabled security group using the `New-DistributionGroup` cmdlet by setting the `-Type` parameter to `Security`. If you do not provide a value for the `-Type` parameter, the group will be created using the `Distribution` group type.

You can mail-enable an existing Active Directory universal distribution group using the `Enable-DistributionGroup` cmdlet.

After creating the *Sales* distribution group in our previous example, we added all of the mailboxes in the *Sales* OU to the group using the `Add-DistributionGroupMember` cmdlet. You can do this in bulk or for one user at a time using the `–Member` parameter:

```
Add-DistributionGroupMember -Identity Sales -Member administrator
```

> Distribution groups are a large topic and we're merely covering the basics here. See *Chapter 5, Distribution Groups and Address Lists* for in-depth coverage of distribution groups.

Dynamic distribution groups determine their membership based on a defined set of filters and conditions. When we created the *Accounting* distribution group, we used the `-IncludedRecipients` parameter to specify that only the `MailboxUsers` and `MailContacts` object types would be included in the group. This eliminates resource mailboxes, groups, or mail users from being included as members. The group will be created in the *Accounting* OU based on the value used with the `-OrganizationalUnit` parameter. Using the `–ConditionalDepartment` parameter, the group will only include users that have a department setting of either *Accounting* or *Finance*. And finally, since the `-RecipientContainer` parameter is set to the FQDN of the domain, any user located in the Active Directory could potentially be included in the group. You can create more complex filters for dynamic distribution groups using a recipient filter; see the recipe titled *Working with Recipient Filters* later in this chapter for an example.

> You can modify both group types using the `Set-DistributionGroup` and `Set-DynamicDistributionGroup` cmdlets.

There's more...

Just as when dealing with other recipient types, there are a couple of considerations that should be taken when it comes to removing distribution groups. You can remove the Exchange attributes from a group using the `Disable-DistributionGroup` cmdlet. The `Remove-DistributionGroup` cmdlet will remove the group object from the Active Directory and Exchange.

See also

▶ *Working with recipient filters*

▶ *Reporting on distribution group membership* in *Chapter 5, Distribution Groups and Address Lists*

▶ *Adding members to a distribution group from an external file* in *Chapter 5, Distribution Groups and Address Lists*

▶ *Previewing dynamic distribution group membership* in *Chapter 5, Distribution Groups and Address Lists*

Managing resource mailboxes

In addition to mailboxes, groups, and external contacts, recipients can also include specific rooms or pieces of equipment. Locations such as a conference room or a classroom can be given a mailbox so they can be reserved for meetings. Equipment mailboxes can be assigned to physical, non-location specific resources such as laptops or projectors and can then be checked out to individual users or groups by booking time with the mailbox. In this recipe, we'll take a look at how you can manage resource mailboxes using the Exchange Management Shell.

How to do it...

When creating a resource mailbox from within the shell, the syntax is similar to creating a mailbox for a regular user. For example, you still use the `New-Mailbox` cmdlet when creating a resource mailbox:

```
New-Mailbox -Name "CR32" -DisplayName "Conference Room 23" `
-UserPrincipalName CR23@contoso.com -Room
```

How it works...

There are two main differences when it comes to creating a resource mailbox as opposed to a standard user mailbox. First, you need to use either the `-Room` switch parameter or the `-Equipment` switch parameter to define the type of resource mailbox that will be created. Second, you do not need to provide a password value for the user account. When using either of these resource mailbox switch parameters to create a mailbox, the `New-Mailbox` cmdlet will create a disabled Active Directory user account that will be associated with the mailbox.

The entire concept of room and equipment mailboxes revolves around the calendars used by these resources. If you want to reserve a room or a piece of equipment, you book time through Outlook or OWA with these resources for the duration that you'll need them. The requests sent to these resources need to be accepted, either by a delegate or automatically using the Resource Booking Attendant.

To configure the room mailbox created in the previous example to automatically accept new meeting requests, we can use the `Set-CalendarProcessing` cmdlet to set the Resource Booking Attendant for that mailbox to `AutoAccept`:

```
Set-CalendarProcessing CR23 -AutomateProcessing AutoAccept
```

When the Resource Booking Attendant is set to `AutoAccept`, the request will be immediately accepted as long as there is not a conflict with another meeting. If there is a conflict, an e-mail message will be returned to the requestor explaining that the request was declined due to scheduling conflicts. You can allow conflicts by adding the `-AllowConflicts` switch parameter to the previous command.

When working with resource mailboxes with `AutomateProcessing` set to `AutoAccept`, you'll get an automated e-mail response from the resource after booking time. This e-mail message will explain whether the request was accepted or declined, depending on your settings. You can add additional text to the response message that the meeting organizer will receive using the following syntax:

```
Set-CalendarProcessing -Identity CR23 `
-AddAdditionalResponse $true `
-AdditionalResponse 'For Assistance Contact Support at Ext. #3376'
```

This example uses the `Set-CalendarProcessing` cmdlet to customize the response messages sent from the CR23 room mailbox. You can see here that we've added a message that tells the user the help desk number to call if assistance is required. Keep in mind that you can only add additional response text when the `AutomateProcessing` property is set to `AutoAccept`.

If you do not want to automate the calendar processing for a resource mailbox then you'll need to add delegates that can accept or deny meetings for that resource. Again, we can turn to the `Set-CalendarProcessing` cmdlet to accomplish this:

```
Set-CalendarProcessing -Identity CR23 `
-ResourceDelegates "joe@contoso.com","steve@contoso.com" `
-AutomateProcessing None
```

In this example, we've added two delegates to the resource mailbox and have turned off automated processing. When a request comes into the CR23 mailbox, both Steve and Joe will be notified and can accept or deny the request on behalf of the resource mailbox.

There's more...

When it comes to working with resource mailboxes, another useful feature is the ability to assign custom resource properties to rooms and equipment resources. For example, you may have a total of 5, 10, or 15 conference rooms, but maybe only four of those have whiteboards. It might be useful for your users to know this information when booking a resource for a meeting where they will be conducting a training session.

Using the shell, we can add custom resource properties to the Exchange organization by modifying the resource schema. Once these custom resource properties have been added, they can then be assigned to specific resource mailboxes.

You can use the following code to add a whiteboard resource property to the Exchange organizations resource schema:

```
Set-ResourceConfig -ResourcePropertySchema 'Room/Whiteboard'
```

Now that the whiteboard resource property is available within the Exchange organization, we can add this to our Conference Room 23 mailbox using the following command:

```
Set-Mailbox -Identity CR23 -ResourceCustom Whiteboard
```

When users access the **Select Rooms** dialog box in Outlook 2007 or 2010, they will see that Conference Room 23 has a whiteboard available.

Converting mailboxes

If you are moving to Exchange 2010 from 2003, you may have a number of mailboxes that were being used as resource mailboxes. Once these mailboxes have been moved over to 2010, they will be identified as Shared mailboxes. You can convert them using the Set-Mailbox cmdlet so that they'll have all of the properties of a resource mailbox:

```
Get-Mailbox conf* | Set-Mailbox -Type Room
```

You can run the Set-Mailbox cmdlet against each mailbox one at a time and convert them to Room mailboxes using the -Type parameter. Or, if you use a common naming convention, you may be able to do them in bulk by retrieving a list of mailboxes using a wildcard and piping them to Set-Mailbox, as shown previously.

See also

> ▸ *Adding, modifying, and removing mailboxes*
> ▸ *Creating recipients in bulk using a CSV file*

Creating recipients in bulk using a CSV file

One of the most common bulk provisioning techniques used in the Exchange Management Shell makes use of comma-separated value (CSV) files. These files act sort of like a database table. Each record in this table is represented by one line in the file, and each field value is separated by a comma, which is used as a delimiter. In this recipe, you'll learn how to set up a CSV file and create recipients in bulk using the Exchange Management Shell.

Getting ready

In addition to the Exchange Management Shell, you'll need to use Microsoft Excel to create a CSV file.

How to do it...

1. In this example, we are going to create some mailboxes in bulk. We'll enter some data into Excel that will include the settings for five new mailboxes:

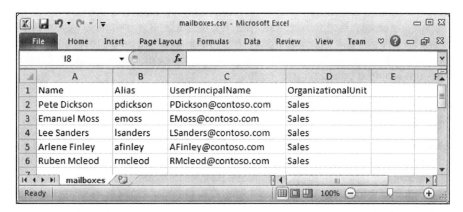

2. Go to **File | Save As** and select **CSV (Comma delimited) (*.csv)** for the file type. Save the file as `C:\Mailboxes.CSV`.

3. Within the Exchange Management Shell, create a secure password object to be used as an initial password for each mailbox:

    ```
    $pass = ConvertTo-SecureString -AsPlainText P@ssw0rd01 -Force
    ```

4. Import the CSV file and create the mailboxes:

    ```
    Import-CSV C:\Mailboxes.CSV | % {
      New-Mailbox -Name $_.Name `
      -Alias $_.Alias `
      -UserPrincipalName $_.UserPrincipalName `
    ```

```
            -OrganizationalUnit $_.OrganizationalUnit `
            -Password $pass `
            -ResetPasswordOnNextLogon $true
    }
```

How it works...

In this example, we're importing the CSV file into the shell and piping that information to the `ForEach-Object` cmdlet (using the `%` alias). For each record in the CSV file, we're running the `New-Mailbox` cmdlet, providing values for the `-Name`, `-Alias`, `-UserPrincipalName`, and `-OrganizationalUnit` parameters. The properties for each record can be accessed inside the loop using the `$_` variable, which is the automatic variable that references the current object in the pipeline. The property names for each record match the header names used in the CSV file. As we create each mailbox, the password is set to the `$pass` variable. The `-ResetPasswordOnNextLogon` parameter is set to `$true`, which will require each user to reset their password after their first logon.

Using this technique, you can literally create thousands of mailboxes in a matter of minutes. This concept can also be applied to other recipient types, such as distribution groups and contacts. You just need to specify the appropriate parameter values in the CSV file and use the corresponding cmdlet for the recipient type. For example, if you want to bulk provision contacts from a CSV file, use the code from the previous example as a guide, and, instead of using the `New-Mailbox` cmdlet, use the `New-MailContact` cmdlet and whatever parameters are required based on your settings.

There's more...

Let's take a look at an alternative approach to the previous example. Let's say that you don't want to set an initial password for each user, and, instead, you want to include this information in the CSV file so each new mailbox gets a unique password. Again, you'll need to set up a CSV file with the required values. For this example, your CSV file would look something like this:

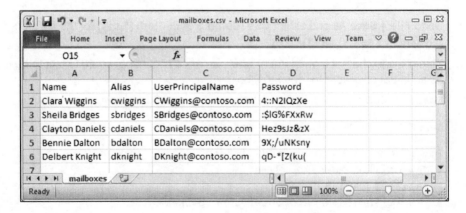

Notice that in the previous screenshot, we are using different column names for this new file. We've removed the `OrganizationalUnit` column and now have a `Password` column which will be used to create each mailbox with a unique password. After you're done creating the file, save it again as `C:\Mailboxes.CSV`.

Next, you can use the following code to create the mailboxes, specifying the path and file name to the CSV file created in the previous step:

```
Import-CSV C:\Mailboxes.CSV | % {
   $pass = ConvertTo-SecureString -AsPlainText $_.Password -Force

   New-Mailbox -Name $_.Name `
   -Alias $_.Alias `
   -UserPrincipalName $_.UserPrincipalName `
   -Password $pass
}
```

As we loop through each record in the CSV file, we create a secure password object that can be used with the `-Password` parameter. The main difference here compared to the previous example is that each user gets a unique password and they do not need to reset their password the first time they log on.

Taking it a step further

When provisioning recipients you'll probably need to do multiple things, such as set Active Directory attributes and configure distribution group membership. Let's take our previous example a step further:

```
Import-CSV C:\NewMailboxes.CSV | % {
   New-Mailbox -Name $_.Name `
   -FirstName $_.FirstName `
   -LastName $_.LastName `
   -Alias $_.Alias `
   -UserPrincipalName $_.UserPrincipalName `
   -Password $pass
   -OrganizationalUnit $_.OrganiationalUnit `
   -Database DB1 `
   -Password (ConvertTo-SecureString -AsPlainText P@ssw0rd -Force)

   Set-User -Identity $_.Name `
   -City $_.City `
   -StateOrProvince $_.State `
   -Title $_.Title `
   -Department $_.Department
```

```
Add-DistributionGroupMember -Identity DL_Sales `
-Member $_.Name

Add-DistributionGroupMember -Identity DL_Marketing `
-Member $_.Name
}
```

Here we're still using a CSV file, but as we loop through each record we're calling multiple cmdlets to first create the mailbox, set some of the Active Directory attributes, and then add the mailbox to two separate distribution groups. In order to use this code, we would just need to create a CSV file that has columns for all of the values we're setting.

Now that we have this framework in place, we can add as many columns as we need to the CSV file and we can call any number of cmdlets for each record in the CSV.

See also

- *Looping through items* in *Chapter 1, PowerShell Key Concepts*
- *Adding, modifying, and removing mailboxes*
- *Managing distribution groups*

Working with recipient filters

Starting with Exchange 2007 and continuing with Exchange 2010, address lists, dynamic distribution groups, e-mail address policies, and global address lists can be customized with recipient filters that use OPATH filtering syntax. This replaces the LDAP filtering syntax that was used in earlier versions of Exchange. We can also perform server-side searches using filters, which can greatly speed up our work. In this recipe, you'll learn how to work with these filters in the Exchange Management Shell.

How to do it...

1. We can filter the results from the recipient `Get-*` cmdlets using the `-Filter` parameter:

   ```
   Get-Mailbox -Filter {Office -eq 'Sales'}
   ```

2. In addition, we can use attribute filters to create distribution groups, e-mail address policies, and address lists using the `-RecipientFilter` parameter:

   ```
   New-DynamicDistributionGroup -Name DL_Accounting `
   -RecipientFilter {
     (Department -eq 'Accounting') -and
     (RecipientType -eq 'UserMailbox')
   }
   ```

How it works...

In our first example, you can see that we've used the `Get-Mailbox` cmdlet to retrieve only the users that have the `Office` property set to the value *Sales*. This is more efficient then performing the following command, which would return the same results:

```
Get-Mailbox | ?{$_.Office -eq 'Sales'}
```

This command uses the `Where-Object` cmdlet (using the `?` alias) to retrieve only the mailboxes with their `Office` property set to *Sales*.We get back the same results, but it is less efficient than our original example. When filtering with `Where-Object`, every mailbox in the organization must be retrieved and evaluated before any results are returned. The benefit of using the `-Filter` parameter with the `Get-Mailbox` cmdlet is that the filtering is done on the server and not our client machines.

There are a number of cmdlets that support this parameter. You can get an entire list with a simple one-liner:

```
get-excommand | ?{$_.parameters.keys -eq 'filter'}
```

This uses the shell function `get-excommand` to retrieve a list of Exchange Management Shell cmdlets that support the `-Filter` parameter. If you are writing scripts or functions that need to query a large amount of recipients, you'll want to try to use server-side filtering whenever possible.

Unfortunately, there are only a certain set of properties that can be filtered. For instance, we were able to filter using the `Office` property when using the `Get-Mailbox` cmdlet. Based on that, you may assume that, since `OrganizationalUnit` is a property of a mailbox object, that you can filter on that as well, but that is not the case. The `Get-Mailbox` cmdlet provides an `-OrganizationalUnit` parameter that can be used to accomplish that task, so it's not always safe to assume that a particular property can be used within a filter. To view a list of common filterable properties that can be used with the `-Filter` parameter, see *Appendix A* at the end of this book.

In our second example, we used the `New-DynamicDistributionGroup` cmdlet to create a query-based group. The membership of this group is determined using the OPATH filter defined with the `-RecipientFilter` parameter. The syntax is similar and the same PowerShell operators can be used. Based on the settings used with our filter when we created the *DL_Accounting* group, only mailboxes with their `Department` attribute set to *Accounting* will be included. Other recipient types, such as mail contacts and mail users, will not be included in the group, even though they may be in the *Accounting* department.

Dynamic distribution groups, address lists, and e-mail address policies can be configured with these filters. Again, to get the list of cmdlets that support this functionality, use the `get-excommand` shell variable:

```
get-excommand | ?{$_.parameters.keys -eq 'recipientfilter'}
```

These cmdlets also have a limited number of filterable properties that can be used. To view a list of the most common properties used with the −RecipientFilter parameter, see *Appendix A* at the end of this book.

There's more...

Instead of using the -RecipientFilter parameter, you have the option of using pre-canned filters. In some cases this may be easier, as it allows you to simply use a set of parameters and values as opposed to an OPATH filter. The following command would create our *DL_Accounting* distribution group with the same members using the pre-canned filter parameters:

```
New-DynamicDistributionGroup -Name DL_Accounting `
-IncludedRecipients MailboxUsers `
-ConditionalDepartment Accounting
```

As you can see, this is a little easier to read and probably easier to type into the shell. Although, there are only a few pre-canned parameters available and they may not always be useful depending on what you are trying to do, but it helps to be aware of this functionality. You can use Get-Help to view the entire list of available parameters for each cmdlet that supports recipient filters.

Understanding variables in filters

One of the issues you may run into when working in the shell is the expansion of variables used within a filter. For example, this syntax is completely valid but will not currently work correctly in the Exchange Management Shell:

```
$office = "sales"
Get-Mailbox -Filter {Office -eq $office}
```

You might get some results from this command, but they will probably not be what you are expecting. This is because, when running the Get-Mailbox cmdlet, the value of the $office variable will not be expanded prior to the command being executed through the remote shell. What you end up with instead is a filter checking for a $null value. In order to fix this, you'll need to use syntax similar to the following:

```
$office = "sales"
Get-Mailbox -Filter "Office -eq '$office'"
```

This syntax will force any variables assigned within the -Filter parameter to be expanded before sending the command through the remote session, and you should get back the correct results.

See also

- *Managing distribution groups*
- *Using the help system* in *Chapter 1, PowerShell Key Concepts*
- *Previewing dynamic distribution group membership* in *Chapter 5, Distribution Groups and Address Lists*

Adding and removing recipient e-mail addresses

There are several recipient types in Exchange 2010 and each one of them can support multiple e-mail addresses. Of course, the typical user mailbox recipient type is probably the first that comes to mind, but we also have distribution groups, contacts, and public folders, each of which can have one or more e-mail addresses. The syntax used for adding and removing e-mail addresses to each of these recipient types is essentially identical: the only thing that changes is the cmdlet that is used to set the address. In this recipe, you'll learn how to add or remove an e-mail address from an Exchange recipient.

How to do it...

1. To add a secondary e-mail address to a mailbox, use the following command syntax:

```
Set-Mailbox dave -EmailAddresses @{add='dave@west.contoso.com'}
```

2. Multiple addresses can also be added using this technique:

```
Set-Mailbox dave -EmailAddresses @{
  add='dave@east.contoso.com',
  'dave@west.contoso.com',
  'dave@corp.contoso.com'
}
```

3. E-mail addresses can also be removed using the following syntax:

```
Set-Mailbox dave -EmailAddresses @{remove='dave@west.contoso.com'}
```

4. Just as we are able to add multiple e-mail addresses at once, we can do the same when removing an address:

```
Set-Mailbox dave -EmailAddresses @{
  remove='dave@east.contoso.com',
  'dave@corp.contoso.com'
}
```

How it works...

Adding and removing e-mail addresses was more challenging in the Exchange 2007 management shell because it required that you work directly with the `EmailAddresses` collection, which is a multi-valued property. In order to modify the collection, you first had to save the object to a variable, modify it, and then write it back to the `EmailAddresses` object on the recipient. This made it impossible to update the e-mail addresses for a recipient with one command.

The `Set-*` cmdlets used to manage recipients in Exchange 2010 now support a new syntax that allows us to use a hash table to modify the `EmailAddresses` property. As you can see from the code samples, we can simply use the `Add` and `Remove` keys within the hash table, and the assigned e-mail address values will be either added or removed as required. This is a nice change that makes it easier to do this in scripts and especially when working interactively in the shell.

The `Add` and `Remove` keywords are interchangeable with the plus (+) and minus (-) characters that serve as aliases:

```
Set-Mailbox dave -EmailAddresses @{
  '+'='dave@east.contoso.com'
  '-'='dave@west.contoso.com'
}
```

In the previous example, we've added and removed e-mail addresses from the mailbox. Notice that the + and - keywords need to be enclosed in quotes so PowerShell does not try to interpret them as the += and -= operators.

This syntax works with all of the `Set-*` cmdlets that support the `-EmailAddresses` parameter:

- `Set-CASMailbox`
- `Set-DistributionGroup`
- `Set-DynamicDistributionGroup`
- `Set-Mailbox`
- `Set-MailContact`
- `Set-MailPublicFolder`
- `Set-MailUser`

Keep in mind that the best way to add an e-mail address to a recipient is through the use of an e-mail address policy. This may not always be an option, but should be used first if you find yourself in a situation where addresses need to be added to a large number of recipients. With that said, it is possible do this in bulk using a simple `foreach` loop:

```
foreach($i in Get-Mailbox -OrganizationalUnit Sales) {
  Set-Mailbox $i -EmailAddresses @{
    add="$($i.alias)@west.contoso.com"
  }
}
```

This code simply iterates over each mailbox in the *Sales* OU and adds a secondary e-mail address using the existing alias at `west.contoso.com`. You can use this technique and modify the syntax as needed to perform bulk operations.

There's more...

Imagine a situation where you need to remove all e-mail addresses under a certain domain from all of your mailboxes. These could be secondary addresses that were added manually to each mailbox, or that used to be applied as part of an e-mail address policy that no longer applies. The following code can be used to remove all e-mail addresses from mailboxes under a specific domain:

```
foreach($i in Get-Mailbox -ResultSize Unlimited) {
  $i.EmailAddresses |
    ?{$_.SmtpAddress -like '*@corp.contoso.com'} | %{
      Set-Mailbox $i -EmailAddresses @{remove=$_}
    }
}
```

This code iterates through each mailbox in the organization and simply uses a filter to discover any e-mail addresses at `corp.contoso.com`. If any exist, the `Set-Mailbox` cmdlet will attempt to remove each of them from the mailbox.

See also

- ▸ *Adding, modifying, and removing mailboxes*
- ▸ *Working with contacts*
- ▸ *Managing distribution groups*

Hiding recipients from address lists

There may be times when you'll need to hide a particular mailbox, contact, or distribution group from your Exchange address lists. This is a common task that is required when you have mailboxes, contacts, or public folders used by applications or staff in your IT department that should not be seen by end-users. In this recipe, we'll take a look at how you can disable these recipient types from the address lists using the Exchange Management Shell.

How to do it...

To hide a mailbox from the Exchange address lists, use the `Set-Mailbox` command:

```
Set-Mailbox dave -HiddenFromAddressListsEnabled $true
```

How it works...

As you can see, hiding a mailbox from address lists is pretty straight forward as it requires only a simple PowerShell one-liner. The `-HiddenFromAddressListsEnabled` parameter accepts a Boolean value, either `$true` or `$false`. To enable this setting, set the value to `$true`, and to disable it, set the value to `$false`.

There are multiple recipient types that can be hidden from address lists. Each of the following cmdlets supports the `-HiddenFromAddressListsEnabled` parameter:

- `Set-DistributionGroup`
- `Set-DynamicDistributionGroup`
- `Set-Mailbox`
- `Set-MailContact`
- `Set-MailPublicFolder`
- `Set-MailUser`
- `Set-PublicFolder`
- `Set-RemoteMailbox`

There's more...

Once you've hidden your recipients from the address lists, you may need to generate a report to list the objects that currently have the `HiddenFromAddressListsEnabled` setting enabled. Use the following command syntax to obtain this information:

```
Get-Mailbox -Filter {HiddenFromAddressListsEnabled -eq $true}
```

This searches for all mailboxes that have been hidden from address lists. It makes use of the `-Filter` parameter which keeps you from having to perform the filtering on the client side with the `Where-Object` cmdlet.

See also

- *Working with recipient filters*

Configuring recipient moderation

Exchange 2010 is the first version of Exchange to implement the moderated transport feature. This allows you to require approval for all e-mail messages sent to a particular recipient by a designated moderator. In this recipe, you'll learn how to configure the moderation settings on recipients using the Exchange Management Shell.

How to do it...

1. To enable moderation for a distribution group, use the `Set-DistributionGroup` cmdlet:

```
Set-DistributionGroup -Identity Executives `
-ModerationEnabled $true `
-ModeratedBy administrator `
-SendModerationNotifications Internal
```

2. These same parameters can be used to configure moderation for a mailbox when using the `Set-Mailbox` cmdlet:

```
Set-Mailbox -Identity dave `
-ModerationEnabled $true `
-ModeratedBy administrator `
-SendModerationNotifications Internal
```

How it works...

When you enable moderation for a recipient, any e-mail message sent to that recipient must be reviewed by a moderator. When a message is sent to a moderated recipient, the moderator will receive the message and determine whether or not it should be accepted. This is done by the moderator through Outlook or OWA by clicking on an **Approve** or **Reject** button in the e-mail message. If the moderator accepts the message, it is delivered to the group. If it is rejected, the message is deleted, and, depending on the `SendModerationNotifications` setting, the sender may receive an e-mail informing them the message has been rejected.

Moderation can be enabled for any recipient, whether it's a mailbox, mail contact, mail user, distribution group, or mail-enabled public folder. The cmdlets for each of these recipient types can be used to configure moderation when a recipient is being created with the `New-*` cmdlets, or after the fact using the `Set-*` cmdlets. To view the list of cmldets that can be used to enable moderation, run the following command:

```
get-excommand | ?{$_.parameters.keys -eq 'ModerationEnabled'}
```

In our first example, we enabled moderation for the *Executives* distribution group, specifying that the administrator account will be used as the moderator for the group. As you can see in the example, we've used multiple parameters when running the command, but only the -ModerationEnabled parameter is required to change the moderation setting for the group. If no value is specified for the -ModeratedBy parameter, the group owner will review and approve the messages sent to the group. You can specify one or more owners when running the Set-DistributionGroup cmdlet with the -ManagedBy parameter.

The -SendModerationNotifications parameter allows you to control the status messages sent to the originator of a message that was sent to a moderated recipient. We have the option of using the following values for this parameter:

- ▸ **Always**: Notifications are sent to all internal and external senders
- ▸ **Internal**: Notifications are only sent to users within the organization
- ▸ **Never**: Notifications are not sent at all

If no value is provided for the -SendModerationNotifications parameter when you enable moderation for a group, the setting will default to Always.

There's more...

There is an exception to every rule, and, of course, there may be times where we need to bypass moderation for certain recipients. Let's say that we need to bypass specific users from moderation on the *Executives* distribution group. The group moderator or group owners are already exempt from moderation. To exclude others we can specify a list of one or more recipients using the -BypassModerationFromSendersOrMembers parameter when running the Set-DistributionGroup cmdlet.

For example, to exclude a recipient named Bob from moderation on the *Executives* distribution group, run the following command:

```
Set-DistributionGroup -Identity Executives `
-BypassModerationFromSendersOrMembers bob@contoso.com
```

If you want the members of the moderated group, or any other distribution group, to be excluded from moderation, simply use the previous syntax and assign the identity of the group to the -BypassModertionFromSendersOrMembers parameter. You can assign multiple users or distribution groups at once; by separating each value with a comma.

Keep in mind that running the previous command will overwrite the existing list of bypassed members if any have been defined. For an example of how to add a new item to a multi-valued property, see the *Working with arrays and hash tables* in *Chapter 1, PowerShell Key Concepts*.

Additionally, you may need to bypass moderation for a group of several individual recipients. While you could add them one by one, this could be very time-consuming if you are dealing with a large number of recipients. Let's say that you want to exclude all the users in the San Diego office from moderation:

```
$exclude = Get-Mailbox -Filter {Office -eq 'San Diego'} |
    Select-Object -ExpandProperty alias


Set-DistributionGroup -Identity Executives `
-BypassModerationFromSendersOrMembers $exclude
```

In this example, we create a collection that contains the alias for each mailbox in the San Diego Office. Next, we use the `Set-DistributionGroup` cmdlet to exclude all of those recipients from moderation using a single command. While this might be useful in certain situations, it's easier to bypass moderation based on groups. If a group has been bypassed for moderation, you can simply manage the membership of the group and you don't need to worry about continuously updating individual recipients that are on the bypass list.

See also

- ▸ *Managing distribution groups*

Configuring message delivery restrictions

Since distribution groups contain multiple members, you may want to place restrictions on who can send messages to these recipients. Exchange allows you to tightly control these settings and provides several options when it comes to placing message delivery restrictions on groups. We can also place restrictions on other recipient types in the organization. This recipe will show you how to configure these options from the Exchange Management Shell.

How to do it...

To restrict who can send messages to a group, use the `Set-DistributionGroup` cmdlet:

```
Set-DistributionGroup -Identity Sales `
-AcceptMessagesOnlyFrom 'Bob Smith','John Jones'
```

After running this command, only the users Bob Smith and John Jones can send messages to the *Sales* distribution group.

How it works...

The `-AcceptMessagesOnlyFrom` parameter allows you to specify one or more recipients who are allowed to send messages to a distribution group. These recipients can be regular users with mailboxes or contacts.

You can add individual recipients and distribution groups to the accepted senders list using the following syntax:

```
Set-DistributionGroup -Identity Sales `
-AcceptMessagesOnlyFromSendersOrMembers Marketing,bob@contoso.com
```

In this example we're allowing both the *Marketing* distribution group and Bob, an individual recipient, to the accepted senders list for the *Sales* distribution group. Doing so will allow Bob and any members of the *Marketing* distribution group to send messages to the *Sales* group.

Keep in mind that, when using these parameters, any existing accepted recipients that have been configured will be overwritten. For an example of how to add a new item to a multi-valued property, see the in *Chapter 1* titled *Working with arrays and hash tables*.

Delivery restrictions can be placed on any recipient, whether it's a mailbox, mail contact, mail user, distribution group, or mail-enabled public folder. The `Set-*` cmdlets for each of these recipient types can be used to configure delivery restrictions. To view the list of cmldets that can be used to do this, run the following command:

```
get-excommand | ?{$_.parameters.keys -eq 'AcceptMessagesOnlyFrom'}
```

If you need to add a large list of users to the accepted senders list, you can create a collection and assign it to the `-AcceptMessagesOnlyFrom` parameter:

```
$finance = Get-Mailbox -Filter {Office -eq 'Finance'}

Set-DistributionGroup -Identity Sales `
-AcceptMessagesOnlyFrom $finance
```

You can wipe out these settings and allow messages from all senders by setting the value to `$null`:

```
Set-DistributionGroup -Identity Sales `
-AcceptMessagesOnlyFromSendersOrMembers $null
```

Similar to the previous examples, we can reject messages from a specific user or member of a distribution list using the `-RejectMessagesFromSendersOrMembers` parameter:

```
Set-DistributionGroup -Identity Executives `
-RejectMessagesFromSendersOrMembers HourlyEmployees
```

In this example, Exchange will reject any message sent from a member of the *HourlyEmployees* distribution group to the *Executives* group.

There's more...

When you create a distribution group, the default configuration is to reject messages from senders who are not authenticated. This means that users outside of your organization will not be able to send messages to your distribution groups. Generally, this is the desired configuration, but if needed, you can modify this setting on a distribution group to accept messages from external users using the following syntax:

```
Set-DistributionGroup -Identity HelpDesk `
-RequireSenderAuthenticationEnabled $false
```

You can see here that we've disabled sender authentication for the *HelpDesk* distribution group. You can re-enable it at any time by setting the previous parameter value to `$true`.

See also

▸ *Managing distribution groups*

Managing automatic replies and out of office settings for a user

Exchange 2010 has introduced a new set of cmdlets that can be used to manage and automate the configuration of a user's Out of Office settings. In this recipe, we'll take a look at how to use these cmdlets from the Exchange Management Shell.

How to do it...

1. To view the Out of Office settings for a mailbox, use the following syntax:

   ```
   Get-MailboxAutoReplyConfiguration dave
   ```

2. You can change the Out of Office settings for a mailbox using the syntax shown next. For example, to disable Out of Office for a mailbox, use the following command:

   ```
   Set-MailboxAutoReplyConfiguration dave -AutoReplyState Disabled
   ```

How it works...

Retrieving the settings for a mailbox simply requires that you run the `Get-MailboxAutoReplyConfiguration` cmdlet and specify the identity of the mailbox, as shown in the previous example. The `Set-MailboxAutoReplyConfiguration` cmdlet supports multiple parameters that can be used to customize the settings use for the mailbox autoreply configuration:

```
Set-MailboxAutoReplyConfiguration dave `
-AutoReplyState Scheduled `
-StartTime 10/10/2011 `
-EndTime 10/15/2011 `
-ExternalMessage "I will be out of the office this week"
```

In this command, we set the `AutoReplyState`, specify a `StartTime` and `EndTime`, and set the `ExternalMessage`. When the `StartTime` date is reached, the mailbox will proceed to automatically reply to messages using the specified `ExternalMessage` until the `EndTime` date is reached. If you want automatic replies to be enabled indefinitely, set the `AutoReplyState` to `Enabled`.

To view the settings configured in the previous command, we can use the `Get-MailboxAutoReplyConfiguration` cmdlet, as shown in the following screenshot:

```
Machine: MBX1.CONTOSO.COM                                        _ □ X
[PS] C:\>Get-MailboxAutoReplyConfiguration dave

RunspaceId       : b577e3a7-75ee-423f-9e04-04d12d259fba
AutoReplyState   : Scheduled
EndTime          : 10/15/2011 12:00:00 AM
ExternalAudience : All
ExternalMessage  : <html>
                   <body>
                   I will be out of the office this week
                   </body>
                   </html>

InternalMessage  :
StartTime        : 10/10/2011 12:00:00 AM
MailboxOwnerId   : contoso.com/Users/Dave Smith
Identity         : contoso.com/Users/Dave Smith
IsValid          : True
```

You can see from viewing the mailbox auto-reply settings for this mailbox that only external replies are enabled. To enable internal Out of Office messages, you could run the previous set command and specify a message using the `-InternalMessage` parameter. Or you can use them both using a single command.

The -`InternalMessage` and -`ExternalMessage` parameters support HTML-formatted messages. If you want to set custom HTML code when configuring the auto-reply configuration from the shell, you can use the following command syntax:

```
Set-MailboxAutoReplyConfiguration dave `
-ExternalMessage (Get-Content C:\oof.html)
```

This command will read in a custom HTML formatted message from an external file and use that data when setting the internal or external message. This will allow you to work on the file from the HTML editor of your choice and import the code using a simple command from the shell.

By default, the -`ExternalAudience` parameter will be set to `None` if no value is specified. The remaining options are `Known` and `All`. Setting the external audience to `Known` will only send automatic replies to external users who are listed as contacts in the users mailbox.

There's more...

These cmdlets can be useful when making mass updates and when running reports. For example, to determine all of the users that currently have Out of Office enabled, you can run the following command:

```
Get-Mailbox –ResultSize Unlimited |
  Get-MailboxAutoReplyConfiguration |
    ?{$_.AutoReplyState -ne "Disabled"} |
      Select Identity,AutoReplyState,StartTime,EndTime
```

This one-liner will check every mailbox in the organization and return only the mailboxes with the auto-reply state set to either `Enabled` or `Scheduled`.

Adding, modifying, and removing server-side inbox rules

Exchange 2010 introduces a new set of cmdlets that can be used to manage server-side inbox rules for mailboxes in your organization. For the first time, we have the ability to add, remove, update, enable, and disable the inbox rules for mailboxes from within the Exchange Management Shell. This new functionality allows administrators to quickly resolve mailbox issues related to inbox rules, and allows them to easily deploy and manage inbox rules in bulk using just a few simple commands. In this recipe, you'll learn how to work with the inbox rules cmdlets in Exchange 2010.

How to do it...

1. To create an inbox rule, use the `New-InboxRule` cmdlet:

    ```
    New-InboxRule -Name Sales -Mailbox dave `
    -From sales@contoso.com `
    -MarkImportance High
    ```

2. You can change the configuration of an inbox rule using the `Set-InboxRule` cmdlet:

    ```
    Set-InboxRule -Identity Sales -Mailbox dave -MarkImportance Low
    ```

3. Use the `Enable-InboxRule` and `Disable-InboxRule` cmdlets to turn a rule on or off:

    ```
    Disable-InboxRule -Identity Sales -Mailbox dave
    ```

4. The `Get-InboxRule` cmdlet will return all of the server-side rules that have been created for a specified mailbox. The output from the command is shown in the following screenshot:

    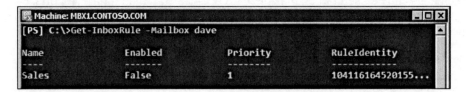

5. To remove an inbox rule, use the `Remove-InboxRule` cmdlet:

    ```
    Remove-InboxRule -Identity Sales -Mailbox dave -Confirm:$false
    ```

How it works...

Inbox rules are used to process messages sent to a mailbox based on a certain set of criteria, and to then take an action on that message if the condition is met. In the previous example, we created an inbox rule for the mailbox that would mark messages from the `sales@contoso.com` address with high importance. The `New-InboxRule` cmdlet provides a number of rule predicate parameters that allow you to define the conditions used for the rules you create.

Let's take a look at another example. Say that we want to create a rule that will check the subject or body of all incoming messages for a certain keyword. If there is a match, we'll send the message to the deleted items folder:

```
New-InboxRule -Name "Delete Rule" `
-Mailbox dave `
-SubjectOrBodyContainsWords "Delete Me" `
-DeleteMessage $true
```

In addition to conditions and actions, we can also add exceptions to these rules. Consider the following example:

```
New-InboxRule -Name "Redirect to Andrew" `
-Mailbox dave `
-MyNameInToOrCcBox $true `
-RedirectTo "Andrew Castaneda" `
-ExceptIfFrom "Alfonso Mcgowan" `
-StopProcessingRules $true
```

In this example, once again we're creating an inbox rule in Dave's mailbox. The condition MyNameInToOrCcBox is set to $true so that any message with the mailbox name in the To or CC fields will be processed by this rule. The action is the RedirectTo setting, and that will redirect the message to Andrews's mailbox, except if the message was sent from Alfonso's mailbox. Finally, the -StopProcessingRules parameter is set to $true, meaning that, once this rule is processed, Exchange will not process any other rules in this mailbox. The -StopProcessingRules parameter is an optional setting and is provided to give you another level of flexibility when it comes to controlling the way the rules are applied.

 It's important to note that when you add, remove, update, enable, or disable server-side rules using the *-InboxRule cmdlets, any client-side rules created by Outlook will be removed.

In all of these examples, we've specified the mailbox identity and have been configuring the rules of a single mailbox. If you do not provide a value for the -Mailbox parameter, the *-InboxRule cmdlets will execute against the mailbox belonging to the user that is running the command.

There's more...

Now let's take a look at a practical example of how you might create inbox rules in bulk. The following code will create an inbox rule for every mailbox in the *Sales* OU:

```
$sales = Get-Mailbox -OrganizationalUnit contoso.com/sales
$sales | %{
  New-InboxRule -Name Junk `
  -Mailbox $_.alias `
  -SubjectContainsWords "[Spam]" `
  -MoveToFolder "$($_.alias):\Junk E-Mail"
}
```

What we are doing here is using the `-SubjectContainsWords` parameter to check for a subject line that starts with "[Spam]". If there is a match, we move the message to the Junk E-Mail folder within that user's mailbox. As you can see, we are looping through each mailbox using the `ForEach-Object` cmdlet (using the `%` alias) and, within the loop, we specify the identity of the user when creating the inbox rule and when specifying the folder id, using the `$_.alias` property.

Even if you are logged in using an account in the Organization Management group, you may receive errors when trying to use the `-MoveToFolder` parameter when creating an inbox rule in another user's mailbox. Assigning `FullAccess` permissions to the mailbox in question should resolve this issue. For more details, see *Granting administrators full access to mailboxes* in *Chapter 10, Exchange Security*.

See also

▶   *Granting users full access permissions to mailboxes* in *Chapter 10, Exchange Security*

Managing mailbox folder permissions

Exchange 2010 introduces a new set of cmdlets that can be used to manage the permissions on the folders inside a mailbox. When it comes to managing recipients, one of the most common tasks that administrators and support personnel perform on a regular basis is updating the permissions on the calendar of a mailbox. In most corporate environments, calendars are shared amongst employees and often special rights need to be delegated to other users allowing them to add, remove, update, or change the items on a calendar. In this recipe, we'll cover the basics of managing mailbox folder permissions from within the shell, but we will focus specifically on calendar permissions since that is a common scenario. Keep in mind that the cmdlets used in this recipe can be used with any folder within a mailbox.

How to do it...

To allow users to view the calendar for a specific mailbox, use the following command:

```
Set-MailboxFolderPermission -Identity dave:\Calendar `
-User Default `
-AccessRights Reviewer
```

How it works...

In this example, we're giving the **Default** user the ability to read all items in the calendar of the specified mailbox by assigning the `Reviewer` access right. This would give every user in the organization the ability to view the calendar items for this mailbox. There are four cmdlets in total that can be used to manage the mailbox folder permissions:

- ▶ `Add-MailboxFolderPermission`
- ▶ `Get-MailboxFolderPermission`
- ▶ `Remove-MailboxFolderPermission`
- ▶ `Set-MailboxFolderPermission`

The `Add` and `Set-MailboxFolderPermission` cmdlets both provide an `-AccessRights` parameter that is used to set the appropriate permissions on the folder specified in the command. In the previous example, instead of assigning the `Reviewer` role, we could have assigned the `Editor` role to the **Default** user, giving all users the ability to completely manage the items in the calendar. The possible values that can be used with the `-AccessRights` parameter are as follows:

- ▶ `ReadItems`: The user assigned this right can read items within the designated folder.
- ▶ `CreateItems`: The user assigned this right can create items within the designated folder.
- ▶ `EditOwnedItems`: The user assigned this right can edit the items that the user owns in the designated folder.
- ▶ `DeleteOwnedItems`: The user assigned this right can delete items that the user owns in the designated folder.
- ▶ `EditAllItems`: The user assigned this right can edit all items in the designated folder.
- ▶ `DeleteAllItems`: The user assigned this right can delete all items in the designated folder.
- ▶ `CreateSubfolders`: The user assigned this right can create subfolders in the designated folder.
- ▶ `FolderOwner`: The user assigned this right has the right to view and move the folder and create subfolders. The user cannot read items, edit items, delete items, or create items.
- ▶ `FolderContact`: The user assigned this right is the contact for the designated folder.
- ▶ `FolderVisible`: The user assigned this right can view the specified folder, but can't read or edit items within the it.

The following roles are made up by one or more of the permissions specified in the previous list and can also be used with the -AccessRights parameter:

▸ **None**: FolderVisible

▸ **Owner**: CreateItems, ReadItems, CreateSubfolders, FolderOwner, FolderContact, FolderVisible, EditOwnedItems, EditAllItems, DeleteOwnedItems, DeleteAllItems

▸ **PublishingEditor**: CreateItems, ReadItems, CreateSubfolders, FolderVisible, EditOwnedItems, EditAllItems, DeleteOwnedItems, DeleteAllItems

▸ **Editor**: CreateItems, ReadItems, FolderVisible, EditOwnedItems, EditAllItems, DeleteOwnedItems, DeleteAllItems

▸ **PublishingAuthor**: CreateItems, ReadItems, CreateSubfolders, FolderVisible, EditOwnedItems, DeleteOwnedItems

▸ **Author**: CreateItems, ReadItems, FolderVisible, EditOwnedItems, DeleteOwnedItems

▸ **NonEditingAuthor**: CreateItems, ReadItems, FolderVisible

▸ **Reviewer**: ReadItems, FolderVisible

▸ **Contributor**: CreateItems, FolderVisible

There's more...

Using the *-MailboxFolderPermission cmdlets makes it easier to perform bulk operations on many mailboxes at once. For example, let's say that you need to assign Reviewer permissions to all employees on every mailbox calendar in the organization. You can use the following code to accomplish this task:

```
$mailboxes = Get-Mailbox -ResultSize Unlimited
$mailboxes | %{
  $calendar = Get-MailboxFolderPermission "$($_.alias):\Calendar" `
  -User Default

  if(!($calendar.AccessRights)) {
    Add-MailboxFolderPermission "$($_.alias):\Calendar" `
    -User Default -AccessRights Reviewer
  }

  if($calendar.AccessRights -ne "Reviewer") {
    Set-MailboxFolderPermission "$($_.alias):\Calendar" `
    -User Default -AccessRights Reviewer
  }
}
```

First, we use the Get-Mailbox cmdlet to retrieve all mailboxes in the organization and store that result in the $mailboxes variable. We then loop through each mailbox in the $mailboxes collection. Within the loop, we retrieve the current calendar settings for the **Default** user, using the Get-MailboxFolderPermission cmdlet, and store the output in the $calendar variable. If the **Default** user has not been assigned any rights to the calendar, we use the Add-MailboxFolderPermission cmdlet to add the Reviewer access right.

If the **Default** user has been assigned calendar permissions, we check to see if the access rights are set to Reviewer. If not, we modify the existing setting for the **Default** user to the Reviewer access right.

See also

▶ *Granting users full access permissions to mailboxes* in *Chapter 10, Exchange Security*

Importing user photos into Active Directory

One of the most popular new features in Exchange 2010 is the ability to view user photos in Outlook 2010. This is made possible by importing an image into the thumbnailPhoto attribute for a given user account in Active Directory. This image can then be displayed when viewing a message or browsing the Global Address List within Outlook 2010. This is a long-awaited enhancement, and the addition of this new feature makes it easier, especially in large organizations, to identify co-workers and get to know the people you are working with. In this recipe, we'll look at how you can import user photographs into Active Directory.

Getting ready

In addition to the Exchange Management Shell, you will need access to the Active Directory administration tools for this recipe. The Remote Server Administration Tools pack (RSAT-ADDS) is a prerequisite required by Exchange 2010 setup, so it will already be installed on an Exchange 2010 server and you can use the tools from there, if needed.

How to do it...

First, you need to update the Active Directory schema to ensure that the thumbnailPhoto attribute will be replicated to the Global Catalog. Your account will need to be a member of the schema admins group in Active Directory. On a machine with the Active Directory administration tools installed, do the following:

1. In the Exchange Management Shell or a cmd console, run the following command to register the Active Directory Schema extension:

    Regsvr32 schmmgmt.dll.

2. Start the MMC console by clicking on **Start | Run**, type MMC, and click **OK**.

3. Go to **File** and click on **Add/Remove Snap-In**.

4. Add the Active Directory Schema Snap-In and click **OK**.

5. Under Active Directory Schema, highlight the **Attributes** node, and locate the **thumbnailPhoto** attribute.

6. Right click on the **thumbnailPhoto** attribute and click on **Properties**.

7. On the Properties page, select **Replicate this attribute to the Global Catalog**, and click **OK**.

At this point, the required Active Directory steps have been completed and you can now import a photo into Active Directory using the Import-RecipientDataProperty cmdlet:

```
Import-RecipientDataProperty -Identity dave `
-Picture `
-FileData (
  [Byte[]] (
    Get-Content -Path C:\dave.jpg `
    -Encoding Byte `
    -ReadCount 0
  )
)
```

How it works...

Each user account or contact object in Active Directory has a thumbnailPhoto attribute that can be used to store binary data. The Get-Content cmdlet is used to read a .jpeg file into a byte array, and we then use the Import-RecipientDataProperty cmdlet to load that data into the thumbnailPhoto attribute of the user account or contact in Active Directory, using the -FileData parameter. Once the data has been imported into Active Directory, Outlook 2010 will query the thumbnailPhoto attribute of each user and display their photo when you receive an e-mail message from them, or when you are viewing their information in the Global Address List.

 If you need to remove a photo for a user or a contact, use the -RemovePicture switch parameter with the Set-Mailbox or Set-MailContact cmdlets.

There are a few things to keep in mind when you decide to load photos into Active Directory for your users. First, the -FileData parameter is limited to 10 kb, so you need to ensure that the images you are trying to import are not too large. Also, the image file must be in jpeg format. The recommended thumbnail photo size in pixels is 96x96 pixels. Finally, be conscious about the size of your NTDS database in Active Directory. If you only have a small amount of users, then this will probably not be a huge issue. If you have hundreds of thousands of users there will be some serious replication traffic if you suddenly import photos for each of those users. Make sure to plan accordingly.

There's more...

Outlook clients operating in cached mode will use the `thumbnailPhoto` attribute configuration of the **Offline Address Book** (**OAB**) to determine how to access photos. By default, the `thumbnailPhoto` attribute is an Indicator attribute, meaning that it points Outlook to Active Directory to retrieve the image. If you want to disable thumbnail photos for cached-mode clients, remove the attribute using the `Remove` method of the `ConfigureAttrbutes` collection:

```
$oab = Get-OfflineAddressBook 'Default Offline Address Book'
$oab.ConfiguredAttributes.Remove('thumbnailphoto,indicator')

Set-OfflineAddressBook 'Default Offline Address Book' `
-ConfiguredAttributes $oab.ConfiguredAttributes
```

If you want offline clients to be able to view thumbnail photos, you can add the `thumbnailPhoto` attribute as a value attribute using the `Add` method:

```
$oab = Get-OfflineAddressBook 'Default Offline Address Book'
$oab.ConfiguredAttributes.Add('thumbnailphoto,value')

Set-OfflineAddressBook 'Default Offline Address Book' `
-ConfiguredAttributes $oab.ConfiguredAttributes
```

If you work in a medium or large organization, this could make for an extremely large OAB. Again, make sure to plan accordingly. Use the following command to update the OAB after these configuration changes have been made:

```
Update-OfflineAddressBook 'Default Offline Address Book'
```

Taking it a step further

If you are going to take advantage of this function, you are likely going to do this in bulk for existing employees, or as new employees are hired, and this may require some automation. Let's say that your company issues a security badge with a photo for each employee. You have each of these photos stored on a file server in jpeg format. The file names of the photos use the Exchange alias for the users associated mailbox. The following script can be used in this scenario to import the photos in bulk:

```
$photos = Get-ChildItem \\server01\employeephotos -Filter *.jpg

foreach($i in $photos) {
[Byte[]]$data = gc -Path $i.fullname -Encoding Byte -ReadCount 0
  Import-RecipientDataProperty $i.basename -Picture -FileData $data
  }
```

First, this code creates a collection of jpeg files in the `\\server01\employeephotos` share and stores the results in the `$photos` object. We're using the `-Filter` parameter with the `Get-ChildItem` cmdlet so that the command only returns files with a `.jpg` extension. The items returned from the `Get-ChildItem` cmdlet are `FileInfo` objects which contain several properties that include detailed information about each file, such as the filename and the full path to the file.

As we loop through each photo in the collection, you can see that inside the loop we're casting the output from `Get-Content` (using the `gc` alias) to `[Byte[]]` and storing the result in the `$data` variable. We can determine the path to the file using the `FullName` property of the `FileInfo` object that represents the current jpeg file being processed in the loop. We then use the `Import-RecipientDataProperty` cmdlet to import the data for the current user in the loop. The `BaseName` property of a `FileInfo` object returns the file name without the extension; therefore we use this property value to identify which user we're importing the photo for when executing the `Import-RecipientDataProperty` cmdlet.

See also

▶ *Transferring files through remote PowerShell* in *Chapter 2, Exchange Management Shell Common Tasks*

4
Managing Mailboxes

In this chapter, we will cover:

- ▶ Reporting on the mailbox size
- ▶ Working with move requests and performing mailbox moves
- ▶ Importing and exporting mailboxes
- ▶ Deleting messages from mailboxes
- ▶ Managing disconnected mailboxes
- ▶ Generating mailbox folder reports
- ▶ Reporting on mailbox creation time
- ▶ Checking mailbox logon statistics
- ▶ Setting storage quotas for mailboxes
- ▶ Finding inactive mailboxes
- ▶ Detecting and fixing corrupt mailboxes
- ▶ Restoring items from mailboxes

Introduction

The concept of the mailbox is the core feature of any Exchange solution, and it's likely that almost everything you do as Exchange administrator will revolve around this component. Exchange 2010 SP1 includes several new cmdlets that make life much easier for any Exchange administrator, allowing you to do just about anything you can think of when it comes to managing mailboxes through scripts and one-liners. This includes tasks such as moving, importing, exporting, removing, and reconnecting mailboxes, just to name a few. In this recipe, you will learn how to generate reports, perform bulk mailbox changes, repair corrupt mailboxes, and more.

Performing some basic steps

To work with the code samples in this chapter, follow these steps to launch the Exchange Management Shell:

1. Log onto a workstation or server with the Exchange Management Tools installed.
2. Open the Exchange Management Shell by clicking on **Start | All Programs | Exchange Server 2010**.
3. Click on the **Exchange Management Shell** shortcut.

Reporting on the mailbox size

Using cmdlets from both the Exchange Management Shell and Windows PowerShell gives us the ability to generate detailed reports. In this recipe, we will use these cmdlets to report on all of the mailboxes within an organization and their total size.

How to do it...

1. Use the following one-liner to generate a report of each mailbox in the organization and the total mailbox size:

```
Get-MailboxDatabase | Get-MailboxStatistics |
  ?{!$_.DisconnectDate} |
    Select-Object DisplayName,TotalItemSize
```

2. Pipe the command even further to export the report to a CSV file that can be opened and formatted in Excel:

```
Get-MailboxDatabase | Get-MailboxStatistics |
  ?{!$_.DisconnectDate} |
    Select-Object DisplayName,TotalItemSize |
      Export-CSV c:\mbreport.csv -NoType
```

How it works...

In both commands, we're using the `Get-MailboxDatabase` cmdlet to pipe each database in the organization to the `Get-MailboxStatistics` cmdlet. Notice that in the next stage of the pipeline we are filtering on the `DisconnectDate` property. Inside the filter we are using the exclamation (`!`) character, which is a shortcut for the `-not` operator in PowerShell. So we are basically saying, give me all the mailboxes in the organization that are not in a disconnected state. This can be standard mailboxes as well as archive mailboxes. We then select the `DisplayName` and `TotalItemSize` properties that give us the name and total mailbox size of each mailbox.

There's more...

When using the first example to view the mailboxes and their total size, you will see the output in the shell is similar to the following screenshot:

```
Machine: MBX1.CONTOSO.COM                                          _ □ X
DisplayName                        TotalItemSize
-----------                        -------------
Gary Busey                         453.2 KB (464,065 bytes)
Anna Dillard                       6.37 MB (6,679,415 bytes)
Pete Dickson                       8.371 MB (8,777,376 bytes)
Kerry Good                         378.8 KB (387,851 bytes)
SystemMailbox{de883e0c-0c71-44d6-b... 2.81 MB (2,946,737 bytes)
```

Here you can see that we get the total size in megabytes as well as in bytes. If you find that this additional information is not useful, you can extend the previous one-liner using a calculated property:

```
Get-MailboxDatabase | Get-MailboxStatistics |
  ?{!$_.DisconnectDate} |
    Select-Object DisplayName,
    @{n="SizeMB";e={$_.TotalItemSize.value.ToMb()}} |
      Sort-Object SizeMB -Desc
```

Running the preceding one-liner will provide output similar to the following:

```
Machine: MBX1.CONTOSO.COM                                          _ □ X
DisplayName                                                  SizeMB
-----------                                                  ------
Administrator                                                    14
Della Conley                                                      9
Carmen Vaughn                                                     8
Pete Dickson                                                      8
Tom Smith                                                         7
```

Notice that we now have a custom property called `SizeMB` that reports only the mailbox size in megabytes. We have also sorted this property in descending order and the mailboxes are now listed from largest to smallest. You can continue to pipe this command down to the `Export-CSV` cmdlet to generate a report that can be viewed outside of the shell.

See also

▸ *Adding, modifying, and removing mailboxes* in *Chapter 3, Managing Recipients*

▸ *Working with move requests and performing mailbox moves*

- ▸ *Reporting on mailbox database size* in *Chapter 6, Mailbox and Public Folder Databases*

- ▸ *Finding the total number of mailboxes in a database* in *Chapter 6, Mailbox and Public Folder Databases*

- ▸ *Determining the average mailbox size per database* in *Chapter 6, Mailbox and Public Folder Databases*

Working with move requests and performing mailbox moves

Even if you performed mailbox moves with PowerShell in Exchange 2007, it's important that you understand that the process is completely different in Exchange 2010 SP1. There is a new set of cmdlets available for performing and managing mailbox moves, and the previously-used Move-Mailbox cmdlet no longer exists. The architecture used by Exchange to perform mailbox moves uses a new concept known as *move requests*, which have been implemented in this latest version. In this recipe, you will learn how to manage move requests from the Exchange Management Shell.

How to do it...

To create a move request and move a mailbox to another database within the Exchange organization, use the New-MoveRequest cmdlet, as shown next:

```
New-MoveRequest –Identity testuser –TargetDatabase DB2
```

How it works...

Mailbox moves are performed asynchronously with this new method and, unlike using the Move-Mailbox cmdlet in Exchange 2007, the New-MoveRequest cmdlet does not perform the actual mailbox move. Mailbox moves are handled by **Client Access Servers** (**CAS**) that run the **Mailbox Replication Service** (**MRS**). This is a major improvement because mailbox data does not move through an administrative workstation when performing a move; instead, the CAS servers are responsible for transferring the data from one database to another. Not only does this make mailbox moves faster, but it also allows you to kick off one or more mailbox moves from any machine in the organization. You can later check on the status of those move requests from any other machine with PowerShell or the Exchange Management Tools installed.

When you create a new move request with the `New-MoveRequest` cmdlet, the command places a special message in the target mailbox database's system mailbox. The MRS scans the system mailboxes on a regular basis looking for queued mailbox move requests and, once they are found, the MRS will start the move process. Once the move has been completed, a record of the mailbox move is saved and can be viewed using the `Get-MoveRequest` cmdlet.

 This recipe only covers local move requests that are performed within an Exchange organization. It is possible to use the `New-MoveRequest` cmdlet to perform a mailbox move across Active Directory forest boundaries. For more details, see *Managing Remote Move Requests* on TechNet at the following URL: `http://technet.microsoft.com/en-us/library/ff841978.aspx`.

If you will be automating mailbox moves using the Exchange Management Shell, it is likely that you will be doing so in bulk. The following example shows how you can move all of the mailboxes from one database to another:

```
Get-Mailbox -Database DB1 | New-MoveRequest -TargetDatabase DB2
```

In this example, we are retrieving all of the mailboxes in the `DB1` database and creating a new move request for each one that will then be moved to the target database of `DB2`. The `-TargetDatabase` parameter is actually an optional parameter. If you have multiple mailbox databases in your organization, you can omit the `-TargetDatabase` parameter in the previous command, and the mailboxes will be moved evenly across the available mailbox databases, as long as those databases have not been suspended or excluded from provisioning and as long as the Mailbox Resources Management Agent is enabled, which is the default setting.

There's more...

In order to view detailed information about move requests, you can use the `Get-MoveRequestStatistics` cmdlet. This will return a great deal of useful information for a given move request such as the move status, percent complete, the total bytes transferred, and more. You can also use the `-IncludeReport` switch parameter when running the cmdlet to provide a debug level details for mailbox moves. This can be very beneficial when troubleshooting an issue.

One of the greatest uses of this cmdlet is reporting on the current status of mailbox moves in progress, especially during large migrations. The following one-liner can be used to gather the statistics for the currently-running mailbox moves and can be run periodically throughout the migration to check the status:

```
Get-MoveRequest |
  ?{$_.Status -ne 'Completed'} |
    Get-MoveRequestStatistics |
        select DisplayName,PercentComplete,BytesTransferred
```

The preceding command would produce an output for each mailbox similar to the following screenshot:

In this example, we're selecting just a few of the properties from the output of the command. Alternatively, it may be useful to export this information to a CSV file or to mail the results to an administrator mailbox. Either way, it gives you a method for monitoring the status of your mailbox moves interactively in the shell or through an automated script.

If you just want to do some basic interactive monitoring from the shell to determine when all moves are complete, you can use the following code:

```
while($true) {
   Get-MoveRequest| ?{$_.Status -ne 'Completed'}
   Start-Sleep 5
   Clear-Host
}
```

The output from this command will give you a view of all the incomplete move requests and will refresh every five seconds. This is done by using an endless while loop that runs Get-MoveRequest, waits for five seconds, clears the screen, and starts over again. Once all moves are completed, just press *Ctrl + C* to break out of the loop.

Removing the move requests

You cannot perform a move request for a mailbox if there is an existing move request associated with that mailbox. This is true regardless of the move request status, whether it is complete, pending, cancelled, or failed. You can use the Remove-MoveRequest to delete an existing move request for a single mailbox, using the following syntax:

```
Remove-MoveRequest -Identity testuser -Confirm:$false
```

If you perform frequent moves you may find it necessary to regularly delete all existing move requests in the organization. To do this, use the following command:

```
Get-MoveRequest -ResultSize Unlimited |
    Remove-MoveRequest -Confirm:$false
```

Keep in mind that stored move requests can provide detailed information that can be used for monitoring or generating reports for mailbox moves. Make sure you no longer need this information before removing these move requests from your organization.

Moving the archive mailboxes

Consider the following example. The *testuser* account has a mailbox in the DB1 database, and also a personal archive mailbox in the DB1 database. We can use the following command to move *testuser* to DB2:

```
New-MoveRequest testuser -TargetDatabase DB2
```

In this case, both the primary mailbox and the archive mailbox will be moved to DB2. We can customize this behaviour by using some additional parameters made available by the New-MoveRequest cmdlet. For example, if we wanted to only move this user's primary mailbox and leave the archive mailbox in its current location, we could use the following command:

```
New-MoveRequest testuser -TargetDatabase DB2 -PrimaryOnly
```

This command adds the -PrimaryOnly switch parameter, which will indicate to the New-MoveRequest cmdlet that we do not want to move the archive mailbox but we do want to move the primary mailbox to the DB2 database. Use the following command to move only the archive mailbox:

```
New-MoveRequest testuser -ArchiveOnly -ArchiveTargetDatabase DB2
```

This time, we have added the -ArchiveOnly switch parameter so that only the archive mailbox will be moved. The -ArchiveTargetDatabase is also used to specify that we want to move the archive mailbox to the DB2 database.

Moving the mailboxes in batches

When performing migrations or moving multiple mailboxes in bulk, it can be useful to move them in batches. The New-MoveRequest cmdlet provides a -BatchName parameter to group multiple mailbox moves into a single, logical collection. Let's say that we are migrating multiple mailboxes to several different databases and we want to easily track the mailbox moves based on a certain criteria:

```
$mailboxes = Get-Mailbox `
    -RecipientTypeDetails UserMailbox `
    -Database DB1 |
      Get-MailboxStatistics |
        ?{$_.TotalItemSize -gt 2gb}
```

```
$mailboxes | %{
  New-MoveRequest -Identity $_.DisplayName `
  -BatchName 'Large Mailboxes' `
  -TargetDatabase DB2
}
```

Here we are retrieving all mailboxes in the `DB1` database that are larger than two gigabytes and storing the results in the `$mailboxes` variable. We then pipe the `$mailboxes` object to the `ForEach-Object` cmdlet (using the `%` alias) and loop through each item. As each mailbox in the collection is processed within the loop, we create a new move request for that mailbox, indicating that it should be included in the *Large Mailboxes* batch and moved to the `DB2` database. At this point, we can easily track the moves in the batch using a simple one-liner:

```
Get-MoveRequest -BatchName 'Large Mailboxes'
```

The preceding command will return each move request included in the *Large Mailboxes* batch and will provide several details including the display name, move status, and target database.

Moving mailboxes with corrupt items

When migrating from a previous version of Exchange, or when migrating large mailboxes, it's not uncommon to run into problems with users that have corrupted items in their mailbox. You can use the `-BadItemLimit` parameter to specify the acceptable number of corrupt, or "bad", items to skip when performing a mailbox move. Keep in mind that if you set the `-BadItemLimit` parameter to a value higher than 50 then you need to also use the `-AcceptLargeDataLoss` switch parameter, as shown in the following example::

```
New-MoveRequest -Identity testuser `
-BadItemLimit 100 `
-AcceptLargeDataLoss `
-TargetDatabase DB2
```

When executing this command, a move request will be created for the *testuser* mailbox. Up to 100 corrupt items in the source mailbox will be allowed in order to perform a successful move to the new database. You will see a warning in the shell when using these parameters and any corrupt items found in the source mailbox will be skipped when the mailbox is moved.

See also

▸ *Reporting on the mailbox size*

▸ *Managing archive mailboxes* in *Chapter 11, Compliance and Audit Logging*

▸ *Adding, modifying, and removing mailboxes* in *Chapter 3, Managing Recipients*

Importing and exporting mailboxes

If you have worked with Exchange for a long time, you have probably used utilities such as ExMerge or the Exchange 2007 Management Shell to import and export data between mailboxes and PST files. While these tools were useful for their time, they had some limitations. For example, ExMerge was the main import and export utility starting with Exchange 5.5 and continuing on to Exchange 2003, but it was difficult to automate. Exchange 2007 included the `Import-Mailbox` and `Export-Mailbox` cmdlets that made it easier to automate these tasks through PowerShell scripts. Unfortunately, the `Export-Mailbox` cmdlet required both a 32-bit workstation running the 32-bit version of the Exchange 2007 Management tools and Microsoft Outlook 2003 SP2 or later.

With the release of Exchange 2010 SP1, we have a new set of cmdlets that can be used to manage the import and export operations for Exchange mailboxes. These new cmdlets have no dependencies on a management workstation and there is no requirement to install Outlook to perform these tasks. The Mailbox Replication Service (MRS) that runs on the Client Access Server (CAS) role introduces a new concept called mailbox import and export requests that implements this functionality as a server-side process. In this recipe, you will learn how to configure your environment and use these cmdlets to automate mailbox import and export requests.

How to do it...

1. Let's start off by exporting a mailbox to a PST file. First, you need to add an RBAC role assignment for your account. Assign the *Mailbox Import Export* role to your account using the following command. You will need to restart the shell after running this command in order for the assigned cmdlets to be visible:

    ```
    New-ManagementRoleAssignment -Role "Mailbox Import Export" `
    -User administrator
    ```

2. Next, you will need to create a network share that can be used to store the PST file. When you create the share, make sure that the Exchange Trusted Subsystem group in Active Directory has at least read/write NTFS permissions on the folder, and also has at least modify share permissions.

3. The last step is to use the `New-MailboxExportRequest` cmdlet to export the data for a mailbox, using the following syntax:

    ```
    New-MailboxExportRequest -Mailbox testuser `
    -Filepath \\contoso-ex01\export\testuser.pst
    ```

How it works...

By default, the built-in *Mailbox Import Export* role is not assigned to anyone, including the administrators. This means that, out of the box, you will not be able to run the `*-MailboxExportRequest` cmdlets, even if you are a member of the *Organization Management* role group. Therefore, the first step in the process is to assign your account to this role using the `New-ManagementRoleAssignment` cmdlet. In the previous example, you can see that we created a direct assignment to the administrator's user account. This can be your administrative account, or an actual role group that you are already a member of. If needed, you can specify that the role be assigned to a role group or an Active Directory security group using the `-SecurityGroup` parameter.

The location used for imported and exported PSTs must be a valid UNC path that the Exchange Trusted Subsystem group has access to. This is because the cmdlets that you execute are actually running under the security context of the Exchange servers in this group group. This is required to implement the new RBAC security model, and, therefore, the Share and NTFS permissions must be assigned to this group and not your user account specifically.

The syntax for the import and export commands is fairly straightforward. Looking at the command used in the previous example, you can see that we were able to easily create an export request for a specified mailbox using a specific file share on the network.

Using additional parameters, we can do other interesting things, such as only exporting specific folders of a mailbox to a PST:

```
New-MailboxExportRequest -Mailbox testuser `
-IncludeFolders "Sent Items" `
-FilePath \\contoso-ex01\export\testuser_sent.pst `
-ExcludeDumpster
```

As you can see from the command, we are only exporting the `Sent Items` folder from the *testuser* mailbox and we are excluding the items in the dumpster.

Here is another example that exports data from an archive mailbox:

```
New-MailboxExportRequest -Mailbox testuser `
-ContentFilter {Received -lt "09/01/2010"} `
-FilePath \\contoso-ex01\export\testuser_archive.pst `
-ExcludeDumpster `
-IsArchive
```

Here we are specifying that we want to only export data from the archive mailbox by using the `-IsArchive` switch parameter. In addition, we are limiting the amount of data exported from the mailbox using the `-ContentFilter` parameter. We are only including items that were received before 09/01/2010. In addition to the `Received` property, the `-ContentFilter` parameter allows you to highly customize the data that is exported.

You can create upto 10 mailbox export requests per mailbox without manually specifying a name for the export request. Once you have reached this limit, you either need to specify a unique name for the export request, or delete some of the previous export requests using the `Remove-MailboxExportRequest` cmdlet.

Using the `-ContentFilter` parameter, you can filter the recipient, types of attachments that were included in a message, text in the body, and more. For a complete list of available property names, check out the *Filterable Properties for the -ContentFilter Parameter* on TechNet at the following URL:

`http://technet.microsoft.com/en-us/library/ff601762.aspx`

There's more...

You can use the `Get-MailboxImportRequest` and `Get-MailboxExportRequest` cmdlets to view the status of your import and export tasks. To view all requests, simply run the appropriate `Get-*` cmdlet. If you want to narrow your search, you can use the `-Mailbox` and `-Status` parameters:

```
Get-MailboxExportRequest -Mailbox testuser -Status Failed
```

This command will return all of the export requests made for the *testuser* mailbox that have a failed status. You can use the same syntax with the import version of this cmdlet to review similar information.

When it comes to advanced reporting of import or export requests, there are two cmdlets available that you can use. `Get-MailboxExportRequestStatistics` and `Get-MailboxImportRequestStatistics` can be used to provide detailed information about the tasks associated with a particular operation. For example, take a look at the following script:

```
foreach($i in Get-MailboxExportRequest) {
  Get-MailboxExportRequestStatistics $i |
    select-object SourceAlias,Status,PercentComplete
}
```

This will provide a brief report for each export request. This can be useful when you are performing multiple import or export operations and need to check the status of each one.

Importing data into mailboxes

The `New-MailboxImportRequest` cmdlet works similarly to the `New-MailboxExportRequest` cmdlet. Most of the parameters shown in the previous examples are available with both cmdlets. For example, we can import data into a specific folder in an inbox with the following command:

```
New-MailboxImportRequest -Mailbox sysadmin `
-IncludeFolders "Sent Items" `
-FilePath \\contoso-ex01\export\testuser_sent.pst
```

This command imports the *testuser* PST into the **Sent Items** folder of the sysadmin mailbox. In addition to exporting data from archive mailboxes, we can also import data into archive mailboxes with the `-IsArchive` switch parameter.

Taking it a step further

Let's create a script that will export all of the mailboxes in your organization to individual PST files stored in a central location. Create a new file called `Export.ps1` and save it in the `C:\` drive. Using a text editor, open the file and add the following code, and then save the file:

```
param($Path, $BatchName)
   foreach($i in Get-Mailbox -ResultSize Unlimited) {
      $filepath = Join-Path -Path $Path -ChildPath "$($_.alias).pst"
      New-MailboxExportRequest -Mailbox $i `
      -FilePath $filepath `
      -BatchName $BatchName
}
```

This script provides a couple of parameters used to control the behavior of the mailbox export requests. First, the `-Path` parameter will allow us to specify a UNC share for our exported mailboxes. Secondly, the `-BatchName` parameter is used to logically group the export requests using a friendly common name.

As we loop through each mailbox, we are doing a few things. We are using the value of the `-Path` parameter as the root directory for the PST file, and we are using the `alias` of the mailbox for the base filename. This will ensure that each PST file is stored centrally in the required location using a unique filename that matches the mailbox alias.

To execute the preceding script, the command might look something like this:

```
$batch = "Export for (Get-Date).ToShortDateString()"
.\Export.ps1 -Path \\contoso\ex01\export -BatchName$batch
```

This will create each mailbox export request using a batch name such as `Export for 10/26/2010`. Then you can easily check the status of all the mailbox export requests that are grouped into that batch name using the following command:

```
Get-MailboxExportRequestStatistics |
  ?{$_.BatchName -eq "Export for 10/26/2010"} |
    select SourceAlias,Status,PercentComplete
```

This one-liner will give you a brief report on each of the export requests performed in the batch created on 10/26/2010 that can be reviewed in the shell, exported to a text or CSV file, or e-mailed to another user.

See also

▸ *Exporting reports to text and CSV files* in *Chapter 2, Exchange Management Shell Common Tasks*

▸ *Sending SMTP e-mails through PowerShell* in *Chapter 2, Exchange Management Shell Common Tasks*

Deleting messages from mailboxes

At one point or another, you are bound to find yourself in a situation where you need to remove an e-mail message from one or more mailboxes. This may be due to a message being sent to one of your distribution lists or as a part of some kind of spam or virus-related outbreak. If you have worked with Exchange 2007, you may be familiar with the `Export-Mailbox` cmdlet that could previously be used to perform this task. With Exchange 2010 SP1, we now have a new cmdlet called `Search-Mailbox` that can be used to clean up the mailboxes in our environment. This cmdlet includes some new features as well, and in this recipe we will take a look at how to use it to delete messages from mailboxes.

How to do it...

1. If you have not already done so, you will need to use the following command syntax to assign your account the *Mailbox Import Export* RBAC role. You will need to restart the shell after running this command in order for the assigned cmdlet to be visible:

    ```
    New-ManagementRoleAssignment –Role "Mailbox Import Export" `
    -User administrator
    ```

2. Next, use the `Search-Mailbox` cmdlet to delete items from a mailbox. In this example, we will use a search query to delete items with a specific phrase in the subject line:

```
Search-Mailbox -Identity testuser `
-SearchQuery "Subject:'Your mailbox is full'" `
-DeleteContent `
-Force
```

How it works...

The key to deleting items from a mailbox is the `-DeleteContent` switch parameter used with the `Search-Mailbox` cmdlet. When executing the command in the previous example, any message matching the subject specified in the search query will be deleted without confirmation and output similar to the following will be displayed:

```
Machine: MBX1.CONTOSO.COM                                    _ □ ×

RunspaceId       : b577e3a7-75ee-423f-9e04-04d12d259fba
Identity         : contoso.com/Users/testuser
TargetMailbox    :
TargetPSTFile    :
Success          : True
TargetFolder     :
ResultItemsCount : 16
ResultItemsSize  : 24.36 KB (24,944 bytes)
```

As you can see, there is a lot of useful information returned that indicates whether or not the delete operation was successful, how many items were deleted, the total item size of the deleted messages, and so on.

Keep in mind that the `Search-Mailbox` cmdlet will include messages in a user's archive mailbox and the dumpster within their primary mailbox as part of the search. To exclude these, use the following syntax:

```
Search-Mailbox -Identity testuser `
-SearchQuery "Subject:'free ipad'" `
-DoNotIncludeArchive `
-SearchDumpster:$false `
-DeleteContent `
-Force
```

There's more...

The `-SearchQuery` parameter is used to specify the criteria of your search using Advanced Query Syntax (AQS), which is the same query syntax used with Windows Search, Exchange Search, and the Instant Search box in Outlook. When composing a command, you want to use the property name, followed by a colon, and then the text you want to query. There are several AQS properties that can be used, some of the more common properties are `Subject`, `Body`, `Sent`, `To`, `From`, and `Attachment`. See *Appendix B* at the end of this book for a list of AQS properties and common search queries.

Running reports before deleting data

Of course, permanently deleting data from someone's mailbox is not something that should be done without total confidence. If you are unsure of the results, or you just want to cover your bases, you can use the following syntax to generate a report of the items that will be deleted:

```
Get-Mailbox |
Search-Mailbox -SearchQuery "from:spammer@contoso.com" `
-EstimateResultOnly | Export-CSV C:\report.csv -NoType
```

This example uses the `-EstimateResultsOnly` parameter when executing the `Search-Mailbox` cmdlet. You can see here that we are executing a one-liner that will search each mailbox for messages sent from `spammer@contoso.com`. The estimate for the result is exported to a CSV file that you can use to determine how much data will be cleaned up out of each individual mailbox.

If you need a more detailed report, we can use the logging capabilities of the `Search-Mailbox` cmdlet. The following command performs a search on the *testuser* mailbox and generates some reports that we can use to determine exactly what will be deleted:

```
Search-Mailbox -Identity testuser `
-SearchQuery "Subject:'Accounting Reports'" `
-TargetMailbox sysadmin `
-TargetFolder "Delete Log" `
-LogOnly `
-LogLevel Full
```

This is made possible by the `-LogOnly` switch parameter. This will generate a message in a target mailbox folder that you specify. In this example, you can see that the target folder for the report is the `Delete Log` folder in the sysadmin mailbox. This report will provide a summary of the items that will be deleted in the search if you were to run this command with the `-DeleteContent` parameter. When setting the `-LogLevel` to parameter value to `Full`, a ZIP file, containing a CSV report listing each of the items returned by the search will be attached to this message.

Deleting messages in bulk

Most likely, you will need to delete items from several mailboxes in a bulk operation. The following one-liner can be used to delete messages from every mailbox in the organization:

```
Get-Mailbox -ResultSize Unlimited |
  Search-Mailbox -SearchQuery 'from:spammer@contoso.com' `
  -DeleteContent -Force
```

In this example, we are piping all the mailboxes in the organization to the `Search-Mailbox` cmdlet. Any messages sent from the `spammer@contoso.com` e-mail address will be deleted.

See also

▶ *Restoring deleted items from mailboxes*

▶ *Performing a discovery search* in *Chapter 11, Compliance and Audit Logging*

▶ *Deleting e-mail items from a mailbox with EWS* in *Chapter 13, Scripting with the Exchange Web Services Managed API*

Managing disconnected mailboxes

Exchange allows us to disassociate a mailbox from an Active Directory user account, and later reconnect that mailbox to an Active Directory account. For some organizations, a mailbox database has a low deleted mailbox retention setting, and once a mailbox has been removed from a user, it is forgotten about and purged from the database once the retention period elapses. However, if you maintain your deleted mailboxes for any amount of time, having the ability to retrieve these mailboxes after they have been removed from a user can be very helpful at times. In this recipe, we will take a look at how to manage disconnected mailboxes using the Exchange Management Shell.

How to do it...

To reconnect a disconnected mailbox to a user account, use the `Connect-Mailbox` cmdlet. The following example reconnects a disconnected mailbox to the *tuser1009* account the Active Directory:

```
Connect-Mailbox -Identity 'Test User' `
-Database DB1 `
-User 'contoso\tuser1009' `
-Alias tuser1009
```

How it works...

When you use the `Remove-Mailbox` or `Disable-Mailbox` cmdlets to delete a mailbox for a user, that mailbox can actually be retained in its source database for a period of time. This is determined by the deleted mailbox retention setting of the database the mailbox resides in. For example, let's say that the deleted mailbox retention for the database hosting the *testuser* mailbox is set to 30 days. After the *testuser* mailbox has been deleted, this gives us 30 days to reconnect that mailbox to an Active Directory user account before the retention period is met and the mailbox is permanently purged.

The `-Identity` parameter, used with the `Connect-Mailbox` cmdlet, specifies the mailbox that should be connected to an Active Directory account and can accept the `MailboxGuid`, `DisplayName`, or `LegacyExchangeDN` values for input. Finding this information requires a little digging, as there is no `Get` cmdlet when it comes to searching for disconnected mailboxes. You can find this information with the `Get-MailboxStatistics` cmdlet:

```
Get-MailboxDatabase |
  Get-MailboxStatistics |
    ?{$_.DisconnectDate} |
      fl DisplayName,MailboxGuid,LegacyExchangeDN,DisconnectDate
```

This command will search each database for mailboxes that have a `DisconnectDate` defined. The values that can be used to identify a disconnected mailbox when running the `Connect-Mailbox` cmdlet will be displayed in the list format.

 It is possible that there could be multiple disconnected mailboxes with the same `DisplayName`. In this case, you can use the `MailboxGuid` value to identify the disconnected mailbox that should be reconnected.

The previous command will return both disconnected mailboxes and also disconnected archive mailboxes, so you may need to filter those out if you have implemented personal archives in your environment. For example:

```
Get-MailboxDatabase |
  Get-MailboxStatistics |
    ?{$_.DisconnectDate -and $_.IsArchiveMailbox -eq $false} |
      fl DisplayName,MailboxGuid,LegacyExchangeDN,DisconnectDate
```

This one-liner will search for disconnected mailboxes in all databases that do not have their `IsArchiveMailbox` property set to `$true`.

All of these commands can be a little cumbersome to type, and if you use them often, it might make sense to write some custom code that makes this easier. Take a look at the following function that has been written to automate the process:

```
function Get-DisconnectedMailbox {
  param(
  [String]$Name = '*',
  [Switch]$Archive
  )

  $databases = Get-MailboxDatabase
  $databases | %{
    $db = Get-Mailboxstatistics -Database $_ |
      ?{$_.DisconnectDate -and $_.IsArchiveMailbox -eq $Archive}

    $db | ?{$_.displayname -like $Name} |
      Select DisplayName,
        MailboxGuid,
        Database,
        DisconnectReason
  }
}
```

This function can be added to your PowerShell profile, and it will then be available every time you start the Exchange Management Shell. You can then run the function just like a regular cmdlet. By default, if you run the cmdlet without parameters all of the disconnected mailboxes in your environment will be returned. You can also narrow your search using wildcards, as shown in the following screenshot:

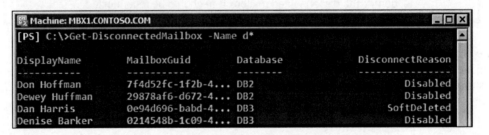

Here you can see that we have used a wildcard with the function to find all the disconnected mailboxes starting with the letter d. To use the function to find disconnected archive mailboxes, simply use the -Archive switch parameter.

There's more...

With the introduction of move requests in Exchange 2010 SP1, some new functionality has been added that you will need to be aware of when managing disconnected mailboxes. When you use the New-MoveRequest cmdlet to move a mailbox from one database to another, the mailbox in the source database is not deleted, and instead, is disconnected and marked as Soft-Deleted. You can check the value of the DisconnectReason property when working with a disconnected mailbox using the Get-MailboxStatistics cmdlet. The Get-DisconnectedMailbox function included earlier in this recipe will also return the value for this property for each disconnected mailbox.

If you move or remove mailboxes frequently, you may end up with hundreds or even thousands of disconnected mailboxes at any given time. Disconnected mailboxes can be purged using the Remove-StoreMailbox cmdlet by specifying the identity of the mailbox, the database it is located in, and the disconnect state that it is in, as shown in the following example:

```
Remove-StoreMailbox -Identity 1c097bde-edec-47df-aa4e-535cbfaa13b4 `
-Database DB1 `
-MailboxState Disabled `
-Confirm:$false
```

Keep in mind that, if you want to delete every single disconnected mailbox in your environment, you will need to run the Remove-StoreMailbox for mailboxes in both the Disabled and Soft-Deleted state. If you want to purge every disconnected mailbox from the organization, regardless of the location or disconnect reason, you can use the following code:

```
$mb = Get-MailboxDatabase |
  Get-MailboxStatistics |
    ?{$_.DisconnectDate}

foreach($i in $mb) {
  Remove-StoreMailbox -Identity $i.MailboxGuid `
  -Database $i.Database `
  -MailboxState $i.DisconnectReason.ToString() `
  -Confirm:$false
}
```

Mailboxes within a recovery database will be reported by the Get-MailboxStatistics cmdlet as disconnected and disabled. You cannot purge them with the Remove-StoreMailbox cmdlet; if you try to do so you will get an error.

See also

▸ *Managing archive mailboxes* in *Chapter 11, Compliance and Audit Logging*

▸ *Setting up a profile* in *Chapter 1, PowerShell Key Concepts*

▸ *Restoring data from a recovery database* in *Chapter 6, Mailbox and Public Folder Databases*

Generating mailbox folder reports

The ability to generate reports based on individual mailbox folders can be extremely useful at times. The Exchange Management Shell provides a versatile cmdlet called `Get-MailboxFolderStatistics` that allows you to obtain detailed information about specific mailbox folders such as the Inbox, Sent Items, Deleted Items, and more. Various pieces of information about these folders can be obtained including the total number of items, the size of the folder, and the folder ID. In this recipe, you will learn how to generate reports using the `Get-MailboxFolderStatistics` cmdlet.

How to do it...

To generate a report for the folders within a user's mailbox, use the following command:

```
Get-MailboxFolderStatistics -Identity testuser -FolderScope All |
  select Name,ItemsInFolder,FolderSize |
    Export-CSV C:\MB_Report.csv -NoType
```

How it works...

In this example, we are executing a one-liner that generates a report of the mailbox folder statistics for the *testuser* mailbox. We specify `All` for the `-FolderScope` so that the cmdlet retrieves information about each folder in the mailbox. From the output, we select a few properties and then export the results to a CSV file.

The information returned by this command can be useful when troubleshooting mailbox quota issues. For example, say you have a user that has reached their mailbox quota limit. We can view the output from the previous command instead of exporting it to a CSV file, as shown in the following screenshot:

```
Machine: MBX1.CONTOSO.COM                                      _ □ ✕
Name                                   ItemsInFolder FolderSize      ▲
----                                   ------------- ----------
Top of Information Store                   0 0 B (0 bytes)
Calendar                                   6 12.57 KB (12,875 bytes)
Contacts                                   4 8.236 KB (8,434 bytes)
Conversation Action Se...                  0 0 B (0 bytes)
Deleted Items                              6 4.01 MB (4,204,424 by...
Drafts                                     0 0 B (0 bytes)
Inbox                                     69 32.47 MB (34,046,610 ...
```

In this example, it's clear that the Inbox folder contains the largest amount of data. You can use this information to inform the user of the current status and recommend they delete some of the data from the Inbox folder.

There's more...

You can run the Get-MailboxFolderStatistics cmdlet against specific folders by specifying the appropriate value for the -FolderScope parameter. There are nearly twenty well-known mailbox folders that can be assigned to the -FolderScope parameter. To view a complete list, run the following command:

```
Get-Help Get-MailboxFolderStatistics -Parameter FolderScope
```

Taking it a step further

We can use this cmdlet in a custom function to generate more sophisticated reports. For example, the following function can be used to generate a report detailing the usage of the Deleted Items folder for one or more mailboxes:

```
function Get-MailboxDeletedItemStats {
  param([string]$id)

  $folder = Get-MailboxFolderStatistics $id `
  -FolderScope DeletedItems

  $deletedFolder = $folder.FolderSize.ToMb()
  $mb = (Get-MailboxStatistics $id).TotalItemSize.value.ToMb()

  if($deletedFolder -gt 0 -and $mb -gt 0) {
    $percentDeleted = "{0:P0}" -f ($deletedFolder / $mb)
  }
  else {
    $percentDeleted = "{0:P0}" -f 0
  }

  New-Object PSObject -Property @{
```

```
        Identity = $id
        MailboxSizeMB = $mb
        DeletedItems = $folder.ItemsInFolder
        DeletedSizeMB = $deletedFolder
        PercentDeleted = $percentDeleted
    }
}
```

This function combines both the `Get-MailboxFolderStatistics` and `Get-MailboxStatistics` cmdlets to determine the total size of the Deleted Items folder and the total size of the mailbox. Several pieces of information are returned, including the percentage of total mailbox size that is comprised of the deleted items. You can add this function to your profile and it will be automatically added to your session every time you start the shell. You can then run the function just like a cmdlet against a single mailbox, as shown in the following screenshot:

This function can also be run against every mailbox, just like any other cmdlet:

```
foreach($mailbox in (Get-Mailbox -ResultSize Unlimited)) {
    Get-MailboxDeletedItemStats $mailbox
}
```

The output from this function can be viewed interactively in the shell or exported to a CSV or text file for later review.

See also

▸ *Using the help system* in *Chapter 1, PowerShell Key Concepts*

▸ *Creating custom objects* in *Chapter 1, PowerShell Key Concepts*

▸ *Exporting reports to text and CSV files* in *Chapter 2, Exchange Management Shell Common Tasks*

Reporting on mailbox creation time

If you work in an environment that frequently hires new employees, you may have a process in place to provision your mailboxes in bulk. You may have already used this book to help you do that. Now you might like to be able to generate reports or retrieve a list of mailboxes that were created during a specific time frame or after a specific date. In this recipe, you will learn a couple of ways to do that using the Exchange Management Shell.

How to do it...

Let's start off with a simple example. To generate a report of mailboxes created in the last week, execute the following command:

```
Get-Mailbox -ResultSize Unlimited |
  ?{$_.WhenMailboxCreated -ge (Get-Date).AddDays(-7)} |
    Select DisplayName, WhenMailboxCreated, Database |
      Export-CSV C:\mb_report.CSV -NoType
```

How it works...

This one-liner searches through every mailbox in the organization checking the `WhenMailboxCreated` property. If the date is within the last seven days, we select a few useful properties for each mailbox and export the list to a CSV file.

Mailboxes also have a property called `WhenCreated`, so why don't we just check this property instead? This is because the `WhenCreated` property is an Active Directory attribute that stores the creation date for the user account and not the mailbox. It is quite possible that your user accounts are created in Active Directory long before they are mailbox-enabled, so using this property may not be reliable in your environment.

There's more...

The `WhenMailboxCreated` property returns a `DateTime` object that can be compared to other `DateTime` objects. In the previous example, we used the following filter with the `Where-Object` cmdlet:

```
$_.WhenMailboxCreated -ge (Get-Date).AddDays(-7)
```

When running the `Get-Date` cmdlet without any parameters, a `DateTime` object for the current date and time is returned. Every `DateTime` object provides an `AddDays` method that can be used to create a new `DateTime` object. So, to get the `DateTime` from seven days ago, we simply provide a negative value when calling this method and the result is the date and time from a week ago. We compare the `WhenMailboxCreated` date to this value, and, if it is greater than or equal to the date seven days ago, the command retrieves the mailbox.

You can use other `DateTime` properties when performing a comparison. For example, let's say last month was March, the third month of the year. We can use the following command to retrieve all the mailboxes created in March:

```
Get-Mailbox | ?{$_.WhenMailboxCreated.Month-eq 3}
```

This gives us the ability to generate very customizable reports, such as reporting only on mailboxes that were created on Mondays in October:

```
Get-Mailbox | ?{
  ($_.WhenMailboxCreated.DayOfWeek -eq "Monday") -and `
  ($_.WhenMailboxCreated.Month -eq 10)
}
```

As you can see, there is a lot of flexibility here that you can use to customize the output to meet your needs. This is a good example of how we can extend the Exchange Management Shell by tapping into the capabilities of the .NET Framework.

See also

▶ *Working with variable and objects* in *Chapter 1, PowerShell Key Concepts*

▶ *Exporting reports to text and CSV files* in *Chapter 2, Exchange Management Shell Common Tasks*

Checking mailbox logon statistics

If you have worked with Exchange 2000 or 2003, you probably remember that you could easily view several mailbox-related details for each mailbox under the *Logons* node of the Exchange System Manager. These details included the user-name, last access time, and more. When viewing mailboxes in the Exchange Management Console in Exchange 2010, these details are not displayed. In this recipe, we will take a look at how we can gather some of this information the `Get-LogonStatistics` cmdlet.

How to do it...

The following command will provide a logon statistics report for all mailboxes in the organization:

```
Get-MailboxServer |
 Get-LogonStatistics |
   Select UserName,ApplicationId,ClientVersion,LastAccessTime
```

How it works...

The `Get-LogonStatistics` cmdlet can be useful for doing some basic checks on client logons, but the information returned from the previous command can be a little confusing and might seem inaccurate. For example, the `ClientVersion` property returned for each logon will always be reported as the same version number for end-user logons. This is due to the fact that client connections go through the Client Access role in Exchange 2010. Whether or not this will be fixed in future versions is unknown.

The `ApplicationId` property will indicate whether clients are connected via RPC or through Outlook Web App. Keep in mind that, depending on the client, multiple connections could be reported. Client's applications initiate multiple connections, so you will likely notice that this cmdlet will return anywhere from three to five records for each user connected to a mailbox. You will also see connections where the username is reported as the name of one or more databases or a system mailbox. These are generated by transport servers and mailbox assistant agents.

There's more...

There are a couple of other ways you can run this cmdlet. First, you can generate a report for an individual user. Instead of selecting individual properties, you can pipe the command to `Format-List` with a wildcard to display all of them:

```
Get-LogonStatistics -Identity testuser | Format-List *
```

You can also retrieve the logon statistics for a particular database using the `-Database` parameter:

```
Get-LogonStatistics -Database DB1
```

When users access their mailbox through Outlook Web App you may find that logon statistics for these sessions are missing or not what you would expect when running the `Get-LogonStatistics` cmdlet. This is because OWA users are not continuously connected to the Exchange server and the OWA client only connects to the server as needed to perform a task.

See also

- ▶ *Reporting on client access server connections*

Setting storage quotas for mailboxes

One thing that has been around for several versions of Exchange is the concept of storage quotas. Using quotas, we can control the size of each mailbox to ensure that our mailbox databases don't grow out of control. In addition to setting storage quotas at the database level, we can also configure storage quotas on a per-mailbox basis. In this recipe, we will take a look at how to configure mailbox storage quotas from the Exchange Management Shell.

How to do it...

Use the following command syntax to set custom limits on mailbox:

```
Set-Mailbox -Identity testuser `
-IssueWarningQuota 1gb `
-ProhibitSendQuota 1.5gb `
-ProhibitSendReceiveQuota 2gb `
-UseDatabaseQuotaDefaults $false
```

How it works...

The `Set-Mailbox` cmdlet is used to configure the quota warning and send and receive limits for each mailbox. In this example, we are setting the `-IssueWarningQuota` parameter to one gigabyte. When the user's mailbox exceeds this size, they will receive a warning message from the system that they are approaching their quota limit.

The `-ProhibitSendQuota` is set to 1.5 gigabytes, and when the total mailbox size exceeds this limit, the user will no longer be able to send messages, although new incoming e-mail messages will still be received.

We've set the `-ProhibitSendReceiveQuota` parameter value to two gigabytes. Once this mailbox reaches this size, the user will no longer be able to send or receive mail.

It's important to point out here that we have disabled the option to inherit the storage quota limits from the database by setting the `-UseDatabaseQuotaDefaults` to `$false`. If this setting were set to `$true`, the custom mailbox quota settings would not be used.

There's more...

By default, mailboxes are configured to inherit their storage quota limits from their parent database. In most cases, this is ideal since you can centrally control the settings for each mailbox in a particular database. However, it is unlikely that having single quota limit for the entire organization will be sufficient. For example, you will probably have a group of managers, VIP users, or executives that require a larger amount of space for their mailboxes.

Even though you could create a separate database for these users with higher quota values, this might not make sense in your environment, and instead, you may want to override the database quota defaults with a custom setting on an individual basis. Let's say that all users with their `Title` set to *Manager* should have a custom quota setting. We can use the following commands to make this change in bulk:

```
Get-User -RecipientTypeDetails UserMailbox `
-Filter {Title -eq 'Manager'} |
  Set-Mailbox -IssueWarningQuota 2gb `
  -ProhibitSendQuota 2.5gb `
  -ProhibitSendReceiveQuota 3gb `
  -UseDatabaseQuotaDefaults $false
```

What we are doing here is searching Active Directory with the `Get-User` cmdlet and filtering the results so that only mailbox-enabled users with their title set to *Manager* are returned. This command is piped further to get the `Set-Mailbox` cmdlet which configures the mailbox quota values and disables the option to use the database quota defaults.

Finding inactive mailboxes

If you support a large Exchange environment, it's likely that users come and go frequently. In this case, it's quite possible over time that you will end up with multiple unused mailboxes. In this recipe, you will learn a couple of techniques used when searching for inactive mailboxes with the Exchange Management Shell.

How to do it...

The following command will retrieve a list of mailboxes that have not been logged on to in over 90 days:

```
$mailboxes = Get-Mailbox -ResultSize Unlimited
$mailboxes | ?{
  (Get-MailboxStatistics $_).LastLogonTime -and `
  (Get-MailboxStatistics $_).LastLogonTime -le `
  (Get-Date).AddDays(-90)
}
```

How it works...

You can see here that we're retrieving all of the mailboxes in the organization using the `Get-Mailbox` cmdlet and storing the results in the `$mailboxes` variable. We then pipe this collection to the `Where-Object` cmdlet (using the `?` alias) and use the `Get-MailboxStatistics` cmdlet to build a filter. This first part of this filter indicates that we only want to retrieve mailboxes that have a value set for the `LastLogonTime` property. If this value is `$null`, it indicates that these mailboxes have never been used, and have probably been recently created, which means that they will probably soon become active mailboxes. The second part of the filter compares the value for the `LastLogonTime`. If that value is less than or equal to the date 90 days ago then we have a match and the mailbox will be returned.

There's more...

Finding unused mailboxes in your environment might be as simple as searching for disabled user accounts in Active Directory that are mailbox-enabled. If that is the case, you can use the following one-liner to discover these mailboxes:

```
Get-User -ResultSize Unlimited -RecipientTypeDetails UserMailbox |
    ?{$_.UserAccountControl -match 'AccountDisabled'}
```

This command uses the `Get-User` cmdlet to search through all of the mailbox-enabled users in Active Directory. Next, we filter the results even further by piping those results to the `Where-Object` cmdlet to find any mailboxes where the `UserAccountControl` property contains the `AccountDisabled` value, indicating that the associated Active Directory user account has been disabled.

Detecting and fixing corrupt mailboxes

For years, Exchange administrators have used the Information Store Integrity Checker, more commonly known as the `ISInteg` utility, to detect and repair mailbox database corruption. You may have used `ISInteg` in previous versions of Exchange to correct a corruption issue preventing a user from opening their mailbox or from opening a particular message. Unfortunately, in order to repair a mailbox with `ISInteg`, you had to dismount the database hosting the mailbox, taking it offline for everyone else that had a mailbox homed on that database. Obviously, taking an entire mailbox database down for maintenance when it is only affecting one user is less than ideal. Exchange 2010 SP1 alleviates this pain point by introducing a new cmdlet that replaces the `ISInteg` tool and allows you to detect and repair mailbox corruption while the database is online and mounted. In this recipe, we will take a look at how to use these cmdlets and automate the detection and repair of corrupt mailboxes.

How to do it...

1. To detect corruption for a single mailbox, use the `New-MailboxRepairRequest` cmdlet with the following syntax:

```
New-MailboxRepairRequest -Mailbox testuser `
-CorruptionType SearchFolder, ProvisionedFolder,FolderView `
-DetectOnly
```

2. The `-DetectOnly` switch parameter indicates that we do not want to perform a repair and that we only want to check for corruption within this mailbox. To perform a repair, simply remove the `-DetectOnly` switch parameter from the previous command:

```
New-MailboxRepairRequest -Mailbox testuser `
-CorruptionType SearchFolder, ProvisionedFolder,FolderView
```

How it works...

The `New-MailboxRepairRequest` cmdlet can be run against a single mailbox or an entire mailbox database. In the previous example, we specified the *testuser* mailbox using the `-Mailbox` parameter. If needed, we could instead use the `-Database` parameter and provide the name of a database that we want to check or repair.

The `-CorruptionType` parameter accepts several values that are outlined as follows:

▶ **SearchFolder**: Used to detect and repair links to folders that no longer exist

▶ **AggregateCounts**: Specifies that aggregate counts on folders that are not indicating the correct values should be repaired or detected

▶ **FolderView**: Used to detect and repair views with incorrect content

▶ **ProvisionedFolder**: Specifies that links between provisioned and unprovisioned folders should be detected and repaired

In the previous example, we specified the `SearchFolder`, `ProvisionedFolder`, and `FolderView` corruption types when performing mailbox repair detection for the *testuser* mailbox. The `-CorruptionType` parameter is required, so you need to provide at least one of the preceding values when running the cmdlet. If you want to check for all of them, just separate each corruption type with a comma when assigning the values to the parameter, as shown previously.

As always, we can take advantage of the PowerShell pipeline to perform operations in bulk. Perhaps you want to perform detection on a group of mailboxes, but not on every mailbox in the entire database. Just pipe the results of the `Get-Mailbox` cmdlet to the `New-MailboxRepairRequest` cmdlet:

```
Get-Mailbox -OrganizationalUnit uss.local/sales |
  New-MailboxRepairRequest `
  -CorruptionType SearchFolder,ProvisionedFolder,FolderView `
  -DetectOnly
```

In this example, we're only performing detection on mailboxes in the *Sales* OU. This is just one example of how you can do this. Use the `-Filter` parameter in combination with `Get-Mailbox` or the `Where-Object` cmdlet to limit which mailboxes are sent down the pipeline.

The `New-MailboxRepairRequest` cmdlet can also be used against archive mailboxes when using the `-Archive` switch parameter.

There's more...

After working with mailbox move requests and mailbox import requests, you might assume that there is an entire set of cmdlets that allow you to get, set, or remove mailbox repair requests, but that is not the case as of Exchange 2010 SP1. In this version, all we have to work with is a single cmdlet: `New-MailboxRepairRequest`. Fortunately, detailed information about the mailbox repair requests are written to the event log so you can still check the status of these operations, but it will either require that you manually check the logs or write some PowerShell code that will check the logs for you.

The following Event IDs will be written to the application log, depending on the parameters used with your command:

- ▶ **10047**: A mailbox repair request has started
- ▶ **10048**: The repair request successfully completed
- ▶ **10049**: The mailbox or database repair request failed
- ▶ **10050**: The mailbox repair request task skipped a mailbox
- ▶ **10059**: A database-level repair request has started
- ▶ **10062**: Corruption was detected

These are some of the more common Events that you will want to keep an eye on. For a complete list, visit the TechNet documentation at the following URL:

`http://technet.microsoft.com/en-us/library/ff628334.aspx`

In order to provide some automation when reviewing the logs, we can use the `Get-EventLog` cmdlet, which is a PowerShell core cmdlet. We can retrieve the logs from the mailbox server where the mailbox resides by filtering the request ID and the event IDs. One way we can do this is by saving the repair request in a variable:

```
$repair = New-MailboxRepairRequest -Mailbox testuser `
-CorruptionType SearchFolder
```

Next, if we want to retrieve the status for event IDs `10047`, `10048`, `10049`, we can use the following command syntax:

```
Get-EventLog -LogName Application -ComputerName ex01 | ?{
    ('10047','10048','10049' -contains $_.EventID) -and `
    ($_.Message -match $repair.RequestID)
}
```

What we should get back here is all events that match the event IDs and the mailbox repair `RequestID` for the *testuser* mailbox. Of course, you can extend this to support multiple mailboxes and simply use PowerShell's looping constructs to iterate through each mailbox repair request and check the logs for each one.

See also

- ▶ *Looping through items* in *Chapter 1, PowerShell Key Concepts*
- ▶ *Creating PowerShell functions* in *Chapter 1, PowerShell Key Concepts*

Restoring deleted items from mailboxes

One of the more common requests that Exchange administrators are asked to perform is restoring deleted items from a user's mailbox. In previous versions of Exchange, there were usually a couple of ways to handle this. First, you could use your traditional brick-level backup solution to restore individual items to a mailbox. Of course, there was also the more time-consuming process of exporting data from a mailbox located in a recovery database. Exchange 2010 reduces the complexity of restoring deleted items by implementing a feature called single item recovery. When this feature is enabled, administrators can recover purged data from an end-users mailbox using the `Search-Mailbox` cmdlet. In this recipe, we will take a look at how this restore process works from within the Exchange Management Shell.

How to do it...

1. If you have not already done so, you will need to use the following command syntax to assign the *Mailbox Import Export* RBAC role to your account. You will need to restart the shell after running this command in order for the assigned cmdlet to be visible:

   ```
   New-ManagementRoleAssignment -Role "Mailbox Import Export" `
   -User administrator
   ```

2. To restore deleted data from an end-user mailbox, use the `Search-Mailbox` cmdlet:

   ```
   Search-Mailbox -Identity testuser `
   -SearchQuery "subject:'Expense Report'" `
   -TargetMailbox restoremailbox `
   ```

```
-TargetFolder "Test Restore" `
-SearchDumpsterOnly
```

How it works...

The `Search-Mailbox` cmdlet provides the capability to search only the dumpster containing the deleted items for a given mailbox using the `-SearchDumpsterOnly` switch parameter. In this example, we've used the `-SearchQuery` parameter to limit the search results to items that contains the term *Expense Report* within the subject line. After this command has been run, an administrator can access the target mailbox to retrieve the restored data. The items that matched the search query will have been restored to a subfolder of the target folder in the target mailbox specified.

 To learn more about Single Item Recovery, see the following Exchange Team blog post: `http://blogs.technet.com/b/ exchange/archive/2009/09/25/3408389.aspx.`

The `-SearchQuery` parameter uses **Advanced Query Syntax** (**AQS**) to define the conditions for your search. See *Appendix B* at the end of this book for a list of AQS properties and common search queries.

There's more...

You can perform very granular searches with AQS and the `-SearchQuery` parameter. Let's say that we wanted to restore all deleted items from the mailbox that were received after a certain date. We can use the following command to accomplish this:

```
Search-Mailbox -Identity testuser `
-SearchQuery "received:>11/01/2010" `
-TargetMailbox administrator `
-TargetFolder "Testuser Restore" `
-SearchDumpsterOnly
```

Similar to the previous example, we are restoring data from the *testuser* mailbox to the same target folder in the administrator mailbox. The difference is that, this time, the search query is only going to look for messages that have been received after November 1 2010. You can see here that we are using the greater than (>) symbol to indicate that any message older than 11/01/2010 should be restored.

You can open the target mailbox in Outlook to retrieve the restored messages or export them using the `New-MailboxExportRequest` cmdlet.

Keep in mind that the `-SearchQuery` parameter is optional. If you want to restore all of the end-user deleted items you can do so by simply omitting this parameter for the commands in the previous examples. Also, you can restore messages when performing a discovery search with the `New-MailboxSearch` cmdlet.

See also

- ▸ *Performing a discovery search* in *Chapter 11, Compliance and Audit Logging*
- ▸ *Restoring data from a recovery database* in *Chapter 6, Mailbox and Public Folder Databases*
- ▸ *Enabling single item recovery* in *Chapter 11, Compliance and Audit Logging*
- ▸ *Importing and exporting mailboxes*

5
Distribution Groups and Address Lists

In this chapter, we will cover the following:

- ▸ Reporting on distribution group membership
- ▸ Adding members to a distribution group from an external file
- ▸ Previewing dynamic distribution group membership
- ▸ Excluding hidden recipients from a dynamic distribution group
- ▸ Converting and upgrading distribution groups
- ▸ Allowing managers to modify group permissions
- ▸ Removing disabled users from distribution groups
- ▸ Working with distribution group naming policies
- ▸ Working with distribution group membership approval
- ▸ Creating address lists
- ▸ Exporting address list membership to a CSV file
- ▸ Configuring hierarchical address books

Introduction

In *Chapter 3*, we looked at managing recipients, which covered the process of creating and modifying the membership of both regular and dynamic distribution groups. In this chapter, we are going to dive deeper into distribution group management within the Exchange Management Shell. The recipes in this chapter provide solutions to some of the most common distribution group management tasks that can, and sometimes must, be handled from the command line. Some of the topics we'll cover include the implementation of group naming policies, allowing group managers to modify the memberships of distribution groups, and more. We'll also go over the process of some basic address list management that can be automated through the shell.

Performing some basic steps

To work with the code samples in this chapter, follow these steps to launch the Exchange Management Shell:

1. Log onto a workstation or server with the Exchange Management Tools installed

2. Open the Exchange Management Shell by clicking on **Start | All Programs | Exchange Server 2010**

3. Click on the **Exchange Management Shell** shortcut

Reporting on distribution group membership

One of the common requests you are likely to receive as an Exchange administrator is to generate a report detailing which recipients are members of one or more distribution groups. In this recipe, we'll take a look at how to retrieve this information from the Exchange Management Shell.

How to do it...

To view a list of each distribution group member interactively, use the following code:

```
foreach($i in Get-DistributionGroup -ResultSize Unlimited) {
  Get-DistributionGroupMember $i -ResultSize Unlimited |
    Select-Object @{n="Member";e={$_.Name}},
      RecipientType,
      @{n="Group";e={$i.Name}}
}
```

This will generate a list of Exchange recipients and their associated distribution group membership.

How it works...

This code loops through each item returned from the `Get-DistributionGroup` cmdlet. As we process each group, we run the `Get-DistributionGroupMember` cmdlet to determine the member list for each group and then use `Select-Object` to construct a custom object that provides `Member`, `RecipientType`, and `Group` properties. Notice that, when running both Exchange cmdlets, we're setting the `-ResultSize` parameter to `Unlimited` to ensure that the details will be retrieved in the event that there are more than 1,000 groups or group members.

There's more...

The previous code sample will allow you to view the output in the shell. If you want to export this information to a CSV file, use the following code:

```
$report=foreach($i in Get-DistributionGroup -ResultSize Unlimited) {
  Get-DistributionGroupMember $i -ResultSize Unlimited |
    Select-Object @{n="Member";e={$_.Name}},
      RecipientType,
      @{n="Group";e={$i.Name}}
}

$report | Export-CSV c:\GroupMembers.csv -NoType
```

The difference this time is that the output from our code is being saved in the `$report` variable. Once the report has been generated, the `$report` object is then exported to a CSV file that can be opened in Excel.

See also

► *Previewing dynamic distribution group membership*
► *Adding members to a distribution group from an external file*

Adding members to a distribution group from an external file

When working in large or complex environments, performing bulk operations is the key to efficiency. Using PowerShell core cmdlets such as `Get-Content` and `Import-CSV`, we can easily import external data into the shell and use this information to perform bulk operations on hundreds or thousands of objects in a matter of seconds. Obviously, this can vastly speed up the time we spend on routine tasks and greatly increase our efficiency. In this recipe, we'll use these concepts to add members to distribution groups in bulk from a text or CSV file using the Exchange Management Shell.

How to do it...

1. Create a text file called `c:\users.txt` that lists the recipients in your organization that you want to add to a group. Make sure you enter them one line at a time, as shown in the following screen shot:

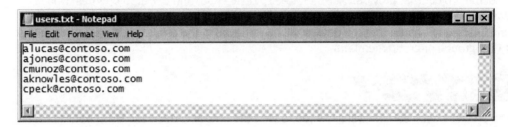

```
users.txt - Notepad
File  Edit  Format  View  Help
alucas@contoso.com
ajones@contoso.com
cmunoz@contoso.com
aknowles@contoso.com
cpeck@contoso.com
```

2. Next, execute the following code to add the list of recipients to a distribution group:

```
Get-Content  c:\users.txt | ForEach-Object {
  Add-DistributionGroupMember –Identity Sales -Member $_
}
```

When the code runs, each user listed in the `c:\users.txt` file will be added to the *Sales* distribution group.

How it works...

When importing data from a plain text file, we use the `Get-Content` cmdlet, which will read the content of the file into the shell one line at a time. In this example, we pipe the content of the file to the `ForEach-Object` cmdlet, and as each line is processed we execute the `Add-DistributionGroupMember` cmdlet.

Inside the `For-EachObject` script block we use the `Add-DistributionGroupMember` cmdlet and assign the `$_` object, which is the current recipient item in the pipeline, to the `-Member` parameter.

 To remove recipients from a distribution group, you can use the `Remove-DistributionGroupMember` cmdlet.

Keep in mind that this text file does not have to contain the SMTP address of the recipient. You can also use the Active Directory account name, User Principal Name, Distinguished Name, GUID, or LegacyExchangeDN values. The important thing is that the file contains a valid and unique value for each recipient. If the identity of the recipient cannot be determined, the `Add-DistributionGroupMember` command will fail.

There's more...

In addition to using plain text files, we can also import recipients from a CSV file and add them to a distribution group. Let's say that you have a CSV file setup with multiple columns, such as `FirstName`, `LastName`, and `EmailAddress`. When you import the CSV file, the data can be accessed using the column headers as the property names for each object. Take a look at the following screenshot:

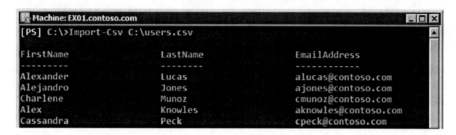

Here you can see that each item in this collection has an `EmailAddress` property. As long as this information corresponds to the recipient data in the Exchange organization, we can simply loop through each record in the CSV file and add these recipients to a distribution group:

```
Import-Csv C:\users.csv | ForEach-Object {
  Add-DistributionGroupMember Sales -Member $_.EmailAddress
}
```

The given code uses the `Import-CSV` cmdlet to loop through each item in the collection. As we process each record, we add the recipient to the *Sales* distribution group using the `$_.EmailAddress` object.

See also

▸   *Managing distribution groups* in *Chapter 3, Managing Recipients*

Previewing dynamic distribution group membership

The concept of the dynamic distribution group was introduced with the initial release of Exchange 2007 and included a new way to create and manage distribution groups. Unlike regular distribution groups whose members are statically defined, a dynamic distribution group determines its members based on a recipient filter. These recipient filters can be very complex, or they can be based on simple conditions, such as including all the users with a common value set for their `Company` or `Department` attributes in Active Directory. Since these dynamic groups are based on a query, they do not actually contain group members and if you want to preview the results of the groups query in the shell you need to use a series of commands. In this recipe, we'll take a look at how to view the membership of dynamic distribution groups in the Exchange Management Shell.

How to do it...

Imagine that we have a dynamic distribution group named `Legal` that includes all of the users in Active Directory with a `Department` attribute set to the word `Legal`. We can use the following commands to retrieve the current list of recipients for this group:

```
$legal= Get-DynamicDistributionGroup -Identity legal
Get-Recipient -RecipientPreviewFilter $legal.RecipientFilter
```

How it works...

Recipient filters for dynamic distribution groups use OPATH filters that are accessible through the `RecipientFilter` property of a dynamic distribution group object. As you can see here, we have specified the `Legal` groups OPATH filter when running the `Get-Recipient` cmdlet with the `-RecipientPreviewFilter` parameter. Conceptually, this would be similar to running the following command:

```
Get-Recipient -RecipientPreviewFilter "Department -eq 'Legal'"
```

Technically, there is a little bit more to it than that. If we were to actually look at the value for the `RecipientFilter` property of this dynamic distribution group, we would see much more information in addition to the filter defined for the `Legal` department. This is because Exchange automatically adds several additional filters when it creates a dynamic distribution group that excludes system mailboxes, discovery mailboxes, arbitration mailboxes, and more. This ends up being quite a bit of information, and creating an object instance of the dynamic distribution group gives us easy access to the existing OPATH filter that can be previewed with the `Get-Recipient` cmdlet.

There's more...

When working with regular distribution groups, you may notice that there is a cmdlet called `Get-DistributionGroupMember`. This allows you to retrieve a list of every user that is a member of a distribution group. Unfortunately, there is no equivalent cmdlet for dynamic distribution groups, and we need to use the method outlined previously that uses the `Get-Recipient` cmdlet to determine the list of recipients in a dynamic distribution group.

If you find yourself doing this frequently, it probably makes sense to wrap these commands up into a function that can be added to your PowerShell profile. This will allow you to determine the members of dynamic distribution group using a single command that will be available to you every time you start the shell. Here is the code for a function called `Get-DynamicDistributionGroupMember`, which can be used to determine the list of recipients included in a dynamic distribution group:

```
function Get-DynamicDistributionGroupMember {
  param(
  [Parameter(Mandatory=$true)]
  $Identity
  )

  $group = Get-DynamicDistributionGroup -Identity $Identity
  Get-Recipient -RecipientPreviewFilter $group.RecipientFilter

}
```

Once this function is loaded into your shell session, you can run it just like a cmdlet:

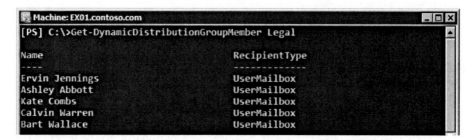

```
Machine: EX01.contoso.com
[PS] C:\>Get-DynamicDistributionGroupMember Legal

Name                          RecipientType
----                          -------------
Ervin Jennings                UserMailbox
Ashley Abbott                 UserMailbox
Kate Combs                    UserMailbox
Calvin Warren                 UserMailbox
Bart Wallace                  UserMailbox
```

You can see that the command returns the recipients that match the OPATH filter for the *Legal* distribution group and is much easier to type than the original example.

See also

▸ *Creating PowerShell functions* in *Chapter 1, PowerShell Key Concepts*

▸ *Reporting on distribution group membership*

▸ *Working with recipient filters* in *Chapter 3, Managing Recipients*

Excluding hidden recipients from a dynamic distribution group

When creating dynamic distribution groups through the Exchange Management Console, you can specify which recipients should be included in the group using a basic set of conditions. If you want to do more advanced filtering, such as excluding hidden recipients, you will need to configure OPATH filters for your dynamic distribution groups through the Exchange Management Shell. In this recipe, you'll learn how to use the shell to create a recipient filter that excludes hidden recipients from dynamic distribution groups.

How to do it...

Let's say that we need to set up a distribution group for our TechSupport department. The following commands can be used to create a dynamic distribution group that includes all the mailboxes for the users in the TechSupport OU that are not hidden from address lists:

```
New-DynamicDistributionGroup -Name TechSupport `
-RecipientContainer contoso.com/TechSupport `
-RecipientFilter {
  HiddenFromAddressListsEnabled -ne $true
}
```

How it works...

When you want to exclude a mailbox, contact, or distribution group from an address list, you set the HiddenFromAddressListsEnabled property of the recipient to $true. This is often done for special purpose recipients that are used for applications or services that should not be visible by the general end-user population. While this takes care of address lists, it does not affect your dynamic distribution groups, and if you want to exclude these recipients you'll need to use a similar filter to the one shown in the previous example. When we created the TechSupport dynamic distribution group, we used a very basic configuration that included all the recipients that exist within the TechSupport OU in Active Directory. Our custom recipient filter specifies that the HiddenFromAddressListEnabled property of each recipient must not be equal to $true. With this filter in place, only recipients that are not hidden from Exchange address lists are included as dynamic distribution group members.

Keep in mind that, when you create a dynamic group using the `-RecipientFilter` parameter, any future changes will have to be made through the Exchange Management Shell. If you need to change the recipient filter at any time, you cannot use Exchange Management Console and will need to use the `Set-DynamicDistributionGroup` cmdlet to make the change.

There's more...

Updating a recipient filter for an existing dynamic distribution group can be a bit tricky. This is because the recipient filters are automatically updated by Exchange to exclude certain types of resource and system mailboxes. Let's go through the process of creating a new dynamic distribution group, and then we'll modify the recipient filter after the fact so that you can understand how this process works.

First, we'll create a new dynamic distribution group for the Marketing department using a basic filter. Only users with e-mail addresses that contain the word `Marketing` will be members of this group:

```
New-DynamicDistributionGroup -Name Marketing `
-RecipientContainer contoso.com/Marketing `
-RecipientFilter {
  EmailAddresses -like '*marketing*'
}
```

Now that the group has been created, let's verify the recipient filter by accessing the `RecipientFilter` property of that object:

```
[PS] C:\>(Get-DynamicDistributionGroup Marketing).RecipientFilter
((EmailAddresses -like '*marketing*') -and (-not(Name -like 'SystemMailbox{
*')) -and (-not(Name -like 'CAS_{*')) -and (-not(RecipientTypeDetailsValue
-eq 'MailboxPlan')) -and (-not(RecipientTypeDetailsValue -eq 'DiscoveryMail
box')) -and (-not(RecipientTypeDetailsValue -eq 'ArbitrationMailbox')))
[PS] C:\>
```

As you can see from the output, we get a lot more back than we originally put in. This is how Exchange prevents the dynamic distribution groups from displaying recipients such as system and discovery mailboxes in your dynamic distribution lists. You do not need to worry about this extraneous code when you update your filters, as it will automatically be added back in for you when you change the recipient filter.

Now that we understand what's going on here, let's update this group so that we can also exclude hidden recipients. To do this, we need to construct a new filter and use the `Set-DynamicDistributionGroup` cmdlet as shown next:

```
Set-DynamicDistributionGroup -Identity Marketing `
```

```
-RecipientFilter {
  (EmailAddresses -like '*marketing*') -and
  (HiddenFromAddressListsEnabled -ne $true)
}
```

Using this command, we've specified the previously-configured filter in addition to the new one that excludes hidden recipients. In order for recipients to show up in this dynamic distribution group, they must have the word `Marketing` somewhere in their e-mail address and their account must not be hidden from address lists.

See also

▸ *Hiding recipients from address lists* in *Chapter 3, Managing Recipients*

▸ *Working with recipient filters* in *Chapter 3, Managing Recipients*

Converting and upgrading distribution groups

When migrating to Exchange 2010 from Exchange 2003, you may be carrying over several mail-enabled non-universal groups. These groups will still function, but the administration of these objects within the Exchange tools will be limited. In addition, several distribution group features provided by Exchange 2010 will not be enabled for a group until it has been upgraded. This recipe covers the process of converting and upgrading these groups within the Exchange Management Shell.

How to do it...

1. To convert all of your non-universal distribution groups to universal, use the following one-liner:

    ```
    Get-DistributionGroup -ResultSize Unlimited `
    -RecipientTypeDetails MailNonUniversalGroup |
      Set-Group -Universal
    ```

2. Once all of your distribution groups have been converted to universal, you can upgrade them using the following command:

    ```
    Get-DistributionGroup -ResultSize Unlimited |
      Set-DistributionGroup -ForceUpgrade
    ```

How it works...

The first command will retrieve all the non-universal mail-enabled distribution groups in your organization and pipe the results to the `Set-Group` cmdlet which will convert them using the `-Universal` switch parameter. It may not be a big deal to modify a handful of groups using the graphical tools, but if you have hundreds of mail-enabled non-universal groups the command in the previous example can save you a lot of time.

If you have a large number of groups to convert, you may find that some of them are members of another global group and cannot be converted. Keep in mind that a universal group cannot be a member of a global group. If you run into errors because of this, you can convert these groups individually using the `Set-Group` cmdlet. Then you can run the command in the previous example again to convert any remaining groups in bulk.

Even after converting non-universal groups to universal, you'll notice that, when viewing the properties of a distribution group created by Exchange 2003, you cannot manage things such as message moderation and membership approval. In order to fully manage these groups, you need to upgrade them using the `-ForceUpgrade` parameter with the `Set-DistributionGroup` cmdlet. Keep in mind that after the upgrade these objects can no longer be managed using anything other than the Exchange 2010 management tools.

There's more...

The Exchange Management tools, both the graphical console and the shell, can only be used to create distribution groups using universal group scope. Additionally, you can only mail-enable existing groups with universal group scope. If you've recently introduced Exchange into your environment, you can convert existing non-universal, non-mail enabled groups in bulk using a one-liner:

```
Get-Group -ResultSize Unlimited `
-RecipientTypeDetails NonUniversalGroup `
-OrganizationalUnit Sales |
  Where-Object {$_.GroupType -match 'global'} |
    Set-Group -Universal
```

As you can see in this example, we are retrieving all non-mail enabled, non-universal global groups from the *Sales* OU and converting them to universal in a single command. You can change the OU or use additional conditions in your filter based on your needs. Once the group is converted it can be mail-enabled using the `Enable-Distribution` group cmdlet and it will show up in the list of available groups when creating new distribution groups in EMC.

See also

▸ *Managing distribution groups*

Allowing managers to modify group membership

Many organizations like to give specific users rights to manage the membership of designated distribution groups. This has been a common practice for years in previous versions of Exchange. While users have typically modified the memberships of the groups they have rights to from within Outlook, they now have the added capability to manage these groups from the web-based **Exchange Control Panel** (**ECP**). Exchange 2010 introduced a new security model that changed the way you can delegated these rights. In this recipe, we'll take a look at what you need to do in Exchange 2010 to allow managers to modify the memberships of distribution groups.

How to do it...

1. The first thing you need to do is assign the built-in `MyDistributionGroups` role to the `Default Role Assignment Policy`:

    ```
    New-ManagementRoleAssignment -Role MyDistributionGroups `
    -Policy "Default Role Assignment Policy"
    ```

2. Next, set the `ManagedBy` property of the distribution group that needs to be modified:

    ```
    Set-DistributionGroup Sales -ManagedBy bobsmith
    ```

After running the given command, Bob Smith has the ability to modify the membership of the *Sales* distribution group through ECP, Outlook, or the Exchange Management Shell.

How it works...

In order to allow managers to modify the membership of a group, we need to do some initial configuration through the new Exchange 2010 security model called **Role Based Access Control** (**RBAC**). The `MyDistributionGroups` role is an RBAC management role that allows end-users to view, remove, and add members to distribution groups where they have been added to the `ManagedBy` property.

By default, the `MyDistribitionGroups` management role is not assigned to anyone. In the first step, we added this role to the `Default Role Assignment Policy` that is assigned to all users by default.

In addition to using the shell, you can assign the `MyDistributionGroups` management role to the `Default Role Assignment Policy` using ECP.

In the next step, we assigned a user to the `ManagedBy` property of the *Sales* distribution group. The `ManagedBy` attribute is a multi-valued property that will accept multiple users if you need to allow several people to manage a distribution group.

The reason that the `MyDistributionGroups` role is not enabled by default is because, in addition to allowing users to modify the groups that they own, it also allows them to create new distribution groups from within the ECP. While some organizations may like this feature, others may not be able to allow this since the provisioning of groups may need to be tightly controlled. Make sure you keep this in mind before implementing this solution.

There's more...

If you need to prevent users from creating their own distribution groups, then you do not want to assign the `MyDistributionGroups` role. Instead, you'll need to create a custom RBAC role. This can only be accomplished using the Exchange Management Shell.

To implement a custom RBAC role that will only allow users to modify distribution groups that they own, we need to perform a few steps. The first thing we need to do is create a child role based on the existing `MyDistributionGroups` management role, as shown next:

```
New-ManagementRole -Name MyDGCustom -Parent MyDistributionGroups
```

After running this command, we should now have a new role called `MyDGCustom` that contains all of the cmdlets that will allow the user to add and remove distribution groups. Using the following commands, we'll remove those cmdlets from the role:

```
Remove-ManagementRoleEntry MyDGCustom\New-DistributionGroup
Remove-ManagementRoleEntry MyDGCustom\Remove-DistributionGroup
```

This modifies the role so that only the cmdlets that can get, add, or remove distribution group members are available to the users.

Finally, we can assign the custom role to the Default Role Assignment Policy, which, out of the box, is already applied to every mailbox in the organization:

```
New-ManagementRoleAssignment -Role MyDGCustom `
-Policy "Default Role Assignment Policy"
```

Now that this custom **RBAC** role has been implemented, we can simply add users to the `ManagedBy` property of any distribution group and they will be able to add members to and remove members from that group. However, they will be unable to delete the group, or create a new distribution group, which accomplishes the goal.

See also

▶ *Working with Role Based Access Control (RBAC)* in *Chapter 10, Exchange Security*

▶ *Troubleshooting Role Based Access Control* in *Chapter 10, Exchange Security*

Removing disabled user accounts from distribution groups

A standard practice amongst most organizations when users leave or have been let go is to disable their associated Active Directory user account. This allows an administrator to easily re-enable the account in the event that the user comes back to work, or if someone else needs access to the account. Obviously, this has become a common practice because the process of restoring a deleted Active Directory user account is a much more complex alternative. Additionally, if these user accounts are left mailbox-enabled, you can end up with distribution groups that contain multiple disabled user accounts. This recipe will show you how to remove these disabled accounts using the Exchange Management Shell.

How to do it...

To remove disabled Active Directory user accounts from all distribution groups in the organization, use the following code:

```
$groups = Get-DistributionGroup -ResultSize Unlimited

foreach($group in $groups){
 Get-DistributionGroupMember $group |
   ?{$_.RecipientType -like '*User*' -and $_.ResourceType -eq $null} |
    Get-User | ?{$_.UserAccountControl -match 'AccountDisabled'} |
     Remove-DistributionGroupMember $group -Confirm:$false
}
```

How it works...

This code uses a `foreach` loop to iterate through each distribution group in the organization. As each group is processed, we retrieve only the members whose recipient type contains the word `User`. We're also filtering out resource mailboxes as these are tied to disabled Active

Directory accounts. These filters will ensure that we only pipe objects with Active Directory user accounts down to the Get-User cmdlet, which will determine whether or not the account is disabled by checking the `UserAccountControl` property of each object. If the account is disabled, it will be removed from the group.

There's more...

Instead of performing the remove operation, we can use a slightly modified version of the previous code to simply generate a report based on disabled Active Directory accounts that are members of a specific distribution group. Use the following code to generate this report:

```
$groups = Get-DistributionGroup -ResultSize Unlimited

$report = foreach($group in $groups){
  Get-DistributionGroupMember $group |
    ?{$_.RecipientType -like '*User*' -and $_.ResourceType -eq $null} |
    Get-User | ?{$_.UserAccountControl -match 'AccountDisabled'} |
      Select-Object Name,RecipientType,@{n='Group';e={$group}}
}

$report | Export-CSV c:\disabled_group_members.csv -NoType
```

After running this code, a report will be generated using the specified file name that will list the disabled account name, Exchange recipient type, and associated distribution group for which it is a member.

See also

▸ *Managing distribution groups* in *Chapter 3, Managing Recipients*

Working with distribution group naming policies

Using group naming policies, you can require that the distribution group names in your organization follow a specific naming standard. For instance, you can specify that all distribution group names are prefixed with a certain word and you can block certain words from being used within group names. In this recipe, you'll learn how to work with group naming policies from within the Exchange Management Shell.

How to do it...

To enable a group naming policy for your organization, use the `Set-OrganizationConfig` cmdlet, as shown next:

```
Set-OrganizationConfig -DistributionGroupNamingPolicy `
"DL_<GroupName>"
```

How it works...

Since Exchange 2010 gives your users the ability to create and manage their own distribution groups, you may want to implement a naming policy that matches your organization's naming standards. In addition, you can implement naming policies so that your administrators are required to follow a specific naming convention when creating groups.

Your distribution group naming policy can be made up of text you specify, or it can use specific attributes that map to the user who creates the distribution group. In the previous example, we specified that all distribution groups should be prefixed with `DL_` followed by the group name. The `<GroupName>` attribute indicates that the group name provided by the user should be used. So, if someone were to create a group named "Help Desk", Exchange would automatically configure the name of the group as `DL_Help Desk`.

The following attributes can be used within your group naming policies:

- Company
- CountryCode
- CountryorRegion
- CustomAttribute1 - 15
- Department
- Office
- StateOrProvince
- Title

Let's take a look at another example to see how we could implement some of these attributes within a group naming policy. Using the following command, we'll update the group naming policy to include both the `Department` and the `State` of the user creating the group:

```
Set-OrganizationConfig -DistributionGroupNamingPolicy `
"<Department>_<GroupName>_<StateOrProvince>"
```

Now let's say that we have an administrator named Dave who works in the IT department in the Arizona office. Based on this information, we know that his `Department` attribute will be set to "IT" and his `State` attribute will be set to "AZ". When Dave uses the `New-DistributionGroup` cmdlet to create a group for the maintenance department, specifying "Maintenance" for the `-Name` parameter value, Exchange will automatically apply the group naming policy, and the distribution group name will be `IT_Maintenance_AZ`.

In addition, we can exclude a list of names that can be used when creating distribution groups. This is also specified by running the `Set-OrganizationConfig` cmdlet. For example, to block a list of words we can use the following syntax:

```
Set-OrganizationConfig `
-DistributionGroupNameBlockedWordsList badword1,badword2
```

If a user tries to create a group using one of the blocked names, they'll receive an error that says The group name contains a word which isn't allowed in group names in your organization. Please rename your group.

There's more...

When a group naming policy is applied in your organization, it is possible to override it from within the Exchange Management Shell. Both the `New-DistributionGroup` and the `Set-DistributionGroup` cmdlets provide an `-IgnoreNamingPolicy` switch parameter that can be used when you are creating or modifying a group. To create a distribution group that will bypass the group naming policy, use the following syntax:

```
New-DistributionGroup -Name Accounting -IgnoreNamingPolicy
```

The graphical management tools (EMC and ECP) can be used to create distribution groups, but if a naming policy is applied to your organization and you need to override it, you must use the shell as shown previously.

You can force administrators to use group naming policies, even if they have access to the Exchange Management Shell. If you plan on doing this, you need to assign them to the `New-DistributionGroup` and `Set-DistributionGroup` cmdlets using a custom Role Based Access Control (RBAC) role that does not allow them to use the `-IgnoreNamingPolicy` switch parameter.

See also

▸ *Managing distribution groups*

Working with distribution group membership approval

You can allow end-users to request distribution group membership through the Exchange Control Panel (ECP). Additionally, you can configure your distribution groups so that users can join a group automatically without having to be approved by a group owner. We'll take a look at how to configure these options in this recipe.

How to do it...

To allow end-users to add and remove themselves from a distribution group, you can set the following configuration using the `Set-DistributionGroup` cmdlet:

```
Set-DistributionGroup -Identity CompanyNews `
-MemberJoinRestriction Open `
-MemberDepartRestriction Open
```

This command will allow any user in the organization to join or leave the `CompanyNews` distribution group without requiring approval by a group owner.

How it works...

The two parameters that control the membership approval configuration for a distribution group are `-MemberJoinRestriction` and `-MemberDepartRestriction`. Both can be set to one of the following values:

- **Open**: Allows the user to add or remove their account from the group without requiring group owner approval

- **Closed**: Users cannot join or leave the grou.

- **ApprovalRequired:** Requests to join or leave a group must be approved by a group owner

These settings are not mutually exclusive. For example, you can allow users to join a group without approval, but you can require approval when users try to leave the group, or vice versa. By default, the `MemberJoinRestriction` property is set to `Closed` and the `MemberDepartRestriction` is set to `Open`.

There's more...

When member join or depart restrictions are set to `ApprovalRequired`, a group owner will receive a message informing them of the request, and they can approve or deny the request using the **Accept** or **Reject** buttons in Outlook or OWA. The user who created the distribution group will automatically be the owner, but you change the owner, if needed, using the `-ManagedBy` parameter when running the `Set-DistributionGroup` cmdlet, as shown:

```
Set-DistributionGroup -Identity AllEmployees `
-ManagedBy dave@contoso.com,john@contoso.com
```

As you can see, the `-ManagedBy` parameter will accept one or more values. If you are setting multiple owners, just separate each one with a comma, as shown previously.

See also

▸ *Reporting on distribution group membership*

▸ *Managing distribution groups* in *Chapter 3, Managing Recipients*

Creating address lists

Just like dynamic distribution groups, Exchange address lists can be comprised of one or more recipient types and are generated using a recipient filter or using a set of built-in conditions. You can create one or more address list(s), made up of users, contacts, distribution groups, or any other mail-enabled objects in your organization. This recipe will show you how to create an address list using the Exchange Management Shell.

How to do it...

Let's say we need to create an address list for the sales representatives in our organization. We can use the `New-AddressList` cmdlet to accomplish this, as shown next:

```
New-AddressList -Name 'All Sales Users' `
-RecipientContainer contoso.com/Sales `
-IncludedRecipients MailboxUsers
```

How it works...

This example uses the `New-AddressList` cmdlet's built-in conditions to specify the criteria for the recipients that will be included in the list. You can see from the command that, in order for a recipient to be visible in the address list, they must be located within the *Sales* OU in Active Directory and the recipient type must be `MailboxUsers`, which only applies to regular mailboxes and does not include other types such as resource mailboxes, distribution groups, and so on. You can use the built-in conditions when you need to configure a basic filter for the list, and they can be easily edited from within the Exchange Management Console.

There's more...

When you need to create an address list based on a more complex set of conditions, you'll need to use the -RecipientFilter parameter to specify an OPATH filter. For example, the following OPATH filter is not configurable when creating or modifying an address list in EMC:

```
New-AddressList -Name MobileUsers `
-RecipientContainer contoso.com `
-RecipientFilter {
HasActiveSyncDevicePartnership -ne $false
}
```

You can see here that we're creating an address list for all the mobile users in the organization. We've set the RecipientContainer to the root domain, and, within the recipient filter, we've specified that all recipients with an ActiveSync device partnership should be included in the list.

 You can create global address lists using the New-GlobalAddress list cmdlet.

You can combine multiple conditions in your recipient filters using PowerShell's logical operators. For instance, we can extend our previous example to add an additional requirement in the OPATH filter:

```
New-AddressList -Name MobileUsers `
-RecipientContainer contoso.com `
-RecipientFilter {
  (HasActiveSyncDevicePartnership -ne $false) -and
  (Phone -ne $null)
}
```

This time, in addition to having an ActiveSync device partnership, the user must also have a number defined within their Phone attribute in order for them to be included in the list.

 If you need to modify a recipient filter after an address list has already been created, use the Set-AddressList cmdlet.

Exchange supports a various number of both common and advanced properties that can be used to construct OPATH filters, as shown in the previous example. To view a list of common filterable properties that can be used with the -RecipientFilter parameter, see *Appendix A* at the end of this book.

See also

▸ *Working with recipient filters* in *Chapter 3, Managing Recipients*
▸ *Export address list membership to a CSV file*

Exporting address list membership to a CSV file

When it comes to working with address lists, a common task is exporting the list of members to an external file. In this recipe, we'll take a look at the process of exporting the contents of an address list to a CSV file.

How to do it...

Let's start off with a simple example. The following commands will export the `All Users` address list to a CSV file:

```
$allusers = Get-AddressList "All Users"
Get-Recipient -RecipientPreviewFilter $allusers.RecipientFilter |
  Select-Object DisplayName,Database |
    Export-Csv -Path c:\allusers.csv -NoTypeInformation
```

When the command completes, a list of user display names and their associated mailbox databases will be exported to `c:\allusers.csv`.

How it works...

The first thing we do in this example is create the `$allusers` variable that stores an instance of the `All Users` address list. We can then run the `Get-Recipient` cmdlet and specify the OPATH filter, using the `$allusers.RecipientFilter` object as the value for the `-RecipientPreviewFilter` parameter. The results are then piped to the `select-object` cmdlet that grabs the `DisplayName` and `Database` properties of the recipient. Finally, the data is exported to a CSV file.

Of course, the given example may not be that practical, as it does not provide the e-mail addresses for the user. We can also export this information, but it requires some special handling on our part. Let's export only the `DisplayName` and `EmailAddresses` for each user. To do so, use the following code:

```
$allusers = Get-AddressList "All Users"
Get-Recipient -RecipientPreviewFilter $allusers.RecipientFilter |
  Select-Object DisplayName,
    @{n="EmailAddresses";e={$_.EmailAddresses -join ";"}} |
      Export-Csv -Path c:\allusers.csv -NoTypeInformation
```

Since each recipient can have multiple SMTP e-mail addresses, the `EmailAddresses` property of each recipient is a multi-valued object. This means we can't simply export this value to an external file, since it is actually an object and not a simple string value. In the given command, we're using the `Select-Object` cmdlet to create a calculated property for the `EmailAddresses` collection. Using the `-Join` operator within the calculated property expression, we are adding each address in the collection to a single string that will be delimited with the semi-colon (;) character.

There's more...

The given method will work for any of the address lists in your organization. For example, you can export the recipients of the **Global Address List** (**GAL**) using the following code:

```
$GAL = Get-GlobalAddressList "Default Global Address List"
Get-Recipient -RecipientPreviewFilter $GAL.RecipientFilter |
    Select-Object DisplayName,
      @{n="EmailAddresses";e={$_.EmailAddresses -join ";"}} |
        Export-Csv -Path c:\GAL.csv -NoTypeInformation
```

As you can see here, the main difference is that this time we are using the `Get-GlobalAddressList` cmdlet to export the default global address list. You can use this technique for any address list in your organization: just specify the name of the address list you want to export when using either the `Get-AddressList` or `Get-GlobalAddress` list cmdlets.

See also

- *Exporting reports to text and CSV files* in *Chapter 2, Exchange Management Shell Common Tasks*
- *Working with recipient filters* in *Chapter 3, Managing Recipients*
- *Creating address lists*

Configuring hierarchical address books

Exchange 2010 SP1 introduced a new feature called the hierarchical address book (HAB). This allows users with Outlook 2010 to browse for recipients using an organizational hierarchy. The idea is that you can give your users the ability to search for recipients based on your organization's structure, versus the Global Address List which only provides a flat view. The configuration of a HAB can only be done using the Exchange Management Shell, and, in this recipe, we'll take a look at an example of how you can configure this feature in your organization.

How to do it...

1. It is recommended that you create an OU in Active Directory to store the root HAB objects. You can create a new OU using your Active Directory administrations tools, or using PowerShell. The following code can be used to create an OU in the root of the Contoso domain called HAB:

    ```
    $objDomain = [ADSI]''
    $objOU = $objDomain.Create('organizationalUnit', 'ou=HAB')
    $objOU.SetInfo()
    ```

2. Next, create a root distribution group for the HAB:

    ```
    New-DistributionGroup -Name ContosoRoot `
    -DisplayName ContosoRoot `
    -Alias ContosoRoot `
    -OrganizationalUnit contoso.com/HAB `
    -SamAccountName ContosoRoot `
    -Type Distribution
    ```

3. Configure the Contoso distribution group as the root organization for the HAB:

    ```
    Set-OrganizationConfig -HierarchicalAddressBookRoot ContosoRoot
    ```

4. At this point, you need to add subordinate groups to the root organization group. These can be existing groups or you can create new ones. In this example, we'll add three existing groups called Executives, Finance, and Sales to the root organization in the HAB:

    ```
    Add-DistributionGroupMember -Identity ContosoRoot -Member
    Executives
    Add-DistributionGroupMember -Identity ContosoRoot -Member Finance
    Add-DistributionGroupMember -Identity ContosoRoot -Member Sales
    ```

5. Finally, we'll designate each of the groups as hierarchical groups and set the seniority index for the subordinate groups:

    ```
    Set-Group -Identity ContosoRoot -IsHierarchicalGroup $true
    Set-Group Executives -IsHierarchicalGroup $true -SeniorityIndex
    100
    Set-Group Finance -IsHierarchicalGroup $true -SeniorityIndex 50
    Set-Group Sales -IsHierarchicalGroup $true -SeniorityIndex 75
    ```

6. After this configuration has been completed, Outlook 2010 users can click on the **Address Book** button and view a new tab called **Organization** that will list our HAB:

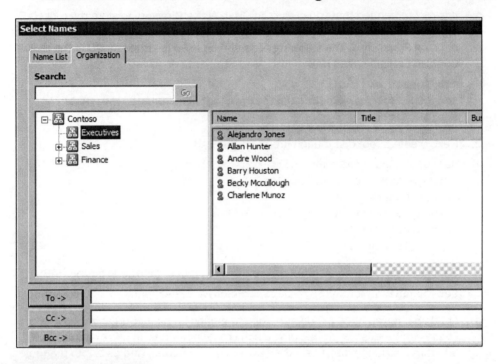

How it works...

The root organization of a HAB is used as the top tier for the organization. Under the root, you can add multiple tiers by adding other distribution groups as members of this root tier and configuring them as hierarchical groups. This allows you to create a HAB that is organized by department, location, or any other structure that makes sense for your environment.

In order to control the structure of the HAB, you can set the `SeniorityIndex` of each sub group under the root organization. This index overrides the automatic sort order based on the `DisplayName` which would otherwise be used if no value was defined. This also works for individual recipients within each group. For example, you can set the `SeniorityIndex` on each member of the `Executives` group using the `Set-User` cmdlet:

```
Set-User cmunoz -SeniorityIndex 100
Set-User awood -SeniorityIndex 90
Set-User ahunter -SeniorityIndex 80
```

The users will be displayed in order, with the highest index number first. This allows you to further organize the HAB and override the default sort order if needed.

There's more...

You may notice that after configuring a HAB that Outlook 2010 users are not seeing the **Organization** tab when viewing the **Address Book**. If this happens, double check the Active Directory schema attribute `ms-Exch-HAB-Root-Department-Link` using ADSIEdit. The `isMemberOfPartialAttributeSet` attribute should be set to `True`. If it is not, change this attribute to `True`, ensure that this has replicated to all DCs in the forest, and restart the Microsoft Exchange Active Directory Topology service on each Exchange server. Of course, this is something you'll want to do during out of hours to ensure there is no disruption of service for end-users. After this work has been completed, Outlook 2010 users should be able to view the Organization tab in the Address Book.

See also

▸   *Managing distribution groups* in *Chapter 3, Managing Recipients*

6

Mailbox and Public Folder Databases

In this chapter, we will cover:

- ► Managing the mailbox and the public folder databases
- ► Moving databases and logs to another location
- ► Configuring the mailbox and public folder database limits
- ► Reporting on mailbox database size
- ► Finding the total number of mailboxes in a database
- ► Determining the average mailbox size per database
- ► Reporting on database backup status
- ► Restoring data from a recovery database
- ► Configuring public folder replication
- ► Managing user access to public folders
- ► Reporting on public folder statistics

Introduction

In this chapter, we will focus on several scenarios in which PowerShell scripting can be used to increase your efficiency when managing databases, which are the most critical resources in your Exchange environment. We will look at how you can add and remove mailbox and public folder databases, configure database settings, generate advanced reports on database statistics, and more from within the shell.

Performing some basic steps

To work with the code samples in this chapter, follow these steps to launch the Exchange Management Shell:

1. Log on to a workstation or the server with the Exchange Management Tools installed

2. Open the Exchange Management Shell by clicking on **Start | All Programs | Exchange Server 2010**

3. Click on the **Exchange Management Shell** shortcut

Managing the mailbox and the public folder databases

The Exchange Management Shell provides a set of cmdlets for both mailbox and public folder database management. In this recipe, we will take a look at how you can use these cmdlets to create, change, or delete mailbox and public folder databases.

How to do it...

The process for managing mailbox and public folder databases is nearly identical: you just need to use the appropriate cmdlet for the job. Let's start off with mailbox databases:

1. To create a mailbox database, use the `New-MailboxDatabase` cmdlet, as shown in the following example:

```
New-MailboxDatabase -Name DB4 `
-EdbFilePath E:\Databases\DB4\DB4.edb `
-LogFolderPath E:\Databases\DB4 `
-Server EX01
```

2. You can mount the database after it has been created using the `Mount-Database` cmdlet:

```
Mount-Database -Identity DB4
```

3. The name of a database can be changed using the `Set-MailboxDatabase` cmdlet:

```
Set-MailboxDatabase -Identity DB4 -Name Database4
```

4. And, finally, you can remove a mailbox database using the `Remove-MailboxDatabase` cmdlet:

```
Remove-MailboxDatabase -Identity Database4 -Confirm:$false
```

How it works...

The `New-MailboxDatabase` cmdlet requires that you provide a name for your database and specify the server name where it should be hosted. In the previous example, you can see that we created the `DB4` database on the `EX01` server. The `-EdbFilePath` parameter specifies the location for your database file. Additionally, you can use the `-LogFolderPath` variable to identify the directory that should hold the transaction logs for this database. If no value is provided for either of these parameters, the database and log directories will be set to the default location within the Exchange installation directory.

Mounting a database is done as a separate step. If you want to create the database and mount it in one operation, pipe your `New-MailboxDatabase` command to the `Mount-Database` cmdlet, as shown in the following line of code:

```
New-MailboxDatabase -Name DB10 -Server EX01 | Mount-Database
```

The `Mount-Database` cmdlet can be used with both mailbox databases and public folder databases. The same is true for its counterpart, `Dismount-Database`, which allows you to dismount a mailbox or public folder database.

As you saw previously, to rename a mailbox database we used the `Set-MailboxDatabase` cmdlet with the `-Name` parameter. It's important to note that, while this will change the database name in the Active Directory and therefore in Exchange, it does not change the filename or path of the database.

Before running the `Remove-MailboxDatabase` cmdlet, you will need to move any regular mailboxes, archive mailboxes, or arbitration mailboxes to another database, using the `New-MoveRequest` cmdlet.

Keep in mind that the removal of a database is only done logically in the Active Directory. Later on, you will need to manually delete the files and directories used by the database running the `Remove-MailboxDatabase` cmdlet.

There's more...

The process for adding, mounting, dismounting, renaming, and removing public folder databases is almost identical to the previous examples. For instance, to create a public folder database, use the following syntax:

```
New-PublicFolderDatabase -Name PFDB1 `
-EdbFilePath E:\Databases\PFDB1\PFDB1.edb `
-LogFolderPath E:\Databases\PFDB1 `
-Server EX01
```

Here you can see that we are using the same parameters that we used when creating a mailbox database. The only difference is that this time we are using the `New-PublicFolderDatabase` cmdlet. The same goes for the `Set-PublicFolderDatabase` and `Remove-PublicFolderDatabase` cmdlets that can be used to rename or remove a public folder. The syntax is the same; you just need to use the appropriate cmdlet.

Understanding automatic mailbox distribution

Exchange 2010 implements a new feature called automatic mailbox distribution. This allows you to omit the `-Database` parameter when creating or moving a mailbox and an agent determines the most appropriate target database based on a number of factors. The Mailbox Resources Management Agent, a cmdlet extension agent, is the application that runs in the background that handles this and it is enabled by default. The benefit of this is that if you provision multiple mailboxes or move multiple mailboxes at one time without specifying a target database, the mailboxes will be distributed across all of the available mailbox databases in the current Active Directory site from where you are running the commands.

Each mailbox database has two properties called `IsExcludedFromProvisioning` and `IsSuspendedFromProvisioning`. These control whether or not a database can be used for automatic mailbox distribution. By default, both are set to `$false`, which means that every mailbox database you create is available for automatic distribution out of the box. If you intend to create a mailbox database used strictly for archive mailboxes or you don't want mailboxes to be placed in a particular database automatically, you can exclude the database from being automatically used. To do so, use the following command syntax after the database has been created:

```
Set-MailboxDatabase -Identity DB1 -IsExcludedFromProvisioning $true
```

When the `IsExcludedFromProvisioning` property is set to `$true`, you can still manually create mailboxes in the database, but it will not be used for automatic distribution.

See also

▶ *Reporting on mailbox database size*

Moving databases and logs to another location

As your environment grows or changes over time, it may be necessary to move one or more databases and their log streams to another location. Like most things, this change can be performed through the Exchange Management Console, but performing this task within the shell gives you some more flexibility. In this recipe, you will learn how to move database and log files to another location.

How to do it...

To move the database file and log stream for the `DB1` database to a new location, use the following command syntax:

```
Move-DatabasePath -Identity DB1 `
-EdbFilePath E:\Databases\DB1\DB1.edb `
-LogFolderPath E:\Databases\DB1 `
-Confirm:$false `
-Force
```

After executing the preceding command, the `DB1` database and log files will be moved to the `E:\Databases\DB1` directory, without prompting you for confirmation.

How it works...

In this example, you can see that we are moving both the database file and the transaction logs to the same directory. You can use different directories or even separate disk spindles as the locations for the database and log folder paths if needed.

To remove the confirmation prompts, we need to set the `-Confirm` parameter to `$false` and also use the `-Force` switch parameter. This may be an important detail if you are running this cmdlet from an automated script. If not used, the cmdlet will not make any changes until an operator confirms it in the shell.

Obviously, in order to move the database file or the logs, the database will need to be taken offline for the duration of the move. The `Move-DatabasePath` cmdlet will automatically dismount the database and remount it when the move process is complete. If the database is already dismounted at the time that you initiate a move, the database will not be automatically mounted upon completion of the command and you will need to mount it manually using the `Mount-Database` cmdlet. Obviously, any users with a mailbox in a dismounted database will be unable to connect to their mailbox. If you need to move a database, ensure that this can be done during a time that will not impact end users.

Keep in mind that databases that are replicated within a **Database Availability Group** (**DAG**) cannot be moved. Each database copy in a DAG needs to use the same local path for the database and logs, so you cannot change this after copies have already been created. If you need to change the paths for a replicated database, you will need to remove all database copies and perform the move. Once this process has been completed, you can create new database copies that will use the new path.

There's more...

Before changing the `EdbfilePath` or the `LogFolderPath` locations for a database, you may want to check the existing configuration. To do so, use the `Get-MailboxDatabase` cmdlet, as shown in the following screenshot:

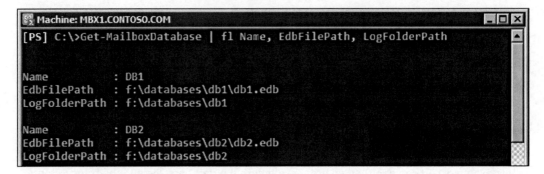

```
Machine: MBX1.CONTOSO.COM                                                    _ □ ✕
[PS] C:\>Get-MailboxDatabase | fl Name, EdbFilePath, LogFolderPath


Name          : DB1
EdbFilePath   : f:\databases\db1\db1.edb
LogFolderPath : f:\databases\db1

Name          : DB2
EdbFilePath   : f:\databases\db2\db2.edb
LogFolderPath : f:\databases\db2
```

Here you can see that we are piping the `Get-MailboxDatabase` cmdlet to `Format-List` (using the `fl` alias) and selecting the `Name`, `EdbFilePath`, and `LogFolderPath` properties, which will display the relevant information for every database in the organization. You can retrieve this information for a single database by specifying the name of the database using the `-Identity` parameter.

Manually moving databases

In certain situations, you may prefer to manually copy or move the database and log files instead of allowing the `Move-DatabasePath` cmdlet to move the data for you. In this case, you can use the following process:

1. Let's say that you need to move the `DB2` database to the `F:\` drive. To do this manually, the first thing you will want to do is dismount the database:

   ```
   Dismount-Database -Identity DB2 -Confirm:$false
   ```

2. Next, use whatever method you prefer to copy the data to the new location on the `F:\` drive. After the data has been copied, use the `Move-DatabasePath` cmdlet, as shown next, to update the configuration information in Exchange:

   ```
   Move-DatabasePath -Identity DB2 `
   -EdbFilePath F:\Databases\DB2\DB2.edb `
   -LogFolderPath F:\Databases\DB2 `
   -ConfigurationOnly `
   -Confirm:$false `
   -Force
   ```

3. The preceding command uses the `-ConfigurationOnly` switch parameter when running the `Move-DatabasePath` cmdlet. This ensures that only the configuration of the database paths is updated and that there is no attempt to copy the data files to the new location.

4. After the files are manually moved or copied and the configuration has been changed, you can re-mount the database, as shown next:

```
Mount-Database -Identity DB2
```

At this point, the database will be brought online and the move operation will be complete.

Taking it a step further

Let's look at an example of how we can use the shell to move databases in bulk. Let's say we have added a new disk to the EX01 server using the `S:\` drive letter and all the databases need to be moved to this new disk under the `Databases` root directory. The following code can be used to perform the move:

```
foreach($i in Get-MailboxDatabase -Server EX01) {
  $DBName = $i.Name

  Move-DatabasePath -Identity $DBName `
  -EdbFilePath "S:\Database\$DBName\$DBName.edb" `
  -LogFolderPath "S:\Database\$DBName" `
  -Confirm:$false `
  -Force
}
```

In this example, we use the `Get-MailboxDatabase` cmdlet to retrieve a list of all the mailbox databases on the EX01 server. As we loop through each mailbox database, we move the EDB file and log path under the `S:\Database` folder in a subdirectory that matches the name of the database.

You can type the preceding code straight into the shell or save it in an external `.ps1` file and execute it as a script.

See also

▶ *Looking through items* in *Chapter 1, PowerShell Key Concepts*

▶ *Using flow control statements* in *Chapter 1, PowerShell Key Concepts*

Configuring the mailbox and public folder database limits

The Exchange Management Shell provides cmdlets that allow you to configure the storage limits for both mailbox and public folder databases. This recipe will show you how to set these limits interactively in the shell or in bulk using automated script.

How to do it...

1. To configure the storage limits for a mailbox database, use the `Set-MailboxDatabase` cmdlet, for example:

   ```
   Set-MailboxDatabase -Identity DB1 `
   -IssueWarningQuota 2gb `
   -ProhibitSendQuota 2.5gb `
   -ProhibitSendReceiveQuota 3gb
   ```

2. You can set the limits for a public folder database using the following command syntax:

   ```
   Set-PublicFolderDatabase -Identity PFDB1 `
   -IssueWarningQuota 25mb `
   -ProhibitPostQuota 30mb `
   -MaxItemSize 5mb
   ```

How it works...

In the first example, we have configured the `IssueWarningQuota`, `ProhibitSendQuota`, and `ProhibitSendRecieveQuota` limits for the `DB1` mailbox database. These are the storage limits that will be applied to each mailbox that is stored in this database. Based on the values used with the command, you can see that users will receive a warning once their mailbox reaches 2 GB in size. When their mailbox reaches 2.5 GB, they will be unable to send outbound e-mail messages and when they hit the 3 GB limit they will be unable to send or receive e-mail messages.

 You can override the database limits on a per mailbox basis using the `Set-Mailbox` cmdlet.

The limits configured in step 2 apply to the folders stored within a public folder database. As you can see, based on the values used in our previous example, a warning will be sent to the folder owner when the size of a folder reaches 25 MB. When it reaches 30 MB, we will no longer allow users to post items to a folder. In addition, the maximum size per item is set to 5 MB. All folders in the `PFDB1` database will inherit these storage limit settings, but you can override them on a per folder basis using the `Set-PublicFolder` cmdlet.

There's more...

Both mailbox and public folder databases support deleted item retention, which allows you to recover items that have been removed from the deleted items folder. By default, the retention period for both mailbox and public folder databases is set to 14 days, but this can be changed using the `-DeletedItemRetention` parameter when using the appropriate cmdlet. For example, to increase the deleted item retention period for the `DB1` database, use the following command:

```
Set-MailboxDatabase -Identity DB1 -DeletedItemRetention 30
```

In this example, we have set the deleted item retention to 30 days. This parameter will also accept input in the form of a time span, and therefore can be specified using the `dd.hh:mm:ss` format. For example, we could have also used `30.00:00:00` as the parameter value, indicating that the deleted item retention should be 30 days, zero hours, zero minutes, and zero seconds, but that would be pointless in this example. However, this format is useful when you need to be specific about hours or minutes, for instance, using `12:00:00` would indicate that deleted items should only be retained for 12 hours. Remember, the `Set-PublicFolderDatabase` cmdlet also supports the `-DeletedItemRetention` parameter, and it works in exactly the same way.

In addition to the deleted item retention, mailbox databases also retain deleted mailboxes for 30 days by default. You can change this value using the `-MailboxRetention` parameter as shown next:

```
Set-MailboxDatabase -Identity DB1 -MailboxRetention 90
```

Like the value used for the `-DeletedItemRetention` parameter, you can specify a time span as the value for the the `-MailboxRetention` parameter. Both of these parameters will accept a maximum of 24,855 days.

Finally, you can configure both mailbox and public folder databases so that items will not be permanently deleted until a database backup has been performed. This is not enabled by default. To turn it on for a particular database, use the `-RetainDeletedItemsUntilBackup` parameter with either the `Set-MailboxDatabase` cmdlet or the `Set-PublicFolderDatabase` cmdlet. For example:

```
Set-MailboxDatabase -Identity DB1 `
-RetainDeletedItemsUntilBackup $true
```

Taking it a step further

To configure these settings in bulk, we can make use of the pipeline to update the settings for a group of databases. For example, the following command will set the database limits for all mailboxes in the organization:

```
Get-MailboxDatabase | Set-MailboxDatabase `
-IssueWarningQuota 2gb `
-ProhibitSendQuota 2.5gb `
-ProhibitSendReceiveQuota 3gb `
-DeletedItemRetention 30 `
-MailboxRetention 90 `
-RetainDeletedItemsUntilBackup $true
```

In this command, we are piping the results of the `Get-MailboxDatabase` cmdlet to the `Set-MailboxDatabase` cmdlet and changing the default settings to the desired values for all databases in the organization.

You can use the `Get-PublicFolderDatabase` and `Set-PublicFolderDatabase` cmdlets in the same way. Simply adjust the parameters and their values to meet your requirements.

See also

▶ *Determining the average mailbox size per database*

Reporting on mailbox database size

In Exchange 2007, it was actually quite difficult to determine the size of a mailbox database using PowerShell. The `Get-MailboxDatabase` cmdlet did not return the size of the database, and instead, you had to use the cmdlet to determine the path to the EDB file and calculate the file size using the `Get-Item` cmdlet or WMI. In Exchange 2010, determining this is very simple and the information can easily be retrieved using the `Get-MailboxDatabase` cmdet. In this recipe, we will take a look at how to report on mailbox database size using the Exchange Management Shell.

How to do it...

To retrieve the total size for each mailbox database, use the following command:

```
Get-MailboxDatabase -Status | select-object Name,DatabaseSize
```

The output from this command might look something like this:

```
Machine: MBX1.CONTOSO.COM                                          _ □ ✕
[PS] C:\>Get-MailboxDatabase -Status | select-object Name,DatabaseSize

Name                              DatabaseSize
----                              ------------
DB1                               648.1 MB (679,542,784 bytes)
DB2                               776.1 MB (813,760,512 bytes)
DB3                               264.1 MB (276,889,600 bytes)
DB4                               8.063 MB (8,454,144 bytes)
```

How it works...

When running the `Get-MailboxDatabase` cmdlet, we can use the `-Status` switch parameter to receive additional information about the database, such as the mount status, the backup status, and the total size of the database, as shown in the previous example. To generate a report with this information, simply pipe the command to the `Export-CSV` cmdlet and specify the path and filename, as shown:

```
Get-MailboxDatabase -Status |
    select-object Name,Server,DatabaseSize,Mounted |
        Export-CSV -Path c:\databasereport.csv -NoTypeInformation
```

This time, we have added the server name that the database is currently associated with and the mount status for that database.

There's more...

When viewing the value for the database size, you probably noticed that we see the total size in megabytes and in parenthesis we see the value in bytes, rather than just seeing a single integer for the total size. The `DatabaseSize` property is of the type `ByteQuantifiedSize`, and we can use several methods provided by this type to convert the value if all we want to retrieve is a numeric representation of the database size.

For example, we can use the `ToKB`, `ToMB`, `ToGB`, and `ToTB` methods of the `DatabaseSize` object to convert the value to kilobytes, megabytes, gigabytes, or terabytes. For example:

```
Get-MailboxDatabase -Status |
    Select-Object Name,
        @{n="DatabaseSize";e={$_.DatabaseSize.ToMb()}}
```

As you can see, this time we have created a calculated property for the `DatabaseSize` and we are using the ToMB method to convert the value of the database. The output we get from the command would look something like this:

```
Machine: MBX1.CONTOSO.COM                                                    _ □ ×
[PS] C:\>Get-MailboxDatabase -Status | Select-Object Name,@{n="DatabaseSize"
;e={$_.DatabaseSize.ToMb()}}

Name                                                             DatabaseSize
----                                                             ------------
DB1                                                                       648
DB2                                                                       776
DB3                                                                       264
DB4                                                                         8
```

This technique may be useful if you are looking to generate basic reports and you don't need all of the extra information that is returned by default. For instance, you may already know that your databases will always be in the range of hundreds of gigabytes. You can simply use a calculated property as shown in the previous example and call the ToGB method for each `DatabaseSize` object.

See also

▶ *Formatting output* in *Chapter 1, PowerShell Key Concepts*

Finding the total number of mailboxes in a database

You can retrieve all kinds of information about a mailbox database using the Exchange Management Shell cmdlets. Surprisingly, the total number of mailboxes in a given mailbox database is not one of those pieces of information. We need to retrieve this data manually. Luckily, PowerShell makes this easy, as you will see in this recipe.

How to do it...

1. There are two ways that you can retrieve the total number of mailboxes in a database. First, we can use the Count property of a collection of mailboxes:

   ```
   @(Get-Mailbox -Database DB1).count
   ```

2. Another way to retrieve this information is to use the Measure-Object cmdlet using the same collection from the preceding example:

   ```
   Get-Mailbox -Database DB1 | Measure-Object
   ```

How it works...

In both steps, we use the `Get-Mailbox` cmdlet and specify the `-Database` parameter, which will retrieve all of the mailboxes in that particular database. In the first example, we have wrapped the command inside the `@()` characters to ensure that PowerShell will always interpret the output as an array. The reason for this is that if the mailbox database contains only one mailbox, the resulting output object will not be a collection, and thus will not have a `Count` property.

 Remember, the default result size for `Get-Mailbox` is 1000. Set the `-ResultSize` parameter to Unlimited to override this.

The second step makes use of the `Measure-Object` cmdlet. You can see that, in addition to the `Count` property, we also get a number of other details. Consider the output as shown in the following screenshot:

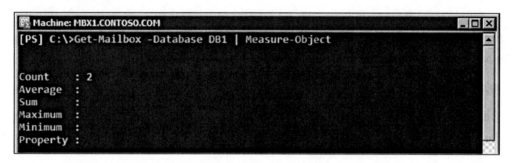

To retrieve only the total number of mailboxes, we can extend this command further in two ways. First, we can enclose the entire command in parenthesis and access the `Count` property:

```
(Get-Mailbox -Database DB1 | Measure-Object).Count
```

In this case, the preceding command would return only the total number of mailboxes in the `DB1` database.

We can also pipe the command to `Select-Object`, and use the `-ExpandProperty` parameter to retrieve only the value of the `Count` property:

```
Get-Mailbox -Database DB1 |
  Measure-Object |
    Select-Object -ExpandProperty Count
```

This command would again only return the total number of mailboxes in the database.

One of the most common questions that comes up when people see both of these methods is, of course, which way is faster? Well, we can use the `Measure-Command` cmdlet to determine this information, but the truth is that your results will vary greatly and there probably won't be a huge difference in this case. The syntax to measure the time it takes to run a script or command is shown next:

```
Measure-Command -Expression {@(Get-Mailbox -Database DB1).Count}
```

Simply supply a script block containing the commands you want to measure and assign it to the `-Expression` parameter as shown previously. The `Measure-Command` cmdlet will return a `TimeSpan` object that reports on the total milliseconds, seconds, minutes that it took to complete the command. You can then compare these values to other commands that produce the same result but use alternate syntax or cmdlets.

 To report on the total number of archive mailboxes, use `Get-Mailbox -Filter {ArchiveName -ne $null} | Measure-Object`.

There's more...

We can easily determine the total number of mailboxes in each database using a single command. The key to this is using the `Select-Object` cmdlet to create a calculated property. For example:

```
Get-MailboxDatabase |
  Select-Object Name,
    @{n="TotalMailboxes";e={@(Get-Mailbox -Database $_).count}}
```

This command would generate output similar to the following:

```
Machine: MBX1.CONTOSO.COM                                          _ □ X
[PS] C:\>Get-MailboxDatabase | Select-Object Name,@{n="TotalMailboxes";e={@(
Get-Mailbox -Database $_).count}}

Name                                                          TotalMailboxes
----                                                          --------------
DB1                                                                        2
DB2                                                                      102
DB3                                                                       45
DB4                                                                        1
```

This command pipes the output from `Get-MailboxDatabase` to the `Select-Object` cmdlet. For each database output by the command, we select the database name and then use the `$_` object when creating the calculated property to determine the total number of mailboxes, using the `Get-Mailbox` cmdlet. This command can be piped further down to the `Out-File` or `Export-CSV` cmdlets that will generate a report saved in an external file.

▶ *Creating custom objects* in *Chapter 1, PowerShell Key Concepts*

Determining the average mailbox size per database

PowerShell is very flexible and gives you the ability to generate very detailed reports. When generating mailbox database statistics, we can utilize data returned from multiple cmdlets provided by the Exchange Management Shell. This recipe will show you an example of this, and you will learn how to calculate the average mailbox size per database using PowerShell.

How to do it...

To determine the average mailbox size for a given database, use the following one-liner:

```
Get-MailboxStatistics -Database DB1 |
  ForEach-Object {$_.TotalItemSize.value.ToMB()} |
    Measure-Object -Average |
      Select-Object -ExpandProperty Average
```

How it works...

Calculating an average is as simple as performing some basic math, but PowerShell gives us the ability to do this quickly with the `Measure-Object` cmdlet. The example uses the `Get-MailboxStatistics` cmdlet to retrieve all the mailboxes in the `DB1` database. We then loop through each one, retrieving only the `TotalItemSize` property, and inside the `ForEach-Object` script block we convert the total item size to megabytes. The result from each mailbox can then be averaged using the `Measure-Object` cmdlet. At the end of the command, you can see that the `Select-Object` cmdlet is used to retrieve only the value for the `Average` property.

The number returned here will give us the average mailbox size in total for regular mailboxes, archive mailboxes, as well as any other type of mailbox that has been disconnected. If you want to be more specific, you can filter out these mailboxes after running the `Get-MailboxStatistics` cmdlet:

```
Get-MailboxStatistics -Database DB1 |
  Where-Object{!$_.DisconnectDate -and !$_.IsArchive} |
    ForEach-Object {$_.TotalItemSize.value.ToMB()} |
      Measure-Object -Average |
        Select-Object -ExpandProperty Average
```

Notice that, in the preceding example, we have added the `Where-Object` cmdlet to filter out any mailboxes that have a `DisconnectDate` defined or where the `IsArchive` property is `$true`.

Another thing that you may want to do is round the average. Let's say the `DB1` database contained 42 mailboxes and the total size of the database was around 392 megabytes. The value returned from the preceding command would roughly look something like `2.39393939393939`. Rarely are all those extra decimal places of any use. Here are a couple of ways to make the output a little cleaner:

```
$MBAvg = Get-MailboxStatistics -Database DB1 |
  ForEach-Object {$_.TotalItemSize.value.ToMB()} |
    Measure-Object -Average |
     Select-Object -ExpandProperty Average


[Math]::Round($MBAvg,2)
```

You can see that this time, we stored the result of the one-liner in the `$MBAvg` object. We then use the `Round` method of the `Math` class in the .NET Framework to round the value, specifying that the result should only contain two decimal places. Based on the previous information, the result of the preceding command would be `2.39`.

We can also use string formatting to specify the number of decimal places to be used:

```
[PS] "{0:n2}" -f $MBAvg
2.39
```

> The `-f Format` operator is documented in PowerShell's help system in about_operators.

Keep in mind that this command will return a string, so if you need to be able to sort on this value, cast it to `double`:

```
[PS] [double]("{0:n2}" -f $MBAvg)
2.39
```

There's more...

The previous examples have only shown how to determine the average mailbox size for a single database. To determine this information for all mailbox databases, we can use the following code:

```
foreach($DB in Get-MailboxDatabase) {
```

```
Get-MailboxStatistics -Database $DB |
ForEach-Object{$_.TotalItemSize.value.ToMB()} |
Measure-Object -Average |
Select-Object @{n="Name";e={$DB.Name}},
@{n="AvgMailboxSize";e={[Math]::Round($_.Average,2)}} |
Sort-Object AvgMailboxSize -Desc
}
```

The result of this command would look something like this:

This example is very similar to the one we looked at previously. The difference is that, this time, we are running our one-liner using a `foreach` loop for every mailbox database in the organization. When each mailbox database has been processed, we sort the output based on the `AvgMailboxSize` property.

See also

▶ *Creating custom objects* in *Chapter 1, PowerShell Key Concepts*

Reporting on database backup status

Using the Exchange Management Shell, we can write scripts that will check on the last full backup time for a database that can be used for monitoring and reporting. In this recipe, you will learn how to check the last backup time for each database and use this information to generate statistics and find databases that are not being backed up on a regular basis.

How to do it...

To check the last full backup time for a database, use the `Get-MailboxDatabase` cmdlet, as shown:

```
Get-MailboxDatabase -Identity DB1 -Status | fl Name,LastFullBackup
```

How it works...

When you run the `Get-MailboxDatabase` cmdlet, you must remember to use the `-Status` switch parameter or else the `LastFullBackup` property will be `$null`. In the previous example, we checked the last full backup for the `DB1` database and piped the output to the `Format-List` (using the `fl` alias) cmdlet. When viewing the `LastFullBackup` for each database, you might find it helpful to pipe the output to the `Select-Object` cmdlet, as shown in the following screenshot:

```
Machine: MBX1.CONTOSO.COM                                              _ □ ✕
[PS] C:\>Get-MailboxDatabase -Status | Select-Object Name,LastFullBackup

Name                                LastFullBackup
----                                --------------
DB1                                 12/5/2010 1:51:33 PM
DB2                                 12/5/2010 1:51:33 PM
DB3                                 12/5/2010 1:51:34 PM
DB4
```

In addition to simply checking the date, it may be useful to schedule this script to run daily and report on the databases that have not recently been backed up. For example, the following command will only retrieve databases that have not had a successful full backup in the last 24 hours:

```
Get-MailboxDatabase -Status |
  ?{$_.LastFullBackup -le (Get-Date).AddDays(-1)} |
    Select-object Name,LastFullBackup
```

Here you can see that the `Get-MailboxDatabase` output is piped to the `Where-Object` cmdlet (using the `?` alias) and we check the value of the `LastFullBackup` property for each database. If the value is less than or equal to 24 hours ago, the database name and last full backup time are retuned.

There's more...

Since the `LastFullBackup` property value is a `DateTime` object, not only can we use comparison operators to find databases that have not been backed up within a certain time frame, but we can also calculate the number of days since that time. This might be a useful piece of information to add to a reporting or monitoring script. The following code will provide this information:

```
Get-MailboxDatabase -Status | ForEach-Object {
  if(!$_.LastFullBackup) {
    $LastFull = "Never"
  }
  else {
```

```
      $LastFull = $_.LastFullBackup
    }
    New-Object PSObject -Property @{
      Name = $_.Name
      LastFullBackup = $LastFull
      DaysSinceBackup = if($LastFull-is [datetime]) {
        (New-TimeSpan $LastFull).Days
      }
      Else {
        $LastFull
      }
    }
  }
}
```

When running this code in the Exchange Management Shell, you would see output similar to the following:

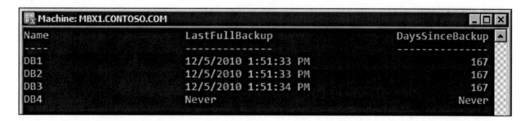

As you can see, we are simply looping through each mailbox database and retrieving the LastFullBackup time. If a database has never been backed up, the value will be $null. With that in mind, this code will return the string **Never** for those databases when reporting on the status. If a value is present for LastFullBackup, we use the New-TimeSpan cmdlet to determine the number of days since the last backup and include that in the data returned.

See also

- ▸ *Creating custom objects* in *Chapter 1, PowerShell Key Concepts*

Restoring data from a recovery database

When it comes to recovering data from a failed database, you have several options depending on what kind of backup product you are using or how you have deployed Exchange 2010 SP1. The ideal method for enabling redundancy is to use a DAG, which will replicate your mailbox databases to one or more servers and provide automatic failover in the event of a disaster. However, you may need to pull old data out of a database restored from a backup. In this recipe, we will take a look at how you can create a recovery database and restore data from it using the Exchange Management Shell.

How to do it...

First, restore the failed database using the steps required by your current backup solution. For this example, let's say that we have restored the `DB1` database file to `E:\Recovery\DB1` and the database has been brought to a clean shutdown state. We can use the following steps to create a recovery database and restore mailbox data:

1. Create a recovery database using the `New-MailboxDatabase` cmdlet:

   ```
   New-MailboxDatabase -Name RecoveryDB `
   -EdbFilePath E:\Recovery\DB1\DB1.edb `
   -LogFolderPath E:\Recovery\DB01 `
   -Recovery `
   -Server MBX1
   ```

2. When you run the preceding command, you will see a warning that the recovery database was created using the existing database file. The next step is to mount the database:

   ```
   Mount-Database -Identity RecoveryDB
   ```

3. Next, we will use the `New-MailboxRestoreRequest` cmdlet to restore the data from the recovery database for a single mailbox:

   ```
   New-MailboxRestoreRequest -SourceDatabase RecoveryDB `
   -SourceStoreMailbox "Joe Smith" `
   -TargetMailbox joe.smith
   ```

How it works...

When you restore the database file from your backup application, you may need to ensure that the database is in a clean shutdown state. For example, if you are using Windows Server Backup for your backup solution, you will need to use the `Eseutil.exe` database utility to play any uncommitted logs into the database to get it in a clean shutdown state. For details on how this works, check out Restoring Mailbox Data from a Recovery Database in Exchange 2010 SP1 at the following URL:

```
http://www.mikepfeiffer.net/2011/07/restoring-mailbox-data-from-a-
recovery-database-in-exchange-2010-sp1/
```

Once the data is restored, we can create a recovery database using the `New-MailboxDatabase` cmdlet, as shown in the first example. Notice that when we ran the command we used several parameters. First, we specified the path to the EDB file and the log files, both of which are in the same location where we restored the files. We have also used the `-Recovery` switch parameter to specify that this is a special type of database that will only be used for restoring data and should not be used for production mailboxes. Finally, we specified which mailbox server the database should be hosted on using the `-Server` parameter. Make sure to run the `New-MailboxDatabase` cmdlet from the mailbox server that you are specifying in the `-Server` parameter, and then mount the database using the `Mount-Database` cmdlet.

The last step is to restore data from one or more mailboxes. As we saw in the previous example, the `New-MailboxRestoreRequest` is the tool to use for this task. This is a new cmdlet in Exchange 2010 SP1, so if you have used this process in the past using the `Restore-Mailbox` cmdlet, you will want to get used to using this new cmdlet.

There's more...

When you run the `New-MailboxRestoreRequest` cmdlet, you need to specify the identity of the mailbox you wish to restore using the `-SourceStoreMailbox` parameter. There are three possible values you can use to provide this information: `DisplayName`, `MailboxGuid`, and `LegacyDN`. To retrieve these values, you can use the `Get-MailboxStatistics` cmdlet once the recovery database is online and mounted:

```
Get-MailboxStatistics -Database RecoveryDB |
    fl DisplayName,MailboxGUID,LegacyDN
```

Here we have specified that we want to retrieve all three of these values for each mailbox in the `RecoveryDB` database.

Understanding target mailbox identity

When restoring data with the `New-MailboxRestoreRequest` cmdlet, you also need to provide a value for the `-TargetMailbox` parameter. The mailbox needs to already exist before running this command. If you are restoring data from a backup for an existing mailbox that has not changed since the backup was done, you can simply provide the typical identity values for a mailbox for this parameter.

If you want to restore data to a mailbox that was not the original source of the data, you need to use the `-AllowLegacyDNMismatch` switch parameter. This will be useful if you are restoring data to another user's mailbox, or if you've recreated the mailbox since the backup was taken.

Learning about other useful parameters

The `New-MailboxRestoreRequest` cmdlet can be used to granularly control how data is restored out of a mailbox. The following parameters may be useful to customize the behaviour of your restores:

▶ **ConflictResolutionOption**: This parameter specifies the action to take if multiple matching messages exist in the target mailbox. The possible values are `KeepSourceItem`, `KeepLatestItem`, or `KeepAll`. If no value is specified, `KeepSourceItem` will be used by default.

▶ **ExcludeDumpster**: Use this switch parameter to indicate that the dumpster should not be included in the restore.

▶ **SourceRootFolder**: Use this parameter to restore data only from a root folder of a mailbox.

▶ **TargetIsArchive**: You can use this switch parameter to perform a mailbox restore to a mailbox archive.

▶ **TargetRootFolder**: This parameter can be used to restore data to a specific folder in the root of the target mailbox. If no value is provided, the data is restored and merged into the existing folders, and, if they do not exist, they will be created in the target mailbox.

These are just a few of the useful parameters that can be used with this cmdlet, but there are more. For a complete list of all the available parameters and full details on each one, run `Get-Help New-MailboxRestoreRequest -Detailed`

Understanding mailbox restore request cmdlets

There is an entire cmdlet set for mailbox restore requests in addition to the `New-MailboxRestoreRequest` cmdlet. The remaining available cmdlets are outlined as follows:

▶ `Get-MailboxRestoreRequest`: Provides detailed status of mailbox restore requests

▶ `Remove-MailboxRestoreRequest`: Removes fully or partially completed restore requests

▶ `Resume-MailboxRestoreRequest`: Resumes a restore request that was suspended or failed

▶ `Set-MailboxRestoreRequest`: Can be used to change the restore request options after the request has been created

▶ `Suspend-MailboxRestoreRequest`: Suspends a restore request any time after the request was created but before the request reaches the status of *Completed*

For complete details and examples for each of these cmdlets, use the `Get-Help` cmdlet with the appropriate cmdlet using the `-Full` switch parameter.

Taking it a step further

Let's say that you have restored your database from backup, you have created a recovery database, and now you need to restore each mailbox in the backup to the corresponding target mailboxes that are currently online. We can use the following script to accomplish this:

```
$mailboxes = Get-MailboxStatistics -Database RecoveryDB
foreach($mailbox in $mailboxes) {
  New-MailboxRestoreRequest -SourceDatabase RecoveryDB `
  -SourceStoreMailbox $mailbox.DisplayName `
  -TargetMailbox $mailbox.DisplayName
}
```

Here you can see that first we use the Get-MailboxStatistics cmdlet to retrieve all the mailboxes in the recovery database and store the results in the $mailboxes variable. We then loop through each mailbox and restore the data to the original mailbox. You can track the status of these restores using the Get-MailboxRestoreRequest cmdlet and the Get-MailboxRestoreRequestStatistics cmdlet.

See also

▶ *Managing disconnected mailboxes* in *Chapter 4, Managing Mailboxes*

Configuring public folder replication

The Exchange Management Shell provides support for public folder replication management both from the shell, and with some built-in scripts located in the Exchange Scripts directory. This recipe will provide a couple of methods that can be used to configure public folder replication.

How to do it...

1. To manage the replication settings for a public folder, use the Set-PublicFolder cmdlet. For example, to configure replicas to the Marketing public folder, use the following command:

   ```
   Set-PublicFolder \Marketing -Replicas PFDB1,PFDB2
   ```

2. To set a custom replication schedule, use the -ReplicationSchedule parameter, as shown in the following example:

   ```
   Set-PublicFolder \Marketing `
   -ReplicationSchedule "Friday.06:00 PM-Monday.05:00 AM"
   ```

3. You can reset this command and switch back to the default setting, which is to always allow replication:

   ```
   Set-PublicFolder \Marketing -ReplicationSchedule Always
   ```

4. To configure a specific folder so that it uses the parent database replication settings, use the following command:

    ```
    Set-PublicFolder \Marketing -UseDatabaseReplicationSchedule $true
    ```

This is the default setting and only needs to be changed if you have modified the replication schedule settings.

How it works...

In the first example, the `Set-PublicFolder` cmdlet uses the `-Replicas` parameter to define each database that should contain a replica of the public folder. Keep in mind that when you set this, you will override the current list that has been configured for the folder. So, if you currently have a replica on PFDB1 and you want to add PFDB2, you will need to specify both database names when you run the command.

When using the `-ReplicationSchedule` parameter to specify a custom replication schedule, the values should use the following format:

```
Weekday.Hour:Minute [AM/PM]-Weekday.Hour:Minute [AM/PM]
```

In the second step, you can see that we modified the schedule so that replication would only take place on the weekends, starting on Friday night and ending on Monday morning.

 You can suspend and resume public folder replication using the `Suspend-PublicFolderReplication` and `Resume-PublicFolderReplication` cmdlets. Use `Get-Help` with these cmdlets for more details.

There's more...

You may have a large number of public folders that need to have replicas added. In this case, Exchange provides a script called `AddReplicaToPFRecursive.ps1` in the scripts directory that is created when you install Exchange.

Let's say that you have a public folder database called PFDB1 on a server called MBX1. You have hundreds of public folders in this database. You then install a new server called MBX2 and create a new public folder database on this server called PFDB2. To add replicas for all of the folders from the PFDB1 database to the PFDB2 database, first switch to the Exchange scripts directory:

```
Set-Location $exscripts
```

Next, run the script as shown next:

```
.\AddReplicaToPFRecursive.ps1 -TopPublicFolder \ -ServerToAdd MBX2
```

This command will recursively add replicas for each folder on **PFDB1** to **PFDB2**.

In addition, you can add replicas to the system folders using the following command:

```
.\AddReplicaToPFRecursive.ps1 -TopPublicFolder \Non_IPM_Subtree `
-ServerToAdd MBX2
```

If you are transitioning to another server, you can move the replicas for good. For example, if you intend to replace MBX1 with MBX2, you can use the MoveAllReplicas.ps1 script to move all the replicas to the PFDB2 database:

```
.\MoveAllReplicas.ps1 -Server MBX1 -NewServer MBX2
```

Keep in mind that it may take some time for public folder replication to kick in, even when the replication schedule is set to "always".

Managing user access to public folders

Client permissions for public folders can be managed using a handful of cmdlets that are available in the Exchange Management Shell. In addition, there are some scripts located in the Exchange scripts directory that can be used to make client permission changes in bulk. In this recipe, we will take a look at how you can use both methods to manage public folder client permissions.

How to do it...

To grant Owner permissions to a user on a public folder, use the following command:

```
Add-PublicFolderClientPermission -Identity \Marketing `
-User Mike `
-AccessRights Owner `
-Server MBX1
```

How it works...

The `Add-PublicFolderClientPermissions` cmdlet can be used to add permissions for a particular user to a public folder. In the previous example, we granted the user *Mike* the *Owner* access right to the `Marketing` public folder using the `-AccessRights` parameter. There are several possible values for this parameter, as shown next:

 ▶ **ReadItems**: The user assigned this right can read items within the designated folder.

 ▶ **CreateItems**: The user assigned this right can create items within the designated folder.

 ▶ **EditOwnedItems**: The user assigned this right can edit the items that the user owns in the designated folder.

 ▶ **DeleteOwnedItems**: The user assigned this right can delete items that the user owns in the designated folder.

 ▶ **EditAllItems**: The user assigned this right can edit all items in the designated folder.

 ▶ **DeleteAllItems**: The user assigned this right can delete all items in the designated folder.

 ▶ **CreateSubfolders**: The user assigned this right can create subfolders in the designated folder.

 ▶ **FolderOwner**: The user assigned this right has the right to view and move the folder and create subfolders. The user cannot read items, edit items, delete items, or create items.

 ▶ **FolderContact**: The user assigned this right is the contact for the designated folder.

 ▶ **FolderVisible**: The user assigned this right can view the specified folder, but can't read or edit items within the designated folder.

The following roles are made up by one or more of the permissions specified in the previous list and can also be used with the `-AccessRights` parameter:

 ▶ **None**: FolderVisible

 ▶ **Owner**: CreateItems, ReadItems, CreateSubfolders, FolderOwner, FolderContact, FolderVisible, EditOwnedItems, EditAllItems, DeleteOwnedItems, and DeleteAllItems

 ▶ **PublishingEditor**: CreateItems, ReadItems, CreateSubfolders, FolderVisible, EditOwnedItems, EditAllItems, DeleteOwnedItems, and DeleteAllItems

 ▶ **Editor**: CreateItems, ReadItems, FolderVisible, EditOwnedItems, EditAllItems, DeleteOwnedItems, and DeleteAllItems

 ▶ **PublishingAuthor**: CreateItems, ReadItems, CreateSubfolders, FolderVisible, EditOwnedItems, and DeleteOwnedItems

 ▶ **Author**: CreateItems, ReadItems, FolderVisible, EditOwnedItems, and DeleteOwnedItems

- ▶ **NonEditingAuthor**: CreateItems, ReadItems, and FolderVisible
- ▶ **Reviewer**: ReadItems and FolderVisible
- ▶ **Contributor**: CreateItems and FolderVisible

You can generate a report that details the client permissions for a public folder using the `Get-PublicFolderClientPermission` cmdlet. For example, the following command returns the permissions set on the `Marketing` public folder:

```
Get-PublicFolderClientPermission \Marketing
```

This command would show each user's access rights to the `Marketing` public folder. To retrieve the client access rights for each public folder, you could use the following commands:

```
Get-PublicFolder -Recurse |
  ?{$_.Name -ne 'IPM_SUBTREE'} |
    Get-PublicFolderClientPermission
```

Keep in mind that this command will return quite a bit of information, even for only a few public folders. You may want to export this information to a text or CSV file for easier review outside the shell.

To remove public folder client permissions for an individual user, use the following command syntax:

```
Remove-PublicFolderClientPermission \Marketing `
-User Mike `
-AccessRights Owner `
-Confirm:$false
```

Here you can see that the syntax is pretty straightforward. We are simply removing the permissions that were set in the first example.

There's more...

The built-in scripts directory on each Exchange server provides some PowerShell scripts that can be used to modify a user's permissions to public folders in bulk. The scripts and their descriptions are outlined as follows:

- ▶ `ReplaceUserWithUserOnPFRecursive.ps1`: You can use this script to replace an existing user with a new user in the client permissions from a public folder recursively
- ▶ `ReplaceUserPermissionOnPFRecursive.ps1`: This script can be used to replace a user's client permissions recursively

> ▶ RemoveUserFromPFRecursive.ps1: You can use this script to recursively remove a user's client permissions from all public folders in the hierarchy

To run these scripts, switch to the scripts directory:

```
Set-Location $exscripts
```

To replace a user with another user on every public folder:

```
.\ReplaceUserWithUserOnPFRecursive.ps1 -TopPublicFolder \ `
-UserOld administrator `
-UserNew Mike
```

To replace a user's permissions on every public folder:

```
.\ReplaceUserPermissionOnPFRecursive.ps1 -TopPublicFolder \ `
-User administrator `
-Permissions Reviewer
```

To remove a user from the client permissions list for all public folders:

```
.\RemoveUserFromPFRecursive.ps1 -TopPublicFolder \ -User sysadmin
```

Reporting on public folder statistics

The Exchange Management Shell provides two cmdlets that can be used to generate detailed reports based on the usage of your public folders. In this recipe, we will take a look at how to report on public folder statistics.

How to do it...

To generate a basic report for each public folder, run the following cmdlet:

```
Get-PublicFolderStatistics | ft Name,ItemCount,TotalItemSize
```

This command would generate an output similar to the following example:

```
Machine: MBX1.CONTOSO.COM                                        _ □ ✕
[PS] C:\>Get-PublicFolderStatistics | ft Name,ItemCount,TotalItemSize

Name                            ItemCount TotalItemSize
----                            --------- -------------
Marketing                              88 515.7 KB (528,053 bytes)
Sales                                 199 367 KB (375,834 bytes)
Finance                                12 20.16 KB (20,641 bytes)
Engineering                            32 50.29 KB (51,500 bytes)
Accounting                              4 14.95 KB (15,306 bytes)
Budget                                 10 16.51 KB (16,904 bytes)
Support                                13 48.88 KB (50,050 bytes)
```

How it works...

As you can see, Get-PublicFolderStatistics provides some very useful and detailed information for each public folder. In addition, you can report on individual items within each folder using the Get-PublicFolderItemStatistics cmdlet. This cmdlet will return each item within a specified public folder and contains detailed information about each item including message size, creation time, last access time, and whether or not it contains an attachment.

You can use the output of the Get-PublicFolderItemStatistics cmdlet to determine which items are no longer being used and can be safely deleted. Simply run the cmdlet and specify the folder name as shown next:

```
Get-PublicFolderItemStatistics -Identity \Marketing
```

You can filter the output based on your needs. For example, if you are only looking for old items which can be safely deleted, you could run something like this:

```
Get-PublicFolderItemStatistics -Identity \Marketing |
    ?{$_.LastModificationTime -le "12/31/2008"}
```

Replace the date in quotes with a date in the past, such as a year or two ago, and then you can find items in the folder that have not been updated in a very long time that can likely be safely deleted.

There's more...

Within the Exchange scripts directory there is a script called AggregatePFData.ps1 which can be used to provide a detailed report on public folder item statistics. This script aggregates the output of the Get-PublicFolderItemStatistics, Get-PublicFolderStatistics, and Get-PublicFolder cmdlets. The last access and last user modification times are returned, in addition to the folder owner and several other properties such as the item count, folder type, whether or not it is mail-enabled, and more.

To run the script, switch to the Exchange server scripts directory:

```
Set-Location $exscripts
```

Next, run the script:

```
.\AggregatePFData.ps1 -Publicfolder \Marketing
```

The output from this command should be similar to the following:

```
Machine: MBX1.CONTOSO.COM                                          _ □ ✕

[PS] C:\Program Files\Microsoft\Exchange Server\V14\scripts>.\AggregatePFDat
a.ps1 -Publicfolder \Marketing


Identity                  : \Marketing
Owner                     : contoso.com/Users/Administrator
ItemTypes                 : IPM.Note, IPM.Note.SMIME.MultipartSigned
FolderType                :
MailEnabled               : False
HasModerator              : False
HasRules                  : False
ItemCount                 : 88
TotalItemSize             : 515.7 KB (528,053 bytes)
LastUserAccessTime        :
LastUserModificationTime  : 5/22/2011 8:24:17 AM
```

From this output, you can see that several useful details about the folder are returned that can be filtered on, or exported to external text or CSV file.

See also

▶ *Exporting reports to text and CSV files* in *Chapter 2, Exchange Management Shell Common Tasks*

7
Managing Client Access

In this chapter, we will cover the following:

- ▶ Creating an RPC Client Access array
- ▶ Configuring the CAS server used by RPC clients
- ▶ Configuring RPC encryption requirements
- ▶ Managing ActiveSync, OWA, POP3, and IMAP4 mailbox settings
- ▶ Setting internal and external CAS URLs
- ▶ Managing Outlook Anywhere settings
- ▶ Blocking Outlook clients from connecting to Exchange
- ▶ Reporting on Active OWA and RPC connections
- ▶ Controlling ActiveSync device access
- ▶ Reporting on ActiveSync devices

Introduction

The **Client Access Server (CAS)** role was introduced in Exchange 2007 to provide a dedicated access point to various services such as Outlook Web Access (OWA), ActiveSync, **POP3**, and **IMAP4** to clients. However, all **MAPI** clients connected directly to the mailbox server role. The CAS role has been extended even further in Exchange 2010 and includes some new features, including functionality that will change the architecture of every Exchange deployment. In this latest release, even though connections to public folders are still made by MAPI clients to the mailbox server role, connections from these clients to Exchange 2010 mailboxes are now handled by the CAS role. This is a major architectural shift, and many of these new features, such as configuring the preferred MAPI endpoint for Outlook clients, can only be managed from the shell.

In addition, with all of the possible ways to connect to Exchange through CAS services such as OWA and ActiveSync, there are a large number of settings and options that can be managed from the command line. The CAS role and the Exchange Management Shell cmdlets used to manage it provide plenty of opportunities for automating repetitive tasks from PowerShell one-liners, scripts, and functions.

In this chapter, we'll take a look at how you can control access to the CAS services in your environment, customize their settings, and generate usage reports using the Exchange Management Shell.

Performing some basic steps

To work with the code samples in this chapter, follow these steps to launch the Exchange Management Shell:

1. Log onto a workstation or server with the Exchange Management Tools installed

2. Open the Exchange Management Shell by clicking on **Start | All Programs | Exchange Server 2010**

3. Click on the **Exchange Management Shell** shortcut

Creating an RPC Client Access array

Since CAS servers are now the MAPI endpoint for Outlook clients accessing Exchange 2010 mailboxes, it is recommended as a best practice that you create arrays of load-balanced CAS servers in order to provide high availability for the CAS server role. In this recipe, you'll learn how to create a CAS array using the Exchange Management Shell.

How to do it...

In order to create a CAS array, you must use the shell since there is no interface within the Exchange Management Console that allows you to perform this task. The following command creates a CAS array for the *CorporateHQ* site in Active Directory:

```
New-ClientAccessArray -Name CASArray01 `
-Fqdn outlook.contoso.com `
-Site CorporateHQ
```

How it works...

CAS arrays are used to group multiple CAS servers together using a logical server name that resolves to a load balanced IP address. This allows your clients to use a single CAS server name at all times, regardless of which CAS server in an array they are connected to. Creating the array allows CAS servers to accept connections using a shared server name, and allows this array name to be associated with a particular mailbox database so that it can be used as the MAPI endpoint configured in a user's Outlook profile. The goal is to provide seamless client access to the CAS role, and if a server in an array goes offline, clients do not need to be reconfigured to point to a different server name.

 You can view the settings for a CAS Array using the `Get-ClientAccessArray` cmdlet. Run `Get-Help Get-ClientAccessArray -full` for details.

You can have only one CAS array per Active Directory site. In the previous example, we created a CAS array in the *CorporateHQ* site. When you create the array using the `New-ClientAccessArray` cmdlet, any existing CAS servers in the Active Directory site will automatically be included. If you deploy a new CAS server in the site at a later time, the server will automatically be added to the array. Even though CAS array membership is automatically configured, you can still allow users to connect directly to an individual CAS server which is controlled by the `RPCClientAccessServer` attribute on each mailbox database.

There's more...

When you create a CAS array, you're basically creating a virtual server object that can be assigned to one or more mailbox databases. You still need to configure a network load-balancing solution that is external to Exchange. For example, when we created the CAS array with the `outlook.contoso.com` FQDN, there are two important steps that would need to take place before this array name could actually be used. First, you would need to configure either Windows Network Load Balancing or a hardware based Load Balancer with a virtual IP address which would load balance traffic across all the CAS servers in the *CorporateHQ* site. Next, you would need to create a host (A) record in DNS for `outlook.contoso.com` that resolves to the load balanced virtual IP address.

See also

▸ *Building a Windows NLB cluster for CAS servers* in *Chapter 9*, *High Availability*
▸ *Configuring the CAS server used by RPC clients*

Configuring the CAS server used by RPC clients

RPC clients such as Outlook 2003, 2007, and 2010 use CAS servers as their MAPI endpoint for mailbox access in Exchange 2010. In this recipe, you will learn how to control which CAS server or CAS array will be used as the MAPI endpoint by configuring the properties of the user's mailbox database using the Exchange Management Shell.

How to do it...

To configure the CAS server that should be used by RPC clients, set the
`RPCClientAccessServer` property of the user's mailbox database. For example:

```
Set-MailboxDatabase -Identity DB1 `
-RpcClientAccessServer outlook.contoso.com
```

After running the previous command, any user with a mailbox in the `DB1` database will use
`outlook.contoso.com` for RPC connections.

How it works...

When creating a mailbox database, the `RpcClientAccessServer` property of the database
will automatically be set to a CAS server in the same Active Directory site as the mailbox
server hosting the database. This is true only if a CAS array has not already been created
for the Active Directory site that the mailbox server is located in. If a CAS array for the Active
Directory site has already been created, the `RpcClientAccessServer` property for the
database being created will be set to the CAS array already defined for that site.

You can control the `RpcClientAccessServer` setting for any mailbox database using the
`Set-MailboxDatabase` cmdlet, as shown in the previous example. In some cases, allowing
Exchange to automatically select the appropriate value for the `RpcClientAccessServer`
setting might be sufficient. If not, you can explicitly set this value to a particular CAS server if
you want all of the users in a particular mailbox database to use a specific CAS server for
RPC access.

There's more...

Ideally, you want to create your CAS arrays before creating your mailbox databases. This
is because, as we discussed previously, once the CAS array for a particular site has been
created, all mailbox databases created within the site will be automatically configured to
use this array as the RPC Client Access server. When a user's Outlook profile is initially
configured and the `RPCClientAccessServer` property for their mailbox database is set to
a specific CAS server, their profile will not be updated if you later change this setting using the
`Set-MailboxDatabase` cmdlet. In this situation, you would need to reconfigure the user's
Outlook profile and set the server name to the FQDN of the CAS array, or you could run a
repair in Outlook to correct the setting. Either way, this requires you or a member of your staff
to touch each workstation used by the affected users. Therefore, it is best practice to set the
RPC Client Access server to the correct value before allowing any users connect to Exchange
using Outlook.

If you've already created multiple mailbox databases across multiple mailbox servers and
have not already created a CAS array, this could end up being a problem for you on the client
side, but updating all of the databases with a new RPC Client Access server setting after the

fact is very easy to do. Let's say that you've created multiple mailbox databases located on several mailbox servers in the default Active Directory site prior to creating a CAS array. You can use the following code to update each database in the site:

```
Get-ExchangeServer |
  Where-Object {$_.Site.Name -eq 'Default-First-Site-Name' `
    -and $_.ServerRole -match 'Mailbox'
  } |
Get-MailboxDatabase |
  Set-MailboxDatabase -RpcClientAccessServer outlook.contoso.com
```

In this example, we first use the `Get-ExchangeServer` cmdlet to create a collection of mailbox servers. You can see that we're filtering two properties, output by this cmdlet. First, we're checking the `Site.Name` property to make sure it is set to `Default-First-Site-Name`, and second, we're filtering the `ServerRole` property to ensure that we're only going to retrieve servers running the Mailbox role. When filtering the `ServerRole` property, you can see that we're using the `-match` operator. This is because comparing the `ServerRole` property using the `-eq` (equals) operator will not evaluate to `$true` if the server is hosting multiple roles. The output of the command returns one or more mailbox servers in the default Active Directory site. Each server object returned is then piped down to the `Get-MailboxDatabase` cmdlet, which retrieves every database hosted by each mailbox server. Finally, those objects are piped down to the `Set-MailboxDatabase` cmdlet, which configures the `RPCClientAccessServer` property of each database in the default site to the `outlook.contoso.com` CAS array.

See also

▸ *Building a Windows NLB cluster for CAS servers* in *Chapter 9, High Availability*

▸ *Creating an RPC Client Access array*

Configuring RPC encryption requirements

In an Exchange 2010 environment, you can control whether or not Outlook clients are required to use encrypted RPC connections. Since this cannot be configured from the Exchange Management Console, you'll need to use the shell in order to modify these settings. Use the steps in this recipe to control RPC encryption requirements using the Exchange Management Shell.

How to do it.

To enable RPC encryption for a CAS server, use the `Set-RPCClientAccess` cmdlet:

```
Set-RpcClientAccess -Server cas1 -EncryptionRequired $true
```

This enables RPC encryption for the `CAS1` client access server.

How it works...

In the RTM version of Exchange 2010, CAS servers were configured to require RPC encryption. Since Outlook 2007 and 2010 are configured by default with encryption enabled, those clients worked without any issues. On the other hand, many organizations are still running Outlook 2003, which by default is not configured to encrypt RPC connections. As such, since the RPC encryption requirements on CAS servers were enabled out of the box, many users running Outlook 2003 could not open their mailboxes. This required administrators to either deploy the client side encryption setting through group policy or to use the command in the previous example to disable RPC encryption on each CAS server so that clients could connect.

In Exchange 2010 SP1, Microsoft decided, due to customer feedback, that the RPC encryption requirement should be disabled by default. So, if you are doing a new deployment of Exchange 2010 SP1, your Outlook 2003 clients will be able to connect just fine after their mailboxes have been moved to an Exchange 2010 SP1 server. Of course, for the most secure environment, you'll want to require RPC encryption and configure your Outlook 2003 clients for RPC encryption.

Keep in mind that any settings that are enabled on an RTM installation will be carried over when upgrading to Exchange 2010 SP1. If you deploy Exchange 2010 RTM and do not modify the default settings, CAS servers will require RPC encryption, even after deploying SP1.

If you have many CAS servers and you'd like to modify this setting in a bulk operation, you can take advantage of PowerShell's pipelining capabilities and looping constructs. For example, the following code would disable RPC encryption on all CAS servers:

```
Get-ClientAccessServer |
    Set-RpcClientAccess -EncryptionRequired $false
```

Additionally, you can accomplish the same thing for all servers in a particular CAS array using the following commands:

```
$servers = (Get-ClientAccessArray -Identity CASArray01).Members
$servers | %{
    Set-RpcClientAccess -Server $_.name -EncryptionRequired $true
}
```

In the previous example, we first create a collection that stores each member of the CAS `Array01` CAS array in the `$servers` variable. We then pipe that object to `ForEach-Object` (using the `%` alias) and then run the `Set-RpcClientAccess` cmdlet to configure the encryption requirement for each server in the collection.

There's more...

As you may already know, all client connections now go through the CAS server role in Exchange 2010. Actually, the truth is that, this statement is not completely accurate. If you are still supporting and using Public Folders in your environment, clients will connect directly to mailbox servers in order to access Public Folder data. In many Exchange 2010 environments, it's not uncommon to see the CAS role running on separate servers to those running the Mailbox role. In this scenario, if you are using Public Folders, you would need to control the encryption requirements on both the CAS and Mailbox server roles, since the client would be establishing RPC connections to both.

In order to control the encryption requirements for the Mailbox server role, use the `Set-MailboxServer` cmdlet, as shown in the following example:

```
Set-MailboxServer -Identity mbx1 -MAPIEncryptionRequired $true
```

After running the previous command, Outlook clients connecting to the `mbx1` server for Public Folder access would need to have the "Encrypt data between Microsoft Outlook and Microsoft Exchange" setting checked in order for RPC encryption to be enabled on the client. As discussed previously, this is enabled by default for both Outlook 2007 and 2010 and is disabled by default for Outlook 2003 clients.

See also

  ▸ *Creating an RPC Client Access array*

Managing ActiveSync, OWA, POP3, and IMAP4 mailbox settings

You can use the Exchange Management Shell to configure a user's ability to access CAS services such as ActiveSync, OWA, POP3, and IMAP4. You can also allow or disallow MAPI connectivity and the ability to connect to Exchange using Outlook Anywhere. In this recipe, you'll learn techniques used to control these settings, whether it is done interactively through the shell or using an automated script.

How to do it...

To control access to CAS services for a mailbox, use the `Set-CASMailbox` cmdlet. Here's an example of how you might use this cmdlet:

```
Set-CasMailbox -Identity 'Dave Smith' `
-OWAEnabled $false `
-ActiveSyncEnabled $false `
-PopEnabled $false `
-ImapEnabled $false
```

This command will disable Outlook Web App (OWA), ActiveSync, POP3, and IMAP4 for the mailbox belonging to Dave Smith.

How it works...

When you create a mailbox, OWA, ActiveSync, POP3, IMAP4, and MAPI access are enabled by default. For most organizations, these default settings are acceptable, but, if that is not the case for your environment, you can use the `Set-CASMailbox` cmdlet to enable or disable access to these services. This can be done for individual users as needed, or you can do this in bulk.

For example, let's say that all of the users in the *Sales* department should only access Exchange internally through Outlook using MAPI, POP, and IMAP. We can use a simple pipeline command to make this change:

```
Get-Mailbox -Filter {Office -eq 'Sales'} |
   Set-CasMailbox -OWAEnabled $false `
   -ActiveSyncEnabled $false `
   -PopEnabled $true `
   -ImapEnabled $true
```

As you can see, we use the `Get-Mailbox` cmdlet and specify a filter that limits the results to users that have their `Office` attribute in Active Directory set to *Sales*. The results are then piped to the `Set-CASMailbox` cmdlet and access to the CAS services is modified for each mailbox. Notice that this time we've used additional parameters to allow POP and IMAP access.

Alternatively, you may want to block MAPI access and only allow users in your organization to connect through OWA. In this case, use the following one-liner:

```
Get-Mailbox -RecipientTypeDetails UserMailbox |
   Set-CasMailbox -OWAEnabled $true `
   -ActiveSyncEnabled $false `
   -PopEnabled $false `
   -ImapEnabled $false `
   -MAPIEnabled $false
```

This time we use `Get-Mailbox` to retrieve all the mailboxes in the organization. We're using the `-RecipientTypeDetails` parameter to specify that we want to find user mailboxes and exclude other types such as discovery and resource mailboxes. The results are piped to the `Set-CASMailbox` cmdlet and access to CAS services is configured with the required settings. You'll notice that this time we've included the `-MAPIEnabled` parameter and set its value to `$false` so that users will only be able to access Exchange through OWA.

There's more...

If you are planning on provisioning all of your new mailboxes through an automated script, you may want to configure these settings at mailbox creation time. Consider the following script named `New-MailboxScript.ps1`:

```
param(
   $name,
   $password,
   $upn,
   $alias,
   $first,
   $last
)


$pass = ConvertTo-SecureString -AsPlainText $password -Force

$mailbox = New-Mailbox -UserPrincipalName $upn `
-Alias $alias `
-Name "$first $last" `
-Password $pass `
-FirstName $first `
-LastName $last

Set-CasMailbox -Identity $mailbox `
-OWAEnabled $false `
-ActiveSyncEnabled $false `
-PopEnabled $false `
-ImapEnabled $false `
-MAPIBlockOutlookRpcHttp $true
```

This script can be used to create a mailbox and configure access to CAS services based on your requirements. If the script is saved in the root of the `C:` drive, the syntax would look like this:

```
[PS] C:\>.\New-MailboxScript.ps1 -first John -last Smith -alias jsmith -
password P@ssw0rd01 -upn jsmith@contoso.com
```

There are basically two phases to the script. First, the mailbox for the user is created using the `New-Mailbox` cmdlet. In this example, the `New-Mailbox` result is saved in the `$mailbox` variable, and the mailbox is created using the parameters provided by the user running the script. Once the mailbox is created, the `Set-CASMailbox` cmdlet is used to configure access to CAS services and uses the `$mailbox` variable to identify the mailbox to modify when the command executes.

See also

> ▸ *Adding, modifying, and removing mailboxes* in *Chapter 3, Managing Recipients*

Setting internal and external CAS URLs

Each CAS server has multiple virtual directories, some of which can only be modified through the Exchange Management Shell. Scripting the changes made to both the internal and external URLs can be a big time-saver, especially when deploying multiple servers in a CAS array. In this recipe, you will learn how to use the set of cmdlets that are needed to modify both the internal and external URLs for each CAS server virtual directory.

How to do it...

To change the external URL of the OWA virtual directory for a server named `CAS1`, use the following command:

```
Set-OwaVirtualDirectory -Identity 'CAS1\owa (Default Web Site)' `
-ExternalUrl https://mail.contoso.com/owa
```

After the change has been made, we can view the configuration using the `Get-OwaVirtualDirectory` cmdlet:

```
[PS] C:\>Get-OwaVirtualDirectory -Server cas1 | fl ExternalUrl


ExternalUrl : https://mail.contoso.com/owa
```

How it works...

Each Client Access server hosts virtual directories in IIS that support Outlook Web App (OWA), Exchange Control Panel (ECP), ActiveSync, Offline Address Book (OAB), and Exchange Web Services (EWS). Each of these services has an associated cmdlet set that can be used to manage the settings of each virtual directory. One of the most common configuration changes made during the deployment process is modifying the internal and external URLs for each of these services. The required configuration varies greatly depending on a number of factors in your environment, especially in larger multi-site environments.

The following cmdlets can be used to modify several settings for each virtual directory, including the values for the internal and external URLs:

- ► `Set-ActiveSyncVirtualDirectory`: Used to configure the internal and external URL values for the /Microsoft-Server-ActiveSync virtual directory. Use the `InternalUrl` and `ExternalUrl` parameters to change the values.

- ► `Set-EcpVirtualDirectory`: Used to configure the internal and external URL values for the /ECP virtual directory. Use the `InternalUrl` and `ExternalUrl` parameters to change the values.

- ► `Set-OabVirtualDirectory`: Used to configure the internal and external URL values for the /OAB virtual directory. Use the `InternalUrl` and `ExternalUrl` parameters to change the values.

- ► `Set-OwaVirtualDirectory`: Used to configure the internal and external URL values for the /OWA virtual directory. Use the `InternalUrl` and `ExternalUrl` parameters to change the values.

- ► `Set-WebServicesVirtualDirectory`: Used to configure the internal and external URL values for the /EWS virtual directory. Use the `InternalUrl` and `ExternalUrl` parameters to change the values.

When running each of these cmdlets, you need to identify the virtual directory in question. For example, when modifying the external URL for the ECP virtual directory, the command might look similar to this:

```
Set-EcpVirtualDirectory -Identity 'CAS1\ecp (Default Web Site)' `
-ExternalUrl https://mail.contoso.com/ecp
```

The syntax is similar to the first example where we modified the OWA virtual directory; the only difference is that the cmdlet name and `ExternalUrl` value have changed. Notice that the identity for the virtual directory is in the format of `ServerName\VirtualDirectoryName (WebsiteName)`. The reason this needs to be done is because it's possible, but not very common, for a particular CAS server to be running more than one site in IIS containing virtual directories for each of these CAS services.

If you are like most folks and have only the default web site running in IIS, you can also take advantage of the pipeline if you forget the syntax needed to specify the identity of the virtual directory. For example:

```
Get-EcpVirtualDirectory -Server cas1 |
    Set-EcpVirtualDirectory -ExternalUrl https://mail.contoso.com/ecp
```

The given pipeline command makes the same change as shown previously. This time we're using the `Get-EcpVirtualDirectory` cmdlet with the `-Server` parameter to identify the CAS server. We then pipe the resulting object to the `Set-EcpVirtualDirectory` cmdlet that makes the change to the `ExternalUrl` value.

There's more...

If you are allowing access to Exchange through Outlook Anywhere, you'll need to configure the external URLs that will be handed to Outlook clients for services such as ECP, OAB, and EWS. These URLs may need to point to a FQDN that resolves to a load balancer VIP or to your reverse proxy infrastructure, such as ISA or TMG.

In addition, you'll probably want to configure your internal URLs to point to a FQDN that resolves to your internal load-balancer VIP. In this situation, you want to make sure you do not modify the internal URL for both the OWA and ECP virtual directories in non-internet-facing sites. This is because OWA and ECP connections from the internet-facing CAS server will be proxied to the servers in the non-internet facing sites, and, if the internal FQDN of the CAS server is not set on each these virtual directories, Kerberos authentication will fail and the user will not be able to access their mailbox.

Finally, for load-balanced CAS servers, you'll want to configure the AutoDiscover internal URL so that it also points to a FQDN that resolves to your load balancer VIP. The syntax for this would look like the following:

```
Set-ClientAccessServer -Identity cas1 `
-AutoDiscoverServiceInternalUri `
https://mail.contoso.com/Autodiscover/Autodiscover.xml
```

Of course, you'll need to make all changes to internal and external URLs on all CAS servers in the array.

Command syntax for the remaining virtual directories

We've already looked at the syntax for modifying both OWA and ECP and internal and external URLs; now let's look at how we can do this for the remaining virtual directories. In these examples, we'll configure the external URL value using the `-ExternalUrl` parameter. If you need to modify the internal URL, simply use the `-InternalUrl` parameter.

To configure the external URL for the OAB, use the following syntax:

```
Set-OABVirtualDirectory -Identity "cas1\oab (Default Web Site)" `
-ExternalUrl https://mail.contoso.com/oab
```

To configure the external URL for the ActiveSync virtual directory, use the following syntax:

```
Set-ActivesyncVirtualDirectory -Identity `
"cas1\Microsoft-Server-ActiveSync (Default Web Site)" `
-ExternalURL https://mail.contoso.com/Microsoft-Server-Activesync
```

To configure the EWS virtual directory, use the following syntax:

```
Set-WebServicesVirtualDirectory -Identity `
"cas1\EWS (Default Web Site)" `
-ExternalUrl https://mail.contoso.com/ews/exchange.asmx
```

In each example, we're setting the value on the CAS1 server. When running these commands or using them in a script, replace the server name with the name of the appropriate CAS server.

See also

▶ *Generating a certificate request* in *Chapter 10, Exchange Security*

▶ *Installing certificates and enabling services* in *Chapter 10, Exchange Security*

▶ *Importing certificates on multiple exchange servers* in *Chapter 10, Exchange Security*

Managing Outlook Anywhere settings

With the release of Exchange 2007 and continuing with Exchange 2010, Microsoft has renamed the RPC over HTTP feature to Outlook Anywhere. This feature allows Outlook clients to connect to Exchange through RPCs encapsulated into an HTTPS connection. This allows easy external access to Exchange from Outlook, as there is no need to open RPC ports on firewalls. In this recipe, we'll take a look at how you can use the Exchange Management Shell to manage Outlook Anywhere settings.

How to do it...

To enable Outlook Anywhere, use the Enable-OutlookAnywhere cmdlet as shown in the following example:

```
Enable-OutlookAnywhere -Server cas1 `
-ExternalHostname mail.contoso.com `
-ClientAuthenticationMethod Basic `
-SSLOffloading $false
```

In this example, Outlook Anywhere is enabled on the CAS1 server.

How it works...

Before enabling Outlook Anywhere, there are two prerequisites that need to be met. First, you need to ensure that your CAS server has a valid SSL certificate installed from a certificate authority (CA) that is trusted by your client machines. Exchange installs a self-signed certificate by default, but this will not be trusted by client workstations.

In addition, you'll need to make sure that Microsoft Windows RPC over HTTP Proxy component is installed on the server. This is typically done before the installation of Exchange when all of the operating system prerequisites are installed.

When running the Enable-OutlookAnywhere cmdlet, you can see that we specified the ExternalHostname. This will be the FQDN that Outlook clients use to connect to Exchange. You'll need to make sure that you have a DNS record created for this FQDN that resolves to your CAS server or to your reverse proxy infrastructure, such as ISA or TMG.

When specifying a value for the ClientAuthenticationMethod parameter, you'll want to use either Basic or NTLM. This setting determines how users authenticate to Outlook Anywhere. When using Basic authentication, the user's password is sent to the server in plain text, but the connection is secured by SSL. If you have workstations that are not domain-joined that will be connecting to Exchange through Outlook Anywhere, you'll need to use Basic authentication.

If only domain-joined clients will be connecting to Outlook Anywhere, such as roaming users with laptops that connect from home, using NTLM authentication is a much more secure option for the ClientAuthenticationMethod. When using NTLM, a user's password is not sent to the server; instead, NTLM sends a hashed value of the user's credentials to the server. Another benefit to using NTLM is that Outlook clients will not be prompted for their credentials when connecting with Outlook Anywhere. Keep in mind that if you are publishing Outlook Anywhere with a reverse proxy solution such as ISA or TMG, you'll need to use **Kerberos Constrained Delegation** (**KCD**), which allows the ISA or TMG server to request a Kerberos service ticket from Active Directory on behalf of the user. Also, remember that NTLM authentication may not work correctly through some firewalls; check with your firewall manufacturer's documentation for details.

Finally, SSLOffloading allows the CAS server to offload the encryption and decryption of the SSL connections to a third party device. Unless you have an SSL offloading solution in place, set the -SSLOffloading parameter to $false.

There's more...

In addition to enabling Outlook Anywhere from the shell, we can also perform some other routine tasks. For example, to view the Outlook Anywhere configuration, use the Get-OutlookAnywhere cmdlet:

```
[PS] C:\>Get-OutlookAnywhere | fl ServerName,ExternalHostname
```

```
ServerName        : CAS1
ExternalHostname : mail.contoso.com
```

The `Get-OutlookAnywhere` cmdlet will return configuration information for servers that have the Outlook Anywhere feature enabled.

If at any time you need to change the authentication method or external host name for Outlook Anywhere, you can use the `Set-OutlookAnywhere` cmdlet:

```
Set-OutlookAnywhere -Identity 'CAS1\Rpc (Default Web Site)' `
-ExternalHostname 'outlook.contoso.com'
```

Notice that the identity of the server needs to be specified in the format of *ServerName\ VirtualDirectoryName (WebsiteName)*.

Finally, you can disable Outlook Anywhere on a server using the `Disable-OutlookAnywhere` cmdlet:

```
Disable-OutlookAnywhere -Server cas1 -Confirm:$false
```

In this case, you only need to specify the server name using the `-Server` parameter when disabling Outlook Anywhere.

See also

- ▶ *Generating a certificate request* in *Chapter 10*, *Exchange Security*
- ▶ *Installing certificates and enabling services* in *Chapter 10*, *Exchange Security*
- ▶ *Importing certificates on multiple exchange servers* in *Chapter 10*, *Exchange Security*

Blocking Outlook clients from connecting to Exchange

Exchange gives you plenty of options to block clients from connecting to mailboxes, depending on the version of the Outlook client and the method used to access the mailbox. In this recipe, you'll learn how to configure these options using the Exchange Management Shell.

How to do it...

1. The `Set-CASMailbox` can be used to block MAPI access to mailboxes based on several factors. For example, we can prevent an individual user from using Outlook to connect using Outlook Anywhere:

   ```
   Set-CASMailbox -Identity dsmith -MAPIBlockOutlookRpcHttp $true
   ```

2. In addition, we can also prevent a user whose Outlook is not configured in cached mode from connecting to their mailbox using the following command:

   ```
   Set-CASMailbox -Identity dsmith `
   -MAPIBlockOutlookNonCachedMode $true
   ```

   In both cases, the user can still access their mailbox using a standard MAPI connection, as long as the `MAPIEnabled` property is set to the default setting of `$true`.

3. You can also block users from connecting from clients based on their version. The following command will block all Outlook versions except 2003, 2007, and 2010 for every mailbox in the organization:

   ```
   Get-CASMailbox -Resultsize Unlimited |
      Set-CASMailbox -MAPIBlockOutlookVersions '-5.9.9;7.0.0-10.9.9'
   ```

4. To find all mailboxes in an organization that have `MAPIBlockOutlookVersions` defined, run the following command:

   ```
   Get-CASMailbox -ResultSize Unlimited |
      ?{$_.MAPIBlockOutlookVersions}
   ```

5. To remove the restriction for a single mailbox, use the following command:

   ```
   Set-CASMailbox dsmith -MAPIBlockOutlookVersions $null
   ```

6. To remove the restriction for the entire organization:

   ```
   Get-CASMailbox -ResultSize Unlimited |
      Set-CASMailbox -MAPIBlockOutlookVersions $null
   ```

How it works...

The `Set-CASMailbox` cmdlet allows you to configure which protocols and services a particular mailbox user can access. To determine the existing settings, we can use the `Get-CASMailbox` cmdlet. For instance, if you need to retrieve all users that have been blocked from connecting to their mailboxes in non-cached mode, use the command shown:

```
Get-CASMailbox | Where-Object{$_.MAPIBlockOutlookNonCachedMode}
```

To find all mailboxes blocked from using Outlook Anywhere, the command is almost identical; just reference the correct property name:

```
Get-CASMailbox | Where-Object{$_.MAPIBlockOutlookRpcHttp}
```

In both examples, we pipe the `Get-CASMailbox` to the `Where-Object` cmdlet. Inside the filter we're checking to see if the property values evaluate as `$true`. If that is the case, the command will return a list of users who have the corresponding setting enabled.

As always, we can use pipelining to enable or disable these settings for multiple users in a single command. Let's say that we want to block all of the users in the *Sales* OU from using Outlook Anywhere:

```
Get-CASMailbox -OrganizationalUnit contoso.com/Sales |
    Set-CASMailbox -MAPIBlockOutlookRpcHttp $true
```

To remove this restriction, use the same command but this time set the parameter value to `$false`:

```
Get-CASMailbox -OrganizationalUnit uss.local/Sales |
    Set-CASMailbox -MAPIBlockOutlookRpcHttp $false
```

In both cases, the `Get-CASMailbox` cmdlet retrieves every mailbox from the *Sales* OU and pipes the object's output by the command to the `Set-CASMailbox` cmdlet that then makes the change.

As we saw earlier, Outlook client versions can be blocked on a per-mailbox basis using the `Set-CASMailbox` cmdlet. This is done by specifying the client version using the `MAPIBlockOutlookVersions` parameter.

In Exchange 2007, you could check the `ClientVersion` property returned by the `Get-LogonStatistics` cmdlet to determine version numbers used by Outlook clients in the organization. In Exchange 2010 SP1, the `ClientVersion` will be reported based on the CAS server making the connection to the mailbox server, not the actual Outlook client. If you need to determine the specific client versions in your environment, you can use the **Help | About** screen in Outlook to determine the exact version number.

A version number is made up of a Major, Minor, and Build number. Here are a few version numbers for some commonly used-versions of Outlook:

- Outlook 2003 SP2 - 11.6568.6568
- Outlook 2007 RTM - 12.4518.1014
- Outlook 2010 RTM – 14.0.4760.1000

The Major build numbers are consistent across the entire Office suite and never change. For example, for Office 2003 the Build number is 11, for Office 2007 the Build number is 12, and for Office 2010 the Build number is 14.

The Minor and Build numbers will change depending on the hotfixes and service packs deployed to the clients. Therefore, the `-MAPIBlockOutlookVersions` parameter will accept a range of values that will allow you to be very specific about which versions should be blocked. You can even specify multiple version ranges and separate each one using a semi-colon.

For example, the following command can be used to block access to Exchange for all versions of Outlook below 2007 and 2010:

```
Set-CASMailbox dsmith -MAPIBlockOutlookVersions '-5.9.9;7.0.0-11.9.9'
```

As you can see here, we've specified two values. The first value indicates that any client version below 5.9.9 will be unable to connect to this mailbox. The second value specifies a range from 7 to 11.9.9 which effectively blocks all access to any client versioned lower than 12.x.x, except for those versioned at 6.x.x. This allows only Outlook 2007 and 2010 clients to connect to this mailbox. It also allows Exchange server MAPI connections from other servers, identified using 6.x.x version numbers.

Keep in mind that when you are making these changes they will not take effect right away. If you want to force this change so it is effective immediately, restart the RPC Client Access service on the CAS server used to access the mailbox. Make sure to do this outside of production hours as it will knock every user connected to that CAS server offline.

There's more...

In addition to blocking Outlook versions at the mailbox level, we can also block them at the server level. Since the MAPI client endpoint is now at the CAS role for mailbox access, we can use the `Set-RPCClientAccess` cmdlet to accomplish this.

```
Set-RpcClientAccess -Server cas1 `
-BlockedClientVersions '-5.9.9;7.0.0-13.9.9'
```

You can see here that we use the `BlockedClientVersions` parameter to define the client versions that should be blocked, and it works in exactly the same way as it does when using the `Set-CASMailbox` cmdlet. In this example, all client versions below Outlook 2010, with the exception of client versions 6.x.x, will be blocked at the CAS server level. Notice that the server name has been specified with this command and you'll need to run it against each CAS server that should block specific Outlook versions.

Reporting on active OWA and RPC connections

One of the nice things about using PowerShell to manage Exchange is that you have a great deal of flexibility when it comes to solving problems. When the Exchange Management Shell does not provide a cmdlet that specifically meets your needs, you can often tap into other resources accessible through PowerShell. This recipe provides a great example for this. In this section, we'll use PowerShell to query performance counter data to determine the number of active OWA and RPC connections on one or more CAS servers.

How to do it...

1. To determine the number of users currently logged into OWA on a CAS server, use the following command syntax:

```
Get-Counter -Counter '\\cas1\MSExchange OWA\Current Users'
```

This retrieves the total number of users logged into OWA on the CAS1 server. The output from this command will look similar to the following:

```
Timestamp                CounterSamples

---------                --------------

11/30/2010 11:57:59 AM   \\cas1\msexchange owa\current users :
                         4
```

Viewing the output, we can see that four users are currently logged on to OWA.

2. To find the total number of RPC connections, we simply need to use another performance counter:

```
Get-Counter '\\cas1\MSExchange RpcClientAccess\User Count'
```

Similar to the previous example, the total number of RPC connects will be reported.

How it works...

The Get-Counter cmdlet is a PowerShell v2 core cmdlet that allows you to retrieve performance counter data from both local and remote machines. In the previous example, we collected the total of current OWA users using the \MSExchange OWA\Current Users counter and the total number of RPC connections using the MSExchange RpcClientAccess\User Count counter on the CAS1 server.

In both of these examples, we've specified the computer name in the counter name assigned to the -Counter parameter. Another way to gather performance counter data from a remote computer is to use the -ComputerName parameter:

```
Get-Counter 'MSExchange OWA\Current Unique Users' `
 -ComputerName cas1,cas2
```

Notice that in the alternate syntax used previously we've removed the computer name from the counter name and have assigned a list of server names using the -ComputerName parameter. This is a quick way to check the number of connections on multiple computers.

There are many Exchange-related performance counters on each Exchange server. You can also use the `Get-Counter` cmdlet to discover these counters:

```
Get-Counter -ListSet *owa* -ComputerName cas1 |
  Select-Object -expand paths
```

This will do a wildcard search and return a list of counters on the specified server that have the letters *owa* in their name. You can use this syntax to quickly find counter names that can be used with the `Get-Counter` cmdlet.

There's more...

To create more advanced and customizable reports, we can create a PowerShell function that returns a custom object with only the information we're interested in. Add the following function to your shell session:

```
function Get-CASActiveUsers {
  [CmdletBinding()]
  param(
    [Parameter(Position=0,
      ValueFromPipelineByPropertyName=$true,
      Mandatory=$true)]
    [string[]]
    $Name
  )

  process {
    $Name | %{
      $RPC = Get-Counter "\MSExchange RpcClientAccess\User Count" `
      -ComputerName $_

      $OWA = Get-Counter "\MSExchange OWA\Current Unique Users" `
      -ComputerName $_

      New-Object PSObject -Property @{
        Server = $_
        'RPC Client Access' = $RPC.CounterSamples[0].CookedValue
        'Outlook Web App' = $OWA.CounterSamples[0].CookedValue
      }
    }
  }
}
```

You can call the function and provide one or more CAS server names that you'd like to generate the report for, as shown in the following screenshot:

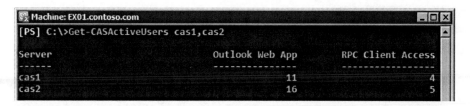

If you look closely at the code in the function you'll notice that we've added some attributes to the $Name parameter. As you can see, in addition to being a mandatory parameter, it also accepts its value from the pipeline by property name. This means that, instead of calling the function and providing a list of server names, we can leverage the objects that are returned by the Get-ClientAccessServer cmdlet to quickly generate a report using a pipeline command:

```
Machine: EX01.contoso.com                                    _ □ X
[PS] C:\>Get-ClientAccessServer | Get-CASActiveUsers

Server                        Outlook Web App        RPC Client Access
------                        ---------------        -----------------
cas1                                       23                       11
cas2                                       15                       11
cas3                                        6                        6
cas4                                       17                        4
```

You can continue to pipe this command down to Export-CSV or ConvertTo-Html to generate an external report file that can be viewed outside of the shell.

See also

▸   *Creating PowerShell functions* in *Chapter 1, PowerShell Key Concepts*

Controlling ActiveSync device access

With the increase of smartphones being deployed and the fact that ActiveSync can now be used across a wide variety of mobile device vendors, Exchange 2010 introduces new functions that allow you to control which devices are able to get connected. Using device access rules, you can define the specific devices or device types that can form an ActiveSync partnership with an Exchange server. This recipe will explore the options that can be used to allow, block, or quarantine ActiveSync devices using the Exchange Management Shell.

How to do it...

1. By default, there is an organization-wide configuration setting that will allow any ActiveSync device to connect to Exchange. You can modify this so that all devices are initially quarantined, and need to be approved by an administrator before they can gain access. To implement this, first run the following command:

```
Set-ActiveSyncOrganizationSettings –DefaultAccessLevel Quarantine `
-AdminMailRecipients administrator@contoso.com
```

   After the previous command completes, all devices that attempt to form an ActiveSync device partnership will be quarantined. When a device is quarantined, the address provided by the `-AdminMailRecipients` parameter will be notified via e-mail. The user will also receive a message on their mobile device informing them that access needs to be granted by an administrator before they'll be able to access any content.

2. Based on the information in the e-mail message, the administrator can choose to enable the device using the `Set-CASMailbox` cmdlet:

```
Set-CASMailbox -Identity dsmith `
-ActiveSyncAllowedDeviceIDs BAD73E6E02156460E800185977C03182
```

   Once the command has been run, the user will be able to connect.

How it works...

In Exchange 2010 RTM, there was no interface to manage any of these settings, and all of these steps had to be performed as shown here using the shell. In Exchange 2010 SP1, you can configure all of these settings in the **Exchange Control Panel** (**ECP**), and, of course, the cmdlets can still be used if you want to do this work from the shell.

When configuring the ActiveSync organization settings, you have the option of adding a custom message that will be sent to the user when they receive the e-mail notification explaining that their device has been quarantined. Use the `-UserMailInsert` parameter when running the `Set-ActiveSyncOrganizationSettings` cmdlet to configure this setting:

```
Set-ActiveSyncOrganizationSettings –DefaultAccessLevel Quarantine `
-AdminMailRecipients helpdesk@contoso.com `
-UserMailInsert 'Call the Help Desk for immediate assistance'
```

In addition to the administrative e-mail notifications, you can find all the devices that are currently in a quarantined state using the `Get-ActiveSync` device cmdlet:

```
Get-ActiveSyncDevice |
  ?{$_.DeviceAccessState -eq 'Quarantined'} |
      fl UserDisplayName,DeviceAccessState,DeviceID
```

This command retrieves ActiveSync devices and is filtered on the `DeviceAccessState` property. The output will provide the username, device access state, and the `DeviceID` that can be used to allow access using the `Set-CASMailbox` cmdlet.

There's more...

Manual approval of ActiveSync devices may not be something you want to take on as an administrative task. An alternative to this is to use device access rules. For instance, let's say that you want to block all ActiveSync devices that are not PocketPC devices. You could set the `DefaultAccessLevel` for the organization to `Block` and create a device access rule allowing only those devices:

```
New-ActiveSyncDeviceAccessRule -QueryString PocketPC `
-Characteristic DeviceModel `
-AccessLevel Allow
```

You can create multiple access rules for different types of devices if needed. To determine the device type, you can use the `Get-ActiveSyncDevice` cmdlet. The property values for `DeviceOS`, `DeviceType`, `DeviceUserAgent`, or `DeviceModel` can be used with the `-QueryString` parameter to define the device type when creating a device access rule.

See also

  ▸ *Reporting on ActiveSync devices*
  ▸ *Managing ActiveSync, OWA, POP3, and IMAP4 mailbox settings*

Reporting on ActiveSync devices

The Exchange Management Shell provides several cmdlets that can be used for generating reports. We can obtain information about users and their devices and we can also generate reports based on end-user activity and server usage. In this recipe, we'll take a look at how we can use these cmdlets to generate multiple ActiveSync reports from the Exchange Management Shell.

How to do it...

1. To generate a report for an individual user's device synchronization status, use the following command:

    ```
    Get-ActiveSyncDeviceStatistics -Mailbox dsmith
    ```

2. This cmdlet will output a lot of information, some of which may not be very interesting. You can limit the data returned by selecting only the properties that provide useful information:

```
Get-ActiveSyncDeviceStatistics -Mailbox dsmith |
   select LastSuccessSync,Status,DevicePhoneNumber,DeviceType
```

The output for the previous command will look similar to the following:

```
LastSuccessSync            Status DevicePhoneNumber DeviceType

---------------            ------ ----------------- ----------

12/31/2010 1:26:45 AM DeviceOk *****0504           PocketPC
```

4. To export this information, you can pipe the command even further to the Export-CSV cmdlet:

```
Get-ActiveSyncDeviceStatistics -Mailbox dsmith |
   select LastSuccessSync,Status,DevicePhoneNumber,DeviceType |
       Export-CSV -Path c:\report.csv -NoType
```

How it works...

Using the Get-ActiveSyncDeviceStatistics cmdlet, we can retrieve the mobile phones that are configured to synchronize with a particular user's mailbox. As you can see from the previous examples, it's quite easy to generate a report for an individual user. This cmdlet requires that you either specify the identity of the ActiveSync device or the mailbox of the owner. In order to generate reports based on statistics for multiple devices, we have a couple of options.

First, we can use the Get-ActiveSyncDevice cmdlet to retrieve a list of allowed devices and then pipe the results to the Get-ActiveSyncDeviceStatistics cmdlet:

```
$dev = Get-ActiveSyncDevice | ?{$_.DeviceAccessState -eq 'Allowed'}
$dev | ForEach-Object {
  $mailbox = $_.UserDisplayName
  $stats = Get-ActiveSyncDeviceStatistics –Identity $_
  $stats | Select-Object @{n="Mailbox";e={$mailbox}},
    LastSuccessSync,
    Status,
    DevicePhoneNumber,
    DeviceType
}
```

This code retrieves all the ActiveSync devices with the Allowed access state. We loop through each device, retrieve the device statistics for each one, and return several properties that provide details about the user and the status of their device. Notice that, in the example, we're using a calculated property to return the mailbox name since that information is not included in the output of the Get-ActiveSyncDeviceStatistics cmdlet.

The other method for obtaining this information is by using the Get-CASMailbox cmdlet to find all users with an ActiveSync device partnership, and then sending those objects down the pipeline to the Get-ActiveSyncDeviceStatistics cmdlet:

```
$mbx = Get-CASMailbox | ?{$_.HasActiveSyncDevicePartnership}
$mbx | ForEach-Object {
  $mailbox = $_.Name
  $stats = Get-ActiveSyncDeviceStatistics -Mailbox $mailbox
  $stats | Select-Object @{n="Mailbox";e={$mailbox}},
    LastSuccessSync,
    Status,
    DevicePhoneNumber,
    DeviceType
}
```

Similar to the previous example, we loop through each mailbox, retrieve the ActiveSync statistics, and then return the same properties as before. This version is considerably slower since it has to first check every mailbox to determine if a device partnership exists, but if you need specific filtering capabilities based on the properties returned by the Get-CASMailbox cmdlet, this may be a useful method.

There's more...

The Exchange Management Shell also provides the Export-ActiveSyncLog cmdlet that can be used to generate reports based on ActiveSync usage. The cmdlet generates reports based on IIS log files and then outputs six separate CSV files that contain detailed information about the usage of ActiveSync devices:

- Users.csv: Provides details on ActiveSync usage for each user that includes the number of sent and received items

- UserAgents.csv: Provides details on the various user agents used by devices to access Exchange

- StatusCodes.csv: Provides the HTTP response codes issued to ActiveSync clients

- Servers.csv: Provides details on server usage including total bytes sent and received

- PolicyCompliance.csv: Provides details on ActiveSync device compliance such as the total number of compliant, non-compliant, and partially compliant devices

- Hourly.csv: Provides an hourly breakdown of device synchronization activity

The cmdlet supports a number of parameters that can be used to generate reports. For example, the following command generates reports for ActiveSync activity taking place on December 30, 2010.

```
Export-ActiveSyncLog `
-Filename C:\inetpub\logs\LogFiles\W3SVC1\u_ex101230.log `
-OutputPath c:\report
```

When running this command, make sure that the directory specified for the output path has already been created. The given command generates the six CSV files discussed previously in the `c:\report` folder.

To generate reports for multiple log files, you'll need to do a little extra work. For example:

```
$path = "C:\inetpub\logs\LogFiles\W3SVC1\"
Get-ChildItem -Path $path -Filter u_ex1012*.log | %{
  Export-ActiveSyncLog -Filename $_.fullname `
  -OutputPrefix $_.basename `
  -OutputPath c:\report
}
```

Here we're using the `Get-ChildItem` cmdlet to retrieve a list of log files from December of 2010. Each time we run the `Export-ActiveSyncLog` cmdlet for a log file, a new set of six CSV reports will be generated. Since we can only define one `OutputPath`, we use the log file base name as a prefix for each CSV report file generated. After the cmdlet has been run, six CSV reports for each day of the month will be located in the `c:\report` directory. You can read these reports in the shell using the `Import-CSV` cmdlet, or open them in **Excel** or **Notepad** for review.

See also

- *Creating custom objects* in *Chapter 1, PowerShell Key Concepts*
- *Controlling ActiveSync device access*
- *Managing ActiveSync, OWA, POP3, and IMAP4 mailbox settings*

8

Managing Transport Servers

In this chapter, we will cover:

- ▶ Managing connectors
- ▶ Configuring transport limits
- ▶ Allowing application servers to relay mail
- ▶ Managing transport rules
- ▶ Working with custom DSN messages
- ▶ Managing connectivity and protocol logs
- ▶ Searching message tracking logs
- ▶ Working with messages in transport queues
- ▶ Searching anti-spam agent logs
- ▶ Implementing a header firewall

Introduction

The Exchange hub and edge transport roles are responsible for handling mail flow inside your organization and can be used to secure messages sent to and received from the Internet. In addition to routing messages, you can apply rules, configure settings, and enforce limits on messages as they pass through the servers in your environment. Transport agents can be used to provide basic anti-spam protection, and both roles implement detailed logging capabilities that can be leveraged from the shell. In this chapter, we'll take a look at several useful scripting techniques that include imposing limits and rules on messages and generating detailed reports on mail flow statistics.

Performing some basic steps

To work with the code samples in this chapter, follow these steps to launch the Exchange Management Shell:

1. Log onto a workstation or server with the Exchange Management Tools installed

2. Open the Exchange Management Shell by clicking on **Start | All Programs | Exchange Server 2010**

3. Click on the **Exchange Management Shell** shortcut

Managing connectors

Exchange 2010 uses both send and receive connectors to transmit and accept messages from other servers. These connectors can be managed from within the Exchange Management Console (EMC), but the addition, configuration, and removal can also be completely managed from the Exchange Management Shell. In this recipe, we'll take a look at the various cmdlets that can be used to manage send and receive connectors.

How to do it...

1. To create a Send connector, use the `New-SendConnector` cmdlet:

```
New-SendConnector -Name Internet `
-Usage Internet `
-AddressSpaces 'SMTP:*;1' `
-IsScopedConnector $false `
-DNSRoutingEnabled $false `
-SmartHosts smtp.contoso.com `
-SmartHostAuthMechanism None `
-UseExternalDNSServersEnabled $false `
-SourceTransportServers hub1
```

2. Receive connectors can be created on each transport server using the `New-ReceiveConnector` cmdlet:

```
New-ReceiveConnector -Name 'Inbound from DMZ' `
-Usage 'Custom' `
-Bindings '192.168.1.245:25' `
-Fqdn mail.contoso.com `
-RemoteIPRanges '172.16.23.0/24' `
-PermissionGroups AnonymousUsers `
-Server hub1
```

How it works...

By default, Exchange does not create send connectors used for routing messages to the Internet, and they need to be created manually using either EMC or the shell. However, there is a hidden implicit send connector that is used to send mail between transport servers within the organization, and you don't need to worry about creating send connectors for internal mail flow. Additionally, you don't need to create send connectors on edge transport servers that have been subscribed to your Exchange organization. Send connectors created on your hub transport servers can be replicated to the edge role through the EdgeSync process.

In the previous example, we used the `New-SendConnector` cmdlet to create an Internet send connector on a hub transport server. This cmdlet provides a number of options that control how the connector is configured. In this case, we've configured an address space of `SMTP:*;1`, which specifies that all messages addressed to recipients outside of the organization will be sent through this connector. Instead of using DNS to route the messages, we're forwarding all messages to a smart host called `smtp.contoso.com`, which in this case, would be an SMTP gateway out in the perimeter network. The source transport server has been configured using the server name `hub1`, which means that any message destined for the Internet will be first routed through this server before being forwarded to the smart host. There are over 30 parameters available with this cmdlet, so you'll want to review the help file to determine how to configure the settings based on your needs. To do this, run `Get-Help New-SendConnector -Full`

After a send connector has been created, its settings can be modified using the `Set-SendConnector` cmdlet. The following example will modify our previous Internet send connector by replacing the associated address spaces:

```
Set-SendConnector -Identity Internet `
-AddressSpaces 'SMTP:*.litwareinc.com;5',
              'SMTP:corp.contoso.com;10'
```

To view all of the properties for a send connector, use the `Get-SendConnector` cmdlet and pipe the command to `Format-List`:

```
Get-SendConnector -Identity Internet | Format-List
```

To disable the connector we can use the following syntax:

```
Set-SendConnector -Identity Internet -Enabled $false
```

And finally, the connector can be removed using the `Remove-SendConnector` cmdlet:

```
Remove-SendConnector -Identity Internet -Confirm:$false
```

Each hub transport will initially be configured during the installation of Exchange with two receive connectors; one for client connections named *Client\<Server Name>* and one for server connections called *Default\<Server Name>*. When installing an Exchange 2010 hub transport server, you don't need to modify any of the default connectors in order for the internal mail flow to work. But if you want to be able to receive mail from other mail systems, such as directly from servers on the Internet or an SMTP gateway in your perimeter network, then you will need to modify either the existing Default server connector, or create a new one for this purpose.

There's more...

Receive connectors are created on a per server basis. In step 2, we used the New-ReceiveConnector cmdlet to create a receive connector on the hub1 server that will be used to accept messages from a remote SMTP server in the perimeter network. You can see that we configured the connector so that the hub1 server is listening on the IP address 192.168.1.245 on TCP port 25 for incoming messages. Based on the RemoteIPRanges and PermissionGroups parameters, any host in the 172.16.23.0/24 subnet will be able to make an unauthenticated connection to hub1 and submit messages to any recipient within the organization. Like send connectors, there are a number of parameters that can be used to create a receive connector. Review the help file for this cmdlet using Get-Help New-ReceiveConnector -Full to determine all of the available options.

Similar to send connectors, receive connectors have Set-* and Remove-* cmdlets that can be used to modify, disable, or remove a receive connector.

To change the settings of a receive connector, use the Set-ReceiveConnector cmdlet:

```
Set-ReceiveConnector -Identity 'hub1\Inbound from DMZ' `
-Banner '220 SMTP OK' `
-MaxInboundConnection 2500 `
-ConnectionInactivityTimeout '00:02:30'
```

Here you can see that we've modified a number of properties on the receive connector. Each of the settings modified here can only be managed from the shell. To view all of the properties available, use the Get-ReceiveConnector cmdlet and pipe the command to Format-List:

```
Get-ReceiveConnector -Identity 'cas1\Inbound from DMZ' |
    Format-List
```

To disable a receive connector, use the Set-ReceiveConnector cmdlet:

```
Set-ReceiveConnector -Identity 'hub1\Inbound from DMZ' `
-Enabled $false
```

You can remove a receive connector using the following syntax:

```
Remove-ReceiveConnector -Identity 'cas1\Inbound from DMZ' `
-Confirm:$false
```

See also

▶ *Configuring transport limits*

▶ *Allowing application servers to relay mail*

Configuring transport limits

Depending on your requirements, transport limits can be configured in multiple ways. We can configure limits on individual mailboxes, on specific connectors, and even at the organization level. In this recipe, you'll learn how to use the Exchange Management Shell to configure limits based on the total number of acceptable recipients for a message, and also the total maximum size of each message that passes through the transport servers in your organization.

How to do it...

To configure mail flow restrictions for an individual mailbox, use the `Set-Mailbox` cmdlet as shown next:

```
Set-Mailbox -Identity dsmith `
-MaxSendSize 10mb `
-MaxReceiveSize 10mb `
-RecipientLimits 100
```

Here you can see that we've set limits for Dave Smith so that the maximum send and receive size for messages sent to or from his mailbox is limited to 10 megabytes. In addition, the maximum number of recipients that can be addressed when he sends an e-mail message is limited to 100.

How it works...

All Exchange recipients provide some type of mail flow settings that can be applied on an individual basis. In the previous example, we applied limits on a mailbox, but you also have the option of applying the `MaxReceiveSize` property on distribution groups and contacts. You may want to implement individual mail flow limits on a subset of recipients, and to do this in bulk, we can take advantage of PowerShell's flexible pipelining capabilities.

For example, let's say that we'd like to configure the mail flow limits shown in the previous example for all the mailbox-enabled users in the *Marketing* OU. The following one-liner would take care of this:

```
Get-Mailbox -OrganizationalUnit contoso.com/Marketing |
   Set-Mailbox -MaxSendSize 10mb `
   -MaxReceiveSize 20mb `
   -RecipientLimits 100
```

Here you can see that we're simply retrieving a list of mailboxes from the *Marketing* OU using the `Get-Mailbox` cmdlet. To configure the limits, we pipe those objects to the `Set-Mailbox` cmdlet and each user is updated with the new settings.

There's more...

In addition to setting limits on individual recipients, we have the option of configuring limits organization-wide. To do this, we use the `Set-TransportConfig` cmdlet:

```
Set-TransportConfig -MaxReceiveSize 10mb `
   -MaxRecipientEnvelopeLimit 1000 `
   -MaxSendSize 10mb
```

This command will enforce a 10 megabyte send and receive limit for messages passing through all transport servers in the organization, as well as limit the total number of recipients per message to 1000.

Limits set on individual users will override these organization limits. For example, if the maximum send and receive size is set to 10 megabytes at the organization level, we can exclude specific users from these restrictions by configuring a higher maximum send and receive size on a per mailbox basis using the `Set-Mailbox` cmdlet.

Limits can also be set on a per connector basis. To set the limits on an Internet receive connector, the command might look something like this:

```
Set-ReceiveConnector -Identity HUB1\Internet `
   -MaxMessageSize 20mb `
   -MaxRecipientsPerMessage 100
```

Notice that the identity is referenced using the format of *ServerName\ConnectorName*. This command will update the `Internet` connector on the `hub1` server. If you have multiple hub transport servers with this receive connector, you can update the settings for each server with one command:

```
Get-ReceiveConnector -Identity *\Internet |
   Set-ReceiveConnector -MaxMessageSize 20mb `
   -MaxRecipientsPerMessage 100
```

This time we use the `Get-ReceiveConnector` cmdlet using an asterisk (*) as a wildcard so that any connector in the organization named `Internet` will be retrieved. We pipe the output down to the `Set-ReceiveConnector` cmdlet and the change is made in bulk.

 If you are operating in co-existence with Exchange 2003, you can also set routing group connector limits using the `Set-RoutingGroupConnector` cmdlet.

Modifying send connectors is a little easier because they are defined at the organization level, so you don't need to iterate through connectors on multiple servers. To modify the maximum message size limits on a send connector named `Internet`, you can run the following command:

```
Set-SendConnector -Identity Internet -MaxMessageSize 5mb
```

In this example, outbound messages through the `Internet` send connector are limited to 5 megabytes in size.

Implementing restrictions at the organization, user, and connector levels should give you plenty of options. However, you can also use transport rules to set a maximum attachment size per message, if needed.

See also

▶ *Managing transport rules*

Allowing application servers to relay mail

When you deploy Exchange 2010, you may be required to allow external devices to relay mail off of your servers. This may be an application server or a physical device such as a copier or printer. In order to allow these external systems to anonymously relay mail, you'll need to configure receive connectors on your hub transport servers that support this. In this recipe, we'll take a look at how you can do this with the Exchange Management Shell.

How to do it...

When implementing an unauthenticated relay, it is wise to use a dedicated receive connector for this purpose:

```
New-ReceiveConnector -Name Relay `
-Usage Custom `
-Bindings '192.168.1.245:25' `
-Fqdn mail.contoso.com `
```

```
-RemoteIPRanges 192.168.1.110 `
-Server HUB1 `
-PermissionGroups ExchangeServers `
-AuthMechanism TLS, ExternalAuthoritative
```

This command creates a receive connector on the `hub1` server named `Relay`. The settings used here specify that the connector listens on the server IP address of 192.168.1.245 on TCP Port 25 and will allow the host at 192.168.1.110 to relay mail, either internally or externally, without requiring authentication.

How it works...

When creating a relay connector using this technique, you want to ensure that only the hosts that are allowed to relay mail are allowed using the `RemoteIPRanges` property. If this connector was configured with a remote IP range of 0.0.0.0-255.255.255.255, this would effectively turn the Exchange server into an open relay. This is because the `AuthMechanism` parameter has been set to `ExternalAuthoritative`, which means that Exchange bypasses all security and fully trusts all messages received from hosts in the `RemoteIPRanges` list. Additionally, messages accepted through this connector will not be scanned by anti-spam agents or be restricted by any of the system-wide message size limits.

There's more...

If the devices or application servers in your environment only need to submit messages to internal recipients and do not need to be completely trusted, creating a receive connector with the following settings is a better option:

```
New-ReceiveConnector -Name Relay `
-Usage Custom `
-Bindings '192.168.1.245:25' `
-Fqdn mail.contoso.com `
-RemoteIPRanges 192.168.1.110 `
-Server HUB1 `
-PermissionGroups AnonymousUsers
```

As you can see, we've removed the `AuthMechanism` parameter from the command and assigned `AnonymousUsers` to the permission groups. This is a more secure approach since messages submitted from external devices or servers will now be subject to anti-spam agents and message restrictions. If you need to allow these devices to route mail to external recipients through this connector, you'll also need to assign the anonymous users the extended right `ms-Exch-SMTP-Accept-Any-Recipient`:

```
Get-ReceiveConnector HUB1\Relay |
  Add-ADpermission -User "NT AUTHORITY\ANONYMOUS LOGON" `
  -ExtendedRights ms-Exch-SMTP-Accept-Any-Recipient
```

After the previous command has been executed, the `Relay` connector on the `hub1` server will be updated and the host at 192.168.1.110 will be able to route messages through the server using unauthenticated relay.

See also

▸ *Configuring Transport Limits*

Managing transport rules

Transport rules can be used within your Exchange organization to take a specific action on a message, based on one or more conditions. For example, you can configure rules that check messages for confidential information or inappropriate content, and then take an action on those messages such as blocking them or forwarding them to another recipient. Exchange 2007 introduced transport rules for the first time, but with Exchange 2010, we now have an upgraded set of cmdlets that provide easier management of transport rules from the shell. In this recipe, you'll learn how to create transport rules using these cmdlets.

How to do it...

To create a transport rule, use the `New-TransportRule` cmdlet:

```
New-TransportRule -Name Confidential `
-Enabled $true `
-SubjectContainsWords Confidential `
-BlindCopyTo Administrator@contoso.com
```

Based on the condition and action for this transport rule, all messages that contain the word `Confidential` in the subject line of a message will be blind copied to the administrator mailbox.

How it works...

In Exchange 2007, if you wanted to create a transport rule from the shell, you first had to create rule predicate objects using the `Get-TransportRulePredicate` cmdlet. These objects were used to define the rule's conditions and exceptions. In order to specify an action, you had to use the `Get-TransportRuleAction` cmdlet to create an object that referenced a specific transport rule action. Once that was complete, you then used those objects with the `New-TransportRule` cmdlet to create a rule. In Exchange 2010, the `New-TransportRule` cmdlet is capable of creating rules using a simple one-liner, as shown in the previous example.

This is possible now because all rule predicates and actions are directly available as parameters of the `New-TransportRule` cmdlet. The side effect of this, of course, is that this cmdlet now provides over 130 parameters, and figuring out the correct combination to create a rule might be a little tricky.

Let's take a look at how we can determine the parameters required to create a transport rule from the shell. Imagine that we need to create a rule based on custom message headers that are added to certain e-mail messages. To determine the available predicates, we can run the `Get-TransportRulePredicate` cmdlet, which will list every predicate available in the organization. When viewing the output from this cmdlet, there is a predicate available called `HeaderMatches`. We can assume, based on the name, that it is probably the one we need in order to create a rule that is triggered on the headers of a message.

Before we can construct a command that can use this predicate, we need to take a closer look at its properties:

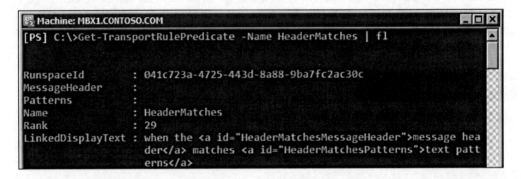

We can tell from examining the `LinkedDisplayText` property in the previous screenshot that this predicate requires two properties. The properties are referenced in each `id` attribute within the `<a></a>` tags.

In this case, the property names are `HeaderMatchesMessageHeader` and `HeaderMatchesPatterns`. These property names correspond to the parameter names that will be required when using the `New-TransportRule` cmdlet to define the condition.

Now that we've identified which parameters will be required for the condition, we need to determine how to define the action. To do this, we can use the `Get-TransportRuleAction` cmdlet:

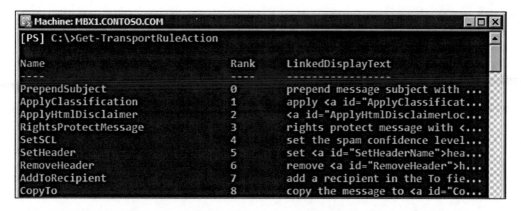

Running this cmdlet will provide all of the available transport rule actions, as shown in the previous screenshot. Based on the output, we may decide that we want to use the `AddToRecipient` action with our rule. Again, we need to view the properties of this item to determine what the parameter name will be:

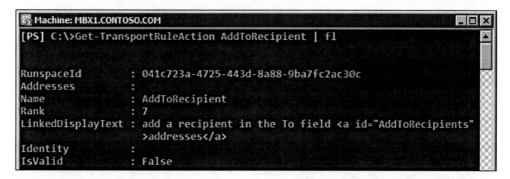

After viewing the details of this action, we can see by examining the `LinkedDisplayText` property that the `id` attribute references `AddToRecipients`, so this will be the parameter name we need to use when defining the action for our rule.

Now that we know what the required parameters are for both the condition and the action, we can create a rule using the `New-TransportRule` cmdlet:

```
New-TransportRule -Name ITSupport `
-Enabled $true `
-HeaderMatchesMessageHeader X-Department `
-HeaderMatchesPatterns ITSupport `
-AddToRecipients administrator@contoso.com
```

In this example, any e-mail message with a custom header named `X-Department` with a value of `ITSupport` will have the administrator mailbox added as a recipient.

When it comes to adding exceptions, we use the same predicate names but prefix them with `ExceptIf`. For example, one of the rule predicate parameters that can be used with the `New-TransportRule` cmdlet is `-From`. If we wanted to create a rule but prevent the rule from firing based on the sender, we can use the `-ExceptIfFrom` parameter when creating the rule:

```
New-TransportRule -Name ITSupport `
-Enabled $true `
-HeaderMatchesMessageHeader X-Department `
-HeaderMatchesPatterns ITSupport `
-ExceptIfFrom administrator@contoso.com `
-AddToRecipients administrator@contoso.com
```

Again, we're creating a rule here based on the headers of the e-mail message. This time, we've added an exception. If the sender is the administrator account, we will not trigger the rule, even if the condition has been met.

As you can see, creating transport rules from the shell can be quite involved. Fortunately, transport rules can be fully managed through the Exchange Management Console (EMC). If you do not have a specific need to manage them from the shell, you may find it easier to create the rules using EMC.

There's more...

You can view the existing transport rules in your Exchange organization using the `Get-TransportRule` cmdlet:

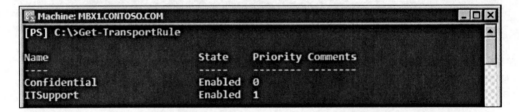

You can examine the details of a particular rule by specifying it by name and viewing the output in list format:

```
Get-TransportRule Confidential | Format-List
```

To view the rule conditions, access the `Conditions` property of the rule and pipe the output to `Format-List`:

```
Machine: MBX1.CONTOSO.COM                                    _ □ ✕
[PS] C:\>(Get-TransportRule Confidential).Conditions | Format-List


Words             : {Confidential}
Name              : SubjectContains
Rank              : 23
LinkedDisplayText : when the Subject field contains <a id="SubjectContainsW
                    ords">specific words</a>
Identity          :
IsValid           : True
```

Transport rule actions can also be viewed by accessing the `Actions` property of the rule:

```
Machine: MBX1.CONTOSO.COM                                    _ □ ✕
[PS] C:\>(Get-TransportRule Confidential).Actions | Format-List


Addresses         : {Administrator@contoso.com}
Name              : BlindCopyTo
Rank              : 9
LinkedDisplayText : Blind carbon copy (Bcc) the message to <a id="BlindCopy
                    To">addresses</a>
Identity          :
IsValid           : True
```

If you want to retrieve specific rules that only contain a certain condition or action, you can use PowerShell's filtering capabilities using the `Where-Object` cmdlet:

```
Get-TransportRule | Where-Object {$_.SubjectContainsWords}
```

In the previous example, we are filtering on the `SubjectContainsWords` property, which is a transport rule condition, and this command will only retrieve the rules where this condition has been defined.

Modifying transport rules

Existing transport rules can be modified using the `Set-TransportRule` cmdlet. If we wanted to change the blind copy mailbox used in the `Confidential` transport rule created earlier, the command might look something like this:

```
Set-TransportRule –Identity Confidential `
  -BlindCopyTo sysadmin@contoso.com
```

If you want to clear the blind copy address and instead redirect the message to another mailbox, you could use the following command syntax:

```
Set-TransportRule –Identity Confidential `
  -BlindCopyTo $null `
  -RedirectMessageTo sysadmin@contoso.com
```

Transport rules are processed based on their priority value in descending order. The first transport rule you create will be given a priority value of zero, and, for each rule you create, the priority number will be incremented by one. To change the priority of a rule, you can use the `Set-TransportRule` cmdlet with the `-Priority` parameter:

```
Set-TransportRule -Identity ITSupport -Priority 0
```

After running the previous command, the `ITSupport` transport rule will be processed first. The previous rule that was assigned priority zero will now be assigned a priority value of one.

Enabling, disabling, and removing transport rules

To disable a rule, use the `Disable-TransportRule` cmdlet:

```
Disable-TransportRule -Identity Confidential -Confirm:$false
```

You can enable a rule using the `Enable-TransportRule` cmdlet:

```
Enable-TransportRule -Identity Confidential
```

When you need to delete a transport rule, use the `Remove-TransportRule` cmdlet:

```
Remove-TransportRule -Identity Confidential -Confirm:$false
```

Understanding regular expressions in transport rules

Exchange 2010 supports the use of simple regular expressions in transport rule predicates that provide pattern properties. This means that any condition or exception that accepts text patterns can be used with a simple regular expression. Consider the following command that creates a new transport rule:

```
New-TransportRule -Name "Block Credit Card Numbers" `
-SubjectOrBodyMatchesPatterns '\d\d\d\d-\d\d\d\d-\d\d\d\d-\d\d\d\d' `
-RejectMessageEnhancedStatusCode "5.7.1" `
-RejectMessageReasonText "Don't send credit card numbers via e-mail!"
```

Here you can see that a transport rule has been created to reject messages that might contain a credit card number. The `\d` pattern matches a single numeric digit. The expression used with the `SubjectOrBodyMatchesPatterns` parameter indicates that any message that contains a 16-digit number where every fourth number is followed by a hyphen (-) should be considered a match. If a match is found, we reject the message and provide a reject reason that will be displayed in the diagnostic information for administrators section of the NDR.

Only a specific set of regular expression pattern strings can be used within transport rules. For a complete list, see the Pattern Strings section in this TechNet article titled Regular Expressions in Transport Rules:

```
http://technet.microsoft.com/en-us/library/aa997187.aspx
```

Working with custom DSN messages

Delivery Status Notification (DSN) messages are system messages generated by transport servers that inform the sender of a message about its status. When a message cannot be delivered to a recipient, Exchange will respond to the sender with a message that is associated with a status message. Sometimes, these status messages may not be detailed enough for your liking. In those cases, you can create new messages associated with the DSN code to provide more details to the sender. This is something that has to be done from the Exchange Management Shell.

How to do it...

You can use the `New-SystemMessage` cmdlet to create a custom DSN message:

```
New-SystemMessage -DSNCode 5.1.1 `
-Text "The mailbox you tried to send an e-mail message to
does not exist. Please contact the Help Desk at extension
4112 for assistance." `
-Internal $true `
-Language En
```

In this example, a **Non Delivery Report** (**NDR**) with the custom DSN message will be delivered to senders that try to send messages to an invalid internal recipient.

How it works...

When creating a custom DSN message, you want to specify whether it will be used for internal or external use. The previous example configured a custom message for DSN code `5.1.1` for internal use. In addition to this, you could create a separate custom DSN message for external users, just set the `-Internal` parameter to `$false`.

Custom DSN messages can also support basic HTML tags. This can be useful when creating an internal custom DSN that directs users to an internal help desk site. Here's another way we could have created the custom DNS message:

```
New-SystemMessage -DSNCode 5.1.1 `
-Text "The mailbox you tried to send an e-mail message to
does not exist. Please visit the
<a href='http://support.contoso.com'>help desk site</a>
forassitance" `
-Internal $true `
-Language En
```

In this example, we've included a hyperlink within the custom DSN message so users can click the link and visit an internal help desk website for additional assistance.

There's more...

To view custom DSN messages, use the `Get-SystemMessage` cmdlet:

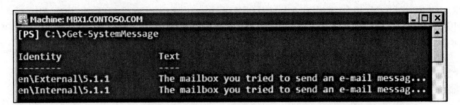

You can also view the default system messages that were installed with Exchange. To do this, run the cmdlet with the `-Original` switch parameter:

```
Get-SystemMessage -Original
```

To modify a system message, use the `Set-SystemMessage` cmdlet:

```
Set-SystemMessage -Identity 'en\External\5.1.1' `
-Text "Sorry, but this recipient is no longer available
or does not exist."
```

As you can see here, we've modified the custom external 5.1.1 message with a new message using the `-Text` parameter.

To remove a custom DSN message, use the `Remove-SystemMessage` cmdlet:

```
Remove-SystemMessage -Identity 'en\Internal\5.1.1' -Confirm:$false
```

The previous command removes the custom message created for the 5.1.1 DSN code without confirmation.

System-generated messages for mailbox and public folder quota warnings can also be customized:

```
New-SystemMessage -QuotaMessageType WarningMailbox `
-Text "Your mailbox is getting too large. Please
 delete some messages to free up space or call
 the help desk at extention 3391." `
-Language En
```

When creating a custom quota message as shown previously, there is no need to specify a DSN code. The `-QuotaMessageType` parameter is used to modify the messages for the various warnings supported by the system. The `-QuotaMessageType` parameter accepts the following values that can be used to customize warning messages:

- ▸ WarningMailboxUnlimitedSize
- ▸ WarningPublicFolderUnlimitedSize
- ▸ WarningMailbox
- ▸ WarningPublicFolder
- ▸ ProhibitSendMailbox
- ▸ ProhibitPostPublicFolder
- ▸ ProhibitSendReceiveMailBox

When creating a custom quota message, you cannot use the -Internal parameter. This is not a problem since quota messages are only intended for internal recipients.

Managing connectivity and protocol logs

Every Exchange hub or edge transport server is capable of logging connection activity and SMTP conversations that take place between servers. You can configure the retention settings for these logs and use them to diagnose mail flow issues within your environment. In this recipe, you'll learn how to configure the logging options on your servers and how to examine the data when troubleshooting problems.

How to do it...

To view the connectivity logging configuration for a transport server, use the Get-TransportServer cmdlet:

```
Get-TransportServer -Identity ex01 | fl ConnectivityLog*
```

The previous command retrieves the default connectivity logging settings for a transport server named ex01. The output returned will be similar to the following screenshot:

```
Machine: MBX1.CONTOSO.COM

[PS] C:\>Get-TransportServer -Identity ex01 | fl ConnectivityLog*


ConnectivityLogEnabled          : True
ConnectivityLogMaxAge           : 30.00:00:00
ConnectivityLogMaxDirectorySize : 1000 MB (1,048,576,000 bytes)
ConnectivityLogMaxFileSize      : 10 MB (10,485,760 bytes)
ConnectivityLogPath             : C:\Program Files\Microsoft\Exchange Serve
                                  r\V14\TransportRoles\Logs\Connectivity
```

How it works...

Connectivity logs record connection details about outbound message delivery queues on a transport server. Connectivity logging is enabled by default on Exchange 2010 SP1 servers. Based on the output from the `Get-TransportServer` cmdlet in the previous example, we can see that by default, the maximum age for connectivity logfiles is 30 days. Once a logfile reaches 10 MB, a new logfile will be created. The directory for connectivity logging will hold up to 1 GB of logs. Transport servers use circular logging for connectivity logs, so once the directory reaches its maximum size, or the logfiles reach their maximum age, those logfiles will be removed to make space for new logfiles.

You can control these settings using the `Set-TransportServer` cmdlet. Here's an example of modifying the connectivity log maximum age and directory size on a hub transport server named `ex01`:

```
Set-TransportServer -Identity ex01 `
-ConnectivityLogMaxAge 45 `
-ConnectivityLogMaxDirectorySize 5gb
```

If you change these settings on a transport server, it is recommended that you also update the remaining transport servers in your organization with a matching configuration.

To make this change to all transport servers at once, use the following one-liner:

```
Get-TransportServer |
  Set-TransportServer -ConnectivityLogMaxAge 45 `
  -ConnectivityLogMaxDirectorySize 5gb
```

There's more...

You can configure protocol logging to record the SMTP conversations between your transport server and other mail servers. Protocol logging can be enabled on a per connector basis, but just like the connectivity logging options, the configuration of the protocol logfile settings are made using the `Set-TransportServer` cmdlet. The following screenshot shows these available properties:

```
Machine: MBX1.CONTOSO.COM                                              _ □ ×
[PS] C:\>Get-TransportServer ex01 | fl ReceiveProtocol*


ReceiveProtocolLogMaxAge           : 30.00:00:00
ReceiveProtocolLogMaxDirectorySize : 250 MB (262,144,000 bytes)
ReceiveProtocolLogMaxFileSize      : 10 MB (10,485,760 bytes)
ReceiveProtocolLogPath             : C:\Program Files\Microsoft\Exchange Se
                                     rver\V14\TransportRoles\Logs\ProtocolL
                                     og\SmtpReceive
```

Here you can see that we've got protocol log settings for receive connectors. The settings shown here are the default values.

Send connectors will use the following protocol log configurations by default:

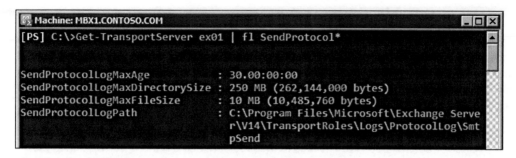

Just like connectivity logs, the send and receive protocol logs have a maximum age and directory size and are controlled by circular logging. The default settings can be changed with the Set-TransportServer cmdlet:

```
Set-TransportServer -Identity hub1 `
-SendProtocolLogMaxAge 45 `
-ReceiveProtocolLogMaxAge 45
```

Again, if you plan on changing this setting, make sure you update all of the transport servers in your organization with the same information.

Before you can capture protocol logging information, you need to enable verbose protocol logging on each connector that you want to report on:

```
Set-SendConnector -Identity Internet -ProtocolLoggingLevel Verbose
```

You can see in the previous command that we've configured the Internet send connector for verbose protocol logging. You can do the same for a receive connector using the Set-ReceiveConnector cmdlet:

```
Get-ReceiveConnector -Identity *\Relay |
    Set-ReceiveConnector -ProtocolLoggingLevel Verbose
```

Here we are using an asterisk (*) as a wildcard to retrieve the Relay connector from each hub transport server in the organization. We can pipe the output to the Set-ReceiveConnector cmdlet to enable verbose protocol logging for the connector on each server.

All hub transport servers use an invisible intra-organization send connector that is used to transmit messages internally to other hub transport servers. You can configure verbose logging for this connector using the Set-TransportServer cmdlet:

```
Set-TransportServer -Identity hub1 `
-IntraOrgConnectorProtocolLoggingLevel Verbose
```

Protocol logfiles for the intra-org connector will be saved in the send protocol log path.

Connectivity and Protocol log files are stored in CSV format and by default, are organized in sub directories under the following path:

```
<install path>\V14\TransportRoles\Logs\
```

Connectivity logs are stored in a sub directory called `Connectivity`, and the logfile naming convention is in the format of *CONNECTLOGyyyymmdd-nnnn.log*, where *yyyymmdd* is the date that the log file was created, and where *nnnn* is an instance number starting with 1 for each day. The instance number will be incremented by one as each logfile reaches the default 10 MB limit and a new log file is created.

Protocol logs are stored in subdirectories of this location in `ProtocolLog\SmtpReceive` and `ProtocolLog\SmtpSend`. The files in these folders use a naming convention in the format of *prefixyyyymmdd-nnnn.log*. The prefix for the log filename will be *SEND* for send connectors and *RECV* for receive connectors. Like connectivity logs, *yyyymmdd* is the date that the logfile was created, and *nnnn* is the instance number that starts with 1 and is incremented as each new logfile is created.

The connectivity logs store details about messages transmitted from local queues to the destination server. For example, a record in a connectivity log file will log the source queue, destination server, DNS resolution details, connection failures, and the total number of messages and bytes transferred.

The protocol logs store SMTP conversations that take place when either sending or receiving a message. The details logged will contain connector and session IDs, the local and remote endpoint of the servers involved, and the SMTP verbs used in the conversation.

Parsing logfiles

Even though connectivity and protocol logs are stored in CSV format, each logfile has header information prepended to the file. The following screenshot shows an example of viewing a connectivity logfile in excel:

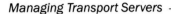

As you can see, the header information includes the Exchange version, the date, and the fields used in the logfiles. This header information, makes it impossible to read these files into the shell using the `Import-CSV` cmdlet. Luckily, PowerShell is so flexible that we can work around this with a little creativity.

Let's say you are interested in finding all errors in the connection log on a transport server named `hub1`. Start the Exchange Management Shell on the `hub1` server and run the following command:

```
$logpath = (Get-TransportServer -Identity hub1).ConnectivityLogPath
```

This will store a reference to the connectivity log folder path that will make the following code easier to read and work with. Now let's say that you want to parse the connectivity logs from the past 24 hours for failures. We'll parse each logfile in the directory and perform a wildcard search based on a keyword:

```
$data = $logs | %{
  Get-Content $_.Fullname | %{
    $IsHeaderParsed = $false
    if($_ -like '#Fields: *' -and !$IsHeaderParsed) {
      $_ -replace '^#Fields: '
      $IsHeaderParsed = $true
    }
    else {
      $_
    }
  } | ConvertFrom-Csv
}


$data | Where-Object{$_.description -like '*fail*'}
```

This code will loop through each log file in the connectivity log folder that has been written to within the past 24 hours. For each logfile, we'll read the content into the shell, excluding the header information, and convert the information to properly-formed CSV data using the `ConvertFrom-CSV` cmdlet. The result will be stored in the `$data` variable that can then be filtered on. In this example, any record within each of the logfiles where the description contains the word `fail` will be returned. You can adjust the `Where-Object` filter based on the information you are searching for.

Message tracking logs

The `Get-MessageTrackingLog` cmdlet is a versatile tool that can be used to search the message tracking logs on mailbox and transport servers. In this recipe, you'll learn how to use this Exchange Management Shell cmdlet to generate detailed reports on various aspects of mail flow within your organization.

How to do it...

The `Get-MessageTrackingLog` cmdlet has a number of available parameters that can be used to perform a search. To retrieve all messages sent from a transport server during a specified time frame, use the following syntax:

```
Get-MessageTrackingLog -Server hub1 `
-Start (Get-Date).AddDays(-1) `
-End (Get-Date) `
-EventId Send
```

Using this command, all messages sent through SMTP from the `hub1` server in the past 24 hours will be returned.

How it works...

Each server running the edge transport, hub transport, and mailbox server roles generates and collects message tracking logs. Message tracking is enabled by default for each of these roles, and the logs are stored in the `<install path>\V14\TransportRoles\Logs\ MessageTracking`directory. Logfiles are limited to 10 megabytes and when a logfile reaches its maximum size, a new logfile will be created. Logfiles are kept for either 30 days or until the maximum size configured for the directory has been reached. Like connectivity and protocol logs, the message tracking logs are removed as needed using circular logging.

You can configure all of these options on transport servers using the `Set-TransportServer` cmdlet. To modify these settings on a mailbox server, use the `Set-MailboxServer` cmdlet.

In the previous example, we ran the `Get-MessageTrackingLog` cmdlet and specified a transport server to execute the search against. Depending on your network topology, you may need to search several servers in order to get accurate results.

For instance, let's say that you've got multiple hub transport servers in your organization. You might want to generate a report for all messages sent by a specific user within a certain time frame. You can search the logs on each transport server using the following syntax:

```
Get-TransportServer |
  Get-MessageTrackingLog -Start (Get-Date).AddDays(-1) `
  -End (Get-Date) `
```

```
     -EventId Send `
     -Sender dmsith@contoso.com
```

Here you can see that we're using the `Get-TransportServer` cmdlet to retrieve a list of all hub transport servers in the organization. Those objects are piped to the `Get-MessageTrackingLog` cmdlet where we specify the start and end time for the search, the `EventId`, and the sender. The records returned by the previous command will provide a number of useful properties such as the sender and recipients of the message, the total size of the message, the IP address of the destination server, the subject of the message, and more. These records can be piped out to `Export-CSV` or `ConvertTo-Html` to generate an external report, or you can pipe the command to `Format-List` to view all of the properties for each log entry.

There's more...

The `-EventID` parameter can be used to specify the event category used to classify a tracking log entry when you perform a search. The following possible event categories can be used:

- **BadMail:** The message was submitted through the pickup or replay directories and cannot be delivered
- **Defer Deliver:** The message delivery has been delayed
- **DSN:** A Delivery Status Notification (DSN) was generated
- **Expand:** Expansion of a distribution group
- **Fail:** Message delivery failed
- **PoisonMessage:** The message was added or removed from the poison message queue
- **Receive:** The message was received either through SMTP or by the StoreDriver
- **Redirect:** The message was redirected to an alternate recipient
- **Resolve:** The recipients listed in the message were resolved to another e-mail address
- **Send:** The message was sent through SMTP to another mail server
- **Submit:** Logged by the mailbox submission service running on a mailbox server
- **Transfer**: Recipients were moved to a forked message because of content conversion, recipient limits, or agents

You can search message tracking logs based on the sender or recipient:

```
Get-MessageTrackingLog -Sender sales@litwareinc.com -EventId Receive
```

In this example, we're searching the message tracking logs for an external sender address and specifying `Receive` as the event category. This would allow us to track all inbound messages from this external sender.

In addition, you can use the `-Recipients` parameter to find messages sent to one or more e-mail addresses:

```
Get-MessageTrackingLog -Recipients dave@contoso.com,john@contoso.com
```

If you know the subject of the message you want to track, use the `-MessageSubject` parameter when running the command:

```
Get-ExchangeServer |
   Get-MessageTrackingLog -MessageSubject 'Financial Report for Q4'
```

Even though CAS servers don't contain message tracking logs, the syntax shown previously is a quick and easy way to perform a search against both mailbox servers and hub transport servers in your environment. This is helpful when you have the server roles separated across multiple servers and you need to view each step in the delivery process.

When it comes to message tracking, you may need to generate reports based on the total number of messages sent or received. Let's say that your boss has asked you to determine the number of individual e-mail messages received by your hub transport servers from the Internet in the past week. Let's start with the following command:

```
Get-TransportServer | Get-MessageTrackingLog -EventId Receive `
-Start (Get-Date).AddDays(-7) `
-End (Get-Date) `
-ResultSize Unlimited |
   Where-Object {$_.ConnectorId -like '*\Internet'}
```

Here we're specifying with the `-EventID` parameter that the event category of the logs returned should be set to `Receive`. Next we specify the date seven days ago as the start time for the search, and the current date for the end time. We set the `-ResultSize` parameter to `Unlimited` because by default, this cmdlet will only return the first 1,000 results. Finally, we filter the output using the `Where-Object` cmdlet based on the connector. Since we have a dedicated receive connector for inbound Internet e-mail, we filter the results so that only received messages through this connector are returned.

Now that we've got an idea of how to construct this command, let's take it a step further. Again, to ensure we're getting all of the required information, we'll search the logs on each transport server and then output the total e-mail items and their total size for the past week:

```
$results = Get-TransportServer |
   Get-MessageTrackingLog -EventId Receive `
   -Start (Get-Date).AddDays(-7) `
   -End (Get-Date) `
   -ResultSize Unlimited |
```

```
        Where-Object {$_.ConnectorId -like '*\Internet'}

$results |
  Measure-Object -Property TotalBytes -Sum |
    Select-Object @{n="Total Items";e={$_.Count}},
    @{n="Total Item Size (MB)";e={[math]::Round($_.Sum /1mb,2)}}
```

Although this could be done on one line, we've separated it out here into two phases for the sake of readability. First, we gather the message tracking logs on each transport server using the desired settings and the output is stored in the `$results` variable.

Next, we pipe `$results` to the `Measure-Object` cmdlet that is used to sum up the `TotalBytes` for all messages accepted from the `Internet` receive connector. The command is piped further to the `Select-Object` cmdlet where we create a custom object with calculated properties that display the total number of e-mail items and the total bytes represented in megabytes. The results from the previous code would look something like this:

Taking it a step further

Message tracking logs can be used to create some pretty advanced reports. Let's say that you want to create a report that shows the total number of messages sent from your organization per external domain. This is possible using the following code:

```
$domain = @{}

$report = Get-TransportServer |
Get-MessageTrackingLog -EventId Send `
-ResultSize Unlimited `
-Start (Get-Date).AddDays(-30) `
-End (Get-Date) |
Where-Object {$_.ConnectorId -eq 'Internet'}

if($report) {
  $domains = $report | %{$_.Recipients | %{$_.Split("@")[1]}}
  $domains | %{$domain[$_] = $domain[$_] + 1}
  Write-Output $domain
}
```

You can see here that first we create a hash table that will be used to keep track of each external domain. We then use the `Get-MessageTrackingLog` cmdlet to build a report for all of the messages sent in the past 30 days using a send connector named `Internet`. Next, we loop through the recipients and retrieve only the domain name from their e-mail addresses and store the results in the `$domains` array. Finally, we loop through each of the domains and add them to the hash table, incrementing the count by one for each matching result. Here's an example of the type of output you might get from the previous code:

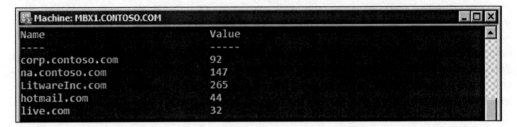

From the output we can see that, in this case, we've sent the majority of our external e-mail in the past 30 days to recipients at `LitwareInc.com`.

See also

▶ *Tracking messages with delivery reports*

Working with messages in transport queues

Transport queues are a temporary storage location for messages that are in transit. Each hub or edge transport server can have multiple queues at any given time depending on the destination of the message. In this recipe, we'll cover several methods that can be used to view queued messages, remove messages from queues, and more.

How to do it...

To view the transport queues that are currently in use on a specific server, use the `Get-Queue` cmdlet:

```
Get-Queue -Server ex01
```

In this example, the transport queues on the `ex01 server` will be returned. The output might look similar to the following:

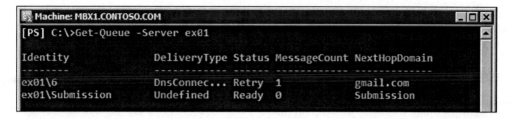

In this example, there is one message awaiting retry due to a DNS resolution problem for the destination domain.

How it works...

When running the Get-Queue cmdlet, the queues displayed will vary depending on what types of messages are currently awaiting delivery. The following queue types are used on transport servers:

- ▶ **Submission Queue**: All messages received by a transport server are first processed in the submission queue. After categorization, each message is moved to either a delivery queue or the retry queue. The queue identity will be listed as *<ServerName>\Submission*, for example: ex01\Submission.

- ▶ **Mailbox Delivery Queue**: All messages destined for direct delivery to a mailbox server using RPC will go through this queue. This queue is used only on hub transport servers. The queue identity will be listed as *<ServerName>\Unique Number*, for example: ex01\15.

- ▶ **Remote Delivery Queue**: All messages being routed to another server through SMTP will go through this queue. The queue identity will be listed as *<ServerName>\Unique Number*, for example: ex01\6.

- ▶ **Poison Message Queue**: Messages that are determined to be potentially harmful will be placed in this queue. The queue identity will be listed as *<ServerName>\Poison*, for example: ex01\Poison.

- ▶ **Unreachable Queue**: Messages that cannot be routed to their destination server will be placed in this queue. The queue identity will be defined as *<ServerName>\Unreachable*, for example: ex01\Unreachable.

In addition to viewing the queues on a single hub transport server, you can use the following command to view the queues on all transport servers in the organization:

```
Get-TransportServer | Get-Queue
```

If you work with busy transport servers, you may want to take advantage of the filtering capabilities of the Get-Queue cmdlet. For example, to filter by delivery type, you can use the following syntax:

```
Get-TransportServer |
  Get-Queue -Filter {DeliveryType -eq 'DnsConnectorDelivery'}
```

This example filters the results based on the DeliveryType. The following values can be used with this filter:

- DNSConnectorDelivery
- NonSMTPGatewayDelivery
- SmartHostConnectorDelivery
- SmtpRelayWithinAdSitetoEdge
- MapiDelivery
- SmtpRelayWithinAdSite
- SmtpRelaytoRemoteAdSite
- SmtpRelaytoTiRg
- Undefined
- Unreachable

The Get-Queue cmdlet also supports several other properties that can be used to construct a filter:

- **Identity**: Specifies the queue identity in the format of server\destination, where destination is a remote domain, mailbox server, or queue name
- **LastError**: Used to search by the last error message recorded for a queue
- **LastRetryTime**: Specifies the time when a connection was last tried for a queue
- **MessageCount**: Allows you to search by the total items in a queue
- **NextHopConnector**: Specifies the identity of the connector used to create a queue
- **NextHopDomain**: The next hop, such as an SMTP domain, server name, AD site, or mailbox database
- **NextRetryTime**: Used to search by when a connection will next be tried by a queue
- **Status**: Shows the status of a queue, such as Active, Ready, Retry, or Suspended

For example, if you want to view queues that have a total message count of more than a certain number of messages, use the MessageCount property with the greater than (-gt) operator:

```
Get-Queue -Server ex01 -Filter {MessageCount -gt 25}
```

Another useful method of finding backed up queues is to use the Status filter:

```
Get-Queue -Server ex01 -Filter {Status -eq 'Retry'}
```

This example searches the queues on the ex01 server for with queues that have messages with a status of Retry. Notice that this time we've used the equals (-eq) comparison operator in the filter to specify the status type.

 To learn about all of the available comparison operators supported by PowerShell, run the following command: Get-Help about_ comparison_operators.

There's more...

To view messages that are queued for delivery, you can use the Get-Message cmdlet. If you want to view all of the messages that are sitting in queues with a status of Retry, use the following command:

```
Get-TransportServer |
   Get-Queue -Filter {Status -eq 'Retry'} |
       Get-Message
```

The Get-Message cmdlet also provides a -Filter parameter that can be used to find messages that match a specific criteria:

```
Get-TransportServer |
   Get-Message -Filter {FromAddress -like '*contoso.com'}
```

The previous command returns all queued messages from every hub transport server in the organization where the sender domain is contoso.com.

 To view the filterable properties for the Get-Message cmdlet, run the following command: Get-Help Get-Message -Parameter Filter.

If you know which server the message is queued on and you just want to view the properties for the message, you can use the following syntax:

```
Get-Message -Server ex01-Filter {Subject -eq 'test'} | Format-List
```

This example filters the Subject of queued messages on the ex01 server. If you want to view all messages queued on a server, you can simply remove the -Filter parameter and value.

To prevent the delivery of a message in a queue, you can use the `Suspend-Message` cmdlet:

```
Get-Message -Server ex01 -Filter {Subject -eq 'test'} |
   Suspend-Message -Confirm:$false
```

To suspend all messages in a particular queue, use the following syntax:

```
Get-Queue -Identity ex01\7 |
  Get-Message |
       Suspend-Message -Confirm:$false
```

Keep in mind that messages in the submission or poison message queue cannot be suspended. When the time comes to allow delivery, you can use the `Resume-Message` cmdlet.

```
Get-Message -Server hub1 -Filter {Subject -eq 'test'} |
   Resume-Message
```

Or we can resume all messages in a particular queue:

```
Get-Queue -Identity ex01\7 |
  Get-Message |
       Resume-Message
```

When you need to force a retry for a queue, you can use the `Retry-Queue` cmdlet:

```
Get-Queue -Identity ex01\7 | Retry-Queue
```

The `Retry-Queue` cmdlet can also be used to resubmit messages to the submission queue, which will allow the categorizer to reprocess the messages. You can resubmit messages with a status of `Retry` in the mailbox or remote delivery queues, or messages that are sitting in the unreachable or poison message queues.

For example, to resubmit all messages in queues with a `Retry` status on all hub transport servers in the organization, use the following command:

```
Get-TransportServer |
  Get-Queue -Filter {Status -eq 'Retry'} |
       Retry-Queue -Resubmit $true
```

Or, to resubmit messages in the unreachable queue on a specific server, use the following command:

```
Retry-Queue -Identity ex01\Unreachable -Resubmit $true
```

Messages with a suspended status cannot be resubmitted using the `Retry-Queue` cmdlet.

You can purge messages from transport queues using the `Remove-Message` cmdlet.

```
Get-TransportServer |
    Get-Queue -Filter {DeliveryType -eq 'DnsConnectorDelivery'} |
        Get-Message | Remove-Message -Confirm:$false
```

This one-liner retrieves queued messages on all transport servers with a specified delivery type and removes them without confirmation. An NDR will be generated and sent to the originator of the message advising them that they'll need to resend the message.

The `Remove-Message` cmdlet provides multiple parameters that can be used to either identify the message based on the message identity, or using a filter with the `-Filter` parameter when you only want to remove a single message:

```
Remove-Message -Identity ex01\10\13 -WithNDR $false -Confirm:$false
```

The previous command removes a single message based on its `MessageIdentity` value. Notice that this time we've set the `-WithNDR` parameter to `$false` and the sender will not be notified that the message will not be delivered.

Searching anti-spam agent logs

Exchange 2010 hub and edge transport servers are capable of using several anti-spam agents to reduce the amount of unwanted e-mail messages that enter your organization. All anti-spam activity is logged by transport servers, and this data can be used to troubleshoot issues and generate reports. In this recipe, you'll learn how to search the anti-spam agent logs using the Exchange Management Shell.

How to do it...

The `Get-AgentLog` cmdlet can be used to parse the anti-spam agent logs. To find all log entries for a particular agent, filter the output based on the `Agent` property:

```
Get-AgentLog | ?{$_.Agent -eq 'Content Filter Agent'}
```

When running this command in a busy environment, you may get back a large number of results, and you may want to consider refining your filter and perhaps limiting the date range to a specific period of time.

How it works...

All of the anti-spam agents use a series of logfiles on each transport server with the anti-spam agents installed. By default, hub transport servers do not have the anti-spam agents installed, but you can install them manually by running the `InstallAntiSpamAgents.ps1` scripts located in the `$exscripts` folder.

By default, the agent logfile directory is set with a maximum size of 250 megabytes. Each individual logfile is limited to 10 megabytes in size, and will be kept for a maximum of 30 days, or until the directory reaches its maximum size. These values can be adjusted by manually editing the `EdgeTransport.exe.config` file on your transport servers.

The following anti-spam filters are available for Exchange transport servers:

▶ **Connection Filtering**: Determines the action for a message based on the IP address of the remote server. Services such as IP Block Lists, IP Block List Providers, IP Allows Lists, and static IP address entries to determine whether or not the message should be blocked.

▶ **Sender Filtering**: Allows you to configure one or more blocked senders and the action that should be taken if a message is received from a specific address.

▶ **Recipient Filtering**: Determines the action to take based on the recipients of an e-mail message.

▶ **Sender ID**: Determines the action to take based on whether or not the sender of a message is transmitting the message from a mail server associated with the sender's domain. This is used to combat domain spoofing.

▶ **Content Filtering**: Uses Microsoft SmartScreen technology to process the contents of each message and determine whether or not the content of the message is appropriate.

▶ **Sender Reputation**: Uses IP reputation information obtained from Microsoft Update services to identify IP address that are known to send spam. Also generates a reputation score on the sending mail server's IP address based on several characteristics including message analysis and external tests.

▶ **Attachment Filtering**: Filters messages based on attachment name, file extension, or file content type.

When viewing agent log entries in the shell, several properties are available that can be used to determine the status of the message:

```
Machine: MBX1.CONTOSO.COM                                        _ □ X
[PS] C:\>Get-AgentLog | ?{$_.Agent -eq 'Sender Filter Agent'}


RunspaceId          : 041c723a-4725-443d-8a88-9ba7fc2ac30c
Timestamp           : 5/29/2011 9:31:26 PM
SessionId           : 08CDEC99390FA985
IPAddress           : 10.100.100.20
MessageId           :
P1FromAddress       : spammer@litwareinc.com
P2FromAddresses     : {}
Recipients          : {}
Agent               : Sender Filter Agent
Event               : OnMailCommand
Action              : RejectCommand
SmtpResponse        : 554 5.1.0 Sender denied
Reason              : ExactMatch
ReasonData          : spammer@litwareinc.com
Diagnostics         :
```

In this example, you can see that the message was blocked because the P1FromAddress
was configured as a blocked sender on the Sender Filtering agent with the action set to
Reject message.

There's more...

When you run the Get-AgentLog cmdlet, every entry in the logfile will be returned.
In an environment that receives a lot of e-mail this can be a little overwhelming and slow.
To narrow your searches, you can specify a time frame using the -StartDate and
-EndDate parameters:

```
Get-AgentLog -StartDate (Get-Date).AddDays(-7) -EndDate (Get-Date)
```

The previous command retrieves the agent logs for the past seven days. In this example, the
start and end dates are specified using Get-Date cmdlet, but, if needed, you can manually
type the date and time for the search:

```
Get-AgentLog -StartDate "1/1/11 9:00 AM" -EndDate "1/8/11 9:00 AM"
```

You can create searches based on the agent as shown in the first example of this recipe.
You can combine this technique with a time frame as well to refine your searches:

```
Get-AgentLog -StartDate (Get-Date).AddDays(-7) -EndDate (Get-Date) |
    ?{$_.Agent -eq 'Sender Filter Agent'}
```

This command pulls the agent logs from the past seven days. The output is piped to the
Where-Object cmdlet (using the ? alias) to filter based on the Agent property of the log
entry. In this example, only the logs for the Sender Filter Agent are retrieved.

The agent logs provide properties that identify both the sender and recipient addresses for the message. To search based on the sender, use the following syntax:

```
Get-AgentLog |
    ?{$_.P1FromAddress -or $_.P2FromAddress -eq 'sales@litwareinc.com'}
```

This command checks both the `P1FromAddress` and `P2FromAddress` properties and only returns the log entries where the sender address is `sales@litwareinc.com`

You can use a similar filter using the `-Like` comparison operator and a wild card to find all messages in the log from a particular sending domain:

```
Get-AgentLog |
    ?{$_.P1FromAddress -or $_.P2FromAddress -like '*@litwareinc.com'}
```

To retrieve the logs for specific recipients, filter on the `Recipients` property:

```
Get-AgentLog | ?{$_.Recipients -eq 'dsmith@contoso.com}
```

You can export the agent logs to a CSV file that can be used in another application, such as Excel. To do this, pipe the desired logs to the `Export-CSV` cmdlet:

```
Get-AgentLog -StartDate (Get-Date).AddDays(-3) -EndDate (Get-Date) |
    ?{$_.Agent -eq 'Content Filter Agent' -and $_.ReasonData -gt 4} |
        Export-CSV c:\contentfilter.csv -NoType
```

In this example, agent logs from the past three days processed by the Content Filter Agent and with an SCL rating of 4 or higher are exported to a CSV file.

You can use the `-Location` parameter to search agent logfiles that are located in an alternate directory. This may be useful when you have specific retention requirements and still need to report on old data that is no longer on your production transport servers. When using this parameter, specify the full path to the directory containing the logfiles:

```
Get-AgentLog -Location e:\logs
```

Keep in mind that this parameter requires a local path, so a UNC path to a shared network folder will not work.

See also

▶ *Exporting reports to text and CSV files* in *Chapter 2, Exchange Management Shell Common Tasks*

Implementing a header firewall

When messages are passed from one server to another through SMTP, Exchange edge and hub transport servers add custom X-Header fields into the message header. These headers can contain a variety of information such as mail server IP addresses, spam confidence levels (SCL), content filtering results, and rules processing status. Header firewalls are used to remove these custom X-Header fields so that unauthorized sources cannot obtain detailed information about your messaging environment. In this recipe, you'll learn how to use the Exchange Management Shell to implement a header firewall that prevents the disclosure of internal information sent to an external source.

How to do it...

One of the most common uses of a header firewall is to remove internal server infrastructure details from SMTP e-mail message headers destined for an external recipient. To do this on an edge transport server, you need to modify the permissions for the Internet send connector using the `Remove-ADPermission` cmdlet:

```
Remove-ADPermission -Identity "EdgeSync - Litware to Internet" `
-User "MS Exchange\Edge Transport Servers" `
-ExtendedRights Ms-Exch-Send-Headers-Routing `
-Confirm:$false
```

In this example, the edge server's Internet send connector named "EdgeSync - Litware to Internet" is modified. The `Ms-Exch-Accept-Headers-Routing` permission is removed from the Internet send connector for the "MS Exchange\Edge Transport Servers" account.

How it works...

By default, all connectors are configured to include routing headers in SMTP e-mail messages. This can be a security concern for many organizations as it exposes the Exchange version in the message header. In addition, for hub transport servers that are configured to send messages directly to the Internet, the internal IP addresses of servers that handled the message are included in the headers.

When viewing the headers of a message received from the `contoso.com` mail server, the following information is available:

```
Received: from EX01.contoso.com ([x.x.x.x]) by ex01.c ...
([10.100.100.20]) with mapi id 14.01.0270.001; Mon, 24 Jan  ...
```

Here we can see the internal IP address of the contoso mail server at 10.100.100.20 and the version number is 14.01.0270.001 which tells us that the server is running Exchange 2010 SP1 with Rollup Update 2. When implementing a header firewall for routing headers, this information will not be sent to external recipients.

There's more...

If you do not use an edge transport server to send Internet e-mail, and instead send messages to the Internet directly from the hub transport role, then you'll need to specify a different user when running the `Remove-ADPermission` cmdlet:

```
Remove-ADPermission -Identity Internet `
-User "NT Authority\Anonymous Logon" `
-ExtendedRights Ms-Exch-Send-Headers-Routing `
-Confirm:$false
```

Again, you'll need to specify the name of the send connector that is used to send outbound Internet e-mail. When dealing with hub transport servers, you can remove the permission for the "NT Authority\Anonymous Logon" account, since the "MS Exchange\Edge Transport Servers" user is specific only to edge transport servers.

9

High Availability

In this chapter, we will cover the following:

- ▶ Building a Windows NLB cluster for CAS servers
- ▶ Creating a Database Availability Group
- ▶ Adding mailbox servers to a Database Availability Group
- ▶ Configuring Database Availability Group network settings
- ▶ Adding mailbox copies to a Database Availability Group
- ▶ Activating mailbox database copies
- ▶ Working with lagged database copies
- ▶ Reseeding a database copy
- ▶ Performing maintenance on Database Availability Group members
- ▶ Reporting on database status, redundancy, and replication

Introduction

If you have worked with previous versions of Exchange, you may have been involved in implementing or supporting a high-availability solution that required a shared storage model. This allowed multiple server nodes to access the same physical storage, and, in the event of an active server node failure, another node in the cluster could take control of the cluster resources since it had local access to the databases and log files. This was a good model for server availability, but did not provide any protection for data redundancy.

With the release of Exchange 2007, Microsoft still supported this shared-storage clustering model, re-branded as **Single Copy Clusters** (**SCC**), but they also introduced a new feature known as continuous replication. Among the three types of continuous replication options provided, **Cluster Continuous Replication** (**CCR**) was the high-availability solution for Exchange 2007 that eliminated the potential risk of a single point of failure at the storage level. With CCR, there were no requirements for shared storage, and database changes were replicated to a passive cluster node using asynchronous log shipping after an initial database seed. Although CCR provided some compelling advantages, there were several limitations. First, you were limited to only two nodes in a CCR cluster. In addition, implementing and managing this configuration required that administrators understand the intricacies of Windows failover clustering.

Microsoft improved on their continuous replication technology and introduced **Database Availability Groups** (**DAGs**) in Exchange 2010. Limitations imposed by CCR in Exchange 2007 were removed by allowing up to 16 nodes to participate within a DAG, while also giving you the option of hosting active copies of individual databases on every server. The reliance on Windows failover clustering administration expertise has been reduced, and you can completely manage all aspects of mailbox server high availability from the Exchange Management Tools.

In this chapter, we'll cover several aspects of managing Exchange high availability using the shell. You'll learn how to create DAGs, manage database copies, perform maintenance on DAG members, and generate reports on mailbox database copies.

In addition to providing high availability for the mailbox server role through DAGs, we can eliminate a single point of failure for servers hosting the CAS role using Network Load Balancing, which we'll cover first.

Performing some basic steps

To make use of all the examples in this chapter, we'll need to use the Exchange Management Shell, and, for one recipe, we have the option of using a standard PowerShell v2 console.

You can launch the Exchange Management Shell using the following steps:

1. Log onto a workstation or server with the Exchange Management Tools installed
2. Open the Exchange Management Shell by clicking on **Start | All Programs | Exchange Server 2010**
3. Click on the **Exchange Management Shell** or the **Exchange ManagementConsole** short cut

To launch a standard PowerShell console, open a standard PowerShell console by clicking on **Start | All Programs | Accessories,** click the **Windows PowerShell** folder and then click the **Windows PowerShell** shortcut.

Unless specified otherwise in the *Getting ready* section, all of the recipes in this chapter will require the use of the Exchange Management Shell.

Building a Windows NLB cluster for CAS servers

High availability for servers running the CAS role is achieved using Network Load Balancing and CAS arrays. While it is recommended that you use a hardware network load balancing (HLB) solution, Windows **Network Load Balancing** (**NLB**) is still supported and may be appropriate for small or medium size organizations. In this recipe, you'll learn how to create a Windows NLB cluster using PowerShell for servers running Windows Server 2008 R2.

Getting ready

For this example, you'll need to run some commands against each of your CAS servers that will be a part of the NLB cluster. You must run these commands from at least one of the CAS servers, and each server in the cluster will need to be running Windows Server 2008 R2 for this to work.

To complete the steps in this recipe, you can use a standard Windows PowerShell console or use the Exchange Management Shell from the server.

How to do it...

1. The first step is to install Windows Network Load Balancing and the Windows Network Load Balancing tools on each CAS server. You can run these commands on each server to install the required components:

    ```
    Import-Module ServerManager
    Add-WindowsFeature NLB, RSAT-NLB
    ```

    If you have PowerShell remoting enabled on all of your CAS servers, you can install the required components on every server at once using `Invoke-Command`:

    ```
    $servers = 'cas1','cas2','cas3','cas4'
    Invoke-Command -ScriptBlock {
      Import-Module servermanager;Add-WindowsFeature NLB,RSAT-NLB
    } -ComputerName $servers
    ```

2. Once each of the CAS servers has the required NLB components installed, import the `NetworkLoadBalancingClusters` module and create the NLB cluster on the first node. The following command assumes that the network interface name on the server has been renamed to "NLB". Yours might be using the default interface name, which would be "Local Area Connection":

```
Import-Module NetworkLoadBalancingClusters

New-NlbCluster -InterfaceName NLB `
-ClusterNameCASArray `
-HostName CAS1 `
-ClusterPrimaryIP 172.16.23.200
```

3. Remove the default port rules that are created for the cluster:

```
Get-NlbClusterPortRule | Remove-NlbClusterPortRule -Force
```

4. Next, create the port rules for the required services:

```
Get-NlbCluster |
  Add-NlbClusterPortRule -StartPort 80 `
  -EndPort 80 `
  -Protocol TCP `
  -Affinity Single

Get-NlbCluster |
  Add-NlbClusterPortRule -StartPort 443 `
  -EndPort 443 `
  -Protocol TCP `
  -Affinity Single

Get-NlbCluster |
  Add-NlbClusterPortRule -StartPort 135 `
  -EndPort 135 `
  -Protocol TCP `
  -Affinity Single

Get-NlbCluster |
  Add-NlbClusterPortRule -StartPort 6005 `
  -EndPort 59530 `
  -Protocol TCP `
  -Affinity Single
```

5. At this point, you can add the remaining nodes to the cluster. In this example, we'll add the `cas2` server to the cluster:

```
Get-NlbCluster |
    Add-NlbClusterNode -NewNodeName cas2 `
    -NewNodeInterface NLB
```

How it works...

Windows Server 2008 R2 servers include the Server Manager PowerShell module, which is a replacement for the `ServerManagerCmd.exe` utility. Using the Server Manager module, we can install various roles and features on the server. In addition, 2008 R2 servers also include the `NetworkLoadBalancingClusters` module that can be used to install and configure Windows NLB, and, as you've seen, we can use both modules to install and configure an NLB cluster for Exchange CAS servers.

Importing the modules and installing the components is fairly straightforward. When installing the `NLB` and `RSAT-NLB` features, you first need to import the `ServerManager` module and install the features using the `Add-WindowsFeature` cmdlet. Once the `RSAT-NLB` tools are installed, we can use the Network LoadBalancing Clusters module, which is loaded using the `Import-Module` cmdlet.

When you initially create the NLB cluster, you use the `New-NLBCluster` cmdlet. In the previous example, we created an NLB cluster using the name `CASArray`, which is assigned using the `-ClusterName` parameter. This name can be anything you like, as it will not be used by clients to access the nodes in the cluster. The `-InterfaceName` and `-ClusterPrimaryIP` parameters are very important. You need to specify the network interface name on the server as the value for the `-InterfaceName` parameter. The cluster primary IP is the shared IP address that will be used to balance the traffic between the CAS servers. You'll need a host (A) record in DNS that resolves to this IP address. This DNS namespace will also be used as the CAS array end-point, which needs to be configured separately.

There's more...

In the previous example, we created port rules for several TCP ports, which are described as follows:

- ▸ **80**: HTTP connections
- ▸ **443**: HTTS connections
- ▸ **135**: RPC End Point Mapper
- ▸ **6005-59530**: Dynamic RPC port range for MAPI connections

Load balancing this set of ports will take care of the web services offered by the CAS role, such as Outlook Web App, Exchange ActiveSync, Offline Address Book, Exchange Web Services, and so on. This will also provide load balancing for connections to the RPC Client Access and Address Book services required for MAPI clients. If you need to provide access to other services such as POP or IMAP, you can use the `Add-NLBPortRule` cmdlet to add additional port rules for those protocols.

As best practice, you should explicitly define the TCP ports that will be load balanced on each node of the cluster. This gives you a little more control when configuring the affinity options for each individual service. For example, the POP and IMAP protocols don't require affinity, so if you wanted to add the ports for those services, you could configure the affinity as `None`, while other protocols such as HTTP/S and RPC will be configured as `Single`.

Exchange 2010 SP1 allows you to configure static RPC ports for the RPC Client Access and Address Book services via the registry. This allows you to restrict MAPI connections to two specific TCP ports, instead of using the dynamic port range. For detailed steps on configuring static RCP ports on CAS servers, see the following article:

Configuring Static RPC Ports on an Exchange 2010 Client Access Server

```
http://social.technet.microsoft.com/wiki/contents/articles/
configuring-static-rpc-ports-on-an-exchange-2010-client-access-
server.aspx
```

Taking it a step further

In Step 5 of the recipe, we looked at an example of adding a CAS server to the WNLB cluster. You can automate this process when adding multiple servers using a simple pipeline command. As long as the servers have matching network interface names (which is recommended), you can use the following code:

```
'cas2','cas3','cas4' | ForEach-Object{
  Get-NlbCluster |
    Add-NlbClusterNode -NewNodeName $_ `
    -NewNodeInterface NLB
}
```

You can see here that we're simply pipelining an array of server names to the `Foreach-Object` cmdlet. For every server in the collection, we add the computer to the NLB cluster.

Since Windows NLB doesn't scale well over eight nodes and doesn't provide service awareness or any affinity options other than single affinity (requests coming from the same client IP), most organizations that are serious about load balancing will implement a hardware-based load balancing solution.

See also

▸ Creating an RPC Client Access array in Chapter 7, Managing Client Access

▸ Configuring the CAS server used by RPC clients in Chapter 7, Managing Client Access

Creating a Database Availability Group

The initial setup and configuration of a Database Availability Group (DAG) is done using a single cmdlet named New-DatabaseAvailabilityGroup. In this recipe, we'll take a look at how you can automate the creation of a DAG using the Exchange Management Shell.

How to do it...

To create a DAG, use the New-DatabaseAvailabilityGroup cmdlet:

```
New-DatabaseAvailabilityGroup -Name DAG `
-WitnessServer HC1 `
-WitnessDirectory C:\FSW `
-DatabaseAvailabilityGroupIPAddresses 192.168.1.55
```

The previous command creates a new Database Availability Group named DAG. The file share witness server is set to a hub transport server named HC1, and the path for the directory is also specified, along with an IP address that will be used only by the DAG cluster resources.

How it works...

When you run the New-DatabaseAvailabilityGroup cmdlet, the only requirement is that you use a unique name for the DAG. In the previous example, we specified the information for the file share witness and IP address, but those values are optional.

 The witness server is a quorum resource used by Windows Failover clustering as a tie-breaker in DAGs with an even number of nodes.

If you do not provide a value for the witness server or witness server directory, Exchange will attempt to locate a hub transport server in the current Active Directory site. If a hub transport server that is not co-located with the mailbox role is available in the site, one will be selected automatically and the configuration of the witness server and its directory will be taken care of by Exchange.

Keep in mind that, if you do not provide an IP address for the DAG, Exchange will attempt to obtain an address for the DAG using DHCP, but it is recommend that you set the IP address statically.

There's more...

If you create a DAG using the minimum amount of information, you can always come back later and modify the configuration. For instance, say we first issue the following command:

```
New-DatabaseAvailabilityGroup -Name DAG
```

At this point, the DAG will attempt to automatically configure the witness server details and will try to obtain an IP address using DHCP. You can view review the settings of the DAG using the `Get-DatabaseAvailabilityGroup` cmdlet:

```
Get-DatabaseAvailabilityGroup -Identity DAG
```

We can update the DAG using the `Set-DatabaseAvailabilityGroup` cmdlet to modify the settings:

```
Set-DatabaseAvailabilityGroup -Identity DAG `
-WitnessServer HC1 `
-WitnessDirectory C:\FSW `
-DatabaseAvailabilityGroupIPAddresses 192.168.1.55
```

You do not have to place the witness directory on another Exchange server. For example, it's quite common for small and medium organizations to utilize two Exchange servers, both running the Mailbox, Hub Transport, and Client Access server roles, as a two-node DAG, along with a hardware load balancer to provide high availability for the CAS role. In this case, you could use a member server in the domain as the witness server; just make sure that the Exchange Trusted Subsystem security group in Active Directory is a member of the local administrator group on that server.

When you are planning on adding servers that are located in separate IP subnets, you'll need to specify an IP address that can be used by the DAG in each of the corresponding networks. For example:

```
New-DatabaseAvailabilityGroup -Name DAG `
-DatabaseAvailabilityGroupIPAddresses 10.1.1.10,192.168.1.10
```

In this example, one of the DAG members is in the 10.1.1.0/24 subnet and the other is located in the192.168.1.0/24 subnet. This will allow the cluster IP address to be brought online by a server in either site.

If you have already created the DAG and need to change the addresses, use the `Set-DatabaseAvailabilityGroup` cmdlet:

```
Set-DatabaseAvailabilityGroup -Identity DAG `
-DatabaseAvailabilityGroupIPAddresses 10.1.1.25,192.168.1.25
```

See also

▸ *Adding mailbox servers to a Database Availability Group*

Adding mailbox servers to a Database Availability Group

Once you've created a Database Availability Group (DAG), you'll need to add DAG members, which are servers running the mailbox server role. In this recipe, you'll learn how to add mailbox servers to a DAG using the Exchange Management Shell.

How to do it...

To add a mailbox server to a DAG, use the `Add-DatabaseAvailabilityGroupServer` cmdlet:

```
Add-DatabaseAvailabilityGroupServer -Identity DAG `
-MailboxServer MBX1
```

In this example, the `MBX1` server is added to a database availability group named `DAG`.

How it works...

In order to run the `Add-DatabaseAvailabilityGroupServer` cmdlet, the servers being added to the DAG must be running an Enterprise Edition of either Windows Server 2008 or 2008 R2. This is due to the requirement of the Windows Failover Clustering component which is required by the DAG. Additionally, the servers must not be a member of an existing DAG for you to successfully run this command.

If you use this cmdlet to add a mailbox server running Windows Server 2008 R2 to a DAG, the Windows Failover Clustering feature will automatically be installed if it has not been already.

When the first mailbox server is added to the DAG, a computer account known as a **Cluster Network Object** (**CNO**) is added to the Active Directory. The name of the computer account will be created using the same name as the DAG. In order for this cmdlet to complete successfully when the first mailbox server is added to the DAG, the Exchange Trusted Subsystem universal security group must have the appropriate permissions in the Active Directory to create the account. In many cases, this should not be an issue, but if you work in an environment where Active Directory security permissions have been modified to restrict access, you may need to pre-stage this CNO object and ensure that the Exchange Trusted Subsystem group has been granted Full Control permissions on the object.

There's more...

The `Add-DatabaseAvailabilityGroupServer` cmdlet will need to be run for each mailbox server that will be included in the DAG. If you want to automate this process, you have a couple of options.

First, if you simply need to add all of the mailbox servers in the organization to the DAG, use the following code:

```
Get-MailboxServer |
  Add-DatabaseAvailabilityGroupServer -Identity DAG
```

If you are working in a more complex environment with multiple Active Directory sites, you'll need to do a little more work. When adding servers to a DAG, you'll probably need to limit this to all of the mailbox servers in a particular AD site. The following code will allow you to accomplish this:

```
$mbx = Get-ExchangeServer | Where-Object{
  $_.Site -match 'Default-First-Site-Name' `
  -and $_.ServerRole -match 'Mailbox'
}

$mbx | ForEach-Object{
  Add-DatabaseAvailabilityGroupServer -Identity DAG `
  -MailboxServer $_
}
```

Here you can see that we're using the `Get-ExchangeServer` cmdlet to retrieve all mailbox servers in the default Active Directory site and storing the results in the `$mbx` variable. We then pipe that variable to the `Add-DatabaseAvailabilityGroupServer` cmdlet and add each server in the site to the DAG.

See also

▸ *Adding mailbox copies to a Database Availability Group*

Configuring Database Availability Group network settings

The Exchange Management Shell includes several cmdlets that allow you to configure the network connections used by servers in a Database Availability Group (DAG). After you have created DAG networks, or after they've been added automatically by DAG network discovery, you can view the DAG networks and their settings, modify the replication configuration, or remove them completely. This recipe provides multiple examples of how you can perform all of these tasks from the shell.

How to do it...

To view the configuration settings of your existing DAG networks, use the Get-DatabaseAvailabilityGroupNetwork cmdlet:

```
Machine: MBX1.CONTOSO.COM                                              _ □ ✕
[PS] C:\>Get-DatabaseAvailabilityGroupNetwork

Identity                   ReplicationEnabled          Subnets
--------                   ------------------          -------
DAG\DAGNetwork01           True                        {{192.168.1.0/24,Up}}
DAG\DAGNetwork02           True                        {{10.1.1.0/24,Up}}
```

The output from the cmdlet shows that there are currently two DAG networks in an organization with a single DAG. The identity of the network, the replication state, and the associated subnets are provided.

How it works...

When you create a DAG, Exchange will automatically discover the existing network connections on each server and create a DAG network for the corresponding IP subnet. Although there is a cmdlet called New-DatabaseAvailabilityGroupNetwork, you should rarely need to use it as this is generally done automatically.

If you need to force Exchange to rediscover the DAG network configuration after changes have been made, you can use the Set-DatabaseAvailabilityGroup cmdlet:

```
Set-DatabaseAvailabilityGroup -Identity DAG –DiscoverNetworks
```

Simply provide the name of the DAG using the -Identity parameter and use the -DiscoverNetworks switch parameter to indicate that Exchange should search for changes in the network configuration.

There's more...

By default, all DAG networks are used for log shipping and seeding. If you do not want to allow replication on a specific network, use the `Set-DatabaseAvailabilityGroup` cmdlet

```
Set-DatabaseAvailabilityGroupNetwork -Identity DAG\DAGNetwork02 `
-ReplicationEnabled $false
```

You may consider doing this if you want dedicated DAG networks for replication and heart beating.

Additionally, you may have other network connections on your mailbox servers that should not be used by the DAG at all. This is commonly seen with iSCSI network adapters used only for connecting to a storage area network. Since Exchange will attempt to discover all network interfaces and add a DAG network for each one, you'll need to completely disable those DAG networks if they should not be used:

```
Set-DatabaseAvailabilityGroupNetwork -Identity DAG\DAGNetwork04 `
-IgnoreNetwork $true
```

In this example, `DAGNetwork04` will be ignored by the DAG. To remove this restriction, use the same cmdlet and set the `-IgnoreNetwork` parameter to `$false` for the required DAG network.

Renaming and removing DAG networks

When making modifications to DAG networks, you may need to rename or remove one or more networks. This can be done easily in the Exchange Management Console, but if you like to work in the shell, you can do this quickly with the built-in cmdlets. For example, assume the output of `Get-DatabaseAvailabilityGroupNetwork` shows the following:

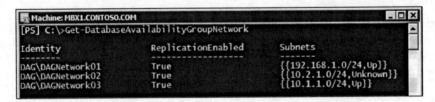

You can see from the output shown here that `DAGNetwork02` is listed as **Unknown**. In this case, this was an automatically-generated DAG network that is no longer in use by any of the servers in the DAG. Use the `Remove-DatabaseAvailabilityGroupNetwork` cmdlet to delete the network:

```
Remove-DatabaseAvailabilityGroupNetwork -Identity DAG\DAGNetwork02 `
-Confirm:$false
```

Once this network has been removed, you can rename DAGNetwork03 to DAGNetwork02:

```
Set-DatabaseAvailabilityGroupNetwork -Identity DAG\DAGNetwork03 `
-Name DAGNetwork02
```

You can run the `Get-DatabaseAvailabilityGroupNetwork` cmdlet again to view the DAG network configuration and verify that the changes have been made.

Adding mailbox copies to a Database Availability Group

Once your Database Availability Group has been created and configured, the next step is to set up database replication by adding new mailbox database copies of existing databases. In this recipe, we'll take a look at how to add mailbox database copies using the Exchange Management Shell.

How to do it...

Use the `Add-MailboxDatabaseCopy` cmdlet to create a copy of an existing database:

```
Add-MailboxDatabaseCopy -Identity DB01 `
-MailboxServer MBX2 `
-ActivationPreference 2
```

When running this command, a copy of the DB01 database is created on the MBX2 server.

How it works...

When creating database copies, keep in mind that this only works for mailbox databases, as public folder databases do not support continuous replication. When creating a copy of a database on another mailbox server, you need to ensure that the server is in the same DAG as the mailbox server hosting the source mailbox database. In addition, a mailbox server can only hold one copy of a given database, and the database path must be identical on every server in the DAG.

 You can remove a database copy using the `Remove-MailboxDatabaseCopy` cmdlet. Run `Get-Help Remove-MailboxDatabaseCopy -Full` for details.

When running the `Add-MailboxDatabaseCopy` cmdlet, you need to specify the identity of the database and the destination mailbox server that will be hosting the database copy. The activation preference for a database can optionally be set when you create the database copy. The value of the activation preference is one of the criteria used by the Active Manager during a failover event to determine the best replicated database copy to activate.

There's more...

In order to create and mount mailbox databases and add database copies to multiple servers in a DAG, several commands must be run from within the shell. If you do deployments on a regular basis or if you build up and tear down lab environments frequently, this is a process that can easily be automated with PowerShell.

The PowerShell function `New-DAGMailboxDatabase` creates new mailbox databases from scratch, mounts them, and then adds passive copies of each database to the remaining servers you specify. The code for this function is as follows:

```
function New-DAGMailboxDatabase {
param(
    $ActiveServer,
    $PassiveServer,
    $DatabasePrefix,
    $DatabaseCount,
    $EdbFolderPath,
    $LogFolderPath
 )

1..$DatabaseCount | Foreach-Object {

    $DBName = $DatabasePrefix + $_
    New-MailboxDatabase -Name $DBName `
    -EdbFilePath "$EdbFolderPath\$DBName\$DBName.edb" `
    -LogFolderPath "$LogFolderPath\$DBName" `
    -Server $ActiveServer

    Mount-Database -Identity $DBName

    $PassiveServer | Foreach-Object {
      Add-MailboxDatabaseCopy -Identity $DBName `
      -MailboxServer $_
    }
  }
}
```

Once you've added this function to your shell session, you can run it using syntax similar to the following:

```
New-DAGMailboxDatabase -ActiveServer mbx1 `
-PassiveServer mbx2,mbx3,mbx4,mbx5 `
-DatabaseCount 3 `
-DatabasePrefix MDB `
-EdbFolderPath E:\Database `
-LogFolderPath E:\Database
```

Running this function with the given parameters will do a number of things. First, you can see, by looking at the function parameter values, that three new databases will be created using a prefix of MDB. This function will create each database using the same prefix, and then number them in order. In this example, the active server MBX1 will have three new databases created, called MDB1, MDB2, and MDB3. The -PassiveServer parameter needs to have one or more servers defined. In this case, you can see that we'll be adding database copies of the three new databases on each of the passive servers specified. All databases and log files on each server will be located in a folder under E:\Database in a sub directory that matches the database name.

In some environments, you might find that trying to mount a database immediately after it was created will fail. What it boils down to is that the mount operation is happening too quickly. If you run into this, you can add a delay before the mount operation; use something like Start-Sleep 5 before calling the Mount-Database cmdlet. This will suspend the script for five seconds, giving Exchange time to catch up and realize that the database has been created before trying to mount it.

See also

▸ *Reporting on database status, redundancy, and replication*

Activating mailbox database copies

After you've created a Database Availability Group (DAG) and have added multiple database copies to the servers in your organization, you'll need to be able to move the active copies to other servers. In this recipe, you'll learn how to do this using the Exchange Management Shell.

How to do it...

Manually moving the active mailbox database to another server in a DAG is a process known as a database switchover. In order to activate passive mailbox database copies on another server, you'll need to use the `Move-ActiveMailboxDatabase` cmdlet:

```
Move-ActiveMailboxDatabase DB01 `
-ActivateOnServer MBX2 `
-Confirm:$false
```

In this example, the passive mailbox database copy of `DB01` is activated on the `MBX2` server.

How it works...

When activating a database copy, you can optionally set the `-MoveComment` parameter to a string value of your choice that will be recorded in the event log entry for the move operation.

You can choose to activate one mailbox database copy at a time or you can move all the active databases on a particular server to one or more servers in the DAG. For example:

```
Move-ActiveMailboxDatabase -Server mbx2 `
-ActivateOnServer mbx1 `
-Confirm:$false
```

As you can see here, all the active databases on `MBX2` will be moved to `MBX1`. Obviously, this requires that you have database copies located on `mbx1` for every mailbox database on `MBX2`.

When moving mailbox database copies, you can also override the auto mount dial settings for the target server by specifying one of the following values for the mount dial override settings:

- ▶ **Lossless**: This is the default value for the `-MountDialOverride` parameter. When performing a lossless mount, all log files from the active copy must be fully replicated to the passive copy.
- ▶ **GoodAvailability**: Specifies that the copy queue length must be less than or equal to six log files in order to activate the passive copy.
- ▶ **BestEffort**: Mounts the database regardless of the copy queue length and could result in data loss.
- ▶ **BestAvailability**: Specifies that the copy queue length must be less than or equal to 12 log files in order to activate the passive copy.

For example, to move the active database of `DB01` from `MBX2` to `MBX1` with good availability, use the `-MountDialOverride` parameter when running the cmdlet:

```
Move-ActiveMailboxDatabase DB01 `
-ActivateOnServer MBX1 `
```

```
-MountDialOverride GoodAvailability `
-Confirm:$false
```

There's more...

If you want to forcefully activate an unhealthy database copy, there are a few parameters available with the `Move-ActiveMailboxDatabase` that can be used, depending on the situation.

For example, if you have a database copy with a corrupt content index state, you can force activation of the database using the `-SkipClientExperienceChecks` parameter:

```
Move-ActiveMailboxDatabase DB01 `
-ActivateOnServer MBX1 `
-SkipClientExperienceChecks `
-Confirm:$false
```

At this point, the search catalog on `DB01` will need to be recrawled or reseeded.

You also have the option of skipping database health checks when attempting to move an active database. It is recommended that you only do this when an initial activation attempt has failed:

```
Move-ActiveMailboxDatabase DB01 `
-ActivateOnServer MBX1 `
-SkipHealthChecks `
-Confirm:$false
```

Finally, you can use the `-SkipLagChecks` parameter to allow activation of a database copy that has copy and replay queue lengths outside of their required thresholds:

```
Move-ActiveMailboxDatabase DB01 `
-ActivateOnServer MBX1 `
-SkipLagChecks `
-Confirm:$false
```

It's important to point out here that activating databases that are missing log files will result in data loss and unhappy users.

See also

- ▸ *Reporting on database status, redundancy, and replication*

Working with lagged database copies

The concept of a lagged database copy is based on functionality introduced with Exchange 2007 that was included with **Standby Continuous Replication** (**SCR**). Using lagged database copies, we can configure a replay lag time in which log files that are replicated to database copies are not played into the database file, therefore lagging behind the active database for a given period of time. The benefit of this is that it gives you the ability to recover point in time data in the event of a logical database corruption. In this recipe, you'll learn how to use the Exchange Management Shell to work with lagged database copies.

How to do it...

1. To create a lagged database copy, specify a replay lag time value when adding a mailbox database copy:

   ```
   Add-MailboxDatabaseCopy -Identity DB03 `
   -MailboxServer mbx2 `
   -ReplayLagTime 3.00:00:00
   ```

   In this example, a new lagged database copy is added to the MBX2 mailbox server with a three day replay lag time.

2. You can also change a regular database copy to a lagged copy:

   ```
   Set-MailboxDatabaseCopy -Identity DB01\mbx2 `
   -ReplayLagTime 12:00:00
   ```

This time, the passive database copy of DB01 on the MBX2 server is configured with a lag replay time of 12 hours. Notice that the Identity is specified in the format of <Database Name>\<Server Name>.

How it works...

When creating lagged database copies, the maximum replay time that can be set is **14 days**. In addition to the -ReplayLagTime parameter, both cmdlets shown in the previous example provide a -TruncationLagTime parameter. Setting the truncation lag time on a lagged database copy allows you to configure the amount of time that Exchange will hold on to any log files that have been played into the database before deleting them.

When using either the -ReplayLagTime or -TruncationLagTime parameters, you need to specify the amount of time in the format of *Days.Hours:Minutes:Seconds*. Alternatively, you can pass a TimeSpan object to either of these parameters:

```
Set-MailboxDatabaseCopy -Identity DB01\mbx2 `
-ReplayLagTime (New-TimeSpan -Hours 12)
```

The `New-TimeSpan` cmdlet is a PowerShell core cmdlet and has parameters that can be used to create a `TimeSpan` object defined in days, hours, minutes, and seconds.

One of the things you need to keep in mind is that you don't want lagged database copies to be automatically activated in the event of a database failover. The first reason for this is that you lose your point in time data recovery options. Secondly, if you have several days of log files that still need to be replayed into a database, the mount time for a lagged database can be very long and can take several hours.

Based on these reasons, you'll want to block activation of your lagged copies after they have been configured. To do this, use the `Suspend-MailboxDatabaseCopy` cmdlet:

```
Suspend-MailboxDatabaseCopy -Identity DB01\MBX2 `
-ActivationOnly `
-Confirm:$false
```

Make sure you use the `-ActivationOnly` switch parameter when running the cmdlet, as shown previously, otherwise it will be suspended indefinitely.

There's more...

Unfortunately, to replay the log files up to a specific point in time, you need to follow a process that cannot be done entirely using the shell. First, you need to suspend the lagged database copy. Next, you have to figure out which log files are required to meet your point in time backup requirements, and move any log files that aren't needed out of the log file path to another location. Finally, you delete the checkpoint file for the database and replay any outstanding log files into the database using the `Eseutil` command line utility. At that point, the database should be clean and you should be able to resume and activate the database copy. Fortunately, database logical corruption is an extremely rare occurrence, but if you need the ability to recover from a specific point in time, you may want to consider using Windows Server Backup or a third-party backup solution, or become familiar with the process of recovering from a lagged database copy.

Reseeding a database copy

There may be times when database replication issues arise in your environment. These issues could be caused by hardware failures, network issues, or, in extremely rare cases, log file corruption, and leave you with failed database copies that need to be reseeded. This recipe outlines the process for reseeding database copies using the Exchange Management Shell.

How to do it...

1. To reseed a database copy, suspend replication using the following command syntax:

   ```
   Suspend-MailboxDatabaseCopy -Identity DB01\MBX2 -Confirm:$false
   ```

2. Next, you're ready to reseed the database. Use the `Update-MailboxDatabaseCopy` cmdlet, as shown:

   ```
   Update-MailboxDatabaseCopy -Identity DB01\MBX2 `
   -DeleteExistingFiles
   ```

How it works...

When using the `Update-MailboxDatabaseCopy` cmdlet to reseed a database copy, you can use the `-DeleteExistingFiles` switch parameter to remove the passive database and log files. Depending on the size of the database, it may take a long time to perform the reseed. Once the reseed is complete, replication for the database will automatically be resumed.

If you don't want replication to resume automatically after a reseed, you can configure it for manual resume:

```
Update-MailboxDatabaseCopy -Identity DB01\MBX2 `
-DeleteExistingFiles `
-ManualResume
```

In this example, we've added the `-ManualResume` switch parameter. After the reseed, we can manually resume replication:

```
Resume-MailboxDatabaseCopy -Identity DB01\MBX2
```

There's more...

One of the things that you may run into is a database with a corrupt content index state. In this situation, it's not necessary to reseed the entire database, and you can reseed the content index catalog independently:

```
Update-MailboxDatabaseCopy -Identity DB01\MBX2 -CatalogOnly
```

Using the `-CatalogOnly` switch parameter as shown previously will allow you to reseed the content index catalog without reseeding the database.

Alternatively, you also have the option of reseeding only the database:

```
Update-MailboxDatabaseCopy -Identity DB01\MBX2 -DatabaseOnly
```

In this example, the DB01 database on the MBX2 server is reseeded without having to seed a copy of the content index catalog.

See also

▶ *Reporting on database status, redundancy, and replication*

Performing maintenance on Database Availability Group members

When it comes to performing maintenance on servers that are part of a Database Availability Group (DAG), you'll need to move any active databases off to another member in the DAG. This will allow you to install patches or take the server down for hardware repairs or upgrades without affecting database availability. This recipe will show you how to use some of the built-in PowerShell scripts installed by Exchange 2010 SP1 that can be used to place a server in and out of maintenance mode.

How to do it...

1. First, switch to the $exscripts directory:

   ```
   Set-Location $exscripts
   ```

2. Next, run the StartDagServerMaintenance.ps1 script and specify the server name that should be put into maintenance mode:

   ```
   .\StartDagServerMaintenance.ps1 -ServerName mbx1
   ```

How it works...

When you run the StartDagMaintenance.ps1 script, it moves all the active databases that are running on the specified server to other members of the DAG. The script will then pause the server node in the cluster and set the DatabaseCopyAutoActivationPolicy mailbox server setting to Blocked. The Suspend-MailboxDatabaseCopy cmdlet is run for each database hosted by the DAG member and the cluster core resources are moved to another server in the DAG, if needed.

After maintenance is complete, run the StopDagServerMaintenance.ps1 script to take the server out of maintenance mode:

```
.\StopDagServerMaintenance.ps1 -ServerName mbx1
```

This will run the `Resume-MailboxDatabaseCopy` cmdlet for each database located on the specified server and resume the node in the cluster. The auto activation policy for the mailbox server will then be set back to `Unrestricted` and the server will be back online, ready for production use.

There's more...

After you've performed maintenance on your DAG members, the databases that were previously active are not moved back, even after running the stop DAG maintenance script. If you are performing maintenance on multiple servers at the same time, you might end up with an uneven distribution of active databases running on other servers in the DAG.

To correct this, the `RedistributeActiveDatabases.ps1` script located in the `$exscripts` folder can be used to re-balance the active database copies across the DAG. There are two options for balancing active database copies within a DAG: by activation preference and by site and activation preference.

When using the `-BalanceDbsByActivationPreference` parameter, the script tries to move the databases to their most preferred copy based on activation preference, regardless of the Active Directory site. If you use the `-BalanceDbsBySiteAndActivationPreference` parameter, the script will attempt to activate the most preferred copy and also try to balance them within each Active Directory site.

When running the script, specify the name of the DAG and the preferred method used to re-balance the databases:

```
.\RedistributeActiveDatabases.ps1 -DagName DAG `
-BalanceDbsByActivationPreference `
-ShowFinalDatabaseDistribution `
-Confirm:$false
```

Notice that the `-ShowFinalDatabaseDistribution` parameter was also used when we ran this script. This will provide a report that displays the actions that were taken to balance the databases:

```
Machine: MBX1.CONTOSO.COM                                    _ □ ×
------------------
Successfully moved         : 2
Moved to less preferred    : 0
Failed to move             : 0
Not moved                  : 2

Start time                 : Sunday, June 05, 2011 8:50:16 PM
End time                   : Sunday, June 05, 2011 8:50:23 PM
Duration                   : 00:00:07.1857520


DbName                     : DB1
ActiveOnPreferenceAtStart  : 2
ActiveServerAtStart        : MBX2
ActiveOnPreferenceAtEnd    : 1
ActiveServerAtEnd          : mbx1
IsOnMostPreferredCopy      : True
MoveStatus                 : MoveSucceeded
```

Here you can see that several key pieces of information are returned, including the success
or failure of the moves and the total duration.

Reporting on database status, redundancy, and replication

When dealing with servers and database copies in a Database Availability Group (DAG), you
need to keep a close eye on your database status, including replication health, as well as
operational events such as database mounts, moves, and failovers. In this recipe, you'll learn
how to use the Exchange Management Shell, along with some built-in PowerShell scripts to
proactively monitor your servers and databases configured for high availability.

How to do it...

To view status information about databases that have been configured with database copies,
use the Get-MailboxDatabaseCopyStatus cmdlet:

```
Get-MailboxDatabaseCopyStatus -Server mbx1 |
    select Name,Status,ContentIndexState
```

In this example, we're viewing all of the database copies on the MBX1 server to determine the health and status of the databases. The output from the previous command will look similar to the following:

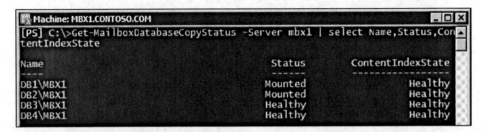

You can see from the above output that the MBX1 server is currently hosting active mailbox databases which are reported with a status of Mounted. The passive database copies hosted on this server are reported as Healthy.

How it works...

In our previous example, we selected only a few of the available properties returned by the Get-MailboxDatabaseCopyStatus cmdlet to get an idea of the health of the databases. The default output for the Get-MailboxDatabaseCopyStatus cmdlet will also provide details about the status of your mailbox database copies and show you the CopyQueueLength and ReplayQueueLength values. Keeping an eye on this information is critical to ensure that database replication is working properly.

If you need to retrieve more detailed information about the database copies on a server, you can pipe this cmdlet to Format-List and review several properties that provide details about copy and replay queue length, log generation and inspection, activation status, and more:

```
Get-MailboxDatabaseCopyStatus -Server mbx1 | Format-List
```

To view the details of a particular database copy, use the -Identity parameter and specify the database and server name in the format of <Database Name>\<Server Name>, as shown in the following command::

```
Get-MailboxDatabaseCopyStatus -Identity DB01\MBX1
```

You can review the status of networks being used for log shipping and seeding using the -ConnectionStatus switch parameter:

```
Get-MailboxDatabaseCopyStatus -Identity DB01\MBX2 `
-ConnectionStatus | Format-List
```

When using this parameter, the `IncomingLogCopyingNetwork` and `SeedingNetwork` properties returned in the output will provide the replication networks being used for these operations.

There's more...

Another way to get a quick overview of the replication status of your mailbox database copies is to use the `Test-ReplicationHealth` cmdlet.

When you run this cmdlet, use the `-Identity` parameter to specify the mailbox server that should be tested, as shown:

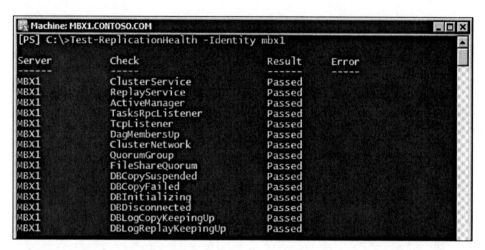

```
Machine: MBX1.CONTOSO.COM                                          _ □ ×
[PS] C:\>Test-ReplicationHealth -Identity mbx1

Server          Check                   Result      Error
------          -----                   ------      -----
MBX1            ClusterService          Passed
MBX1            ReplayService           Passed
MBX1            ActiveManager           Passed
MBX1            TasksRpcListener        Passed
MBX1            TcpListener             Passed
MBX1            DagMembersUp            Passed
MBX1            ClusterNetwork          Passed
MBX1            QuorumGroup             Passed
MBX1            FileShareQuorum         Passed
MBX1            DBCopySuspended         Passed
MBX1            DBCopyFailed            Passed
MBX1            DBInitializing          Passed
MBX1            DBDisconnected          Passed
MBX1            DBLogCopyKeepingUp      Passed
MBX1            DBLogReplayKeepingUp    Passed
```

As you can see from the output, all of the cluster services and resources are tested. In addition, several aspects of database copy health will be checked, including log replay, log copy queues, and the status of the database and whether it is suspended, disconnected, or initializing.

To proactively monitor replication health on an on-going basis, you can schedule the following script to run every hour or so. It will send a message to a specified e-mail address with any errors that are being reported:

```
param(
    $To,
    $From,
    $SMTPServer
)

$DAGs = Get-DatabaseAvailabilityGroup
$DAGs | Foreach-Object{
    $_.Servers | Foreach-Object {
```

```
$test = Test-ReplicationHealth -Identity $_.Name
$errors = $test | Where-Object{$_.Error}
if($errors) {
  $errors | Foreach-Object {
    Send-MailMessage -To $To `
   -From $From `
   -Subject " Replication Health Error" `
   -Body $_.Error `
   -SmtpServer $SMTPServer
  }
 }
}
}
```

This script iterates though every DAG in your environment and every mailbox server that is a member of a DAG. The `Test-ReplicationHealth` cmdlet is run for each server, and any errors reported will be e-mailed to the specified recipient.

To use this script, save the previous code to a file such as `ReplicationHealth.ps1`. When you schedule the script to run, call the script and provide values for the recipient e-mail address, the sender address, and the SMTP server used to send the message:

```
c:\ReplicationHealth.ps1 -To administrator@contoso.com `
-From sysadmin@contoso.com `
-SMTPServer hc1.contoso.com
```

Remember, depending on where your script is running from, if you are using one of your hub transport servers as the SMTP server, you may need to configure your receive connectors to allow SMTP relay.

Understanding switchover and failover metrics

The `CollectOverMetrics.ps1` script can be used to read the event logs from the mailbox servers that are configured in a DAG, and it gathers information about database mounts, moves, and failovers. This script is installed with Exchange 2010 and is located in the `$exscripts` directory.

To run the script, switch to the `$exscripts` directory:

```
Set-Location $exscripts
```

Next, run the script and specify the name of the DAG you want to to receive a report for, and the location where the report should be saved:

```
.\CollectOverMetrics.ps1 -DatabaseAvailabilityGroup DAG `
-ReportPath c:\Reports
```

When running this command, you'll see output similar to the following:

```
Machine: MBX1.CONTOSO.COM                                    _ □ X
Get statistics from MBX2
Get statistics from MBX1
Found total of 47 entries
Searching for ACLL loss reports on MBX2.
Searching for ACLL loss reports on MBX1.

Generated the following per-DAG reports:
c:\Reports\FailoverReport.DAG.2011_06_05_20_57_28.csv
```

As you can see, each server in the DAG will be processed and a CSV file will be generated in the specified report path. At this point, you can read the CSV file into the shell using the `Import-CSV` cmdlet:

```
Import-Csv c:\Reports\FailoverReport.DAG.2011_06_05_20_57_28.csv
```

You can then view details about switchover or failover events in each database, which will be similar to the following:

```
Machine: MBX1.CONTOSO.COM                                    _ □ X
DatabaseName           : DB1
TimeRecoveryStarted    : 6/5/2011 8:50:20 PM
TimeRecoveryEnded      : 6/5/2011 8:50:23 PM
ActionInitiator        : Admin
ActionCategory         : Move
ActionReason           : Rebalance
Result                 : Success
DurationOutage         : 2.7050062
DurationDismount       : 0.4566823
DurationBcs            : 0.1245223
DurationAcll           : 0.5068131
DurationMount          : 1.5350646
DurationOther          : 0.2064462
ActiveOnStart          : mbx2.contoso.com
ActiveOnFinish         : MBX1.contoso.com
```

You can limit the reports to specific databases when running the script and also specify a start and end time so you can limit the information returned to meet your requirements.

Understanding Replication Metrics

The `CollectReplicationMetrics.ps1` is also included in the `$exscripts` directory on Exchange 2010 SP1 servers. This script can be used to collect data from performance counters related to database replication, and it needs to be run for a period of time in order for it to gather information. Similar to the `CollectOverMetrics.ps1` script, you specify a DAG name and a path used to save the report in CSV or HTML format. When running `CollectReplicationMetrics.ps1`, you need to specify a duration which defines the amount of time the script will run. You also need to specify a frequency interval for which metrics will be collected.

To run the script, switch to the $exscripts directory:

```
Set-Location $exscripts
```

Next, run the script and specify the DAG name, duration, frequency, and report path that should be used:

```
.\CollectReplicationMetrics.ps1 -DagName DAG `
-Duration '01:00:00' `
-Frequency '00:01:00' `
-ReportPath c:\reports
```

Using the given parameter values, the script will run for one hour, and collect replication metrics every minute. When the script completes, you can read the CSV files that were generated into the shell using the Import-CSV cmdlet, or open them up in Excel for review.

See also

▶ *Scheduling scripts to run at a later time* in *Chapter 2, Exchange Management Shell Common Tasks*

10
Exchange Security

In this chapter, we will cover the following:

- ▶ Granting users full access permissions to mailboxes
- ▶ Finding users with full access to mailboxes
- ▶ Sending e-mail messages as another user or group
- ▶ Working with Role Based Access Control (RBAC)
- ▶ Creating a custom RBAC role for administrators
- ▶ Creating a custom RBAC role for end users
- ▶ Troubleshooting Role Based Access Control
- ▶ Generating a certificate request
- ▶ Installing certificates and enabling services
- ▶ Importing certificates on multiple exchange servers

Introduction

When it comes to managing security in Exchange 2010, you have several options, depending on the resources that you're dealing with. For example, you can allow multiple users to open a mailbox by assigning them full access permissions on a mailbox object, but granting administrators the ability to create recipient objects needs to be done through Role Based Access Control (RBAC). Obviously, since the security for both of these components is handled differently, we have unrelated sets of cmdlets that need to be used to get the job done, and managing each of them through the shell will require a unique approach.

In this chapter, we'll take a look at several solutions implemented through the Exchange Management Shell that address each of the components described previously, as well as some additional techniques that can be used to improve your efficiency when dealing with Exchange security.

Performing some basic steps

To work with the code samples in this chapter, follow these steps to launch the Exchange Management Shell:

1. Log onto a workstation or server with the Exchange Management Tools installed

2. Open the Exchange Management Shell by clicking on **Start | All Programs | Exchange Server 2010**

3. Click on the **Exchange Management Shell** shortcut

Granting users full access permissions to mailboxes

One of the most common administrative tasks that Exchange administrators need to perform is managing the access rights to one or more mailboxes. For example, you may have several users that share access to an individual mailbox, or you may have administrators and help desk staff that need to be able to open end users, mailboxes when troubleshooting a problem or providing technical support. In this recipe, you'll learn how to assign the permissions required to perform these tasks through the Exchange Management Shell.

How to do it...

To assign full access rights for an individual user to a specific mailbox, use the Add-MailboxPermission cmdlet:

```
Add-MailboxPermission -Identity dsmith `
-User hlawson `
-AccessRights FullAccess
```

After running this command, the user hlawson will be able to open the mailbox belonging to dsmith and read or modify the data within the mailbox.

How it works...

When you assign full access rights to a mailbox, you may notice that the change does not take effect immediately, and the user that has been granted permissions to a mailbox still cannot access that resource. This is because the Information Store service uses a cached mailbox configuration that by default is only refreshed every two hours. You can force the cache to refresh by restarting the Information Store service on the mailbox server that is hosting the active database where the mailbox resides. Obviously this is not something that should be done during business hours on production servers since it will disrupt mailbox access for end users.

Since we can grant permissions to a mailbox using the `Add-MailboxPermission` cmdlet, you would be correct when assuming that this change can also be reversed, if needed. To remove the permissions assigned in the previous example, use the `Remove-MailboxPermission` cmdlet:

```
Remove-MailboxPermission -Identity dsmith `
-User hlawson `
-AccessRights FullAccess `
-Confirm:$false
```

In addition to assigning full access permissions to individual users, you can also assign this right to a group:

```
Add-MailboxPermission -Identity dsmith `
-User "IT Help Desk" `
-AccessRights FullAccess
```

In this example, the `IT Help Desk` is a mail-enabled universal security group, and it has been granted full access to the `dsmith` mailbox. All users who are members of this group will be able to open the mailbox and access its contents through Outlook or OWA.

Of course, you may need to do this for multiple users, and doing so one mailbox at a time is not very efficient. To make this a little easier, we can make use of a simple pipeline command. For example, let's say that you want to grant full access rights to all mailboxes in the organization:

```
Get-Mailbox -ResultSize Unlimited -RecipientTypeDetails UserMailbox |
   Add-MailboxPermission -User "IT Help Desk" `
   -AccessRights FullAccess
```

The given command retrieves all user mailboxes in the organization, and sends them down the pipeline to the `Add-MailboxPermission` cmdlet, where full access rights are assigned to the `IT Help Desk` group.

There's more...

If you need to assign access permissions to all the mailboxes in your organization, you probably should consider doing this at the database level, rather than on an individual mailbox basis. In the previous example, we used a pipeline operation to apply the permissions to all mailboxes with a one-liner. The limitation with this is that the command only sets the permissions on the existing mailboxes; any new mailbox created afterwards will not inherit these permissions. You can solve this problem by assigning the `Receive-As` extended right to a user or group on a particular database.

For example, if all of our mailboxes are located in the `DB01` database, we can allow a user access to every mailbox in the database using the following command:

```
Add-ADPermission -Identity DB01 `
-User support `
-ExtendedRights Receive-As
```

After running this command, the support account will be able log on to every mailbox in the `DB01` database, as well as any mailboxes created in that database in the future.

Of course, you'll likely have more than one database in your organization. If you want to apply this setting to every mailbox database in the organization, pipe the output from the `Get-MailboxDatabase` cmdlet to the `Add-ADPermission` cmdlet using the appropriate parameters:

```
Get-MailboxDatabase |
Add-ADPermission –User support `
-ExtendedRights Receive-As
```

Once this command has been run, the user account `support` will be able connect to any mailbox in the Exchange organization.

See also

▶ *Sending e-mail messages as another user or group*

Finding users with full access to mailboxes

One of the issues with assigning full mailbox access to users and support personnel is that things change over time. People change roles, move to other departments, or even leave the organization. Keeping track of all of this and removing full access permissions when required can be challenging in a fast-paced environment. This recipe will allow you to solve that issue using the Exchange Management Shell to find out exactly who has full access permissions for the mailboxes in your environment.

How to do it...

To find all of the users or groups who have been assigned full access rights to a mailbox, use the `Get-MailboxPermission` cmdlet:

```
Get-MailboxPermission -Identity administrator |
    Where-Object {$_.AccessRights -like "*FullAccess*"}
```

You can see here that we are limiting the results using a filter by piping the output to the `Where-Object` cmdlet. Only the users with the `FullAccess` access rights will be returned.

How it works...

The previous command is useful for quickly viewing the permissions for a single mailbox while working interactively in the shell. The first problem with this approach is that it also returns a lot of information that we're probably not interested in. Consider the truncated output from our previous command:

```
Machine: MBX1.CONTOSO.COM                                        _ □ ✕
[PS] C:\>Get-MailboxPermission -Identity administrator | Where-Object {$_.Ac
cessRights -like "*FullAccess*"}

Identity              User                AccessRights      IsInherited Deny
--------              ----                ------------      ----------- ----
contoso.com/Users...  NT AUTHORITY\SELF   {FullAccess,...   False       False
contoso.com/Users...  CONTOSO\sysadmin    {FullAccess}      False       False
contoso.com/Users...  CONTOSO\IT Help Desk {FullAccess}     False       False
contoso.com/Users...  CONTOSO\Domain Ad... {FullAccess}     True        True
```

Notice that both the `IT Help Desk` and `sysadmin` have full access permissions to the administrator mailbox. This is useful, because we know that someone assigned these permissions to the mailbox since this is not something Exchange is going to do on its own. What is not so useful is that we also see all of the built-in full access permissions that apply to every mailbox, such as the `NT AUTHORITY\SELF` and other default permissions. To filter out this information, we can use a more complex filter:

```
Get-MailboxPermission administrator |
    Where-Object {
        ($_.AccessRights -like "*FullAccess*") `
        -and ($_.User -notlike "NT AUTHORITY\SELF") `
        -and ($_.IsInherited -eq $false)
    }
```

You can see that we're still filtering based on the `AccessRights` property, but now we're excluding the `SELF` account and any other accounts that receive their permissions through inheritance. The output now gives us something that's a little easier to work with when reviewing a report:

```
Machine: MBX1.CONTOSO.COM                                              _ □ ✕
Identity              User              AccessRights    IsInherited Deny
--------              ----              ------------    ----------- ----
contoso.com/Users...  CONTOSO\sysadmin      {FullAccess}    False       False
contoso.com/Users...  CONTOSO\IT Help Desk {FullAccess}    False       False
```

This is an easy way to figure out which accounts have been assigned full access to a mailbox via the `Add-MailboxPermission` cmdlet. Keep in mind that users who have been assigned these permissions at the database level receive their permissions through inheritance, so you may need to adjust the filter to meet your specific needs.

There's more...

Finding out which users have full access rights to an individual mailbox can be useful for quick troubleshooting, but chances are you're going to need to figure this out for all the mailboxes in your organization. The following code will generate the output that provides this information:

```
foreach($mailbox in Get-Mailbox -ResultSize Unlimited) {
  Get-MailboxPermission $mailbox |
    Where-Object {
    ($_.AccessRights -like "*FullAccess*") `
    -and ($_.User -notlike "NT AUTHORITY\SELF") `
    -and ($_.IsInherited -eq $false)
  }
}
```

As you can see here, we use a `foreach` loop to process all of the mailboxes in the organization. Inside the loop, we're using the same filter from the previous example to determine which users have full access rights to each mailbox.

Sending e-mail messages as another user or group

In some environments, it may be required to allow users to send e-mail messages from a mailbox as if the owner of that mailbox had actually sent this message. This can be accomplished by granting `Send-As` permissions to a user on a particular mailbox. In addition, you can also allow a user to send e-mail messages that are sent using the identity of a distribution group. This recipe explains how you can manage these permissions from the Exchange Management Shell.

How to do it...

To assign `Send-As` permissions to a mailbox, we use the `Add-ADPermission` cmdlet:

```
Add-ADPermission -Identity "Frank Howe" `
-User "Eric Cook" `
-ExtendedRights Send-As
```

After running the previous command, Eric Cook can send messages from Frank Howe's mailbox.

How it works...

The `Add-ADPermission` cmdlet uses the `-Identity` parameter to classify the object to which you will assign the permissions. Unlike many of the Exchange cmdlets, you cannot use the alias of the mailbox when assigning a value to the `-Identity` parameter. You can use the user's display name, as shown previously, as long as it is unique) or you can use the distinguished name of the object. If you do not know a user's full name, you can use the `Get-Mailbox` cmdlet and pipe the object to the `Add-ADPermission` cmdlet:

```
Get-Mailbox fhowe |
    Add-ADPermission -User ecook -ExtendedRights Send-As
```

You might find this syntax useful when assigning the `Send-As` right in bulk. For example, to grant a user `Send-As` permission for all users in a particular OU, use the following syntax:

```
Get-Mailbox -OrganizationalUnit contoso.com/Sales |
    Add-ADPermission -User ecook -ExtendedRights Send-As
```

If you ever need to remove these settings, simply use the `Remove-ADPermission` cmdlet. This command will remove the permissions assigned in the first example:

```
Remove-ADPermission -Identity "Frank Howe" `
-User ecook `
-ExtendedRights Send-As `
-Confirm:$false
```

There's more...

To assign `Send-As` permissions to a distribution group, the process is exactly the same as for a mailbox. Use the `Add-ADPermission` cmdlet:

```
Add-ADPermission -Identity Marketing `
-ExtendedRights send-as `
-User ecook
```

You can also provide the identity of the group to the `Add-ADPermission` cmdlet via a pipeline command, just as we saw earlier with the `Get-Mailbox` cmdlet. To do this with a distribution group, use the `Get-DistributionGroup` cmdlet:

```
Get-DistributionGroup -ResultSize Unlimited |
    Add-ADPermission -User ecook -ExtendedRights Send-As
```

In the given example, the user `ecook` is given the `Send-As` right for all distribution groups in the organization.

Working with Role Based Access Control (RBAC)

The security model in Exchange 2010 has completely changed and no longer resembles the way we used to manage security in previous versions of Exchange. Exchange 2010 introduces the Role Based Access Control (RBAC) permissions model, which essentially determines which cmdlets administrators and end users are allowed to use in order to change settings within the system. This recipe will show you how to work with the predefined RBAC permissions in Exchange 2010.

How to do it...

Let's say that you need to allow a member of your staff to manage the settings of the Exchange servers in your organization. This administrator only needs to manage server settings, and should not be allowed to perform any other tasks, such as recipient management.

Exchange 2010 provides a large set of predefined permissions that can be used to address common tasks like this. In this case, we can use the `Server Management` role group that allows administrators to manage the servers in the organization.

All we need to do to assign the permission is to add the required user account to this role group:

```
Add-RoleGroupMember -Identity "Server Management" -Member bwelch
```

At this point, the user can use the Exchange Management Console or the Exchange Management Shell to perform server-related management tasks.

How it works...

In Exchange 2010, the graphical tools (the Exchange Management Console and the Exchange Control Panel) use Exchange Management Shell cmdlets to make configuration changes, create recipient objects, and more. Any change made within the organization is carried out by one or more cmdlets, regardless of whether or not you are performing the task through the GUI or the shell.

Exchange 2010 implements RBAC by grouping sets of cmdlets used to perform specific tasks into management roles. Think of a management role simply as a list of cmdlets. For example, one of the roles assigned via the `Server Management` role group is called `Exchange Servers`. This role allows an assigned user the ability to use over 30 separate cmdlets that are specifically related to managing servers, such as `Get-ExchangeServer`, `Set-ExchangeServer`, and more.

There are a number of built-in role groups that you can use to delegate typical management tasks to the administrators in your environment. You can view all of the built-in role groups using the `Get-RoleGroup` cmdlet.

Role groups can assign many different management roles to a user. In the previous example, we were working with the `Server Management` role group, which assigns a number of different management roles to any user that is added to this group. To view a list of these roles, we can use the `Get-ManagementRoleAssignment` cmdlet:

```
Get-ManagementRoleAssignment -RoleAssignee 'Server Management' |
    Select-Object Role
```

The output from this command is shown in the following screenshot:

As you can see, each management role assigned through this role group is returned. To determine which cmdlets are made available by each of these roles, we can run the `Get-ManagementRoleEntry` cmdlet against each of them individually. An example of this can be seen in the following screenshot:

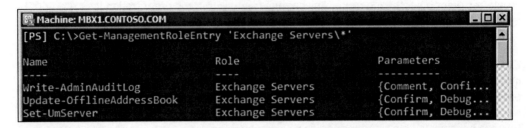

Management role entries are listed in the format of `<Role Name>\<Cmdlet Name>`. The `Get-ManagementRoleEntry` cmdlet can be used with wildcards, as shown with the previous command. The output from the `Get-ManagementRoleEntry` command in the previous example is truncated for readability, but, as you can see, there are several cmdlets that are part of the `Exchange Servers` management role, which can be assigned via the `Server Management` role group. If only this role is assigned to a user, they are given access to these specific cmdlets and will not see other cmdlets, such as `New-Mailbox`, since that is part of another management role.

To view all of the management roles that exist in the organization, use the `Get-ManagementRole` cmdlet. You can then use the `Get-ManagementRoleEntry` cmdlet to determine which cmdlets belong to that role.

There's more...

Many of the management roles installed with Exchange 2010 can be assigned to users by adding them to a role group. Role groups are associated with management roles through something called role assignments. Although the recommended method of assigning permissions is through the use of role groups, you can still directly assign a management role to a user with the `New-ManagementRoleAssignment` cmdlet:

```
New-ManagementRoleAssignment -Role 'Mailbox Import Export' `
-User administrator
```

In this example, the administrator is assigned the `Mailbox Import Export` role, which is not associated with any of the built-in role groups. In this case, we can create a direct assignment as shown previously, or use the `-SecurityGroup` parameter to assign this role to an existing role group or a custom role group created with the `New-RoleGroup` cmdlet.

RBAC is for end-users too

Everything we've looked at so far is RBAC for administrators, but end users need to be able to run cmdlets too. Now, this doesn't mean that they need to fire up EMS and start executing commands, but other things that they change will require the use of PowerShell cmdlets behind the scenes.

A good example of this is the **Exchange Control Panel** (**ECP**). When a user logs into ECP, the very first thing they see is the **Account Information** screen, which allows them to change various settings that apply to their user account, such as their address, city, state, zip code, and phone numbers. When users change this information in ECP, those changes are carried out in the background with Exchange Management Shell cmdlets.

Here's the confusing part. End users are also assigned permissions from management roles, but not through role groups or role assignments as they are applied to administrators. Instead, end users are assigned their management roles through something called a role assignment policy.

When you install Exchange, a single role assignment policy is created. Mailboxes that are created or moved over to Exchange 2010 will use the `Default Role Assignment Policy`, which gives users some basic rights, such as modifying their contact information, creating Inbox rules through ECP, and more.

To determine which management roles are applied to the default role assignment policy, use the following command:

```
Get-RoleAssignmentPolicy "Default Role Assignment Policy" |
    Format-List AssignedRoles
```

See also

- ▸ *Creating a custom RBAC role for administrators*
- ▸ *Creating a custom RBAC role for end users*
- ▸ *Troubleshooting Role Based Access Control*

Creating a custom RBAC role for administrators

Sometimes, the management roles that are installed by Exchange are not specific enough to meet your needs. When you are faced with this issue, the solution is to create a custom RBAC role. The process can be a little tricky, but the level of granular control that you can achieve is quite astounding. This recipe will show you how to create a custom RBAC role that can be assigned to administrators based on a very specific set of requirements.

How to do it...

Let's say that your company has decided that a group of support personnel should be responsible for the creation of all new Exchange recipients. You want to be very specific about what type of access this group will be granted and you plan on implementing a custom management role based on the following requirements:

- ▸ Support personnel should be able to create Exchange recipients in the Employees OU in the Active Directory
- ▸ Support personnel should not be able to create Exchange recipients in any other OU in the Active Directory
- ▸ Support personnel should not be able to remove recipients in the Employees OU, or any other OU in the Active Directory

Use the following steps to implement a custom RBAC role for the support group based on the previous requirements:

1. First, we need to create a new custom management role:

   ```
   New-ManagementRole -Name "Employee Recipient Creation" `
   -Parent "Mail Recipient Creation"
   ```

2. Next, we need to modify the role so that the support staff cannot remove recipients from the organization:

   ```
   Get-ManagementRoleEntry "Employee Recipient Creation\*" |
     Where-Object {$_.name -like "remove-*"} |
       Remove-ManagementRoleEntry -Confirm:$false
   ```

3. Now we need to scope this role to a specific location in Active Directory:

   ```
   New-ManagementScope -Name Employees `
   -RecipientRoot contoso.com/Employees `
   -RecipientRestrictionFilter {
      (RecipientType -eq "UserMailbox") -or
      (RecipientType -eq "MailUser") -or
      (RecipientType -eq "MailContact")
   }
   ```

4. Finally, we can create a custom role group and add the support staff as members:

   ```
   New-RoleGroup -Name Support `
   -Roles "Employee Recipient Creation" `
   -CustomRecipientWriteScope Employees `
   -Members bjacobs,dgreen,jgordon
   ```

How it works...

The built-in management roles cannot be modified, so, when we want to customize an existing role to meet our needs, we need to create a new custom role based on an existing parent role. Since we know that the built-in `Mail Recipient Creation` role provides the cmdlets that our support group will need, the first thing we must do is create a new role as a child of the `Mail Recipient Creation` role called `Employee Recipient Creation`.

One of the requirements in our scenario was that support personnel should not be able to remove recipients from the organization, so we edited our custom role to get rid of any cmdlets that could be used to remove recipients from the *Employees* OU, or any other location in the Active Directory. We used the `Remove-ManagementRoleEntry` cmdlet to delete all of the `Remove-*` cmdlets from our custom role, and therefore this will prevent users assigned to the custom role from removing recipient objects.

Next, we created a management scope that defines what the support group can access. We used the `New-ManagementScope` cmdlet to create the `Employee` management scope. As you can see from the command, we specified the recipient root as the *Employees* OU, per the requirements in our scenario. When specifying a `RecipientRoot`, we are also required to specify a `RecipientRestrictionFilter` which will be limited to the `UserMailbox`, `MailUser`, and `MailContact` recipient types.

Finally, we created our management role group using the `New-RoleGroup` cmdlet. The command used created a role group named `support`, which created a universal security group in the Microsoft Exchange Security Groups OU in Active Directory. The role group was created using the `Employees` management scope, limiting access to the *Employees* OU. Also, notice that we added three users to the group using the `-Members` parameter. Doing it this way automatically creates the management role assignment for us. You can view management role assignments using the `Get-ManagementRoleAssignment` cmdlet.

There's more...

One of the things making custom RBAC role assignments so powerful is the use of the management scope. When we created the `Employees` management scope, we used the `-RecipientRestrictionFilter` parameter to limit the types of recipients that would apply to that scope. When creating the role group, we specified this scope using the `-CustomRecipientWriteScope` parameter. This locks the administrator down to only writing to recipient objects that match the scope's filter and recipient root.

Keep in mind that scopes can be created with a `ServerRestrictionFilter`, and role groups and role assignments can be configured to use these scopes by assigning them to the `CustomConfigWriteScope` parameter. This can be useful when assigning custom RBAC roles for administrators who will be working on servers, as opposed to recipients. For example, instead of limiting your staff to working with recipient objects in a specific OU, you could create a custom role that only applies to specific servers in your organization, such as ones that are located in another city or Active Directory site.

See also

- ▸ *Working with Role Based Access Control (RBAC)*
- ▸ *Creating a custom RBAC role for end-users*
- ▸ *Troubleshooting Role Based Access Control*

Creating a custom RBAC role for end users

Like custom RBAC roles for administrators, you can also create custom roles that apply to your end users. This may be useful when you need to allow them to modify additional configuration settings that apply to their own accounts through the Exchange Control Panel (ECP). This recipe will provide a real world example of how you might implement a custom RBAC role for end users in your Exchange organization.

How to do it...

When users log on to ECP, they have the ability to modify their work phone number, their fax number, their home phone number, and their mobile phone number, among other things. Let's say that we need to limit this so that they can only update their home phone number, as their work, fax, and mobile numbers will be managed by the administrators in your organization.

Since built-in roles cannot be modified, we need to create a custom role based on one of the existing built-in roles. Use the following steps to implement a custom RBAC role for end users based on the previous requirements:

1. The `MyContactInformation` role allows end users to modify their contact information, so we'll create a new custom role based on this parent role:

    ```
    New-ManagementRole -Name MyContactInfo `
    -Parent MyContactInformation
    ```

2. The `Set-User` cmdlet is what executes in the background when users modify their contact information. This is done using several parameters made available through this cmdlet. We'll create an array that contains all of these parameters so we can modify them later:

    ```
    $parameters = Get-ManagementRoleEntry "MyContactInfo\Set-User" |
        Select-Object -ExpandProperty parameters
    ```

3. Next, we'll create a new array that excludes the parameters that allow the end users to change their business related phone numbers:

```
$parameters = $parameters |
  Where-Object{
    ($_ -ne "Phone") -and `
    ($_ -ne "MobilePhone") -and `
    ($_ -ne "Fax")
  }
```

4. Now we'll modify the `Set-User` cmdlet so that it only provides our custom list of parameters:

```
Set-ManagementRoleEntry -Identity "MyContactInfo\Set-User" `
-Parameters $parameters
```

5. The `MyContactInformation` role is assigned to end users through the default role assignment policy, so we need to remove that assignment from the policy:

```
Remove-ManagementRoleAssignment -Identity `
"MyContactInformation-Default Role Assignment Policy" `
-Confirm:$false
```

6. Finally, we can add our custom RBAC role to the default role assignment policy:

```
New-ManagementRoleAssignment -Role MyContactInfo `
-Policy "Default Role Assignment Policy"
```

When users log in to ECP, they'll only be able to modify their home phone numbers.

How it works...

As you can see from these steps, not only do management roles provide users with access to cmdlets, but also to specific parameters available on those cmdlets. We're able to limit the use of the `Set-User` cmdlet by removing access to the parameters that allow users to modify properties of their account that we do not want them to change.

End user management roles are assigned through a role assignment policy. By default, only one role assignment policy is created when you deploy Exchange 2010, called the `Default Role Assignment Policy`. In the first example, we created a custom role based on the existing `MyContactInformation` role, which allows end users to update their personal contact details.

One of the questions you may be asking at this point is how did we determine that the `MyContactInformation` role was the one that needed to be modified? Well, we can come to this conclusion by first checking which roles assign the `Set-User` cmdlet with the `-Phone` parameter:

All of the built-in end user management roles are prefixed with "My", and, as you can see from the previous output, the only two roles that apply here are listed at the bottom. Now we need to check the default role assignment policy:

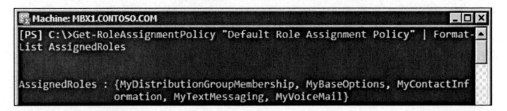

As you clearly see from the output, the only roles assigned to the end users that contain the `Set-User` cmdlet are assigned by the `MyContactInformation` role, and we know that this is the role that needs to be replaced with a custom role.

There's more...

If you don't want to modify the existing role assignment policy, you can create a new role assignment policy that can be applied to individual users. This may be useful if you need to test things without affecting other users. To do this, use the `New-RoleAssignmentPolicy` cmdlet, and specify a name for the policy and all roles that should be applied via this role assignment policy:

```
New-RoleAssignmentPolicy -Name MyCustomPolicy `
-Roles MyDistributionGroupMembership,
        MyBaseOptions,
        MyTextMessaging,
        MyVoiceMail,
        MyContactInfo
```

Once this is complete, you can assign the role assignment policy to an individual user with the `Set-Mailbox` cmdlet:

```
Set-Mailbox -Identity "Ramon Shaffer" `
-RoleAssignmentPolicy MyCustomPolicy
```

If you later decide that this new policy should be used for all of your end users, you'll need to do two things. First, you'll need to set this role assignment policy as the default policy for new mailboxes:

```
Set-RoleAssignmentPolicy MyCustomPolicy -IsDefault
```

Then you'll need to modify the existing users so that they'll be assigned the new role assignment policy:

```
Get-Mailbox -ResultSize Unlimited |
   Set-Mailbox -RoleAssignmentPolicy MyCustomPolicy
```

See also

▸ *Working with Role Based Access Control (RBAC)*

▸ *Creating a custom RBAC role for administrators*

▸ *Troubleshooting Role Based Access Control*

Troubleshooting Role Based Access Control

Troubleshooting permission issues can be challenging, especially if you've implemented custom RBAC roles. In this recipe we'll take a look at some useful troubleshooting techniques that can be used to troubleshoot issues related to RBAC.

How to do it...

There are several scenarios in which you can use the Exchange Management Shell cmdlets to solve problems with RBAC, and there are a couple of cmdlets that you'll need to use to do this. The following steps outline solutions for some common troubleshooting situations:

1. To determine which management roles have been assigned to a user, use the following command syntax:

```
Get-ManagementRoleAssignment -GetEffectiveUsers |
   Where-Object {$_.EffectiveUserName -eq 'sysadmin'}
```

2. To retrieve a list of users that have been assigned a specific management role, run the following command and specify a role name such as the `Legal Hold` role, as shown next:

```
Get-ManagementRoleAssignment -Role 'Legal Hold' -GetEffectiveUsers
```

3. You can determine if a user has write access to a recipient, server, or database. For example, use the following syntax to determine if the `sysadmin` account has the ability to modify the Dave Jones mailbox:

```
Get-ManagementRoleAssignment -WritableRecipient djones `
  -GetEffectiveUsers |
    Where-Object{$_.EffectiveUserName -eq 'sysadmin'}
```

After running the previous command, any roles that give the `sysadmin` write access to the specified recipient will be returned.

How it works...

The `Get-ManagementRoleAssignment` cmdlet is a useful tool when it comes to troubleshooting RBAC issues. If an administrator is unable to modify a recipient or make a change against a server, it is very possible that the role assignment is either incorrect or it might not exist at all. In each step shown previously, we used the `-GetEffectiveUsers` parameter with this cmdlet, which provides a quick way to find out if certain roles have been assigned to a specific user.

In addition to the `-WritableRecipient` parameter, you have the option of using either the `-WritableServer` or `-WritableDatabase` parameters. These can be used to determine if an administrator has write access to a server or database object. This can be useful in determining if a role assignment has not been made for an administrator that should be able to modify one of these objects. You can also use this as a method of determining if some administrators have been granted too much control in your environment.

There's more...

If someone is not receiving the permissions you think they should, they may not be a member of the required role group. The steps outlined previously should help you make this determination, but it may be as simple as making sure the administrator has been added to the right role group that will assign the appropriate roles. You can retrieve the members of a role group in the shell using the `Get-RoleGroupMember` cmdlet. This command will return all members of the Organization Management role group:

```
Get-RoleGroup 'Organization Management' | Get-RoleGroupMember
```

You can also use these cmdlets to generate a report of all the members of each role group. For example, this will display the member of each role group in the shell:

```
foreach($rg in Get-RoleGroup) {
  Get-RoleGroupMember $rg |
    Select-Object Name,@{n="RoleGroup";e={$rg.Name}}
}
```

See also

▸ *Working with Role Based Access Control (RBAC)*

▸ *Creating a custom RBAC role for administrators*

▸ *Creating a custom RBAC role for end users*

Generating a certificate request

In order to create a new certificate, you need to generate a certificate request using the either the Exchange Management Console, or through the shell using the `New-ExchangeCertificate` cmdlet. Once you have a certificate request generated, you can obtain a certificate from an internal Certificate Authority or a third party external Certificate Authority. In this recipe, we'll take a look at the process of generating a certificate request from the Exchange Management Shell.

How to do it...

1. In this example, we'll generate a request using two **Subject Alternative Names (SANs)**. This will allow us to support multiple URLs with one certificate:

    ```
    $cert = New-ExchangeCertificate -GenerateRequest `
    -SubjectName "c=US, o=Contoso, cn=mail.contoso.com" `
    -DomainName autodiscover.contoso.com,mail.contoso.com `
    -PrivateKeyExportable $true
    ```

2. After the request has been generated, we can export it to a file that can be used to submit a request to a certificate authority:

    ```
    $cert | Out-File c:\cert_request.txt
    ```

How it works...

When you install Exchange 2010, self-signed certificates are automatically generated and installed to encrypt data passed between hub transport servers, and between clients and CAS Servers. Since these self-signed certificates will not be trusted by your client machines when accessing the CAS role, it is recommended that you replace these certificates with new certificates issued from a trusted certificate authority. If you do not replace these certificates, clients such as Outlook 2010 and Outlook Web App users will receive certificate warnings informing them that the certificates are not issued from a trusted source. This can create some confusion for end-users and could generate calls to your help desk.

You can get around these certificate warnings by installing the server's self-signed certificates in the Trusted Root Certificate Authority store on the client machines, but even in a small environment this can become an administrative headache. That's why it is recommended to replace the self-signed certificates before placing your Exchange 2010 servers into production.

When using the `New-ExchangeCertificate` cmdlet to generate a certificate request, you can use the `-SubjectName` parameter to specify the common name of the certificate. This value is set using an X.500 distinguished name, and, as you saw in step two, the common name for the certificate was set to `mail.contoso.com`. If you do not provide a value for the `-SubjectName` parameter, the hostname of the server where the cmdlet is run to generate the request will be used.

The `-DomainName` parameter is used to define one or more FQDNs that will be listed in the Subject Alternative Names field of the certificate. This allows you to generate certificates that support multiple FQDNs that can be installed on multiple Exchange servers. For example, you may have several CAS servers in your environment, and, instead of generating multiple certificates for each one, you can simply add Subject Alternative Names to cover all of the possible FQDNs that users will need to access, and then install a single certificate on multiple CAS servers.

The `New-ExchangeCertificate` cmdlet outputs a certificate request in Base64 format. In the previous example, we saved the output of the command in a variable so we could simply output the data to a text file. Once the request is generated, you'll need to supply the data from this request to the issuing **Certificate Authority** (**CA**). This is usually done through a web form hosted by the CA where you submit the certificate request. You can simply open the request file in Notepad, copy the data and paste it into the submission form on the CA website. Once the information is submitted, the CA will generate a certificate that can be downloaded and installed on your servers. See the next recipe in this chapter titled *Installing Certificates and Enabling Services* for steps on how to complete this process.

There's more...

It's recommended as a best practice that you limit the number of Subject Alternative Names on your certificates, so your name space design should be completely defined before creating your certificates. For example, let's say that you've got four CAS servers in a CAS array and all of your servers are located in a single Active Directory site. Even though you have multiple servers, you only need to include the FQDNs that your end users will use to access these servers. If you configure your CAS URLs appropriately, there's no requirement to include the server's FQDN or hostname as a Subject Alternative Name in this scenario.

If you plan on installing a certificate on multiple servers, make sure that you mark the certificate as exportable by setting the `-PrivateKeyExportable` parameter to `$true`. This will allow you to export the certificate and install it on the remaining servers in your environment.

See also

 - ▸ *Installing certificates and enabled services*
 - ▸ *Importing certificates on multiple exchange servers*

Installing certificates and enabling services

After you've generated a certificate request and have obtained a certificate from a certificate authority, you will need to install the certificate on your server using the `Import-ExchangeCertificate` cmdlet. This recipe will show you how to install certificates issued from a certificate authority and how to assign services to the certificate using the Exchange Management Shell.

How to do it...

1. Let's say that you have requested and downloaded a certificate from an Active Directory Enterprise CA and downloaded the file to the root of the `C:\` drive. First, read the certificate data into a variable in the shell:

   ```
   $certificate = Get-Content -Path c:\certnew.cer `
   -Encoding Byte `
   -ReadCount 0
   ```

2. Next, we can import the certificate and complete the pending request:

   ```
   Import-ExchangeCertificate -FileData $certificate
   ```

3. Now that the certificate is installed, we can enable it for specific services:

```
Get-ExchangeCertificate -DomainName mail.contoso.com |
    Enable-ExchangeCertificate -Services IIS,SMTP
```

At this point, the certificate has been installed and will now be used for Client Access services, such as Outlook Web App and the Exchange Control Panel, and also for secure SMTP used by the Hub Transport role.

How it works...

Since the Exchange Management Shell uses remote PowerShell sessions, the `Import-ExchangeCertificate` cmdlet cannot use a local file path to import a certificate file. This is because the cmdlet could be running on any server within your organization and a local file path may not exist. This is why we need to use the `-FileData` parameter to provide the actual data of the certificate. In the first step, we read the certificate data into a byte array using the `Get-Content` cmdlet, which is a PowerShell core cmdlet, and is not run through the remote shell on the Exchange server. The content of the certificate is stored as a byte array in the `$certificate` variable, and we can assign this data to the `-FileData` parameter of the `Import-ExchangeCertificate` cmdlet, which allows us to import the certificate to any Exchange server through the remote shell.

 Use the -Server parameter with the Get-ExchangeCertificate cmdlet to target a specific server. Otherwise, the cmdlet will run against the server you are currently connected to.

There's more...

As shown previously, once the certificate has been imported, it needs to have one or more services assigned before it can be used by an Exchange server. After importing a certificate, you can use the `Get-ExchangeCertificate` cmdlet to view it:

You can see that we have two certificates installed. When assigning services to a certificate, we need to be specific about which one needs to be modified. We can do this either by specifying the thumbprint of the certificate when running the `Enable-ExchangeCertificate` cmdlet, or by using the method shown previously, where we used the `Get-ExchangeCertificate` cmdlet with the `-DomainName` parameter to retrieve a particular certificate, and send it down the pipeline to the `Enable-ExchangeCertificate` cmdlet.

Let's say that we're connected to a server named EXCH01. We've imported a certificate, and now we need to view all of the installed certificates so we can figure out which one needs to be enabled and assigned the appropriate services. We can do this by viewing a few key properties of each certificate, using the Get-ExchangeCertificate cmdlet:

```
Machine: MBX1.CONTOSO.COM                                           _ □ ×
[PS] C:\>Get-ExchangeCertificate | Format-List Thumbprint,CertificateDomains
,Services,IsSelfSigned


Thumbprint         : 0F3FC9DB7BBE409E4E66D8422A37518041E907E0
CertificateDomains : {mbx1, mbx1.contoso.com}
Services           : IMAP, POP, IIS, SMTP
IsSelfSigned       : True

Thumbprint         : CF61E66A6BE1A286471B30DFCEA1126F6BC7DCBB
CertificateDomains : {mail.contoso.com, autodiscover.contoso.com}
Services           : None
IsSelfSigned       : False
```

Here you can see that we've retrieved the Thumbprint, CertificateDomains, and assigned Services for each installed Exchange certificate in list format. We've also selected the IsSelfSigned property that will tell us whether or not the certificate was issued from a certificate authority, or installed by Exchange as a self-signed certificate. It's pretty clear from the output that the second certificate in the list is the one that was issued from a certificate authority, since the IsSelfSigned property is set to $false. At this point, we can use the certificate thumbprint to assign services to this certificate:

```
Enable-ExchangeCertificate `
-Thumbprint CF61E66A6BE1A286471B30DFCEA1126F6BC7DCBB `
-Services IIS,SMTP
```

If you have multiple certificates installed, especially with duplicate domain names, use the method shown here to assign services based on the certificate thumbprint. Otherwise, you may find it easier to enable certificates based on the domain name, as shown in the first example.

See also

▶ *Importing certificates on multiple exchange servers*

▶ *Generating a certificate request*

Importing certificates on multiple exchange servers

If your environment contains multiple Exchange servers, you'll likely want to use the same certificate on multiple servers. If you have a large amount of servers, importing certificates one at a time, even with the Exchange Management Shell, could end up being quite time-consuming. This recipe will provide a method for automating this process using the Exchange Management Shell.

How to do it...

Once you've gone through the process of generating a certificate request, installing a certificate, and assigning the services on one server, you can export that certificate and deploy it to your remaining servers. The following steps outline the process of exporting an installed certificate on a server named CAS1 and importing that certificate on a server named CAS2:

1. In order to export a certificate, we'll first need to assign a password to secure the private key that will be exported with the certificate:

   ```
   $password = ConvertTo-SecureString -String P@ssword `
   -AsPlainText `
   -Force
   ```

2. Now we can export the certificate data with the Export-ExchangeCertificate cmdlet. We'll retrieve the certificate from the CAS1 server and export the data to a binary-encoded value stored in a variable:

   ```
   $cert = Get-ExchangeCertificate `
     -DomainName mail.contoso.com -Server cas1 |
       Export-ExchangeCertificate –BinaryEncoded:$true `
       -Password $password
   ```

3. Next, we can import the certificate file data into the CAS2 server as a certificate:

   ```
   Import-ExchangeCertificate -FileData $cert.FileData `
   -Password $password `
   -Server cas2
   ```

4. Finally, we can assign the services to the certificate that was recently imported on the CAS2 server:

   ```
   Get-ExchangeCertificate `
     -DomainName mail.contoso.com -Server cas2 |
       Enable-ExchangeCertificate -Services IIS,SMTP
   ```

How it works...

As you can see from these steps, exporting a certificate from one server and importing it on an additional server is rather complex, and would be even more so if you want to do this on something like 5 or 10 servers. If this is a common task that needs to be done frequently, then it makes sense to automate it even further. The following PowerShell function will automate the process of exporting a certificate from a source server and importing the certificate on one or more target servers:

```
function Deploy-ExchangeCertificate {
  param(
    $SourceServer,
    $Thumbprint,
    $TargetServer,
    $Password,
    $Services
  )

  $password = ConvertTo-SecureString -String $Password `
  -AsPlainText `
  -Force

  $cert = Get-ExchangeCertificate -Thumbprint $Thumbprint `
  -Server $SourceServer |
    Export-ExchangeCertificate -BinaryEncoded:$true `
    -Password $Password

  foreach($Server in $TargetServer) {
    Import-ExchangeCertificate -FileData $cert.FileData `
    -Password $Password `
    -Server $Server

    Enable-ExchangeCertificate -Thumbprint $Thumbprint `
    -Server $Server `
    -Services $Services `
    -Confirm:$false `
    -Force
  }
```

This function allows you to specify a certificate that has been properly set up and installed on a source server, and then deploy that certificate and enable a specified list of services on one or more servers. The function accepts a number of parameters and requires that you specify the thumbprint of the certificate that you want to deploy.

Let's say that you've got a Client Access server array that contains six CAS servers. You've gone through the certificate generation process, obtained the certificate from a trusted certificate authority, and installed the certificate on the first CAS server. Now you can add the `Deploy-ExchangeCertificate` function to your PowerShell session and deploy the certificate to the remaining servers in the array.

First, you need to determine the thumbprint on the source server you want to deploy, and you can do this using the `Get-ExchangeCertificate` cmdlet. The next step is to run the function with the following syntax:

```
Deploy-ExchangeCertificate -SourceServer cas1 `
-TargetServer cas2,cas3,cas4,cas5,cas6 `
-Thumbprint DE4382508E325D27D2D48033509EE5F9C621A07B `
-Services IIS,SMTP `
-Password P@ssw0rd
```

The function will export the certificate on the CAS1 server with the thumbprint value assigned to the `-Thumbprint` parameter. The value assigned to the `-Password` parameter will be used to secure the private key when the certificate data is exported. The certificate will then be installed on the five remaining CAS servers in the array, and will have the IIS and SMTP services assigned.

There's more...

You may want to export your certificates to an external file that can be used to import the certificate on another server at a later time. For example:

```
$password = ConvertTo-SecureString `
-String P@ssword `
-AsPlainText `
-Force

$file = Get-ExchangeCertificate `
-Thumbprint DE4382508E325D27D2D48033509EE5F9C621A07B –Server cas1 |
  Export-ExchangeCertificate –BinaryEncoded:$true -Password $password

Set-Content -Path c:\cert.pfx -Value $file.FileData -Encoding Byte
```

This is similar to the previous examples, except this time we're exporting the certificate data to an external `.pfx` file.

You can use the following commands to import this certificate at a later time on another server in your environment:

```
$password = ConvertTo-SecureString `
-String P@ssword `
```

```
-AsPlainText `
-Force

$filedata = Get-Content -Path c:\cert.pfx -Encoding Byte -ReadCount 0

Import-ExchangeCertificate -FileData ([Byte[]]$filedata) `
-Password $password `
-Server cas2
```

This will import the certificate from the external `.pfx` file to the CAS2 server. Once this is complete, you can use the `Enable-ExchangeCertificate` cmdlet to assign the required services to the certificate.

See also

- ▸ *Generating a certificate request*
- ▸ *Installing certificates and enabling services*

11
Compliance and Audit Logging

In this chapter, we will cover the following:

- ▶ Managing archive mailboxes
- ▶ Configuring archive mailbox quotas
- ▶ Creating retention tags and policies
- ▶ Applying retention policies to mailboxes
- ▶ Placing mailboxes on retention hold
- ▶ Performing a discovery search
- ▶ Placing mailboxes on litigation hold
- ▶ Enabling mailbox audit logging
- ▶ Generating mailbox audit log reports
- ▶ Configuring Administrator Audit Logging
- ▶ Searching administrator audit logs

Introduction

One of the biggest changes introduced in Exchange 2010 was the inclusion of several new compliance and audit logging features. Over the years, many organizations have relied on third-party products for archiving and retaining of e-mail messages for legal protection and regulatory compliance. Fortunately, this function is now built into the product, along with some very powerful auditing capabilities that can track which users are accessing and modifying items in mailboxes and which administrators are making changes throughout the Exchange organization.

In this chapter, we'll look at some of the most common tasks related to compliance and audit logging that can be automated through the Exchange Management Shell. This includes managing retention polices, performing legal searches, and restoring items from mailboxes, along with generating detailed reports based on mailbox and administrator audit logs.

Performing some basic steps

To work with the code samples in this chapter, follow these steps to launch the Exchange Management Shell:

1. Log on to a workstation or server with the Exchange Management Tools installed
2. Open the Exchange Management Shell by clicking on **Start | All Programs | Exchange Server 2010**
3. Click on the **Exchange Management Shell** shortcut

Managing archive mailboxes

Starting with Exchange 2010, a new personal storage concept was introduced, called an archive mailbox. The idea is that you can give one or more users a secondary mailbox that can be accessed from anywhere, just like their regular mailbox, and it can be used to store older mailbox data, eliminating the need for a PST file. With the release of Exchange 2010 SP1, archive mailboxes can now be located on a database separate from the primary mailbox, allowing administrators to put low-priority, archived mailbox data on an inexpensive lower tier of storage. In this chapter, we'll look at how you can manage archive mailboxes for your users through the Exchange Management Shell.

How to do it...

To create an archive mailbox for an existing mailbox, use the `Enable-Mailbox` cmdlet, as shown in the following example:

```
Enable-Mailbox -Identity administrator -Archive
```

How it works...

When you create an archive mailbox for a user, they can access their personal archive when connecting to Outlook 2007 or 2010, or the Outlook Web App. In the previous example, we created an archive mailbox for an existing user. Using a one-liner, we can easily do this in bulk for multiple users. For example, to create an archive mailbox for all users in the DB01 database, you could use the following command:

```
Get-Mailbox -Database DB01 |
    Enable-Mailbox -Archive -ArchiveDatabase DB02
```

As you can see, we're making use of the pipeline here to perform a bulk operation on all of the mailboxes in the DB01 database. The result of the Get-Mailbox command is piped to the Enable-Mailbox cmdlet. The -Archive switch parameter tells the cmdlet that we know this user already has a mailbox, and we just want to create a personal archive for the user. In addition, we've specified the -ArchiveDatabase parameter so that the archives for each mailbox will not be created in the same database as the primary mailbox, but, instead, in the DB02 database.

In addition to creating an archive for an existing user, we can enable a personal archive for a mailbox as it is created. For example, the following commands will create a mailbox and a personal archive for a new user:

```
$password = ConvertTo-SecureString P@ssword -AsPlainText -Force

New-Mailbox -Name "Dave Smith" -alias dsmith `
-UserPrincipalName dave@contoso.com `
-Database DB01 `
-Archive `
-ArchiveDatabase DB02 `
-Password $password
```

In this command, we've created the primary mailbox in the DB01 database, and, again, we've made use of the -Archive and -ArchiveDatabase parameters so that the archive is created in the DB02 database.

There's more...

If you need to turn off an archive mailbox for a user, you can use the Disable-Mailbox cmdlet with the -Archive switch parameter. The command to disable the personal archive for Dave Smith is as simple as this:

```
Disable-Mailbox -Identity dsmith -Archive –Confirm:$false
```

When you run this command, the archive mailbox for the user goes into a disconnected state, but the user can still access their primary mailbox. The disconnected archive mailbox is retained in the database until the deleted mailbox retention period for the database has elapsed.

See also

- *Adding, modifying, and removing mailboxes* in *Chapter 3, Managing Recipients*
- *Configuring archive mailbox quotas*

Configuring archive mailbox quotas

As you enable archive mailboxes for end users and set up retention policies, you may find that the default limitations configured for archive mailboxes do not meet your needs. In this recipe, you'll learn how to modify archive mailbox quotas using the Exchange Management Shell.

How to do it...

1. To modify the archive quota settings for a single mailbox, use the `Set-Mailbox` cmdlet:

   ```
   Set-Mailbox dsmith -ArchiveQuota 10gb -ArchiveWarningQuota 8gb
   ```

2. To do this in bulk, use the `Get-Mailbox` cmdlet to retrieve the mailboxes that need to be updated and pipe the results to the `Set-Mailbox` cmdlet. For example, this one-liner would update all users in the `DB01` database:

   ```
   Get-Mailbox -Database DB01 |
     Where-Object {$_.ArchiveName} |
       Set-Mailbox -ArchiveQuota 10gb -ArchiveWarningQuota 8gb
   ```

As you can see here, we're filtering the results of the `Get-Mailbox` cmdlet based on the `ArchiveName` property. If this property is defined, then we know that the user has an archive mailbox enabled.

How it works...

There are two settings that can be used to configure quotas for archive mailboxes:

- `ArchiveWarningQuota`: When an archive mailbox exceeds the size set for the archive warning quota, a warning message is sent to the mailbox owner and an event is logged on the mailbox server that hosts the archive mailbox

- `ArchiveQuota`: When an archive mailbox exceeds the size set for the archive quota, a warning message is sent to the mailbox owner and items can no longer be moved to the archive mailbox

In Exchange 2010 SP1, archive mailboxes are configured with default limitations. The archive warning quota is set to 40 GB and the archive quota is set to 50 GB. These settings can only be applied on a per-mailbox basis, unlike regular mailboxes, which can receive their limits from the parent database.

If you implement custom archive quotas, you may need to run a script on a regular basis in order to update any new archives that have been recently created. For example, let's say that you've decided that archive mailboxes should be no larger than 5 GB. You could run a script regularly, either manually or through a scheduled task, that will update any new users that have been added to the organization:

```
Get-Mailbox –ResultSize Unlimited |
  Where-Object {$_.ArchiveName -and $_.ArchiveQuota -ge 50gb} |
    Set-Mailbox -ArchiveQuota 5gb -ArchiveWarningQuota 4gb
```

Again, we're using the `Where-Object` cmdlet to filter on the `ArchiveName` property, but we've added another filter to check if the `ArchiveQuota` is greater than or equal to 50 GB. If so, we send those mailboxes down the pipeline to the `Set-Mailbox` cmdlet and modify the archive quota settings.

There's more...

You can view the current settings for these values using the `Get-Mailbox` cmdlet. For example, to check the values for a specific user, run the following command:

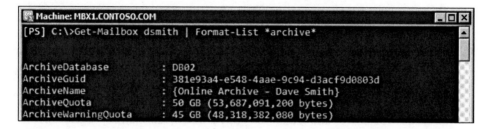

This uses a wildcard to display all the properties for a mailbox that contain the word *archive*. This will provide the quota settings, as well as the database location for the archive mailbox, which may be different than that of the user's primary mailbox.

See also

- *Managing archive mailboxes*

Creating retention tags and policies

Retention policies are the recommended method for implementing messaging records management in Exchange 2010. Retention policies use retention tags to apply settings to mailbox folders and individual items. Retention tags are configured with a retention action that can be taken when an item reaches its retention age limit. In this recipe, you'll learn how to create retention tags and policies in the Exchange Management Shell.

How to do it.

There are three types of retention tags that can be used to apply retention settings to a mailbox through a retention policy. The following steps outline the process of creating custom retention tags based on these types and assigning them to a new retention policy:

1. The following command will create a retention policy tag for the `Inbox` folder specifying that items older than 90 days be deleted permanently:

```
New-RetentionPolicyTag -Name AllUsers-Inbox `
-Type Inbox `
-Comment "Items older than 90 days are deleted" `
-RetentionEnabled $true `
-AgeLimitForRetention 90 `
-RetentionAction PermanentlyDelete
```

2. In addition, we can create a default policy tag for the entire mailbox. To do this, we need to set the type to `All`. A default retention policy tag of type `All` will apply to any item that does not have a retention tag applied:

```
New-RetentionPolicyTag -Name AllUsers-Default `
-Type All `
-Comment "Items older than 120 days are permanently deleted" `
-RetentionEnabled $true `
-AgeLimitForRetention 120 `
-RetentionAction PermanentlyDelete
```

3. We can also create personal tags that can be used by end users for personal items:

```
New-RetentionPolicyTag -Name Critical `
-Type Personal `
-Comment "Use this tag for all critical items" `
-RetentionEnabled $true `
-AgeLimitForRetention 730 `
-RetentionAction DeleteAndAllowRecovery
```

4. After creating these tags, we can create a new retention policy and add the previously-created tags:

```
New-RetentionPolicy -Name AllUsers `
-RetentionPolicyTagLinks AllUsers-Inbox,AllUsers-Default,Critical
```

At this point, the `AllUsers` retention policy can be assigned to one or more mailboxes, and the settings defined by the retention tags will be applied.

How it works...

In the RTM version of Exchange 2010, we had to completely manage retention tags and policies using the shell. Starting with Exchange 2010 SP1, retention policies and tags can be managed from the Exchange Management Console, and you may find it much easier to deal with policies and tags through the GUI. In either case, the cmdlets used to create and manage tags and policies can still be used if automation or command line administration is required.

As we saw from the previous example, there are three types of retention tag that can be used to apply retention settings to mailbox folders and messages. These types are outlined in detail as follows:

- **Retention Policy Tags**: These are used to apply settings to default folders such as Inbox and Sent Items.

- **Default Policy Tags**: These apply to any item that does not have a retention tag set. A retention policy can contain only one default policy tag.

- **Personal Tags**: These can be applied by users who access their mailboxes from Outlook 2010 or the Outlook Web App. Personal tags can be applied to custom folders and individual items.

When you create one or more retention tags to be applied to a policy, you'll need to define the type using one of these settings. Additionally, retention tags have actions that will be used when the age limit for retention is met. The available retention actions are outlined as follows:

- `DeleteAndAllowRecovery`: This action will perform a hard delete, sending the message to the dumpster. The user will be able to recover the item using the Recover Deleted Items dialog box in Outlook 2010 or the Outlook Web App.

- `MarkAsPastRetentionLimit`: This action will mark an item as past the retention limit, displaying the message using strikethrough text in Outlook 2007 or 2010 or the Outlook Web App.

- `MoveToArchive`: This action moves the message to the user's archive mailbox.

- `MoveToDeletedItems`: This action will move the message to the Deleted Items folder.

- `PermanentlyDelete`: This action will permanently delete the message. It cannot be restored using the Recover Deleted Items dialog box.

When working with retention tags and policies, there are a few things you should keep in mind. First, mailboxes can only be assigned one policy at a time, and you cannot have multiple retention policy tags for a single default folder in the same retention policy. For example, you can't have two retention policy tags for the `Inbox` default folder in the same retention policy.

Retention Policies can contain one default policy tag of type All.You can assign multiple personal tags to a policy, but be careful not to go overboard as this could be confusing for users. Also, keep in mind that retention tags are not applied to mailboxes until they have been linked to an enabled retention policy and the managed folder assistant has run against each mailbox.

There's more...

You can create a retention policy without initially linking any retention tags to it. You can also go back and add retention tags to a policy later if needed. If you need to add or remove tags to an existing policy, you can use the Set-RetentionPolicy cmdlet. For example, to add the Sales-Inbox and Sales-DeletedItems retention policy tag to the Sales-Users retention policy, your command would look like this:

```
Set-RetentionPolicy -Identity Sales-Users `
-RetentionPolicyTagLinks Sales-Inbox,Sales-DeletedItems
```

The thing to note here is that this command will overwrite the policy's current tag list. If you need to add tags and keep the policy's existing tags, you will need to use special syntax. For example:

```
$Tags = (Get-RetentionPolicy Sales-Users).RetentionPolicyTagLinks
$NewTags = Get-RetentionPolicyTag Sales-Critical
$Tags += $NewTags
Set-RetentionPolicy Sales-Users -RetentionPolicyTagLinks $Tags
```

What we're doing here is saving the existing tag list applied to the Sales-Users policy in the $Tags variable. We then add a new tag to the list and store that result in the $NewTags variable. Finally, we add the $NewTags to the existing $Tags collection and assign that back to the retention policy when running the Set-RetentionPolicy cmdlet.

Understanding default tags

When you install Exchange 2010, several retention tags are created by default. These may be specific enough to meet your needs, so you might want to take a look at these before creating any custom tags. To view the current list of available retention tags, use the Get-RetentionPolicyTag cmdlet:

```
Machine: MBX1.CONTOSO.COM                                      _ □ X
[PS] C:\>Get-RetentionPolicyTag | select Name,Type,RetentionAction

Name                                   Type          RetentionAction
----                                   ----          ---------------
Personal 1 year move t...              Personal      MoveToArchive
Default 2 year move to...              All           MoveToArchive
Personal 5 year move t...              Personal      MoveToArchive
```

In addition, Exchange automatically creates retention policies for use with personal archives and arbitration mailboxes. There are two retention policies created by default:

1. **Default Archive Policy**: This policy can be applied to mailboxes that contain a personal archive and it provides a built-in set of retention tags.

2. **ArbitrationMailbox**: This policy is applied by default to the system mailbox. It contains two system tags by default.

Some of the retention tags used within these policies are considered system tags, and, by default, are not visible when running the `Get-RetentionPolicyTag` cmdlet. You can view the tags included with these policies by using the `-IncludeSystemTags` switch parameter:

```
Get-RetentionPolicyTag -IncludeSystemTags
```

See also

▶ *Applying retention policies to mailboxes*

Applying retention policies to mailboxes

Retention policies are not automatically applied to end user mailboxes and must be set manually using either the Exchange Management Console or the Exchange Management Shell. In this recipe, you'll learn how to apply retention policies to mailboxes from the command line, which will be useful when performing a retention policy assignment on a large number of mailboxes, or on a regular basis as new mailboxes are created.

How to do it...

1. To apply a retention policy to a mailbox, you use the `Set-Mailbox` cmdlet, specifying the retention policy name using the `-RetentionPolicy` parameter. For example, to do this for one user, the command would look something like this:

```
Set-Mailbox dsmith -RetentionPolicy AllUsers
```

2. In addition, you may need to perform this operation on all mailboxes at once. In this case, you could use the following syntax:

```
Get-Mailbox -RecipientTypeDetails UserMailbox |
    Set-Mailbox -RetentionPolicy AllUsers
```

How it works...

Retention policies are set on a per-mailbox basis. Unfortunately, there is no default setting that allows you to apply retention policies for new mailboxes. This can become a problem if your organization regularly creates new mailboxes and administrators forget to assign a retention policy during the provisioning process.

To get around this, you can schedule the following command to run on a regular basis:

```
Get-Mailbox -RecipientTypeDetails UserMailbox |
    Where-Object {$_.RetentionPolicy -eq $null} |
        Set-Mailbox -RetentionPolicy AllUsers
```

This one-liner will retrieve all of the user mailboxes in the organization that do not have a retention policy setting. This is done by piping the results of the Get-Mailbox cmdlet to a filter that checks that the RetentionPolicy property is $null. Any mailboxes retrieved based on this filter will be piped down to the Set-Mailbox cmdlet where a retention policy will be applied.

Another option would be to set the retention policy as mailboxes are created using the scripting agent. See the recipe in *Chapter 2, Exchange Management Shell Common Tasks* titled *Automating tasks with the Scripting Agent* for more details.

There's more...

Once a retention policy is set on a mailbox, the retention settings defined by the policy's retention tags will be applied to each mailbox by the Managed Folder Assistant. The Managed Folder Assistant is a service that runs on each mailbox server, and, by default, it is set to process every mailbox on the server within one day.

The Managed Folder Assistant can be a resource-intensive task, especially when processing new mailboxes for the first time. With that said, it is possible to force the Managed Folder Assistant to run immediately, but keep in mind that it could impact the performance of the mailbox server.

To force the Managed Folder Assistant to process a particular mailbox, use the Start-ManagedFolderAssistant cmdlet:

```
Start-ManagedFolderAssistant -Identity dsmith@contoso.com
```

To force the Managed Folder Assistant to run against all mailboxes in a particular database, use the following syntax:

```
Get-Mailbox -Database DB01 | Start-ManagedFolderAssistant
```

See also

- *Placing mailboxes on retention hold*
- *Scheduling scripts to run at a later time* in *Chapter 2, Exchange Management Shell Common Tasks*
- *Automating tasks with the scripting agent* in *Chapter 2, Exchange Management Shell Common Tasks*

Placing mailboxes on retention hold

When a user goes on vacation or will be out of the office for an extended period of time, you may need to suspend the processing of the retention policy applied to their mailbox. This recipe will show you how to use the Exchange Management Shell to place mailboxes on retention hold, as well as remove retention hold and discover which mailboxes are currently configured for retention hold.

How to do it...

1. To place a mailbox on retention hold, use the `Set-Mailbox` cmdlet:

   ```
   Set-Mailbox -Identity dsmith -RetentionHoldEnabled $true
   ```

2. To remove the retention hold setting from the mailbox, use the same command, but set the `-RetentionHoldEnabled` parameter to `$false`:

   ```
   Set-Mailbox -Identity dsmith -RetentionHoldEnabled $false
   ```

How it works...

When retention hold is enabled for a mailbox, the user who owns that mailbox can still open their mailbox, send and receive messages, delete items, and so on. The only difference is that any items that are past the retention period for any assigned tags will not be processed.

You can include a retention comment when placing a user on retention hold. Users running Outlook 2010 will see retention comments in the backstage area of Outlook. To add a comment, use the same command used previously, but supply a message using the `-RetentionComment` parameter:

```
Set-Mailbox -Identity dsmith `
-RetentionHoldEnabled $true `
-RetentionComment "You are currently on retention hold"
```

Since the retention hold setting is enabled using the `Set-Mailbox` cmdlet, you can easily apply this setting to many mailboxes at once with a simple one-liner. Let's say that you need to do this for all users in the `Marketing` distribution group:

```
Get-DistributionGroupMember -Identity Marketing |
    Set-Mailbox -RetentionHoldEnabled $true
```

Or maybe you need to do this for all users in a particular database:

```
Get-Mailbox -Database DB01 |
    Set-Mailbox -RetentionHoldEnabled $true
```

In addition to simply enabling this setting, you also have the option of configuring a start and end date for the retention hold period. For example:

```
Set-Mailbox -Identity dsmith -RetentionHoldEnabled $true `
-StartDateForRetentionHold '1/10/2011 8:00:00 AM' `
-EndDateForRetentionHold '1/14/2011 5:30:00 PM'
```

This command will pre-configure the start date for the retention hold period, and remove that setting when the end date elapses.

There's more...

If you are not sure which users are currently configured with the retention hold setting, you can use the following one-liner to retrieve all mailboxes that have retention hold enabled:

```
Get-Mailbox –ResultSize Unlimited |
    Where-Object{$_.RetentionHoldEnabled}
```

Any mailboxes with the `RetentionHoldEnabled` property set to `$true` will be retrieved using this command.

See also

▶ *Placing mailboxes on litigation hold*

Performing a discovery search

Exchange 2010 provides the ability to search through mailboxes for content that might be required during an investigation, such as a violation of organizational policy or regulatory compliance, or due to a lawsuit. Although this can be done through the Exchange Control Panel, you may need to do this from the command line, and, in this recipe, you'll learn how to perform discovery searches from the Exchange Management Shell.

How to do it...

In order to perform a discovery search, you'll need special permissions. By default, no one, not even the user who installed Exchange 2010, is assigned the right to perform searches. Using an account that is a member of the Organization Management role group, you can assign the required permissions in one of two ways and then perform a discovery search. These tasks are outlined in the following steps:

1. For example, if you are using the administrator account that is already a part of the `Organization Management` role group, you can assign yourself the permission to perform discovery searches by adding your account to the `Discovery Management` role group:

   ```
   Add-RoleGroupMember -Identity "Discovery Management" `
   -Member administrator
   ```

   As an alternative, you can also give yourself or another user a direct role assignment to the `Mailbox Search` role:

   ```
   New-ManagementRoleAssignment -Role "Mailbox Search" `
   -User administrator
   ```

2. After you have been assigned permissions, you'll need to restart the Exchange Management Shell so that the cmdlets required to perform the search will be loaded. Then you can use the `New-MailboxSearch` cmdlet to create a new search:

   ```
   New-MailboxSearch -Name Case1 `
   -TargetMailbox "Discovery Search Mailbox" `
   -SearchQuery 'Subject:"Corporate Secrets"' `
   -StartDate "1/1/2010" `
   -EndDate "12/31/2010" `
   -MessageTypes Email `
   -IncludeUnsearchableItems `
   -LogLevel Full
   ```

The previous command will search all mailboxes in the organization for messages sent or received in the year 2010 with a subject of "Corporate Secrets". Any messages found matching this criteria will be copied to the Discovery Search mailbox.

How it works...

One of the benefits to using the shell versus the Exchange Control Panel (ECP) when performing a discovery search is that you can specify the target mailbox. The ECP requires that you use a Discovery Search mailbox to store the results. With the `New-MailboxSearch` cmdlet, you can provide a value for the `-TargetMailbox` parameter and specify another mailbox.

If you perform a search without specifying any source mailboxes, all of the mailboxes in the organization will be searched, as in our previous example. One thing to keep in mind is that, to successfully perform a search, you need to have healthy database indexes, and indexing needs to be enabled (it is, by default) for each database that contains the mailboxes you are searching.

Let's take a look at another example. This time, we'll search a specific mailbox and store the results in an alternate mailbox:

```
New-MailboxSearch -Name Case2 `
-SourceMailboxes dsmith,jjones `
-TargetMailbox administrator `
-SearchQuery 'Subject:"Corporate Secrets"' `
-MessageTypes Email `
-StatusMailRecipients legal@contoso.com
```

This time, we've specified two source mailboxes to search and the results will be stored in the administrator mailbox. The `-StatusMailRecipients` parameter is also used to send an e-mail notification to the legal department when the search is complete. Also notice that, this time, we did not specify a start or end date, so the search will be performed against all items in each source mailbox.

The key to performing a precise search is using the `-SearchQuery` parameter. This allows you to use keywords and specific property values when searching for messages with Advanced Query Syntax (AQS). See Appendix B at the end of this book for details on creating an AQS query.

Once a discovery search has completed, you can export the items captured by the search by accessing the target mailbox. Whether it is the Discovery Search mailbox or an alternate mailbox that you specified when running the command, you can give your account full access permissions to the mailbox and access the items using Outlook or OWA.

There's more...

Once you start a discovery search, it may take some time to complete, depending on the size and number of mailboxes you are working with. These searches can be completely managed from the shell. For example, if you want to remove a search before it completes, you can use the `Remove-MailboxSearch` cmdlet. You can also stop a search, modify its properties, and restart the search. Let's say we've just created a new search; we can check its status with the `Get-MailboxSearch` cmdlet:

```
Get-MailboxSearch | Select-Object Name,Status,Percentcomplete
```

If needed, we can stop the search before it is completed, modify the properties, and then restart the search using the mailbox search cmdlets:

```
Stop-MailboxSearch -Identity Case3
Set-MailboxSearch -Identity Case3 -SourceMailboxes Finance,HR
Start-MailboxSearch -Identity Case3
```

As you can see in these commands, we first stop the Case3 search, then modify the source mailboxes it is configured to run against, and finally restart the search.

See also

▸ *Deleting messages from mailboxes* in *Chapter 4, Managing Mailboxes*

Placing mailboxes on litigation hold

When an organization is dealing with the possibility of legal action, data such as documents and e-mail messages related to the case usually need to be reviewed, and an effort to preserve this information must be made. Exchange 2010 allows you to protect and maintain this data by placing mailboxes on litigation hold. This prevents users or retention policies from modifying or removing any messages that may be required during the legal discovery process. In this recipe, you'll learn how to manage litigation hold settings for mailboxes from the Exchange Management Shell.

How to do it...

1. To place a mailbox on litigation hold, use the Set-Mailbox cmdlet:

   ```
   Set-Mailbox -Identity dsmith -LitigationHoldEnabled $true
   ```

2. To remove the retention hold setting from the mailbox, use the same command, but set the -LitigationHold parameter to $false:

   ```
   Set-Mailbox -Identity dsmith -LitigationHoldEnabled $false
   ```

How it works...

At first glance, it may seem that litigation hold and retention hold are essentially the same, but the truth is they are quite different. When you place a mailbox on litigation hold, retention policies are not suspended, which gives the end user the impression that the policies are still in place and that data can be removed from the mailbox.

When a user empties their Deleted Items folder or performs a *Shift+Delete* on messages, these items are moved to the Recoverable Items folder. Users can recover these items by default for up to 14 days, but they can also delete items from the Recoverable Items folder using the Recover Deleted Items tool in an attempt to permanently purge the data from their mailbox. Deleting items for the Recoverable Items folder places the data in the Purges sub folder, which is hidden from the user. When a mailbox is on litigation hold, an administrator can access the items in the Purges folder using a Discovery Search, and the mailbox assistant does not purge the items in this folder when the database deleted item retention period elapses.

Messages located in the Recoverable Items folder do not count against a user's mailbox storage quota, but each mailbox does have a `RecoverableItemsQuota` that is set to 30 GB by default. This property can be changed at the database level, using the `Set-MailboxDatabase` cmdlet, or at the mailbox level, using the `Set-Mailbox` cmdlet.

 Keep in mind that when you place a mailbox on litigation hold, it may take up to 60 minutes to take effect. You'll receive a warning message in the shell explaining this when you enable the setting for a mailbox.

Like retention hold, you can include a retention comment when placing a user on litigation hold, as some organizations are required to inform users of this for legal purposes. Users running Outlook 2010 will see retention comments in the backstage area of Outlook. To add a comment, provide a message using the `-RetentionComment` parameter when placing the mailbox on litigation hold:

```
Set-Mailbox -Identity dsmith `
-LitigationHoldEnabled $true `
-RetentionComment "You are currently on litigation hold"
```

There's more...

To determine which users are currently on litigation hold, use the `Get-Mailbox` cmdlet and filter the `LitigationHoldEnabled` property:

```
Get-Mailbox -ResultSize Unlimited `
-Filter {LitigationHoldEnabled -eq $true}
```

When a mailbox has been placed on litigation hold, you can view the date it was placed on litigation hold and which user enabled the setting by viewing the litigation properties for a mailbox:

```
Machine: MBX1.CONTOSO.COM                                    _ □ ✕
[PS] C:\>Get-Mailbox dsmith | Format-List *litigation*         ▲


LitigationHoldEnabled : True
LitigationHoldDate    : 6/12/2011 11:37:34 AM
LitigationHoldOwner   : Administrator
```

See also

▶   *Performing a discovery search*

Enabling mailbox audit logging

You can enable mailbox audit logging to track logons to mailboxes and determine which actions are being taken against a mailbox. Audit log entries for a mailbox keep track of important details such as the username, client IP address, and hostname of the computer used by the person that made the change, and the actions made, such as accessing, moving, or deleting messages. In this recipe, we'll look at what needs to be done in order to enable and configure mailbox audit logging.

How to do it...

1. To enable mailbox audit logging, use the `Set-Mailbox` cmdlet:

    `Set-Mailbox -Identity dsmith -AuditEnabled $true`

2. By default, audit logs entries are retained per mailbox based on the `AuditLogAgeLimit` property which, by default, is set to 90 days. You can increase this value using the `Set-Mailbox` cmdlet:

    `Set-Mailbox -Identity dsmith -AuditLogAgeLimit 120`

3. To disable mailbox audit logging, set the `-AuditEnabled` parameter to `$false`:

    `Set-Mailbox -Identity dsmith -AuditEnabled $false`

Mailbox audit logging cannot be enabled through the Exchange Management Console or the Exchange Control Panel, and can only be enabled through the shell.

How it works...

When you enable mailbox audit logging, only a subset of actions performed by administrators and delegates are tracked by default. Actions taken by the mailbox owner are not logged. This is due to the fact that the owner of the mailbox is regularly making changes, and logging this information could generate an undesirable amount of logs.

To view the default settings, we can look at the audit properties for a mailbox:

As you can see, several actions for both administrators and delegates are enabled by default, and no actions are logged for the mailbox owner. Users with full mailbox access are considered delegates.

You can customize the actions that will be audited to meet your requirements. For example, let's say that you only want to audit delete operations on items in a mailbox. You can configure these settings using the `Set-Mailbox` cmdlet:

```
$actions = "SoftDelete","HardDelete"
Set-Mailbox dsmith -AuditEnabled $true `
-AuditAdmin $actions `
-AuditDelegate $actions `
-AuditOwner $actions
```

In this example, `SoftDelete` and `HardDelete` actions will be logged for delegates, administrators, and the mailbox owner.

These settings can also be configured independently. For example:

```
Set-Mailbox -Identity dsmith -AuditEnabled $true `
-AuditDelegate SendAs,SendOnBehalf
```

This time, only the audit delegate actions have been modified. These values can be used with delegates, administrators, or mailbox owners.

Audit logs are stored in the Audits subfolder of the Recoverable Items folder in the user's mailbox, which the user cannot see. If you move the mailbox to another database, the audit logs are still available because they are stored within the user's mailbox.

There's more...

In some cases, you may have a third-party application that uses a service account to access mailboxes within your organization. When you have mailbox audit logging enabled, this can generate a large number of logs that you have to try to filter through later. In this scenario, you can exclude a specific account from being audited by mailbox audit logging.

To exclude a service account from audit logging, use the following syntax:

```
Set-MailboxAuditBypassAssociation -Identity BESAdmin `
-AuditBypassEnabled $true
```

In this example, the BESAdmin account will be excluded from any mailbox audit logs in the organization. You can disable this later, if needed, by setting the `AuditByPassEnabled` parameter to `$false`:

```
Set-MailboxAuditBypassAssociation -Identity BESAdmin `
-AuditBypassEnabled $false
```

See also

▶   *Generating mailbox audit log reports*

Generating mailbox audit log reports

After you've enabled mailbox audit logging, there are two ways from within the Exchange Management shell that you can search the logs and generate reports. In this recipe, you'll learn how to use both synchronous and asynchronous mailbox audit log searches from the Exchange Management Shell.

How to do it...

1. To perform a synchronous mailbox audit log search, use the `Search-MailboxAuditLog` cmdlet. After executing the following command, the results will be displayed in the shell:

    ```
    Search-MailboxAuditLog -Identity dsmith -ShowDetails
    ```

2. To perform an asynchronous search, use the `New-MailboxAuditLogSearch` cmdlet:

    ```
    New-MailboxAuditLogSearch -Name Search1 `
    -Mailboxes dsmith,bjones `
    -LogonTypes admin,delegate `
    -StartDate 1/1/11 `
    -EndDate 1/15/11 `
    ```

```
-ShowDetails `
-StatusMailRecipients admin@contoso.com
```

The asynchronous search will run in the background, and the results will be sent via e-mail in XML format to address specified with the `-StatusMailRecipients` cmdlet.

How it works...

When working interactively, it's easier to use the `Search-MailboxAuditLog` cmdlet to view mailbox audit log reports because you can view the results in the shell. Using the `New-MailboxAuditLogSearch` requires that you work with an XML document that contains the results of the search.

The key to getting useful information out of the mailbox audit log reports from the shell is to use the `-ShowDetails` switch parameter. For example, if we want to determine which items have been deleted from a user's mailbox within a specified time frame, assuming mailbox audit logging is enabled for this mailbox, we could use the following command:

```
Search-MailboxAuditLog -Identity dsmith `
-StartDate 1/1/2011 `
-EndDate 3/14/11 `
-ShowDetails| ?{$_.Operation -like '*Delete*'}
```

Here you can see that we're searching a single mailbox, start and end dates have been specified, the `-ShowDetails` parameter is used, and the results are piped to the `Where-Object` cmdlet (using the `?` alias) where we filter on the `Operation` property. Since we're using the `-like` operator with the `*Delete*` wildcard, both `SoftDelete` and `HardDelete` operations will be returned. We can take this a step further by selecting several properties that provide useful information:

```
Search-MailboxAuditLog -Identity dsmith `
-StartDate 1/1/2011 `
-EndDate 3/14/11 `
-ShowDetails | ?{$_.Operation -like '*Delete*'} |
   select LogonUserDisplayName,Operation,OperationResult,SourceItems
```

This will provide details about each delete operation, the delegate or administrator that performed the operation, the result, and the source items.

When generating reports on deleted items, the `SourceItems` property is actually a collection that contains several pieces of information about each deleted item, such as the message ID, the subject, and the parent folder it was deleted from. By default, when viewing the output from the `Search-MailboxAuditLog` cmdlet, the only information you will see is the message ID, which is not that useful in most cases. To get to the details about each message that was deleted, we need to loop through each of the items contained within the `SourceItems` property. Consider the following code:

```
$logs = Search-MailboxAuditLog -Identity dsmith `
        -LogonTypes Delegate,Admin `
        -ShowDetails | ?{$_.Operation -like '*Delete*'}

$logs | Foreach-Object{
  $mailbox = $_.MailboxResolvedOwnerName
  $deletedby = $_.LogonUserDisplayName
  $LastAccessed = $_.LastAccessed
  $operation = $_.Operation
  $_.sourceitems | Foreach-Object {
    New-Object PSObject -Property @{
      Mailbox = $mailbox
      Subject = $_.SourceItemSubject.Trim()
      Operation = $operation
      Folder = $_.SourceItemFolderPathName.Trim()
      DeletedBy = $deletedby
      TimeDeleted = $LastAccessed
    }
  }
}
```

In this example, we first search the mailbox audit logs for a mailbox where the logon types are either an administrator or delegate, and filter the results so that only `SoftDelete` and `HardDelete` operations are returned. We then loop through each entry and create a custom object that will return important information about each deleted message, such as the subject of the message, the user who deleted the message, the folder it was deleted from, and the time it was deleted. The output from the command would look something like this:

```
Machine: mbx1.contoso.com                                      _ □ ✕
TimeDeleted : 6/12/2011 12:20:32 PM
Subject     : Sales Forecast
Folder      : \Inbox
DeletedBy   : Jacob Craig
Operation   : SoftDelete
Mailbox     : Dave Smith

TimeDeleted : 6/12/2011 12:20:31 PM
Subject     : Finance Report
Folder      : \Inbox
DeletedBy   : Jacob Craig
Operation   : SoftDelete
Mailbox     : Dave Smith
```

Since start and end times were not provided when running the `Search-MailboxAuditLog` cmdlet, this code will provide a report for any deleted item entries in the log.

When using the `Search-MailboxAuditLog` cmdlet, you can only specify one mailbox using the `-Identity` parameter. The cmdlet does provide a `-Mailboxes` parameter, but unfortunately, you cannot use the `-ShowDetails` switch parameter when searching multiple mailboxes. If you need to generate detailed reports for multiple mailboxes, use the `ForEach-Object` cmdlet to search the mailbox audit logs for multiple mailboxes:

```
$mailboxes = Get-Mailbox | ?{$_.AuditEnabled}
$mailboxes | ForEach-Object {
  Search-MailboxAuditLog -Identity $_.name -ShowDetails
}
```

In this example, we first create a collection of mailboxes where mailbox auditing is enabled. We then loop through each one and call the `Search-MailboxAuditLog` cmdlet.

There's more...

Most of the parameters provided by the `New-MailboxAuditLogSearch` are similar to the ones we looked at when using the `Search-MailboxAuditLog` cmdlet. One of the main differences, besides the results being e-mailed to a recipient in XML format, is that both the `-StartDate` and `-EndDate` parameters are required.

See also

▶ *Enabling mailbox audit logging*

Configuring Administrator Audit Logging

Administrator Audit Logging allows you to track which cmdlets are being run within your Exchange organization. The log entries provide details about the cmdlet and parameters used when a command was executed, which objects were affected by the command, and the user who ran the cmdlet. In this recipe, you'll learn how to configure the options used to define the Administrator Audit Logging settings in your environment.

How to do it...

For new installations of Exchange 2010 SP1, Administrator Audit Logging is enabled by default. If you have upgraded to SP1 from the RTM version of Exchange 2010, then you may need to enable Administrator Audit Logging before you can report on which cmdlets are being run within your organization.

1. To determine the current configuration, use the `Get-AdminAuditLogConfig` cmdlet:

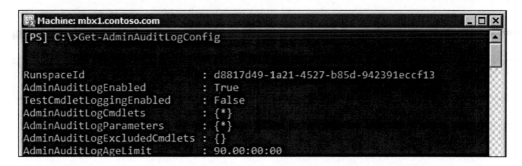

```
Machine: mbx1.contoso.com                                          _ □ ×
[PS] C:\>Get-AdminAuditLogConfig


RunspaceId                      : d8817d49-1a21-4527-b85d-942391eccf13
AdminAuditLogEnabled            : True
TestCmdletLoggingEnabled        : False
AdminAuditLogCmdlets            : {*}
AdminAuditLogParameters         : {*}
AdminAuditLogExcludedCmdlets    : {}
AdminAuditLogAgeLimit           : 90.00:00:00
```

2. You can review the output and check the `AdminAuditLogEnabled` property. If this is set to false, use the `Set-AdminAuditLogConfig` cmdlet to enable administrator audit logging:

```
Set-AdminAuditLogConfig -AdminAuditLogEnabled $true
```

The Administrator Audit Log settings are an organization-wide setting. The previous command only needs to be run once from a server within the Exchange organization.

How it works...

Once administrator audit logging has been enabled, the default settings are configured so that all cmdlets are audited. Cmdlets run through the Exchange Management Shell, the Exchange Management Console, or in the Exchange Control Panel are all subject to the administrator audit log settings.

If you take another look at the output from the `Get-AdminAuditLogConfig` cmdlet, you'll notice that `AdminAuditLogCmdlets` is set to the asterisk (*) character, meaning that all cmdlets by default are configured for auditing. This is true only with cmdlets that make changes to the environment. Any `Get-*` or `Search-*` cmdlets are not subject to auditing, since they do not make any changes and would generate a large number or logs.

You can override this setting using the `Set-AdminAuditLogConfig` cmdlet. For example, if you only wanted to audit one or two specific cmdlets, you can assign each cmdlet name, separated by a comma, to the `-AdminAuditLogCmdlets` parameter:

```
Set-AdminAuditLogConfig `
-AdminAuditLogCmdlets Set-Mailbox,Set-CASMailbox
```

The same goes for cmdlet parameters. If you want to limit which parameters are audited for each cmdlet, specify a list of parameter names using the `–AdminAuditLogParameters` parameter.

 When making changes with the `Set-AdminAuditLogConfig` cmdlet, you'll receive a warning message that it may take up to one hour for the change to take effect. To apply the changes immediately, simply close and reopen the shell.

You can also exclude specific cmdlets from being audited. To do so, use the following syntax:

```
Set-AdminAuditLogConfig -AdminAuditLogExcludedCmdlets New-Mailbox
```

In this example, the `New-Mailbox` cmdlet will not be audited. You can exclude multiple cmdlets by supplying a list of cmdlet names separated by a comma.

By default, the administrator audit log will keep up to 90 days of log entries. This setting can also be modified using the `Set-AdminAuditLogConfig` cmdlet. Audit log entries are stored in a hidden, dedicated arbitration mailbox.

There's more...

The Exchange Management Shell provides a number of troubleshooting cmdlets that use the verb *Test*. By default, these cmdlets are not audited due to the fact that they can generate a significant amount of data in a short amount of time. If you need to enable logging of the `Test-*` cmdlets, use the `Set-AdminAuditLogConfig` cmdlet:

```
Set-AdminAuditLogConfig -TestCmdletLoggingEnabled $true
```

It is recommended that you only leave test cmdlet logging enabled for short periods of time. Once you are done, you can disable the setting by setting the value back to `$false`:

```
Set-AdminAuditLogConfig -TestCmdletLoggingEnabled $false
```

See also

▸ *Searching administrator audit logs*

Searching administrator audit logs

You can use the Exchange Management Shell to search the administrator audit logs and generate reports based on the cmdlets and parameters used to modify objects within your Exchange environment. Like mailbox audit log reports, we have two ways in which we can view the audit logs from the Exchange Management Shell, and in this recipe we'll take a look at both methods.

How to do it...

1. To perform a synchronous administrator audit log search in the shell, we can use the `Search-AdminAuditLog` cmdlet. For example, after executing the following command, the results will be displayed in the shell:

```
Search-AdminAuditLog -Cmdlets Set-Mailbox `
-StartDate 01/1/2011 `
-EndDate 01/31/2011 `
-IsSuccess $true
```

This command would return all of the log entries for the `Set-Mailbox` cmdlet for the month of January. Only the log entries from successful commands will be returned.

2. To perform an asynchronous search, use the `New-AdminAuditLogSearch` cmdlet:

```
New-AdminAuditLogSearch -Cmdlets Set-Mailbox `
-StartDate 01/1/2011 `
-EndDate 01/31/2011 `
-IsSuccess $true `
-StatusMailRecipients admin@contoso.com
```

Based on the parameters used here, the results of the search will be the same, the difference is that the search will take place in the background, and instead of displaying the results in the shell, a message will be e-mailed to a recipient and the report will be attached in XML format.

How it works...

The administrator audit log entries provide the complete details of every cmdlet that was used to make a change in your environment. When using the `Search-AdminAuditLog` cmdlet, we can limit the results based on a specific time frame and by the name of the cmdlet or parameters that were used. If you run the cmdlet without any parameters, all of the entries in the administrator audit log will be returned.

One of the most useful things about this cmdlet is that you can quickly determine how and why something has recently been changed. For example, let's say that a user named Richard Sutton reports that he suddenly cannot log onto the network, let alone receive his e-mail. You could consult the administrator audit logs to determine what might have happened to his account:

```
Machine: mbx1.contoso.com                                              _ □ X
[PS] C:\>Search-AdminAuditLog | ?{$_.ObjectModified -like '*sutton*'}


RunspaceId          : d8817d49-1a21-4527-b85d-942391eccf13
ObjectModified      : contoso.com/Sales/Richard Sutton
CmdletName          : Remove-Mailbox
CmdletParameters    : {Identity}
ModifiedProperties  : {}
Caller              : contoso.com/Users/Administrator
Succeeded           : True
Error               : None
RunDate             : 6/12/2011 12:11:40 PM
OriginatingServer   : MBX1 (14.01.0218.011)
Identity            : RgAAAABzOVavK3SXQJphjuU6RCbVBwAekZy0tVySQbAoBiSmcL42AA
                      AATELrAAAekZy0tVySQbAoBiSmcL42AAAATIQSAAAJ
IsValid             : True
```

Using the previous command, we search the administrator audit log and pipe the results to the `Where-Object` cmdlet, filtering on the `ObjectModfied` property where the object contains the user's last name. The most recent command used to modify this object will be returned first. Viewing the output, we can see that the `Remove-Mailbox` cmdlet was run against this object by the administrator account, therefore removing the Active Directory account and mailbox, which explains why the user cannot log on.

There's more...

The default view of each administrator audit log entry provides a lot of detailed information, but we can work with the properties of each log entry to gain even more insight into what was changed. One good example of this is the ability to view the new and old values that have been set on an object.

For example, let's say that we want to review the audit logs to determine the changes made by the 10 most recent commands. First, we can save the results in a variable:

```
$logs = Search-AdminAuditLog | Select-Object -First 10
```

Each of the log entries are now stored in the $logs variable, which at this point is an array of audit log entries. To view the first entry in the list, we can access the zero element of the array:

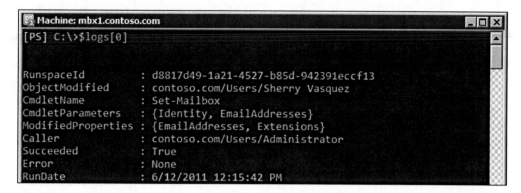

```
Machine: mbx1.contoso.com                                          _ □ ×
[PS] C:\>$logs[0]


RunspaceId           : d8817d49-1a21-4527-b85d-942391eccf13
ObjectModified       : contoso.com/Users/Sherry Vasquez
CmdletName           : Set-Mailbox
CmdletParameters     : {Identity, EmailAddresses}
ModifiedProperties   : {EmailAddresses, Extensions}
Caller               : contoso.com/Users/Administrator
Succeeded            : True
Error                : None
RunDate              : 6/12/2011 12:15:42 PM
```

After reviewing the details, we can see that the Set-Mailbox cmdlet modified two properties of an account. To determine those values, we can view the ModifiedProperties property of the current array element:

```
Machine: mbx1.contoso.com                                          _ □ ×
[PS] C:\>$logs[0].ModifiedProperties | Format-List


Name     : EmailAddresses
NewValue : SMTP:svasquez@contoso.com
OldValue : smtp:svasquez@corp.contoso.com;SMTP:svasquez@contoso.com
```

Viewing the output in list format we can see that the user previously had two smtp addresses configured for their account. When the cmdlet was executed, only one of those values was added back as a new value, so clearly the other address was removed from the mailbox.

See also

▸ *Configuring Administrator Audit Logging*

12
Server Monitoring and Troubleshooting

In this chapter, we will cover the following:

- ▸ Managing and monitoring services
- ▸ Verifying server connectivity
- ▸ Working with the event logs
- ▸ Reporting on disk usage
- ▸ Checking CPU utilization
- ▸ Monitoring memory utilization
- ▸ Reporting on Exchange Server uptime
- ▸ Troubleshooting the Mailbox role
- ▸ Troubleshooting the Client Access Server role
- ▸ Troubleshooting Transport servers
- ▸ Verifying certificate health

Introduction

One of the most important aspects of managing Exchange 2010 is the day-to-day monitoring and maintenance of the servers in your organization. In order to ensure that all systems are operating reliably, it is critical that you proactively monitor the health of each server in your environment. While this task is probably better suited for a robust enterprise monitoring solution such as Microsoft System Center Operations Manager, it is possible to write PowerShell scripts to monitor your systems and troubleshoot issues that may arise. In this chapter, we'll take a look at several ways to monitor the health of server resources such as memory, CPU, and disk utilization, verify service availability, track errors written to the event logs, and more. We'll also explore various methods that can be used to troubleshoot issues when things have gone wrong.

Performing some basic steps

To work with the code samples in this chapter, follow these steps to launch the Exchange Management Shell:

1. Log onto a workstation or server with the Exchange Management Tools installed

2. Open the Exchange Management Shell by clicking on **Start | All Programs | Exchange Server 2010**

3. Click the **Exchange Management Shell** shortcut

Managing and monitoring services

One of most critical aspects of server monitoring requires you to keep an eye on all of the Exchange services that need to be running to ensure the application is online and servicing end users. In this recipe, we'll take a look at how to monitor and manage both Windows operating system services and Exchange Server specific services.

How to do it...

1. One of the ways we can monitor the state of one or more services is using the PowerShell core cmdlets. For example, to view all Exchange-related services, run the following command:

   ```
   Get-Service *exch*
   ```

2. To view only the Exchange-related services that are currently running, pipe the previous command to Where-Object and filter the results:

   ```
   Get-Service *exch* | Where-Object {$_.Status -eq 'Running'}
   ```

3. The `Get-Service` cmdlet can be run against remote machines as well. The following example retrieves the services from every Exchange server in the organization:

```
Get-ExchangeServer | ForEach-Object {
  Get-Service *exch* -ComputerName $_.Name |
    Where-Object {$_.Status -eq 'Running'}
}
```

4. We can also stop, start, or restart services. For example, the following screenshot shows the commands that perform all three operations on the `IISAdmin` service on the local server:

```
Machine: MBX1.CONTOSO.COM                                           _ □ ×
[PS] C:\>Stop-Service IISADMIN
WARNING: Waiting for service 'IIS Admin Service (IISADMIN)' to finish
stopping...
[PS] C:\>Start-Service IISADMIN
[PS] C:\>Restart-Service IISADMIN
WARNING: Waiting for service 'IIS Admin Service (IISADMIN)' to finish
stopping...
WARNING: Waiting for service 'IIS Admin Service (IISADMIN)' to finish
stopping...
[PS] C:\>Get-Service IISADMIN

Status    Name             DisplayName
------    ----             -----------
Running   IISADMIN         IIS Admin Service
```

5. In addition to using the built-in `*-Service` cmdlets, we can use WMI to monitor and manage services. In the following example, we create an instance of the `IISAdmin` service using the `Win32_Service` WMI class:

```
Machine: MBX1.CONTOSO.COM                                           _ □ ×
[PS] C:\>$s = Get-WmiObject Win32_Service -Filter "Name = 'IISAdmin'"
[PS] C:\>$s


ExitCode  : 0
Name      : IISADMIN
ProcessId : 4824
StartMode : Auto
State     : Running
Status    : OK


[PS] C:\>$s.StopService()
```

As you can see from the previous screenshot, an instance of the `IISAdmin` service is saved in the `$s` variable and we can view several details about the service, as well as use its methods to stop and start the service.

How it works...

The `*-Service` cmdlets are PowerShell core cmdlets used to manage services on Windows Servers. They can be quite useful, but there are a few limitations. For example:

```
Machine: MBX1.CONTOSO.COM                                           _ □ X
[PS] C:\>Get-Service MSExchangeAB -ComputerName cas1 | Format-List *


Name                 : MSExchangeAB
RequiredServices     : {MSExchangeADTopology}
CanPauseAndContinue  : False
CanShutdown          : True
CanStop              : True
DisplayName          : Microsoft Exchange Address Book
DependentServices    : {}
MachineName          : cas1
ServiceName          : MSExchangeAB
ServicesDependedOn   : {MSExchangeADTopology}
ServiceHandle        : SafeServiceHandle
Status               : Running
ServiceType          : Win32OwnProcess
Site                 :
Container            :
```

Notice here that, while there are several useful details shown about the `MSExchangeAB` service, the service start-up type is not listed. This is a key property because you may not want to attempt to start a service through an automated script when a service might be set to manual or disabled start-up.

Another limitation is the fact that the `Get-Service` and `Set-Service` cmdlets are the only `*-Service` cmdlets that provide a `-ComputerName` parameter. Fortunately, we can use WMI to write scripts like the one shown next:

```
$servers = Get-ExchangeServer | Select-Object -ExpandProperty Name

Get-WmiObject Win32_Service -ComputerName $servers `
-Filter "Name Like '%exch%'AND StartMode='Auto' AND State='Stopped'" |
Foreach-Object {$_.StartService()}
```

Here we're using a WQL query with the `Get-WmiObject` cmdlet to retrieve all of the Exchange services from each server. We then loop through the collection, and any services set for automatic start-up that are not currently running will be started.

There's more...

Another way to monitor Exchange Server-specific services is using the built-in Exchange Management Shell cmdlet `Test-ServiceHealth`. This cmdlet will check the Exchange services for each role and report the running and non-running services. To check the services on the local server, simply run the cmdlet without any parameters.

To run the cmdlet against each server in the organization and view the status of the Exchange services, use the following command:

```
Get-ExchangeServer | Test-ServiceHealth
```

Starting non-running Exchange services with this cmdlet on the local server is as simple as the following one-liner:

```
Test-ServiceHealth |
  Select-Object -ExpandProperty ServicesNotRunning |
    Start-Service
```

Due to the limitations of the `Start-Service` cmdlet, this command will not work remotely, but you can use WMI, as shown previously, to start or restart services on remote computers.

We can combine both `Test-ServiceHealth` and WMI in a script that will monitor and start any non-running Exchange services on an on-going basis:

```
$servers = "mbx1","mbx2","cas1","cas2"

while($true){
  $servers | Foreach-Object {
    $name = $_
    $s = Test-ServiceHealth -Server $name |
          Select-Object -ExpandProperty ServicesNotRunning

    if($s) {
      $s | Foreach-Object {
        $date = Get-Date

        $wmi = Get-WmiObject Win32_Service -Filter "Name = '$_'" `
        -ComputerName $name

        $wmi.StartService()

        Send-MailMessage -To administrator@contoso.com `
        -From powershell@contoso.com `
        -Subject "Service Failure on $name" `
        -Body "Attempted to start the $_ service at $date" `
        -SmtpServer hub1
```

```
        }
      }
    }
    Start-Sleep -Seconds 300
}
```

You can save this code to a `.ps1` script and run it manually or at system start-up. The script will check each of the defined Exchange servers every five minutes. If any of the Exchange services are not running, an attempt to start the service will be made and an e-mail will notify an administrator's mailbox informing them of the server name, service name, and the date and time that an attempt to start the service was made.

Obviously, if certain Exchange services are not running, you may not be able to send an e-mail message, and you might want to replace that portion of the code to perform some other action, such as logging the operation to a log file.

See also

▶ *Sending SMTP e-mails through PowerShell* in *Chapter 2, Exchange Management Shell Common Tasks*

Verifying server connectivity

When writing your own monitoring and troubleshooting scripts, you need a way to verify that remote systems are online and responding. This can be useful when building a script that needs to poll servers on a regular basis, or to do a routine check within a script to verify that a server is online before invoking one or more commands. In this recipe, we'll take a look at how you can use the shell to verify connectivity of remote servers.

How to do it...

1. To verify that a remote system is available, use the `Test-Connection` cmdlet:

   ```
   Test-Connection -ComputerName mbx1
   ```

2. The `-ComputerName` parameter accepts an array of arguments, so you can test multiple systems at once by specifying multiple server names separated by a comma:

   ```
   Test-Connection -ComputerName mbx1,mbx2
   ```

3. Like the ping command, the cmdlet will send four echo requests to the remote host by default. You can override this using the -Count parameter:

```
Test-Connection -ComputerName mbx1,mbx2 -Count 1
```

4. To verify that all of the Exchange servers in the organization are online and responding, iterate through the server names returned by the Get-ExchangeServer cmdlet:

```
Get-ExchangeServer |
  ForEach-Object{Test-Connection -ComputerName $_.Name -Count 1}
```

How it works...

The Test-Connection cmdlet uses the Win32_PingStatus WMI class to send ICMP echo request packets to one or more remote systems. The benefit to using this cmdlet instead of the traditional ping utility is that we get back objects that can be evaluated, as opposed to plain text, which would require string parsing.

By default, if a remote system is offline, the Test-Connection cmdlet will throw an exception. Perhaps one of the most useful features of this cmdlet is the function provided by its -Quiet parameter. When using this parameter, all errors are suppressed and the cmdlet simply returns a Boolean result: $true if the remote system is online, and $false otherwise. This is useful in a script that can be used to execute a series of commands only if a remote host is available. For example:

```
Get-Content C:\servers.txt |
  Where-Object {Test-Connection $_ -Quiet -Count 1} |
    Foreach-Object {
      Get-Service *exch* -ComputerName $_
    }
```

In this example, we have a script that will display the Exchange related services on each server listed in a text file. We read the list into the shell, and as we loop through each server name, we use the Test-Connection cmdlet to ensure that each server is online. Those names are piped to the ForEach-Object cmdlet where we run the Get-Service cmdlet against each server. You can replace Get-Service by one or more commands that you only want to run against servers that are online.

Working with the event logs

Detailed messages about informational events, warnings, and errors are logged in both the Windows event logs, and the Applications and Services event logs. The messages provide deep insight into what is going on with the operating system and your Exchange servers. In this recipe, you'll learn how PowerShell makes it easier than ever to monitor these logs using simple commands that can be used to troubleshoot issues and generate reports.

How to do it...

1. To determine the available Windows logs that you can work with on a server, use the `Get-EventLog` cmdlet with the `-List` parameter:

```
Machine: MBX1.CONTOSO.COM                                    _ □ X
[PS] C:\>Get-EventLog -List

Max(K) Retain OverflowAction        Entries Log
------ ------ --------------        ------- ---
20,480      0 OverwriteAsNeeded      11,133 Application
20,480      0 OverwriteAsNeeded           0 HardwareEvents
   512      7 OverwriteOlder              0 Internet Explorer
20,480      0 OverwriteAsNeeded           0 Key Management Service
```

2. The names listed under the Log column are the log names you can use with the `Get-EventLog` cmdlet. For example, to view the events in the application log that were logged by Exchange, you could use the following command:

```
Get-EventLog -LogName Application -Source *exch* -EntryType Error
```

3. In addition to specifying the log name and the entry type, you can retrieve a specific number of log entries from multiple servers:

```
$servers = Get-ClientAccessServer | select -expand name

Get-EventLog -LogName "MSExchange Management" `
-EntryType Error `
-After (Get-Date).AddDays(-7) `
-Newest 10 `
-ComputerName $servers |
   select MachineName,TimeWritten,EventID,Message |
      Export-CSV c:\errors.csv -NoTypeInformation
```

These commands will retrieve the last 10 errors from the past week in the MS Exchange Management log on each CAS server in the organization, and store the results in an external CSV file.

How it works...

The `Get-EventLog` cmdlet works only with classic Windows event logs such as the Application, Security, System, Setup, and the `ForwardedEvents` logs. In fact, any cmdlet using the EventLog noun is restricted to these logs and does not work with the new Windows event logs that were added starting with Windows Vista and Windows Server 2008. In addition to retrieving logs with the `Get-EventLog` cmdlet, you can also clear the logs, modify the log settings, and create custom logs and event log entries. To learn more about the cmdlets used for these tasks, run `Get-Help *-EventLog`.

There's more...

Starting with Windows Server 2008, a new category of event logs, the Applications and Services logs, was added to the operating system. The purpose of this is to store application-specific events to their own dedicated logs, which are referred to as an application's crimson channel.

Exchange 2010 servers running the mailbox role log events to crimson channels in the Application and Services logs. To view the Exchange related channels, use the following command:

```
Machine: MBX1.CONTOSO.COM                                    _ □ X
[PS] C:\>Get-WinEvent -ListLog *exch* | select LogName

LogName
-------
MSExchange Management
Microsoft-Exchange-HighAvailability/BlockReplication
Microsoft-Exchange-HighAvailability/Debug
Microsoft-Exchange-HighAvailability/Operational
```

As you can see from the output, there are several logs available for several high-availability components and mailbox database failures. To search these logs, we can use the Get-WinEvent cmdlet. The following code shows how to extract recent errors from the Exchange High Availability/Operational log and send the output in the body of an HTML-formatted e-mail message:

```
[string]$report = ""
Get-MailboxServer | select -expand Name | Foreach-Object{
  $date = (Get-Date).AddDays(-7)
  $report += Get-WinEvent `
  -LogName Microsoft-Exchange-HighAvailability/Operational `
  -ComputerName $_ |
    Where-Object {($_.LevelDisplayName -eq 'Error') -and `
    ($_.TimeCreated -gt $date)} |
      select MachineName,TimeCreated,Id,ProviderName,Message |
        ConvertTo-Html
}

Send-MailMessage -To administrator@contoso.com `
-From powershell@contoso.com `
-Subject "Event Log Errors" `
-Body $report `
-BodyAsHtml `
-SmtpServer cas1
```

This code iterates through each mailbox server in the organization and retrieves the errors from the Operational log that have occurred within the last seven days. Notice that we initialize a string variable called $report before processing each mailbox server. As the code loops through each server, we call the Get-WinEvent cmdlet and filter the results based on those that are errors and the time that the event was created. We select a few key properties and convert the data to HTML using the ConvertTo-Html cmdlet. The output from the logs are appended to the $report variable, and after each server has been processed, the HTML data is used as the body of the e-mail message when sending the information to an administrator's mailbox using the Send-MailMessage cmdlet. The key here is to include the -BodyAsHtml switch parameter with the Send-MailMessage cmdlet, so that the data is viewable in the body of the message.

Reporting on disk usage

Keeping an eye on hard disk utilization is a key component in any monitoring solution. Depending on the environment, Exchange databases can grow quickly, and several gigabytes of log files can be generated in a short period of time. Obviously, you need to know if you are getting low on free disk space. In addition, you may want to track your disk utilization over time to plan upgrades and changes to your systems. This recipe will show you how you can quickly report on the disk usage on each of your servers.

How to do it...

1. One of the quickest ways to determine disk usage is using WMI. Use the following code to display the capacity and free space of each local fixed disk:

```
Get-WmiObject Win32_LogicalDisk -Filter "DriveType='3'" |
    select @{n="Drive";e={$_.DeviceId}},
           @{n="Size";e={[math]::Round($_.Size/1gb,2)}},
           @{n="FreeSpace";e={[math]::Round($_.FreeSpace/1gb,2)}}
```

The output from the command will look similar to the following:

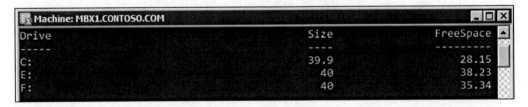

2. As you can see from the output in the previous step, the size of each disk is shown in gigabytes. We can extend this code even further by adding a slight modification and encapsulating it into a function that can be used to gather this information from multiple servers:

```
function Get-DiskUsage {
  param(
    [Parameter(
      Position=0,
      ValueFromPipelineByPropertyName=$true,
      Mandatory=$true)]
    [String]$Name
  )

  process {
    Get-WmiObject Win32_LogicalDisk `
    -ComputerName $Name -Filter "DriveType='3'" |
      select @{n="Server";e={$_.SystemName}},
        @{n="Drive";e={$_.DeviceId}},
        @{n="Size";e={[math]::Round($_.Size/1gb,2)}},
        @{n="FreeSpace";e={[math]::Round($_.FreeSpace/1gb,2)}}
  }
}
```

3. The function in the previous step is written to support pipeline input. You can easily generate a report detailing the disk usage on all of the CAS servers in the organization using the following one-liner:

4. The information can also be sorted, filtered, or even exported to a CSV file. The following one-liner would generate a report for any Exchange server in the organization with a disk less than 20 gigabytes free:

```
Get-ExchangeServer |
  Get-DiskUsage | Where-Object {$_.FreeSpace -lt 20} |
    Export-CSV C:\Disk_Report.csv -NoTypeInformation
```

How it works...

The Win32_LogicalDisk WMI class returns several details about each disk installed on a system. The FreeSpace and Size properties are represented in bytes, and you can see this by simply running the following command:

```
Get-WmiObject Win32_LogicalDisk
```

The `DriveType` property represents fixed disks, and this is why the code from the previous examples filtered on this value where the property was equal to three, returning only the installed hard disks, and excluding other types such as floppy or DVD drives.

When we retrieve each instance of a disk using this class, it's much more useful to convert the values returned in bytes to gigabytes. We do this by using the `gb` multiplier. Consider the following example:

```
Machine: MBX1.CONTOSO.COM                                              _ □ X
[PS] C:\>$c = Get-WmiObject Win32_LogicalDisk -Filter "DeviceID='C:'"
[PS] C:\>$c.Size
42841665536
[PS] C:\>$c.Size/1gb
39.8994102478027
[PS] C:\>[math]::Round($c.Size/1gb,2)
39.9
[PS] C:\>_
```

Here we've stored an instance of the C: drive in the `$c` variable. Looking at the `Size` property, we can see that we get back the value in bytes. We then convert the `$c.Size` value to gigabytes by dividing the value by `1gb`. The value returned is better, but there are more decimal places provided than we need. To take care of this, we use the static `Round` method of the `Math` class to round the number using only two decimal places.

We've streamlined this process using our `Get-DiskUsage` function. Inside the process block of the function, we pipe the output of `Get-WmiObject` to `Select-Object` where we create custom properties with new header names and values that have been converted using the techniques shown previously.

There's more...

In addition to WMI, we can also use performance counters to access detailed information about disk resources on servers. For example, using the `Get-Counter` cmdlet, we can determine the percentage of freespace available on each logical disk:

```
Get-Counter "\LogicalDisk(*)\% Free Space"
```

By default, we get back the free space for each disk as well as the total free space across each disk installed in the system.

We can borrow the structure of our `Get-DiskUsage` function to create a new function that queries performance counter data and returns the free space percentage for each disk on an Exchange server:

```
function Get-DiskFreeSpacePercentage {
  param(
    [Parameter(
      Position=0,
```

```
        ValueFromPipelineByPropertyName=$true,
        Mandatory=$true)]
     [String]$Name
  )

  process {
    $free = Get-Counter "\LogicalDisk(*)\% Free Space" -comp $Name
    $free.CounterSamples | ?{$_.InstanceName -match ":"} |
      select @{n="Server";e={$Name}},
             @{n="Drive";e={$_.InstanceName}},
             @{n="PercentFree";e={[Math]::Round($_.CookedValue,2)}}
  }
}
```

This function can be run against one server at a time, or we can leverage the pipeline to report on multiple servers within the organization:

This can be useful when performing a quick check interactively from the shell, or we can export the data to an external file for later review. Remember the PercentFree property can be filtered, which might be useful when monitoring disks that fall below a certain percentage of free space.

See also

- *Creating custom objects* in *Chapter 1, PowerShell Key Concepts*
- *Creating PowerShell functions* in *Chapter 2, Exchange Management Shell Common Tasks*

Checking CPU utilization

One of the best ways to monitor CPU utilization with PowerShell is by querying performance counters. We can also get this information using WMI. In this recipe, you'll learn a few techniques that can be used to monitor CPU utilization using the Get-Counterand Get-WmiObject cmdlets.

How to do it...

1. To get an idea of the current CPU utilization for a server, we can gather data for the `Processor(_Total)\% Processor Time` performance counter:

```
Get-Counter "\Processor(_Total)\% Processor Time" -Continuous
```

This would continuously output the total utilization across each CPU, as shown:

```
Machine: MBX1.CONTOSO.COM                                          _ □ ×
[PS] C:\>Get-Counter "\Processor(_Total)\% Processor Time" -Continuous

Timestamp                    CounterSamples
---------                    --------------
6/18/2011 5:45:40 PM         \\mbx1\processor(_total)\% processor time :
                             0.0984629549116378
```

2. In addition, we can use the `Win32_Processor` class and select the `LoadPercentage` property to determine the utilization for each CPU:

```
Get-WmiObject Win32_Processor | select LoadPercentage
```

Both `Get-Counter` and `Get-WmiObject` support the `-ComputerName` parameter and can be run against remote machines.

How it works...

The `Processor(_Total)\% Processor Time` performance counter measures the total utilization of all the processors in a machine. It is likely that your servers will have multiple processors with multiple cores. Keep in mind that this utilization value is averaged over all processors.

We can customize the output of the `Get-Counter` cmdlet and make things is a little easier to read. For example, the following function will output the total processor utilization in a custom object:

```
function Get-ProcessorUsage {
  param(
    [Parameter(
      Position=0,
      ValueFromPipelineByPropertyName=$true,
      Mandatory=$true)]
    [String]$Name
  )

  process {
    $CPU = (Get-Counter "\Processor(_total)\% Processor Time" `
```

```
-ComputerName $Name).CounterSamples[0].CookedValue.ToString('N2')

    New-Object PSObject -Property @{
      Server = $Name
      "CPU Usage (%)" = [int]$CPU
    }
  }
}
```

After adding this function to the shell, we can run it against every Exchange server in the organization:

```
Machine: MBX1.CONTOSO.COM                                          _ □ ×
[PS] C:\>Get-ExchangeServer | Get-ProcessorUsage

Server                                                    CPU Usage (%)
------                                                    -------------
MBX1                                                                 92
MBX2                                                                  8
CAS2                                                                  2
CAS1                                                                  0
```

To monitor the usage over a period of time, you can run the function inside a loop:

```
while($true) {
  Get-ExchangeServer | Get-ProcessorUsage
  Start-Sleep -Seconds 5
}
```

This code will report the total CPU usage for each Exchange server in the organization, every five seconds.

Now let's switch back and try doing this with WMI. When using the `Win32_Processor` class, we can select the `LoadPercentage` property, but we'll get one result for each CPU in the machine. Since there is no total value reported, we have to average the result ourselves:

```
Get-WmiObject Win32_Processor |
  Measure-Object -Average LoadPercentage |
    select -expand Average
```

Using the `Measure-Object` cmdlet, we can calculate an average based on the `LoadPercentage` property returned from each CPU. Now that we have the syntax figured out, we can use a `foreach` loop to run this code on multiple servers:

```
foreach($server in Get-ExchangeServer) {
  Get-WmiObject Win32_Processor -ComputerName $server.Name |
    Measure-Object -Average –Property LoadPercentage |
```

```
        select @{n="Server";e={$server.Name}},
               @{n="CPU Usage (%)";e={$_.Average}}
}
```

This will return the same objects as the `Get-ProcessorUsage` function, and the output from both examples will be the same.

There's more...

You could reuse the structure of the `Get-ProcessorUsage` function and use WMI instead of the `Get-Counter` cmdlet. Here is the function rewritten using WMI:

```
function Get-ProcessorUsage {
  param(
    [Parameter(
      Position=0,
      ValueFromPipelineByPropertyName=$true,
      Mandatory=$true)]
    [String]$Name
  )

  process {
   [int]$CPU = Get-WmiObject Win32_Processor `
    -ComputerName $Name |
      Measure-Object -Average –Property LoadPercentage |
        Select-Object -ExpandProperty Average

   New-Object PSObject -Property @{
    Server = $Name
    "CPU Usage (%)" = $CPU
   }
  }
}
```

Then, we can reuse the code that uses the while loop to continuously monitor the CPU usage of every server in the organization:

```
while($true) {
  Get-ExchangeServer | Get-ProcessorUsage
  Start-Sleep –Seconds 5
}
```

See also

> ▸ *Monitoring memory utilization*

> ▸ *Creating PowerShell functions* in *Chapter 2, Exchange Management Shell Common Tasks*

Monitoring memory utilization

To retrieve memory information from local and remote computers using PowerShell, we can use WMI, or query performance counters. In this recipe, you'll learn a few techniques that can be used to monitor memory utilization using the `Get-WmiObject` cmdlet.

How to do it...

1. To gather memory utilization with WMI, we need to query two separate classes:

   ```
   $OS = Get-WmiObject Win32_OperatingSystem
   $CS = Get-WmiObject Win32_ComputerSystem
   ```

2. Next, we can access the free and total physical memory from each object:

```
Machine: MBX1.CONTOSO.COM                                          _ □ ✕
[PS] C:\>$OS.FreePhysicalMemory
160036
[PS] C:\>$CS.TotalPhysicalMemory
2147016704
[PS] C:\>
```

3. To convert the values to gigabytes, we need to use the `mb` and `gb` multipliers:

```
Machine: MBX1.CONTOSO.COM                                          _ □ ✕
[PS] C:\>$OS.FreePhysicalMemory/1mb
0.152622222900391
[PS] C:\>$CS.TotalPhysicalMemory/1gb
1.99956512451172
[PS] C:\>
```

Now we can easily see that the local system has a total of 2 GB of RAM. If we subtract the `FreePhysicalMemory` from the `TotalPhysicalMemory`, we can determine that we're using about 1.8 GB of RAM on this machine.

How it works...

When working with the `Win32_OperatingSystem` class, the `FreePhysicalMemory` property is represented in kilobytes, as opposed to bytes. Therefore, when we calculate the size in gigabytes, we need to use the `mb` multiplier.

There's more...

Querying two separate WMI classes to get the free and used physical memory for a computer eliminates the possibility of doing this in a clean one-liner. Instead, we can use a function to do this, which will also make it easier when running this code against multiple servers:

```
function Get-Memory {
  param(
    [Parameter(
      Position=0,
      ValueFromPipelineByPropertyName=$true,
      Mandatory=$true)]
    [String]$Name
  )

  process {
    $OS = Get-WmiObject Win32_OperatingSystem `
    -ComputerName $Name
    $CS = Get-WmiObject Win32_ComputerSystem `
    -ComputerName $Name

    $free = [math]::Round($OS.FreePhysicalMemory /1mb,2)
    $total = [math]::Round($CS.TotalPhysicalMemory /1gb)

    New-Object PSObject -Property @{
      Server = $Name
      "Memory Total (GB)" = $total
      "Free Memory (GB)" = $free
    }
  }
}
```

Once we've added this function into the shell, we can easily determine the memory usage on a single server, or we can pipe the `Get-ExchangeServer` cmdlet to this function and generate a report for every server in the organization:

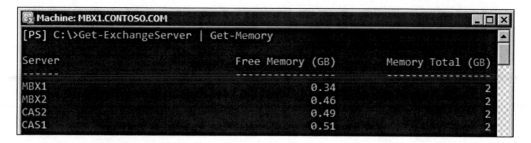

You could continue to pipe this command to other cmdlets to generate an HTML report or export to a CSV or text file.

See also

▶ *Checking CPU utilization*

▶ *Creating PowerShell functions* in *Chapter 2, Exchange Management Shell Common Tasks*

Reporting on Exchange Server uptime

Using WMI and PowerShell, we can quickly determine how long a server has been online based on the last boot time of the operating system. This information can be useful for monitoring scripts that report on availability, or even when you just want to do a quick check on how long each server has been online. In this recipe, we'll take a look at how to use PowerShell to extract this information.

How to do it...

1. To determine the total uptime for a server, we can query the `Win32_OperatingSystem` class by first running this command:

   `$OS = Get-WmiObject Win32_OperatingSystem`

2. Next, we can access the `LastBootUpTime` property of this object to determine how long the system has been online:

3. The problem with this, as you can see from the output shown previously, is that the value is stored in UTC (Universal Time Coordinate) format. So we'll convert the value to a readable date time format:

```
$OS.ConvertToDateTime($OS.LastBootUpTime)
```

4. To get the total uptime, we can subtract the LastBootUpTime from the current date and time:

```
(Get-Date) - $OS.ConvertToDateTime($OS.LastBootUpTime)
```

5. So far we've only been querying the local machine, so now we need to wrap this code up into a script that can gather this information from multiple servers. Add the following function to your shell session:

```
function Get-Uptime {
  param(
    [Parameter(
      Position=0,
      ValueFromPipelineByPropertyName=$true,
      Mandatory=$true)]
    [String]$Name
  )

  process {
    $OS = Get-WmiObject Win32_OperatingSystem -ComputerName $Name
    $lastBoot = $OS.ConvertToDateTime($OS.LastBootUpTime)
    $upTime = (Get-Date) - `
    $OS.ConvertToDateTime($OS.LastBootUpTime)

    New-Object PSObject -Property @{
      Server = $Name
      LastBoot = $lastBoot
      DaysUp = $upTime.Days
      HoursUp = $upTime.Hours
      MinutesUp = $upTime.Minutes
    }
  }
}
```

6. The function will accept pipeline input from other commands, or you can run it against one server at a time, as shown in the following screenshot:

```
Machine: MBX1.CONTOSO.COM                              _ □ X
[PS] C:\>Get-Uptime mbx1


LastBoot  : 6/12/2011 10:15:38 PM
Server    : mbx1
MinutesUp : 51
HoursUp   : 19
DaysUp    : 5
```

How it works...

The `ConvertToDateTime` method used to convert `LastBootUpTime` to a .NET `DateTime` object is not part of the `Win32_OperatingSystem` class. It's actually a `ScriptMethod` added by the `Types.ps1xml` file.

 Run `Get-Help about_Types.ps1xml` to learn how .NET Framework types can be extended in PowerShell.

In order to determine the server uptime, we use `(Get-Date)`, which gives us a `DateTime` object for the current date and time, and then subtract the `LastBootUpTime`. The results are in a `TimeSpan` object that tells us how long the server has been online:

[PS] (Get-Date) - $OS.ConvertToDateTime($OS.LastBootUpTime)

Days	**: 14**
Hours	**: 20**
Minutes	**: 38**
Seconds	**: 14**
Milliseconds	**: 551**

As shown here, each `TimeSpan` object has several properties, such as `Days`, `Hours`, `Minutes`, and so on. The `Get-UpTime` function reports the uptime for a server using this technique and returns a subset of these properties, including other information, as a custom object.

There's more...

You can also use the `Get-UpTime` function to generate a report for all of the Exchange servers in an organization:

```
Get-ExchangeServer | Get-UpTime |
    Export-CSV c:\uptime.csv -NoTypeInformation
```

This one-liner pipes the uptime details for each server to a CSV file on the `C:` drive.

See also

▶ *Verifying connectivity*

▶ *Creating PowerShell functions* in *Chapter 2, Exchange Management Shell Common Tasks*

Troubleshooting the Mailbox role

The Exchange Management Shell provides several built-in troubleshooting cmdlets that you can use to diagnose issues when they arise. In this recipe, we'll take a look at how you can use the `Test-MapiConnectivity` cmdlet to monitor and troubleshoot the mailbox server role.

How to do it...

To verify that a mailbox server can accept logons, you can use the built-in shell cmdlet `Test-MapiConnectivity` using a number of parameters:

1. Use the `-Database` parameter to test the ability to log on to a specific database:

   ```
   Test-MAPIConnectivity -Database DB1
   ```

2. Use the `-Identity` parameter to test the ability to log on to a specific mailbox:

   ```
   Test-MAPIConnectivity -Identity administrator
   ```

3. Use the `-Server` parameter to test the ability to log on to each system mailbox on a particular mailbox server:

   ```
   Test-MAPIConnectivity -Server MBX1
   ```

How it works...

The `Test-MAPIConnectivity` cmdlet verifies that both client connections via the MAPI protocol and LDAP connections for authentication are working correctly on a mailbox server. This ensures that the Exchange Store and DSAccess components are working by authenticating the request and retrieving a list of items from a mailbox.

When you use the `-Identity` parameter, the cmdlet logs on to the mailbox server that hosts the database where the mailbox resides. When using the `-Database` parameter, the cmdlet logs on to the `SystemMailbox` for the database. Additionally, the cmdlet will log on to the `SystemMailbox` in each database if you use the `-Server` parameter to specify a particular mailbox server.

You can also use the -MonitoringContext parameter to include logon latency values for each database or mailbox.

You can run the cmdlet locally when connected to a mailbox server without providing any parameters, and the tests will be performed against the local server.

You can test all mailbox servers within the organization by using this one-liner:

```
[PS] C:\>Get-MailboxServer | Test-MAPIConnectivity

MailboxServer      Database           Result      Error
------------       --------           ------      -----
MBX1               DB01               Success
MBX2               DB02               Success
```

See also

- ▸ *Reporting on database status, redundancy, and replication* in *Chapter 9, High Availability*

Troubleshooting the Client Access Server role

The Exchange Management Shell provides several built-in cmdlets that you can use to troubleshoot and diagnose issues. The Client Access Server role has a number of cmdlets that can be used to perform tests on several different services. In this recipe, we'll take a look at how you can use these cmdlets to monitor and troubleshoot the Client Access Server role.

How to do it...

1. We can test RPC connectivity to a CAS server using the Test-OutlookConnectivity cmdlet. To specify a mailbox that the cmdlet should use, we'll need to provide the credentials for that user:

```
$user = "contoso\administrator"
$pass = ConvertTo-SecureString -AsPlainText "P@ssw0rd01" -Force
$creds = New-Object System.Management.Automation.PSCredential `
-ArgumentList $user,$pass
```

2. After we have the credential object created, we can try to connect using RPC:

    ```
    Test-OutlookConnectivity -Identity administrator `
    -Protocol:TCP `
    -MailboxCredential $creds
    ```

3. We can also verify Outlook Anywhere connectivity by specifying HTTP as the protocol:

    ```
    Test-OutlookConnectivity -Identity administrator `
    -Protocol:HTTP `
    -MailboxCredential $creds
    ```

4. In addition to RPC and HTTP connections, one of the most critical services on the CAS role is the Mailbox Replication Service. Use the `Test-MRSHealth` cmdlet to verify this service is functioning properly:

    ```
    Test-MRSHealth -Identity CAS1
    ```

How it works...

The `Test-OutlookConnectivity` cmdlet verifies that a connection can be made from Outlook to a CAS server. In the previous example, we used the `-Identity` parameter to specify a particular mailbox to test. This parameter is optional if you create a test account using the `New-TestCasConnectivityUser.ps1` script. Simply switch to the `$exscripts` directory and execute the script to create the test account. You'll be prompted for a password, but from then on you will not need to provide an identity when running the cmdlet.

When specifying the protocol, we have the option to use TCP or HTTP. Using TCP will simulate an Outlook connection using RPC and using HTTP will simulate the logon via Outlook Anywhere.

The Mailbox Replication Service is the component on the CAS responsible for doing things like moving mailboxes or importing and exporting data to and from mailboxes. The `Test-MRSHealth` cmdlet ensures that the Mailbox Replication Service is running on the target CAS and responding to RPC ping checks.

You can test the Mailbox Replication Service on each server using a one-liner:

```
Get-ClientAccessServer | Test-MRSHealth
```

There's more...

The CAS role provides many services to clients and there are a number of test cmdlets available to troubleshoot these components. The cmdlets outlined here are a few of the cmdlets that can be used to perform these tasks:

-   `Test-ActiveSyncConnectivity`: Performs a test against a mailbox to ensure ActiveSync connectivity

- ▶ `Test-CalendarConnectivity`: Verifies that anonymous calendar sharing is functioning by checking the Calendar virtual directory under the OWA virtual directory

- ▶ `Test-EcpConnectivity`: Validates the ECP virtual directory on a specified CAS server

- ▶ `Test-ImapConnectivity`: Ensures that the IMAP4 service is running and that a connection can be made to a mailbox through a specified CAS server

- ▶ `Test-OutlookWebServices`: Verifies that the correct service information is being returned to a recipient using the Autodiscover service

- ▶ `Test-OwaConnectivity`: Validates the OWA virtual directory on a specified CAS server

- ▶ `Test-WebServicesConnectivity`: Verifies Exchange Web Service's functionality on a specified CAS server

For examples on usage and syntax run `Get-Help <cmdlet name> -Examples`.

See also

- ▶ *Troubleshooting the mailbox role*
- ▶ *Troubleshooting Transport Servers*

Troubleshooting Transport servers

Like the Mailbox and Client Access Server roles, Transport servers also have a couple of cmdlets dedicated to testing the flow of messages to servers running the Mailbox and Hub Transport roles. In this recipe, you'll learn how to use these cmdlets to troubleshoot mail flow and connectivity issues using the Exchange Management Shell.

How to do it...

1. To test mail flow from one server to another, use the following syntax:

   ```
   Test-Mailflow -Identity MBX1 -TargetMailboxServer MBX2
   ```

2. You can use the following syntax to test mail flow from a specific server to a mailbox:

   ```
   Test-Mailflow -Identity MBX1 `
   -TargetEmailAddress dsmith@contoso.com
   ```

3. To validate SMTP connections, use the `Test-SmtpConnectivity` cmdlet:

   ```
   Test-SmtpConnectivity -Identity HUB2
   ```

How it works...

The `Test-Mailflow` cmdlet sends an e-mail message from a system mailbox on a Mailbox server to another mailbox. If you do not provide a target mailbox server or e-mail address, the message will be sent and delivered to a system mailbox on the specified mailbox server. This cmdlet verifies that the Mailbox Submission Service, and the Transport server components are functioning correctly.

When you run the `Test-MailFlow` cmdlet, the output will provide the status of the test, the message latency time, and whether or not the test message was sent locally or to a destination mailbox on another server:

```
Machine: MBX1.CONTOSO.COM                                    _ □ X
[PS] C:\>Test-Mailflow -Identity mbx1 -TargetMailboxServer mbx1


RunspaceId          : 45580ab6-643c-4640-8b7d-d4ffee4fd834
TestMailflowResult  : Success
MessageLatencyTime  : 00:00:04.2371645
IsRemoteTest        : True
Identity            :
IsValid             : True
```

The `Test-SmtpConnectivity` cmdlet does something completely different. This cmdlet ensures that an SMTP connection can be made to the receive connectors on a Hub Transport server. This cmdlet was designed for use by a Microsoft System Center Operations Manager to validate the receive connectors on a Hub Transport server, but feel free to use the cmdlet for troubleshooting.

You can run `Test-SmtpConnectivity` against one server at a time, as shown previously, or against every transport server in the organization using a one-liner:

```
Get-TransportServer | Test-SmtpConnectivity
```

See also

▸ *Troubleshooting the Mailbox role*

▸ *Troubleshooting the Client Access server role*

Verifying certificate health

Exchange 2010 relies on certificates to secure several aspects of communication with clients and servers. X.509 certificates are used with **Transport Layer Security** (**TLS**) and **Secure Sockets Layer** (**SSL**) to secure communication over protocols such as HTTPS, SMTP, POP, and IMAP. In this recipe, you'll learn how to verify the validity of the certificates installed on your Exchange servers using the Exchange Management Shell.

How to do it...

1. To verify the health of certificates installed on the local server, use the following command:

```
Get-ExchangeCertificate |
  select Status,
         Thumbprint,
         IsSelfSigned,
         @{n="Expires";e={$_.NotAfter}},
         @{n="DaysLeft";e={($_.NotAfter - $_.NotBefore).Days}}
```

The output from this command displays several details about each installed certificate, as in the following screenshot:

```
Machine: MBX1.CONTOSO.COM                                          _ □ ×
Status       : Valid
Thumbprint   : 48F50E020F5398D0DDE0D71FC2AAF7B08C37499D
IsSelfSigned : True
Expires      : 12/9/2015 5:47:29 PM
DaysLeft     : 1826
```

2. To validate the certificates on every server in your organization, use the following code:

```
foreach($server in Get-ExchangeServer) {
  Get-ExchangeCertificate -Server $Server |
    select @{n="Server";e={$Server}},
           Status,
           Thumbprint,
           IsSelfSigned,
           @{n="Expires";e={$_.NotAfter}},
           @{n="DaysLeft";e={($_.NotAfter - $_.NotBefore).Days}}
}
```

3. This code will generate output similar to the previous example, but will add the server name to each record returned:

```
Machine: MBX1.CONTOSO.COM                                          _ □ ×
Server       : CAS1
Status       : Valid
Thumbprint   : FAEAF1EA2DF4776F5A369CA712A558992E78F0B0
IsSelfSigned : False
Expires      : 6/5/2013 9:51:32 PM
DaysLeft     : 730
```

How it works...

By itself, the `Get-ExchangeCertificate` provides a great deal of information about each certificate installed. In each of the previous examples, we've customized the output generated by this cmdlet to show only a few key details about each certificate installed on one or more servers.

Using the previous examples, we can quickly determine if any certificates have been installed incorrectly or are in a pending state waiting for completion by checking the Status property. In addition, we can also see when the certificate expires, by checking the `Expires` and `DaysLeft` properties.

There's more...

Let's take the previous example and rewrite it as a PowerShell function. Add the following code to your shell session:

```
function Test-CertificateHealth {
  param(
    [Parameter(
      Position=0,
      ValueFromPipelineByPropertyName=$true,
      Mandatory=$true)]
    [String]$Name
  )

  process {
    Get-ExchangeCertificate -Server $Name |
      select @{n="Server";e={$Name}},
             Status,
             Thumbprint,
             IsSelfSigned,
             @{n="Expires";e={$_.NotAfter}},
             @{n="DaysLeft";e={($_.NotAfter - $_.NotBefore).Days}}
  }
}
```

Wrapping this code up into a function provides a nice clean method for writing some useful one-liners. For example, we can do a quick check against every server in the organization to see if any of the installed certificates are going to expire in the next three months:

```
$servers = Get-ExchangeServer
$servers | Test-CertificateHealth |
  Where-Object {$_.DaysLeft -le 90}
```

For those with large enterprise environments, with a mix of Exchange 2007 and 2010 servers, this code may be especially helpful when it comes to tracking down certificates that will soon expire.

See also

- *Generating a certificate request* in *Chapter 10, Exchange Security*
- *Installing certificates and enabling services* in *Chapter 10, Exchange Security*
- *Importing certificates on Multiple Exchange servers* in *Chapter 10, Exchange Security*
- *Creating PowerShell functions* in *Chapter 2, Exchange Management Shell Common Tasks*

13

Scripting with the Exchange Web Services Managed API

In this chapter, we will cover the following:

- ▸ Getting connected to EWS
- ▸ Sending e-mail messages with EWS
- ▸ Working with impersonation
- ▸ Searching mailboxes
- ▸ Retrieving the headers of an e-mail message
- ▸ Deleting e-mail items from a mailbox
- ▸ Creating calendar items
- ▸ Exporting attachments from a mailbox

Introduction

Exchange Web Services (EWS) was introduced with Exchange 2007 and it gave developers the ability to write applications that previously required the use of multiple APIs such as CDOEx, Exchange OLEDB, WebDAV, and more. Today, developers can call Exchange Management Shell cmdlets from .NET-managed applications to perform administrative tasks programmatically. When it comes to manipulating the contents of a mailbox, such as creating or modifying calendar items, e-mail messages, contacts, or tasks, developers now use EWS.

Working with EWS requires formatting and sending an XML request over HTTP and parsing the XML response from an Exchange server. Initially, developers used either raw XML or auto-generated proxy classes in Visual Studio to do this, and it required some very verbose code that was difficult to read and debug. Fortunately, the Exchange Web Services team developed and released the EWS Managed API in April of 2009. The EWS Managed API is a fully object-oriented .NET wrapper for the EWS XML protocol that makes life much easier for application developers.

Applications written using the Managed API require a fraction of the code that developers had to write previously when working with raw XML or auto-generated proxy classes. This makes for a huge increase in productivity because the code is easier to read and troubleshoot, and the learning curve for new developers is much lower. The good news is that this is also true for Exchange administrators that want to write advanced PowerShell scripts that utilize EWS. The EWS Managed API can be used to do things in PowerShell that are not possible with Exchange Management Shell cmdlets. The EWS Managed API assembly can be loaded into the shell, and, with the right permissions, you can immediately start building scripts that can access and manipulate the data within any mailbox inside the organization.

In this chapter, we will cover some of the key concepts of using EWS in your PowerShell scripts, such as connecting to EWS, sending e-mail messages, and working with items in one or more mailboxes. The end goal is to give you a basic understanding of the EWS Managed API so that you can start building some basic scripts or deciphering the code samples you come across on the internet or within the TechNet documentation.

Performing some basic steps

To work with the code samples in this chapter, follow these steps to download the EWS Managed API:

1. Download the EWS Managed API from the following URL:
    `http://www.microsoft.com/downloads/en/details.aspx?FamilyID=c3342fb3-fbcc-4127-becf-872c746840e1`

2. For x64 (64-bit) computers, download and run `EwsManagedApi.msi`. For x86 (32-bit) computers, download and run `EwsManagedApi32.msi`.

3. During the installation, select a destination folder such as `C:\EWS` or choose the default directory `C:\Program Files\Microsoft\Exchange\Web Services\1.1`. You will need to note the location so you can import the `Microsoft.Exchange.WebServices.dll` assembly into the shell.

You can use either a standard PowerShell console or the Exchange Management Shell to run the code for each recipe in this chapter.

Getting connected to EWS

When working with EWS, you first need to create an instance of the `ExchangeService` class that can be used to send SOAP messages to an Exchange server. This class has several properties and methods that can be used to specify explicit credentials, set the web service's end-point URL, or make a connection using the built-in AutoDiscover client. In this recipe, you'll learn how to make a connection to EWS that can be used to run custom scripts against the web service.

How to do it...

1. The first thing we need to do is load the EWS Managed API assembly into the shell:

   ```
   Add-Type -Path C:\EWS\Microsoft.Exchange.WebServices.dll
   ```

2. Now we can create an instance of the `ExchangeService` class:

   ```
   $svc = New-Object Microsoft.Exchange.WebServices.Data.
   ExchangeService
   ```

3. At this point, we can use the `AutoDiscoverUrl` method to determine the EWS end-point on the closest Client Access Server for the mailbox with a particular SMTP address:

   ```
   $svc.AutoDiscoverUrl("administrator@contoso.com")
   ```

Now that we have an Exchange service connection created, we can send e-mail messages, create and modify items within a mailbox, and perform other tasks.

How it works...

Before we can start working with the classes in the EWS Managed API, the assembly must be loaded so that the .NET Framework types are available when running scripts that utilize the API. This is only valid for the current shell session, and, if you will be creating scripts, you'll want to make sure that this is always the first thing that is done before invoking any code. We used the `Add-Type` cmdlet in the previous example to load the assembly, but this is also valid:

```
[System.Reflection.Assembly]::LoadFile(
  "C:\ews\Microsoft.Exchange.WebServices.dll"
)
```

This is basically the longhand method of doing the same thing we did before: loading an unreferenced assembly into the shell environment. Notice that in both examples, we are using the path `C:\EWS`. This is not the default path where the assembly is installed, but you can copy it to any folder of your choice.

When creating an instance of the `ExchangeService` class, we have the option of versioning the connection. For example:

```
$svc=New-Object Microsoft.Exchange.WebServices.Data.ExchangeService `
-ArgumentList "Exchange2010_SP1"
```

Here we are passing the Exchange version to the `ExchangeService` class constructor. When you do not provide a value, the most recent version of Exchange will be used, which in this case would be Exchange 2010 SP1, since were using the 1.1 version of the API. The values for that can be used for Exchange are `Exchange2007_SP1`, `Exchange2010`, and `Exchange2010_SP1`.

Since we didn't specify credentials when creating the `ExchangeService` object, we need to provide the SMTP address associated with the mailbox of the currently logged on user when calling the `AutoDiscoverUrl` method.

There's more...

If you want to use explicit credentials when creating your `ExchangeService` object rather than using the credentials of the currently logged on user, you need to do a couple of things differently. The following code will create an instance of the `ExchangeService` class using an alternate set of credentials:

```
$svc = New-Object Microsoft.Exchange.WebServices.Data.ExchangeService
$svc.Credentials = New-Object `
Microsoft.Exchange.WebServices.Data.WebCredentials `
-ArgumentList "administrator","P@ssw0rd01","contoso.com"
```

In addition, you also have the option of setting the EWS URL manually:

```
$url = "https://ex1.contoso.com/EWS/Exchange.asmx"
$svc.Url = New-Object System.Uri -ArgumentList $url
```

Although it is possible to set the URL manually, developers use AutoDiscover as a best practice because it allows the API to determine the best Client Access Server that should be used as the web service's end-point. A hard-coded URL value could potentially mean a broken script if things change later on in your environment.

Certificates matter

Just like Outlook Web App, the EWS virtual directory is secured with an SSL certificate. If you are still using the self-signed certificates that are installed by default on Client Access Servers, you'll need to override a security check done by the API to validate the certificate, otherwise you will be unable to connect. To do this, we can use the `ServicePointManager` class in the `System.Net` namespace. This class can be used to hook up a certificate validation callback method, and, as long as that method returns `$true`, the API will consider the self-signed certificate to be trusted:

```
$svc = New-Object Microsoft.Exchange.WebServices.Data.ExchangeService

$spm = [System.Net.ServicePointManager]
$spm::ServerCertificateValidationCallback = {$true}

$svc.AutoDiscoverUrl("administrator@contoso.com")
```

Certificate validation callback methods are written to perform additional checks on a certificate. These callback methods return a `Boolean` value that indicates whether or not a certificate can be trusted. Instead of writing a callback method, we're assigning a script block that returns `$true` to the `ServerCertificateValidationCallback` property. This forces the API to consider any EWS end-point to be secure, regardless of the status of the certificate used to secure it. Keep in mind, that self-signed certificates are considered to be a bootstrap security configuration so connections to Exchange can be secured out of the box. The best practice is to replace these certificates with trusted commercial or enterprise PKI certificates.

Sending e-mail messages with EWS

As we saw back in *Chapter 2, Exchange Management Shell Common Tasks*, we can use the built-in PowerShell v2 cmdlet `Send-MailMessage` to send e-mail messages. This can be a useful tool when writing scripts that need to send notifications, but the EWS Managed API has several distinct advantages over this approach. In this recipe, we'll take a look at how to send e-mail messages through EWS and why this might be a better option for organizations that have an Exchange infrastructure in place.

How to do it...

1. First, we'll import the EWS Managed API assembly, create an instance of the `ExchangeService` class, and set the EWS end-point using AutoDiscover:

    ```
    Add-Type -Path C:\EWS\Microsoft.Exchange.WebServices.dll

    $svc = New-Object `
    -TypeName Microsoft.Exchange.WebServices.Data.ExchangeService

    $svc.AutoDiscoverUrl("administrator@contoso.com")
    ```

2. Next, we'll create an instance of the `EmailMessage` class:

    ```
    $msg = New-Object `
    -TypeName Microsoft.Exchange.WebServices.Data.EmailMessage `
    -ArgumentList $svc
    ```

3. At this point, we can set specific properties on the $msg object such as the subject, body, and one or more recipients:

```
$msg.Subject = "Test E-Mail"
$msg.Body = "This is a test"
$msg.From = "administrator@contoso.com"
$msg.ToRecipients.Add("sysadmin@contoso.com")
$msg.SendAndSaveCopy()
```

Once this code has been executed, the message is sent to sysadmin@contoso.com.

How it works...

When we send e-mail messages through EWS, we don't have to worry about specifying an SMTP server since the message is transmitted through the web service. This allows our code to run on any machine that has PowerShell v2 installed, and we don't need to modify the receive connectors on the hub transport servers to allow a specific host to relay mail. Additionally, EWS will allow us to use AutoDiscover to automatically find the correct end-point, which prevents the need to hardcode server names into our scripts.

Setting the Subject, Body, and From properties of an EmailMessage object is pretty straightforward. We simply need to assign a value as we would with any other object. Adding recipients requires that we use the Add method of the ToRecipients property. If you have multiple recipients that must be addressed, you can call this method for each one, or you can loop through a collection using the ForEach-Object cmdlet:

```
$to = "sysadmin@contoso.com","IT@contoso.com","help@contoso.com"
$to | ForEach-Object {$msg.ToRecipients.Add($_)}
```

When you call the Add method, you'll notice that the ToRecipients property will be returned for each address added to the message. If you want to simply call this method without having anything returned to the screen, pipe the command to Out-Null:

```
$msg.ToRecipients.Add("sales@contoso.com") | Out-Null
```

In addition, we can also carbon copy and blind copy recipients on the message:

```
$msg.CcRecipients.Add("sales@contoso.com") | Out-Null
$msg.BccRecipients.Add("dmsith@contoso.com") | Out-Null
```

Finally, if you do not want to save a copy of the message in the Sent Items folder, you can simply use the Send method:

```
$msg.Send()
```

Keep in mind that, since we did not provide credentials when connecting to EWS, the user running this code will need to have a mailbox on the server which corresponds to the From address being used. Since we are connecting with our currently logged on credentials, the message must be sent from the mailbox of the user running the code.

There's more...

Instead of typing all of the commands required to instantiate the Exchange service object, it makes much more sense to put this code into a reusable function. Call AutoDiscover, create the e-mail message object, and set all of the required properties, Consider the following example:

```
function Send-EWSMailMessage {
  param(
  [Parameter(
    Position=0,
    Mandatory=$true,
    ValueFromPipelineByPropertyName=$true
  )]
  [String[]]
  $PrimarySmtpAddress,

  [Parameter(
    Position=1, Mandatory=$true
  )]
  [String]
  $From,

  [Parameter(
    Position=2, Mandatory=$true
  )]
  [String]
  $Subject,

  [Parameter(
    Position=3, Mandatory=$true
  )]
  [String]
  $Body
  )

  begin {
    Add-Type -Path C:\EWS\Microsoft.Exchange.WebServices.dll
  }
```

```
  process {
     $svc = New-Object `
     -TypeName Microsoft.Exchange.WebServices.Data.ExchangeService

     $svc.AutodiscoverUrl($From)

     $msg = New-Object `
     -TypeName Microsoft.Exchange.WebServices.Data.EmailMessage `
     -ArgumentList $svc

     $msg.Subject = $Subject
     $msg.Body = $Body

     $PrimarySmtpAddress | %{
       $msg.ToRecipients.Add($_) | Out-Null
     }

     $msg.SendAndSaveCopy()
  }
}
```

This is an advanced function that can be run in a couple of different ways. Notice that the first parameter is called `PrimarySmtpAddress` and it accepts a value from the pipeline by property name. This will allow us to add the function to the Exchange Management Shell and take advantage of the pipeline to send e-mail messages. For example, once this function has been loaded into EMS, we can do something like this:

```
Get-Mailbox -OrganizationalUnit contoso.com/sales |
   Send-EWSMailMessage -From administrator@contoso.com `
   -Subject 'Sales Meeting' `
   -Body 'Tomorrows sales meeting has been cancelled'
```

Here, you can see that we're retrieving all the users from the `Sales` OU and piping those objects to our `Send-EWSMailMessage` function. One message will be addressed and sent to each recipient because the `PrimarySmtpAddress` parameter receives its value from each object that comes across the pipeline.

Since the `PrimarySmtpAddress` parameter also accepts an array of string objects, we can run the function and specify a list of recipients, as shown in the following example:

```
Send-EWSMailMessage -From administrator@contoso.com `
-PrimarySmtpAddress help@contoso.com,IT@contoso.com `
-Subject 'Critical alert on EXCH-MBX-02' `
-Body 'EXCH-MBX-02 Server is low on disk space'
```

If needed, you could extend this function by adding parameters for `Cc` and `Bcc` recipients and call the `RecipientsTo.Add` method for each type inside the process block.

See also

▸ *Sending SMTP e-mails through PowerShell* in *Chapter 2, Exchange Management Shell Common Tasks*

Working with impersonation

When building PowerShell scripts that leverage the EWS Managed API, we can use impersonation to access a user's mailbox on their behalf without having to provide their credentials. In order to utilize impersonation, we need permissions inside the Exchange organization, and then we need to configure the `ExchangeService` connection object with the impersonated user ID. In this recipe, you'll learn how to assign the permissions and write a script that uses EWS impersonation.

Getting ready

You will need to use the Exchange Management Shell in this recipe in order to assign permissions for Application Impersonation.

How to do it...

The first thing you need to do is assign your account the `ApplicationImpersonation` RBAC role from the Exchange Management Shell:

```
New-ManagementRoleAssignment -Role ApplicationImpersonation `
-User administrator
```

After we've been granted the permissions, we need to import the EWS Managed API assembly and configure the `ExchangeService` connection object:

```
Add-Type -Path C:\EWS\Microsoft.Exchange.WebServices.dll

$svc = New-Object -TypeName `
Microsoft.Exchange.WebServices.Data.ExchangeService

$id = New-Object -TypeName `
Microsoft.Exchange.WebServices.Data.ImpersonatedUserId `
-ArgumentList "SmtpAddress","dsmith@contoso.com"
```

```
$svc.ImpersonatedUserId = $id
$svc.AutoDiscoverUrl("dsmith@contoso.com")
```

We now have an `ExchangeService` connection to EWS as the impersonated user `dsmith`.

How it works...

In order to access a mailbox using the permissions of an impersonated user, we use RBAC to create a management role assignment for the user that will be calling the code. Like any other management role assignment, this can be done directly for one user or to a group. Keep in mind that you can also associate scopes when assigning the `ApplicationImpersonation` role. The command shown in our example would give the administrator account impersonation rights to any mailbox in the organization.

Once we have impersonation rights, we load the EWS Managed API assembly and create an instance of the `ExchangeService` class to bind to an EWS end-point on a CAS server.

Notice that, when we create the `$id` object, we're creating an instance of the `ImpersonatedUserId` class and passing two values to the constructor. First, we specify that we want to identify the user to impersonate, using a data type of `SmtpAddress`. The next value passed to the constructor is the actual e-mail address for the impersonated user. The final step is to assign this object to the `$svc.ImpersonatedUserId` property.

Now that our `ExchangeService` connection is configured for impersonation, we can do things like send e-mails, modify calendar items, or search the mailbox of the impersonated user.

There's more...

Let's take a look at how we could use impersonation using a modified version of the `Send-EwsMailMessage` function, included in the *Sending e-mail messages with EWS* recipe earlier in this chapter. Add the following function to your shell session:

```
function Send-EWSMailMessage {
  param(
  [Parameter(
    Position=0,
    Mandatory=$true,
    ValueFromPipelineByPropertyName=$true
  )]
  [String[]]
  $PrimarySmtpAddress,

  [Parameter(
    Position=1, Mandatory=$true
```

```
)]
[String]
$From,

[Parameter(
  Position=2, Mandatory=$true
)]
[String]
$Subject,

[Parameter(
  Position=3, Mandatory=$true
)]
[String]
$Body
)

begin {
  Add-Type -Path C:\EWS\Microsoft.Exchange.WebServices.dll
}

process {
  $svc = New-Object `
  -TypeName Microsoft.Exchange.WebServices.Data.ExchangeService

  $id = New-Object -TypeName `
  Microsoft.Exchange.WebServices.Data.ImpersonatedUserId `
  -ArgumentList "SmtpAddress",$From

  $svc.ImpersonatedUserId = $id

  $svc.AutodiscoverUrl($From)

  $msg = New-Object `
  -TypeName Microsoft.Exchange.WebServices.Data.EmailMessage `
  -ArgumentList $svc

  $msg.Subject = $Subject
  $msg.Body = $Body

  $PrimarySmtpAddress | %{
    $msg.ToRecipients.Add($_) | Out-Null
  }
```

```
    $msg.SendAndSaveCopy()
  }
}
```

As you can see, we've modified this version of the function so that the SMTP address specified using the -From parameter is used as the impersonated user ID. Let's say that you are logged into Windows using the domain administrator account, which has been assigned the ApplicationImpersonation RBAC role. Once the function has been loaded into the shell you could execute the following command:

```
Send-EWSMailMessage -From sysadmin@contoso.com `
-PrimarySmtpAddress help@contoso.com `
-Subject 'Critical alert on EXCH-MBX-04' `
-Body 'EXCH-MBX-04 Server is low on disk space'
```

Using this command, the e-mail message is sent through EWS from the sysadmin mailbox. The message appears to the recipient as if the sysadmin account had sent it.

Searching mailboxes

The EWS Managed API can be used to search one or more folders within an Exchange mailbox. The latest version of the API supports searches using Advanced Query Syntax, allowing us to search folders using the indexes created by the Exchange Search service. This makes searching a mailbox folder very fast and less resource intensive than methods that were used with previous versions of the API. In this recipe, you'll learn how to search the contents of a mailbox through PowerShell and the EWS Managed API.

How to do it...

1. First, load the assembly, create the ExchangeService object and connect to EWS:

   ```
   Add-Type -Path C:\EWS\Microsoft.Exchange.WebServices.dll
   $svc = New-Object Microsoft.Exchange.WebServices.Data.
   ExchangeService
   $svc.AutoDiscoverUrl("administrator@contoso.com")
   ```

2. Next, create a view for the total number of items that should be returned from the search:

   ```
   $view = New-Object -TypeName `
   Microsoft.Exchange.WebServices.Data.ItemView `
   -ArgumentList 100
   ```

3. The next step is to create a property set containing all the properties of each message we want returned, and then associate that property set with the $view object created in the last step:

```
$propertyset = New-Object Microsoft.Exchange.WebServices.Data.
PropertySet (
    [Microsoft.Exchange.WebServices.Data.BasePropertySet]::IdOnly,
    [Microsoft.Exchange.WebServices.Data.ItemSchema]::Subject,
    [Microsoft.Exchange.WebServices.Data.ItemSchema]::
HasAttachments,
    [Microsoft.Exchange.WebServices.Data.ItemSchema]::DisplayTo,
    [Microsoft.Exchange.WebServices.Data.ItemSchema]::DisplayCc,
    [Microsoft.Exchange.WebServices.Data.ItemSchema]::DateTimeSent,
    [Microsoft.Exchange.WebServices.Data.ItemSchema]::
DateTimeReceived
)

$view.PropertySet = $propertyset
```

4. Next, define a search query using AQS syntax:

```
$query = "Subject:sales"
```

5. We can then perform the search using the FindItems method of our Exchange Service object:

```
$items = $svc.FindItems("Inbox",$query,$view)
```

6. Finally, loop through each item and return a custom object that contains the properties for each message:

```
$items | Foreach-Object{
  New-Object PSObject -Property @{
    Id = $_.Id.ToString()
    Subject = $_.Subject
    To = $_.DisplayTo
    Cc = $_.DisplayCc
    HasAttachments = [bool]$_.HasAttachments
    Sent = $_.DateTimeSent
    Received = $_.DateTimeReceived
  }
}
```

When executing this code, any of the last 100 items in the administrator inbox that have the word "sales" in the subject line will be returned.

How it works...

Since we are not supplying credentials when creating the `ExchangeService` object and we're not using impersonation, the search will be performed in the administrator mailbox, as this is the logged-on user. You probably noticed that the property set only contains a few key properties of each message. Although there are many more available properties that can be returned, as a best practice we should only retrieve the properties that interest us. That way, if we are executing the code over and over, perhaps even against multiple mailboxes, we are not burdening the Exchange servers by requesting unnecessary data.

The key to a successful search is constructing the appropriate AQS query. You can use an AQS query for specific properties of a message using word phrase restriction, date range restriction, or message type restriction. For example, instead of querying using the `Subject` property, we can search for messages retrieved within a certain time frame:

```
$svc.FindItems(
   "Inbox",
   "Sent:01/01/2011..04/15/2011",
   $view
)
```

Notice that the first value passed in the call to `FindItems` is the folder that we want to search, next is the AQS query that specifies that we only want to retrieve items that were sent between specific dates in January and April, and finally we pass in the `$view` object that specifies the total items to return with a defined property set.

There are a number of well-known mailbox folders that can be searched using the `FindItems` method:

- ► `ArchiveDeletedItems`: The Deleted Items folder in the archive mailbox
- ► `ArchiveMsgFolderRoot`: The root of the message folder hierarchy in the archive mailbox
- ► `ArchiveRecoverableItemsDeletions`: The root of the folder hierarchy of recoverable items that have been soft-deleted from the Deleted Items folder of the archive mailbox
- ► `ArchiveRecoverableItemsPurges`: The root of the hierarchy of recoverable items that have been hard-deleted from the Deleted Items folder of the archive mailbox
- ► `ArchiveRecoverableItemsRoot`: The root of the Recoverable Items folder hierarchy in the archive mailbox
- ► `ArchiveRecoverableItemsVersions`: The root of the Recoverable Items versions folder hierarchy in the archive mailbox

- ▸ `ArchiveRoot`: The root of the folder hierarchy in the archive mailbox
- ▸ `Contacts`: The Contacts folder
- ▸ `DeletedItems`: The Deleted Items folder
- ▸ `Drafts`: The Drafts folder
- ▸ `Inbox`: The Inbox folder
- ▸ `JunkEmail`: The Junk E-mail folder
- ▸ `RecoverableItemsDeletions`: The root of the folder hierarchy of recoverable items that have been soft-deleted from the Deleted Items folder
- ▸ `RecoverableItemsPurges`: The root of the folder hierarchy of recoverable items that have been hard-deleted from the Deleted Items folder
- ▸ `RecoverableItemsRoot`: The root of the Recoverable Items folder hierarchy
- ▸ `RecoverableItemsVersions`: The root of the Recoverable Items versions folder hierarchy in the archive mailbox
- ▸ `SearchFolders`: The Search Folders folder, also known as the Finder folder
- ▸ `SentItems`: The Sent Items folder

For details, see the list of members for the `WellKnownFolderName` enumeration in the Exchange Web Services Managed API 1.1 SDK documentation on MSDN:

`http://msdn.microsoft.com/en-us/library/dd633710(v=exchg.80).aspx`

There's more...

One piece of interesting information not returned by the code in the previous example is the body of the message. This is because there are a number of properties that the `FindItems` method will not return, one of which is the message body. In order to retrieve the message body, we can bind to the message after the search has been performed using the ID of the message.

Let's extend the previous code so that we can retrieve the body of the message and add the ability to impersonate the target mailbox. Add the following code to a file called `MailboxSearch.ps1`:

```
Param($query,$mailbox)

Add-Type -Path C:\EWS\Microsoft.Exchange.WebServices.dll
$svc = New-Object Microsoft.Exchange.WebServices.Data.ExchangeService

$id = New-Object -TypeName `
Microsoft.Exchange.WebServices.Data.ImpersonatedUserId `
-ArgumentList "SmtpAddress",$mailbox
```

```
$svc.ImpersonatedUserId = $id
$svc.AutoDiscoverUrl($mailbox)

$view = New-Object -TypeName `
Microsoft.Exchange.WebServices.Data.ItemView `
-ArgumentList 100

$propertyset = New-Object Microsoft.Exchange.WebServices.Data.
PropertySet (
  [Microsoft.Exchange.WebServices.Data.BasePropertySet]::IdOnly,
  [Microsoft.Exchange.WebServices.Data.ItemSchema]::Subject,
  [Microsoft.Exchange.WebServices.Data.ItemSchema]::HasAttachments,
  [Microsoft.Exchange.WebServices.Data.ItemSchema]::DisplayTo,
  [Microsoft.Exchange.WebServices.Data.ItemSchema]::DisplayCc,
  [Microsoft.Exchange.WebServices.Data.ItemSchema]::DateTimeSent,
  [Microsoft.Exchange.WebServices.Data.ItemSchema]::DateTimeReceived
)

$view.PropertySet = $propertyset

$items = $svc.FindItems("Inbox",$query,$view)

$items | Foreach-Object{
  $emailProps = New-Object -TypeName `
  Microsoft.Exchange.WebServices.Data.PropertySet(
    [Microsoft.Exchange.WebServices.Data.BasePropertySet]::IdOnly,
    [Microsoft.Exchange.WebServices.Data.ItemSchema]::Body
  )

  $emailProps.RequestedBodyType = "Text"
  $email = [Microsoft.Exchange.WebServices.Data.EmailMessage]::Bind(
    $svc, $_.Id, $emailProps
  )

  New-Object PSObject -Property @{
    Id = $_.Id.ToString()
    Subject = $_.Subject
    To = $_.DisplayTo
    Cc = $_.DisplayCc
    HasAttachments = [bool]$_.HasAttachments
    Sent = $_.DateTimeSent
    Received = $_.DateTimeReceived
    Body = $email.Body
  }
}
```

When running the script, provide values for the `-Query` and `-Mailbox` parameters:

```
c:\MailboxSearch.ps1 -query "Sent:04/01/2011..04/16/2011" `
-mailbox sysadmin@contoso.com
```

When the script executes, the first 100 items in the `sysadmin` mailbox that were sent between April 1 and 16 will be returned. The script will output a custom object for each item that contains the `Id`, `Subject`, `To`, `Cc`, `HasAttachments`, `Sent`, `Received`, and `Body` properties. Notice that, even though the body might be composed as HTML, we've only requested the text type for the body in the property set used when binding to the message.

See also

▶   *Exporting attachments from a mailbox*

Retrieving the headers of an e-mail message

When troubleshooting mail flow issues, you may need to take a look at the headers of an e-mail message. This is easy to do through Outlook for items in your own mailbox, but if you want to do this on behalf of another user, it requires you to have permissions to their mailbox, and then you need to open their mailbox in Outlook to view the headers. In this recipe, we'll take a look at how you can retrieve the headers of a message in your own mailbox, as well as another user's mailbox, using the EWS Managed API and PowerShell.

How to do it...

1. First, load the assembly, create the `ExchangeService` object, and connect to EWS:

    ```
    Add-Type -Path C:\EWS\Microsoft.Exchange.WebServices.dll
    $svc = New-Object Microsoft.Exchange.WebServices.Data.
    ExchangeService
    $svc.AutoDiscoverUrl("administrator@contoso.com")
    ```

2. Next, create a view for the total number of items that should be returned from the search:

    ```
    $view = New-Object -TypeName `
    Microsoft.Exchange.WebServices.Data.ItemView `
    -ArgumentList 100
    ```

3. The next step is to create a property set that will include the message ID. We then need to associate that property set with the `$view` object created in the last step:

```
$schema = [Microsoft.Exchange.WebServices.Data.ItemSchema]

$propertyset = New-Object -TypeName `
Microsoft.Exchange.WebServices.Data.PropertySet (
  $schema::IdOnly
)

$view.PropertySet = $propertyset
```

4. Next, define a search query using AQS syntax:

```
$query = "Subject:'Important Sales Information'"
```

5. We can then perform the search, using the `FindItems` method of our Exchange Service object:

```
$items = $svc.FindItems("Inbox",$query,$view)
```

6. Loop through each item returned by the search and retrieve the message header information:

```
$items | Foreach-Object{

  $headerview = New-Object -TypeName `
  Microsoft.Exchange.WebServices.Data.ItemView `
  -ArgumentList 1

  $headerprops = New-Object -TypeName `
    Microsoft.Exchange.WebServices.Data.PropertySet (
    $schema::InternetMessageHeaders
  )

  $headerview.PropertySet = $headerprops

  $message = [Microsoft.Exchange.WebServices.Data.Item]::Bind(
    $svc, $_.Id, $headerview.PropertySet
  )

  $message.InternetMessageHeaders
}
```

How it works...

The code in this example is very similar to what we used in the recipe for *Searching mailboxes*. Again, since we are not supplying credentials when creating the `ExchangeService` object, and we're not using impersonation, the search will be performed in the administrator mailbox. When calling the `FindItems` method, we're specifying the folder to search, the AQS search query to be used, and the item view.

For each item returned by the search, we need to create a new view and property set for the single instance of the message that returns only the message headers. We then bind to the message and return the header information.

The header information returned will provide details of which server received the message, the content type of the message, the subject and date, and all of the X-Headers included with the message.

There are a number of well-known mailbox folders that can be searched using the `FindItems` method. For details, see the recipe earlier in this chapter titled *Searching mailboxes*.

There's more...

Of course, we'll primarily need to retrieve the message headers for an item in another user's mailbox. Here is an extended version of our previous code that implements EWS impersonation and provides parameters for the mailbox and folder to be searched. Add the following code to a script called `GetMessageHeaders.ps1`:

```
Param($query, $mailbox, $folder)

Add-Type -Path C:\EWS\Microsoft.Exchange.WebServices.dll
$svc = New-Object Microsoft.Exchange.WebServices.Data.ExchangeService

$id = New-Object -TypeName `
Microsoft.Exchange.WebServices.Data.ImpersonatedUserId `
-ArgumentList "SmtpAddress",$mailbox

$svc.ImpersonatedUserId = $id
$svc.AutoDiscoverUrl($mailbox)

$view = New-Object -TypeName `
Microsoft.Exchange.WebServices.Data.ItemView `
-ArgumentList 100

$schema = [Microsoft.Exchange.WebServices.Data.ItemSchema]

$propertyset = New-Object -TypeName `
```

```
Microsoft.Exchange.WebServices.Data.PropertySet (
  $schema::IdOnly
)

$view.PropertySet = $propertyset

$query = $query

$items = $svc.FindItems($folder,$query,$view)

$items | Foreach-Object{

  $headerview = New-Object -TypeName `
  Microsoft.Exchange.WebServices.Data.ItemView `
  -ArgumentList 1

  $headerprops = New-Object -TypeName `
    Microsoft.Exchange.WebServices.Data.PropertySet (
    $schema::InternetMessageHeaders
  )

  $headerview.PropertySet = $headerprops

  $message = [Microsoft.Exchange.WebServices.Data.Item]::Bind(
    $svc, $_.Id, $headerview.PropertySet
  )

  $message.InternetMessageHeaders
}
```

To run the script against an alternate mailbox, provide the query and the SMTP address associated with the mailbox:

```
c:\GetMessageHeaders.ps1 -query "subject:critical information" '
-mailbox sysadmin@contoso.com `
-folder Inbox
```

When the script executes, the headers for each message matching the AQS query will be returned.

See also

► *Working with impersonation*

Deleting e-mail items from a mailbox

The Exchange Management Shell provides cmdlets that allow you to delete items from one or more mailboxes. This can also be done with the EWS Managed API, and you can get a little more control over how the items are deleted compared to what the built-in cmdlets provide. In this recipe, you'll learn how to use the EWS Managed API to delete items from one or more mailboxes using PowerShell.

How to do it...

1. First, load the assembly, create the `ExchangeService` object, and connect to EWS:

```
Add-Type -Path C:\EWS\Microsoft.Exchange.WebServices.dll
$svc = New-Object Microsoft.Exchange.WebServices.Data.
ExchangeService
$svc.AutoDiscoverUrl("administrator@contoso.com")
```

2. Next, create a view for the total number of items that should be returned from the search:

```
$view = New-Object -TypeName `
Microsoft.Exchange.WebServices.Data.ItemView `
-ArgumentList 100
```

3. Create a property set that will include the message id. We then need to associate that property set with the `$view` object created in the last step:

```
$propertyset = New-Object Microsoft.Exchange.WebServices.Data.
PropertySet (
   [Microsoft.Exchange.WebServices.Data.BasePropertySet]::IdOnly
)

$view.PropertySet = $propertyset
```

4. Next, define a search query using AQS syntax:

```
$query = "Body:'inappropriate content'"
```

5. We can then perform the search using the `FindItems` method of our Exchange Service object:

```
$items = $svc.FindItems("Inbox",$query,$view)
```

6. For each item returned by the search, bind to the message and call the `Delete` method, specifying the delete mode that should be used:

```
$items | Foreach-Object{
  $message = [Microsoft.Exchange.WebServices.Data.Item]::Bind(
    $svc, $_.Id
  )

  $message.Delete("SoftDelete")
}
```

How it works...

The code in this example is very similar to what we used in the recipe for *Searching mailboxes*. Again, since we are not supplying credentials when creating the `ExchangeService` object and we're not using impersonation, the search will be performed in the administrator mailbox. When calling the `FindItems` method, we're specifying the folder to search, the AQS search query to be used, and the item view.

Notice that this time we only need to specify the ID of the message in the property set. This is because we only want to call the Delete method on the item class and we don't need to retrieve any other data from the message. In this example, we've defined a string of inappropriate content that should be found in the message body.

We loop through each item returned by the search and create an instance of the message using the item class `Bind` method. At that point, we call the `Delete` method, which accepts one of three values from the `DeleteMode` enumeration. The valid values for this method are defined as follows:

- ▸ `HardDelete`: Permanently deletes the item
- ▸ `MoveToDeletedItems`: Moves the item to the Deleted Items folder of the target mailbox
- ▸ `SoftDelete`: The item is moved to the dumpster and can be recovered by the mailbox owner using the Recoverable Items feature of Outlook and OWA

Having the ability to specify the delete mode gives you a little more control when deleting items in a mailbox than the built-in Exchange Management Shell cmdlets.

There are a number of well-known mailbox folders that can be searched for using the `FindItems` method. For details, see the recipe earlier in this chapter titled *Searching mailboxes*.

There's more...

Whenever you are executing code that can perform a destructive operation, it makes sense to implement the `ShouldProcess` method introduced with PowerShell v2 advanced functions. Implementing `ShouldProcess` in an advanced function gives you the ability to add the common risk mitigation parameters such as `-Whatif` and `-Confirm`. The following function takes our previous code up a notch, written as an advanced function that implements `ShouldProcess`. Add the following function to your Exchange Management Shell session:

```
function Remove-MailboxItem {
  [CmdletBinding(
    SupportsShouldProcess = $true, ConfirmImpact = "High"
  )]
  param(
    [Parameter(
      Position=0,
      Mandatory=$true,
      ValueFromPipelineByPropertyName=$true
    )]
    [String]
    $PrimarySmtpAddress,

    [Parameter(
      Position = 1, Mandatory = $true
    )]
    [String]
    $SearchQuery,

    [Parameter(
      Position = 2, Mandatory = $false
    )]
    [int]
    $ResultSize = 100,

    [Parameter(
      Position = 3, Mandatory = $false
    )]
    [string]
    $Folder = "Inbox",

    [Parameter(
      Position = 4, Mandatory = $false
    )]
    [ValidateSet(
     'HardDelete',
     'SoftDelete',
     'MoveToDeletedItems'
```

```
    )]
    $DeleteMode = "MoveToDeletedItems"
)

begin {
  Add-Type -Path C:\EWS\Microsoft.Exchange.WebServices.dll
}

process {
  $svc = New-Object -TypeName `
  Microsoft.Exchange.WebServices.Data.ExchangeService

  $id = New-Object -TypeName `
  Microsoft.Exchange.WebServices.Data.ImpersonatedUserId `
  -ArgumentList "SmtpAddress",$PrimarySmtpAddress

  $svc.ImpersonatedUserId = $id
  $svc.AutoDiscoverUrl($PrimarySmtpAddress)

  $view = New-Object -TypeName `
  Microsoft.Exchange.WebServices.Data.ItemView `
  -ArgumentList 100

  $propertyset = New-Object –TypeName `
  Microsoft.Exchange.WebServices.Data.PropertySet (
    [Microsoft.Exchange.WebServices.Data.BasePropertySet]::IdOnly
  )

  $view.PropertySet = $propertyset

  $items = $svc.FindItems($Folder,$SearchQuery,$view)

  $items | %{
    $message = [Microsoft.Exchange.WebServices.Data.Item]::Bind(
      $svc, $_.Id
    )

    if ($pscmdlet.ShouldProcess($message.Subject)) {
     $message.Delete($DeleteMode)
    }
  }
}
}
```

We now have a `Remove-MailboxItem` function that supports impersonation, allowing the code to execute against one or more mailboxes. In addition, it supports pipeline input by property name, so you can utilize the `Get-Mailbox` cmdlet to delete items from multiple mailboxes using a simple one-liner. Consider the following example:

```
Get-Mailbox -ResultSize Unlimited |
    Remove-MailboxItem -SearchQuery "body:free ipad" `
    -DeleteMode HardDelete
```

In this example, we pipe every mailbox in the organization down to the `Remove-MailboxItem` function , which will perform a hard delete on each message that matches the AQS query. Since the `ConfirmImpact` property is set to `High`, you'll be prompted for confirmation before each message is deleted.

To force a delete operation without confirmation, you can set the `–Confirm` parameter to `$false`. To do this on a single mailbox, you could use the following syntax:

```
Remove-MailboxItem -PrimarySmtpAddress sysadmin@contoso.com `
-SearchQuery "body:buy cheap drugs" `
-DeleteMode HardDelete `
-Confirm:$false
```

You can also use the `-Whatif` parameter here to test the command to ensure that the correct messages will be deleted:

```
Remove-MailboxItem -PrimarySmtpAddress sysadmin@contoso.com `
-SearchQuery "body:buy cheap drugs" `
-DeleteMode HardDelete `
-Whatif
```

See also

▶ *Searching mailboxes*

Creating calendar items

Imagine that you have a monitoring script written in PowerShell that checks memory, CPU, or disk utilization on all of your Exchange servers. In addition to alerting your team of any critical problems via e-mail, it might also be nice to schedule a reminder in the future for non-critical issues by creating a calendar item in one or more mailboxes. The EWS Managed API makes it easy to create a calendar item through PowerShell with just a few commands.

How to do it...

1. First, load the assembly, create the `ExchangeService` object, and connect to EWS:

```
Add-Type -Path C:\EWS\Microsoft.Exchange.WebServices.dll
$svc = New-Object Microsoft.Exchange.WebServices.Data.
ExchangeService
$svc.AutoDiscoverUrl("administrator@contoso.com")
```

2. Next, create a new Appointment object:

```
$appt = New-Object -TypeName `
Microsoft.Exchange.WebServices.Data.Appointment `
-ArgumentList $svc
```

3. Fill out the subject and body for the appointment:

```
$appt.Subject = "Review Disk Space Utilization on Server(s)"
$appt.Body = "EXCH-01 has only 40% free disk space on drive c:"
```

4. Set the start and end times for the appointment:

```
$start = (Get-Date).AddDays(1)
$appt.Start = $start
$appt.End = $start.AddHours(1)
```

5. Add one or more required attendees to the appointment:

```
$appt.RequiredAttendees.Add("help@contoso.com")
$appt.RequiredAttendees.Add("sysadmin@contoso.com")
```

6. Finally, save the appointment and send a copy to all attendees:

```
$mode = [Microsoft.Exchange.WebServices.Data.SendInvitationsMode]
$appt.Save($mode::SendToAllAndSaveCopy)
```

How it works...

Using the code in this example, we are creating the calendar item in the mailbox of the user calling the code. The `Appointment` class is used to create the item and, after we've created an instance of this class, we set the details of the appointment using the `Subject` and `Body` properties.

The `Start` and `End` properties need to be assigned a `DateTime` object. In our example, we're using the `AddDays` method of the current date and time to set the start time for the meeting in exactly 24 hours in the future. We then use the same object to increment the time by one hour and assign that to the `End` property for the appointment.

When adding attendees to the appointment, we use the `RequiredAttendees.Add` method. When you call the `Add` method, you'll notice that the `RequiredAttendees` property will be returned for each required attendee added to the appointment. If you want to simply call this method without having anything returned to the screen, there's a few ways you can accomplish this. First, you can pipe the command to `Out-Null`:

```
$appt.RequiredAttendees.Add("help@contoso.com") | Out-Null
$appt.RequiredAttendees.Add("sysadmin@contoso.com") | Out-Null
```

Another way you'll see this written is by casting the commands to `[void]`:

```
[void]$appt.RequiredAttendees.Add("help@contoso.com")
[void]$appt.RequiredAttendees.Add("sysadmin@contoso.com")
```

Finally, you can assign the commands to `$null`, which is said to be the fastest method:

```
$null = $appt.RequiredAttendees.Add("help@contoso.com")
$null = $appt.RequiredAttendees.Add("sysadmin@contoso.com")
```

In addition to adding required attendees, we can also add one or more optional attendees to the item:

```
$null = $appt.OptionalAttendees.Add("IT@contoso.com")
```

Finally, when calling the `Save` method for the appointment, you need to pass in a value from the `SendInvitationsMode` enumeration. The valid values that can be used are `SendOnlyToAll`, `SendToAllAndSaveCopy`, and `SendToNone`.

There's more...

Let's make this easier by wrapping all of the code up into a reusable function. Add the following code to your PowerShell session:

```
function New-CalendarItem {
  [CmdletBinding()]
  param(
  [Parameter(
    Position=1, Mandatory=$true
  )]
  [String]
  $Subject,
  [Parameter(
    Position=2, Mandatory=$true
  )]
  [String]
  $Body,
  [Parameter(
```

```
    Position=3, Mandatory=$true
)]
[String]
$Start,
[Parameter(
    Position=4, Mandatory=$true
)]
[String]
$End,
[Parameter(
    Position=5
)]
[String[]]
$RequiredAttendees,
[Parameter(
    Position=8
)]
[String]
$Mailbox
)

begin{
    Add-Type -Path C:\EWS\Microsoft.Exchange.WebServices.dll
}

process {
    $svc = New-Object -TypeName `
 Microsoft.Exchange.WebServices.Data.ExchangeService

    $id = New-Object -TypeName `
    Microsoft.Exchange.WebServices.Data.ImpersonatedUserId `
    -ArgumentList "SmtpAddress",$Mailbox

    $svc.ImpersonatedUserId = $id
    $svc.AutodiscoverUrl($Mailbox)

    $appt = New-Object -TypeName `
    Microsoft.Exchange.WebServices.Data.Appointment `
    -ArgumentList $svc

    $appt.Subject = $Subject
    $appt.Body = $Body
    $appt.Start = $Start
    $appt.End = $End
```

```
   if($RequiredAttendees) {
     $RequiredAttendees | Foreach-Object{
       $null = $appt.RequiredAttendees.Add($_)
     }
   }

   $mode = [Microsoft.Exchange.WebServices.Data.SendInvitationsMode]
   $appt.Save($mode::SendToAllAndSaveCopy)
 }
}
```

This function can be used to create a calendar item in the mailbox of another user. For this to work, you'll need to be assigned the `ApplicationImpersonation` RBAC role. To run the function, you might do something like this:

```
New-CalendarItem -Subject "Reboot Server" `
-Body "Reboot EXCH-SRV01 server after 5PM today" `
-Start (Get-Date).AddHours(6) `
-End (Get-Date).AddHours(7) `
-Mailbox sysadmin@contoso.com `
-RequiredAttendees help@contoso.com, IT@contoso.com
```

In this example, the calendar item is created in the sysadmin mailbox. Multiple attendees will be added to the item and will receive an invitation for the meeting when it is saved. Notice that the meeting is scheduled for six hours in the future, with a total duration of one hour.

If you want to create calendar items in multiple mailboxes, loop through a collection with the `Foreach-Object` cmdlet and run the function for each user:

```
$start = Get-Date "Monday, April 18, 2011 8:00:00 AM"
$end = $start.AddHours(1)

Get-DistributionGroupMember ITSupport | Foreach-Object{
   New-CalendarItem -Subject "Install Hotfixes" `
   -Body "Start patching servers after 5PM today" `
   -Start $start `
   -End $end `
   -Mailbox $_.PrimarySMTPAddress
}
```

In this example, each member of the IT Support distribution group will have a calendar item created in their mailbox that will serve as a reminder; no attendees will be added to the item.

See also

▸ *Sending e-mail messages with EWS*

Exporting attachments from a mailbox

The Exchange Management Shell provides cmdlets that allow you to export e-mail messages from one mailbox to another mailbox. These e-mails can then be exported to a PST file, or you can open an alternate mailbox and access the data. The only limitation is that this provides no option to export only the message attachments. The EWS Managed API has this functionality built in. In this recipe, you'll learn how to export e-mail attachments from an Exchange mailbox using PowerShell.

How to do it...

1. First, load the assembly, create the `ExchangeService` object, and connect to EWS:

    ```
    Add-Type -Path C:\EWS\Microsoft.Exchange.WebServices.dll
    $svc = New-Object Microsoft.Exchange.WebServices.Data.
    ExchangeService
    $svc.AutoDiscoverUrl("administrator@contoso.com")
    ```

2. Next, create a view for the total number of items that should be returned from the search:

    ```
    $view = New-Object -TypeName `
    Microsoft.Exchange.WebServices.Data.ItemView `
    -ArgumentList 100
    ```

3. Next, create a property set and then associate that property set with the `$view` object:

    ```
    $base = [Microsoft.Exchange.WebServices.Data.BasePropertySet]

    $propertyset = New-Object -TypeName `
    Microsoft.Exchange.WebServices.Data.PropertySet (
      $base::FirstClassProperties
    )

    $view.PropertySet = $propertyset
    ```

4. Define a query for the type of attachments you are looking for. For example, if you are looking for attachments in Microsoft Word format, use the following:

```
$query = "Attachment:docx"
```

5. We can then perform the search using the `FindItems` method of our Exchange Service object:

```
$items = $svc.FindItems("Inbox",$query,$view)
```

6. Finally, we loop through each item returned and export the attachments to the specified folder on the file system, such as `c:\export`:

```
$items | ForEach-Object{
  if($_.HasAttachments ) {
    $_.Load()
    $_.Attachments | ForEach-Object {
      $_.Load()
      $filename = $_.Name
      Set-Content -Path c:\export\$filename `
      -Value $_.Content `
      -Encoding Byte `
      -Force
    }
  }
}
```

How it works...

The code in this example is very similar to what we used in the recipe for *Searching Mailboxes*. Again, since we are not supplying credentials when creating the `ExchangeService` object and we're not using impersonation, the search will be performed in the administrator mailbox. When calling the `FindItems` method, we're specifying the folder to search, the AQS search query to be used, and the item view.

As you can see, we're using the `Attachment` property in the AQS query. This allows us to search for a string within the file name or inside the file itself. When the results are returned, we loop through each message, and use the Load method to load the attachment, which allows us to then access the `Content` property of each attachment. The `Content` property stores the message attachment as a byte array, which can easily be used to recreate the file using the `Set-Content` cmdlet by specifying the encoding as `Byte`.

There are a number of well-known mailbox folders that can be searched using the `FindItems` method. For details, see the recipe earlier in this chapter titled *Searching mailboxes*.

There's more...

Like many of our previous examples, reusability is key. Let's take this code and add a few enhancements so it can be run via a PowerShell script. Add the following code to a file called `AttachmentExport.ps1`:

```
Param($folder, $query, $path, $mailbox)

Add-Type -Path C:\EWS\Microsoft.Exchange.WebServices.dll
$svc = New-Object Microsoft.Exchange.WebServices.Data.ExchangeService

$id = New-Object -TypeName `
Microsoft.Exchange.WebServices.Data.ImpersonatedUserId `
-ArgumentList "SmtpAddress",$mailbox

$svc.ImpersonatedUserId = $id
$svc.AutoDiscoverUrl($mailbox)

$view = New-Object -TypeName `
Microsoft.Exchange.WebServices.Data.ItemView `
-ArgumentList 100

$base = [Microsoft.Exchange.WebServices.Data.BasePropertySet]

$propertyset = New-Object –TypeName `
Microsoft.Exchange.WebServices.Data.PropertySet (
   $base::FirstClassProperties
)

$view.PropertySet = $propertyset

$items = $svc.FindItems($folder,$query,$view)

$items | Foreach-Object{
  if($_.HasAttachments) {
    $_.Load()
    $_.Attachments | ForEach-Object {
      $_.Load()
      $filename = $_.Name

      Set-Content -Path $path\$filename `
      -Value $_.Content `
      -Encoding Byte `
      -Force
```

```
        }
      }
   }
```

Using this script, we can export the attachments from one or more mailboxes since we've included the code to support impersonation. Just make sure your account has been assigned the `ApplicationImpersonation` RBAC role when running this script against another mailbox. Let's say we wanted to export all of the Excel files that are attached to messages in the `sysadmin` mailbox. Run this script with the following syntax:

```
c:\AttachmentExport.ps1 -folder inbox `
-mailbox sysadmin@contoso.com `
-query "attachment:xls" `
-path c:\Attachments
```

You can also export all attachments simply by using a wildcard in the search query:

```
c:\AttachmentExport.ps1 -folder inbox `
-mailbox sysadmin@contoso.com `
-query "attachment:*" `
-path c:\Attachments
```

Keep in mind that, since our item view is set to 100, we may need to increase the number if we want to search through mailbox folders with a higher item count.

See also

▶   *Searching mailboxes*

Exchange Management Shell reference

This appendix provides additional information related to the **Exchange Management Shell** (**EMS**). You can use this section as a reference for finding commonly-used automatic shell variables and type accelerators, along with a listing of commonly-used EMS scripts that are installed with Exchange 2010. Additionally, common filterable properties supported by EMS cmdlets that include filter parameters are outlined in detail.

Commonly-used shell variables

PowerShell and the Exchange Management Shell provide several automatic variables. The following table provides a list of commonly-used automatic variables with a description for each one:

Variable Name	Description
$$	Contains the last token in the last command received.
$?	Contains the execution status of the last command.
$^	Contains the first token in the last command received.
$_	Contains the current object being processed within a pipeline.
$Args	Contains an array of undeclared arguments received by function, script, or script block.
$Error	Contains an array of error objects recorded in the current shell session. The latest error can be accessed using the zero index of the array, that is, $error[0].
$Exbin	References the full path to the Exchange Server\Bin directory. This variable is only present when starting the shell using the Exchange Management Shell shortcut on a machine with the Exchange tools installed.

Variable Name	Description
$ExScripts	References the full path to the Exchange scripts directory. This variable is only present when starting the shell using the Exchange Management Shell shortcut on a machine with the Exchange tools installed.
$False	Provides a Boolean false value when used in commands and scripts.
$ForEach	Contains the enumerator inside a *ForEach-Object* loop.
$Home	Contains the full path to the user's home directory.
$Host	Contains an object that represents the current PowerShell host application.
$Input	Contains the enumerator for items passed to a function. The $Input variable can access the current object being processed within a pipeline.
$MaximumHistoryCount	Specifies the maximum number of entries that can be saved in the command history in the current shell session.
$Null	Provides a NULL or empty value when used in commands and scripts.
$Profile	Contains the full path to the PowerShell profile for the current user and current host application.
$PSHome	Contains the full path to the installation directory of Windows PowerShell.
$Pwd	Contains the path to the current location.
$True	Provides a Boolean true value.

To view the variables currently defined in your shell session, run Get-Variable. You can also read more about PowerShell variables by running the Get-Help <TopicName> cmdlet on the following About topics:

- about_Automatic_Variables
- about_Environment_Variables
- about_Preference_Variables

The preceding topics only reference PowerShell specific variables, and not the shell variables that are specific to the Exchange Management Shell.

Commonly-used type accelerators

Type accelerators, also referred to as type shortcuts, allow you to create an object of a specific .NET Framework type without having to enter the entire type name. This is a feature that is supported by both PowerShell and the Exchange Management Shell, and allows you to reduce the amount of typing required when creating an object or explicitly typing a variable. The following table lists some of the most commonly-used type shortcuts:

Type shortcut	.NET framework type
[int]	System.Int32
[long]	System.Int64
[string]	System.String
[bool]	System.Boolean
[byte]	System.Byte
[double]	System.Double
[decimal]	System.Decimal
[datetime]	System.DateTime
[array]	System.Array
[hashtable]	System.Collections.HashTable
[switch]	System.Management.Automation.SwitchParameter
[adsi]	System.DirectoryServices.DirectoryEntry

Scripts available in the $ExBin directory

The following table lists some of the most commonly-used EMS PowerShell scripts that are installed with Exchange 2010:

Name	Description
`AddReplicaToPFRecursive.ps1`	Adds a new server to the replication list for a public folder and all folders beneath it in the hierarchy
`AddUsersToPFRecursive.ps1`	Adds a user and their permissions to the client permissions list for a public folder and all folders beneath it in the hierarchy
`AggregatePFData.ps1`	Aggregates and reports information collected by multiple EMS public folder cmdlets
`CheckDatabaseRedundancy.ps1`	Monitors the redundancy of replicated mailbox databases
`CheckInvalidRecipients.ps1`	Fixes recipient objects that have multiple primary SMTP addresses defined
`CollectOverMetrics.ps1`	Reports on database availability group, switchover, and failover metrics
`CollectReplicationMetrics.ps1`	Reports on replication status and statistics for databases
`ConvertTo-MessageLatency.ps1`	Provides end-to-end latency information gathered from message tracking logs
`DatabaseMaintSchedule.ps1`	Generates maintenance and quota notification schedule time based on a set of input values
`enable-CrossForestConnector.ps1`	Configures a send connector for cross forest trust for anonymous users
`Export-RetentionTags.ps1`	Exports retention tags to an external file
`get-setuplog.ps1`	Displays analysis of the Exchange setup log created during installation
`get-AntispamFilteringReport.ps1`	Generates a report on anti-spam filtering
`get-AntispamSCLHistogram.ps1`	Reports on all entries for the Content Filter and groups by SCL values
`get-AntispamTopBlockedSenderDomains.ps1`	Reports on the top 10 (unless specified otherwise) sender domains blocked by anti-spam agents

Name	Description
`get-AntispamTopBlockedSenderIPs.ps1`	Reports on the top 10 (unless specified otherwise) sender IPs blocked by anti-spam agents.
`get-AntispamTopBlockedSenders.ps1`	Reports on the top 10 (unless specified otherwise) senders blocked by anti-spam agents.
`get-AntispamTopRBLProviders.ps1`	Reports on the top 10 (unless specified otherwise) reasons for rejection by blocklist providers.
`get-AntispamTopRecipients.ps1`	Reports on the top 10 (unless specified otherwise) recipients rejected by anti-spam agents.
`install-AntispamAgents.ps1`	Installs the anti-spam agents on a transport server.
`Reset-AntispamUpdates.ps1`	Removes the anti-spam agents from a transport server.
`Import-RetentionTags.ps1`	Imports retention tags from an external file
`MailboxDatabaseReseedUsingSpares.ps1`	Validates the safety of the environment, before swapping failed database copy to a spare disk and reseeding.
`Move-TransportDatabase.ps1`	Moves the queue database to an alternate disk on a transport server.
`MoveAllReplicas.ps1`	Moves all public folder content from one server to another.
`MoveMailbox.ps1`	Works like the Move-Mailbox cmdlet in Exchange 2007 and performs synchronous mailbox moves.
`new-TestCasConnectivityUser.ps1`	Creates a test user that can be used when testing connectivity on CAS servers.
`Prepare-MoveRequest.ps1`	Prepares mailboxes for cross-forest mailbox moves.
`RedistributeActiveDatabases.ps1`	Attempts to redistribute active databases evenly across a number of mailbox servers within a DAG.
`RemoveReplicaFromPFRecursive.ps1`	Removes a public folder replica and all folders beneath it in the hierarchy.
`RemoveUserFromPFRecursive.ps1`	Removes a user from the client permissions list for a public folder and all folders beneath it in the hierarchy.

Name	Description
ReplaceReplicaOnPFRecursive.ps1	Replaces a server with a new server in the replication list for a public folder and all folders beneath it in the hierarchy
ReplaceUserPermissionOnPFRecursive.ps1	Replaces the permissions of a user for a public folder with a new set of permissions and applies it to all folders beneath it in the hierarchy
ReplaceUserWithUserOnPFRecursive.ps1	Replaces a user for a new user on the client permissions list for a public folder and applies to all folders beneath it in the hierarchy
ResetCasService.ps1	Resets virtual directory on CAS
ResetSearchIndex.ps1	Rebuilds full-text index catalog
StartDagServerMaintenance.ps1	Initiates DAG server maintenance
StopDagServerMaintenance.ps1	Stops DAG server maintenance and resumes mailbox database copies
Troubleshoot-DatabaseLatency.ps1	Diagnoses disk subsystem issues (used by SCOM)
Troubleshoot-DatabaseSpace.ps1	Troubleshoots log growth (used by SCOM)

Scripts may be added to this directory as you install rollup updates and service packs, and some of them will only be present when a specific server role is installed. For example, the anti-spam scripts will only be available on transport servers. To view all scripts in the $ExScripts folder, run Get-ChildItem $exscripts –Filter *.ps1.

Properties that can be used with the Filter parameter

There are a number of EMS cmdlets that provide a -Filter parameter which can be used to narrow searches based on the value of an OPATH property. These properties can also map to a particular LDAP attribute.

The following table lists some of the commonly-used properties and the cmdlets that can be used to query their values using the -Filter parameter:

Property Name	Attribute	Cmdlets Supported	Input Value
Alias	mailNickname	Get-DistributionGroup	String/Wildcard
		Get-DynamicDistributionGroup	
		Get-Mailbox	
		Get-MailContact	
		Get-MailPublicFolder	
		Get-MailUser	
		Get-Recipient	
City	City	Get-Contact	String/Wildcard
		Get-Recipient	
		Get-User	
Company	Company	Get-Contact	String/Wildcard
		Get-Recipient	
		Get-User	
Database	homeMDB	Get-Mailbox	Mailbox database
		Get-Recipient	Identity
			DN
Department	department	Get-Contact	String/Wildcard
		Get-Recipient	
		Get-User	

Property Name	Attribute	Cmdlets Supported	Input Value
DisplayName	displayName	Get-CASMailbox	String/Wildcard
		Get-Contact	
		Get-DistributionGroup	
		Get-DynamicDistributionGroup	
		Get-Group	
		Get-Mailbox	
		Get-MailContact	
		Get-MailPublicFolder	
		Get-MailUser	
		Get-Recipient	
		Get-UMMailbox	
		Get-User	
DistinguishedName	distinguishedName	Get-CASMailbox	DN
		Get-Contact	
		Get-DistributionGroup	
		Get-DynamicDistributionGroup	
		Get-Group	
		Get-Mailbox	
		Get-MailContact	
		Get-MailPublicFolder	
		Get-MailUser	
		Get-Recipient	
		Get-UMMailbox	
		Get-User	

Property Name	Attribute	Cmdlets Supported	Input Value
EmailAddresses	proxyAddresses	Get-CASMailbox	E-mail Address
		Get-DistributionGroup	
		Get-DynamicDistributionGroup	
		Get-Mailbox	
		Get-MailContact	
		Get-MailPublicFolder	
		Get-MailUser	
		Get-Recipient	
		Get-UMMailbox	
FirstName	givenName	Get-Contact	String/Wildcard
		Get-Recipient	
		Get-User	
HiddenFromAddress ListsEnabled	msExchHideFrom AddressLists	Get-DistributionGroup	$true $false
		Get-DynamicDistributionGroup	
		Get-Mailbox	
		Get-MailContact	
		Get-MailPublicFolder	
		Get-MailUser	
		Get-Recipient	
HomePhone	homePhone	Get-Contact	String/Wildcard
		Get-User	
LastName	sn	Get-Contact	String
		Get-Recipient	
		Get-User	
Manager	manager	Get-Contact	String/Wildcard
		Get-Recipient	
		Get-User	

Property Name	Attribute	Cmdlets Supported	Input Value
Name	name	Get-CASMailbox	String
		Get-Contact	
		Get-DistributionGroup	
		Get-DynamicDistributionGroup	
		Get-Group	
		Get-Mailbox	
		Get-MailContact	
		Get-MailPublicFolder	
		Get-MailUser	
		Get-Recipient	
		Get-UMMailbox	
		Get-User	
Phone	telephoneNumber	Get-Contact	String/Wildcard
		Get-Recipient	
		Get-User	
PrimarySmtpAddress	N/A	Get-CASMailbox	E-mail Address
		Get-DistributionGroup	
		Get-DynamicDistributionGroup	
		Get-Mailbox	
		Get-MailContact	
		Get-MailPublicFolder	
		Get-MailUser	
		Get-Recipient	
		Get-UMMailbox	

Property Name	Attribute	Cmdlets Supported	Input Value
SamAccountName	SamAccountName	Get-CASMailbox	String
		Get-DistributionGroup	
		Get-Group	
		Get-Mailbox	
		Get-MailUser	
		Get-Recipient	
		Get-UMMailbox	
		Get-User	
StateOrProvince	st	Get-Contact	String/Wildcard
		Get-Recipient	
		Get-User	
StreetAddress	streetAddress	Get-Contact	String
		Get-User	
Title	title	Get-Contact	String
		Get-Recipient	
		Get-User	
UserPrincipalName	userPrincipalName	Get-Mailbox	User logon name User principal name/Wildcard
		Get-MailUser	
		Get-Recipient	
		Get-User	

The preceding table only includes a list of commonly-used filterable properties that can be used with the -Filter parameter. In addition to this list, there are several other properties that can be filtered. See this article in the TechNet documentation for a complete list:

http://technet.microsoft.com/en-us/library/bb738155(EXCHG.80).aspx

Properties that can be used with the RecipientFilter parameter

There are a number of EMS cmdlets that provide a `-RecipientFilter` parameter and can be used to define the criteria used for dynamic distribution groups, e-mail address policies, and address lists. The following cmdlets support this parameter:

- New-AddressList
- New-DynamicDistributionGroup
- New-EmailAddressPolicy
- New-GlobalAddressList
- Set-AddressList
- Set-DynamicDistributionGroup
- Set-EmailAddressPolicy
- Set-GlobalAddressList

The following table lists some of the common properties used when creating a recipient filter using the `-RecipientFilter` parameter:

Property Name	LDAP Attribute	Input Value
Alias	mailNickname	String/Wildcard
City	L	String/Wildcard
Company	company	String/Wildcard
Database	homeMDB	Mailbox database
		Identity
		DN
DisplayName	displayName	String/Wildcard
EmailAddresses	proxyAddresses	E-mail address
ExternalEmailAddress	targetAddress	E-mail address
FirstName	givenName	String/Wildcard
HiddenFromAddressListsEnabled	msExchHideFromAddressLists	$true $false
LastName	Sn	String/Wildcard
Manager	Manager	String/Wildcard
Name	Name	String
Office	physicalDeliveryOfficeName	String
SamAccountName	SamAccountName	String/Wildcard

Property Name	LDAP Attribute	Input Value
StateOrProvince	st	String/Wildcard
StreetAddress	streetAddress	String
Title	title	String
UserPrincipalName	userPrincipalName	User logon name
		User principal name/ Wildcard

The preceding table only includes a list of commonly used filterable properties that can be used with the `-RecipientFilter` parameter. In addition to this list, there are several other properties that can be filtered. See this article in the TechNet documentation for a complete list:

```
http://technet.microsoft.com/en-us/library/bb738157(EXCHG.80).aspx
```

Advanced Query Syntax

This appendix provides additional information related to working with **Advanced Query Syntax (AQS)** when performing queries with Exchange Search. Exchange 2010 SP1 introduces new cmdlets that leverage Exchange Search for discovery purposes, and in addition, AQS can be used to perform searches with the Exchange Web Services Managed API.

The following Exchange Management Shell cmdlets provide a `-SearchQuery` parameter that can be used to define an AQS query:

- New-MailboxSearch
- Search-Mailbox
- Set-MailboxSearch

The tables in this appendix outline the AQS keywords that can be used with these cmdlets to perform queries in Exchange Search, along with the EWS Managed API.

Using the word phrase search

The following table outlines the properties that can be used to define an AQS query using a word phrase restriction:

Property	Examples	Description

Attachments	`attachment:report.xlsx`
	
	`attachment:salesreport.docx`
	
	`attachment:pptx`
		Searches for items that have an attachment with a specific name such as `report.xlsx` or `salesreport.docx`. You can include partial file names, as shown in the last example, to find all messages with a certain extension. The file body of attachments will also be searched.

Cc	`Cc:administrator`
	
	`Cc:sales@contoso.com`
		Searches for items where `administrator` or `sales@contoso.com` is included in the carbon copy line.

Property	Example	Description
From	`From:Bob` `From:Bob Smith`	Searches for items sent from Bob or Bob Smith.
To	`To:Bob` `To:Bob Smith`	Searches for items sent to Bob or Bob Smith.
Bcc	`Bcc:Bob` `Bcc:Bob Smith`	Searches for items where Bob was included in the blind carbon copy line.
Subject	`Subject:sales` `Subject:(Sales Meeting)`	Searches for items with the word sales in the subject line. Searches for items with the words "sales" or "meeting" in the subject line.
Body	`Body:financial` `Content:financial`	Searches for items where the word "financial" appears in the message body.
Participants	`Participants:Bob Smith`	Searches for items with Bob Smith in the To, Cc, or Bcc fields.
RetentionPolicy	`Retentionpolicy:` `critical`	Searches for items that have the critical retention tag applied.
(Not Defined)	Financial Report	Searches for items that contain both "Financial" and "Report" in all word phrase properties.

When performing a word phrase search, the property names and search terms are case insensitive. If you want an exact match, enclose the search query in double quotes, otherwise the search will default to a prefix match. For example, searching for the term *report* would match the word *reporting* unless enclosed in double quotes, indicating an exact search.

Examples

If you want to delete all messages in the administrator mailbox where the sender's e-mail address is `sales@contoso.com,` use the following code:

```
Search-Mailbox -Identity administrator `
-SearchQuery "from:sales@contoso.com" `
-DeleteContent `
-Force
```

If you want to create a discovery search based on messages that contain the phrase *Employee Salary* in every mailbox, use the following code:

```
New-MailboxSearch -Name MySearch `
-TargetMailbox "Discovery Search Mailbox" `
-SearchQuery 'Body:"Employee Salary"' `
-MessageTypes Email `
-IncludeUnsearchableItems `
-LogLevel Full
```

Using a date range search

The following table outlines the properties that can be used to define an AQS query using a date range restriction:

Property	Example	Description
Received	Received:today	Searches for items received today
	Received:04/22/2011	Searches for items received on April 22
	Received:01/01/2011..04/01/2011	Searches for items received between January 1 and April 1
Sent	Sent:today	Searches for items sent today
	Sent:01/22/2011	Searches for items sent on January 22

You can use relative dates when performing a date range restricted search. For example, today, tomorrow, or yesterday can be used with the Received or Sent keywords.

You can use a specific day of the week: (Sunday, Monday, Tuesday, Wednesday, Thursday, Friday, or Saturday) with the Received or Sent keywords.

You can also use a specific month: (January, February, March, April, May, June, July, August, September, October, November, or December) with the Received or Sent keywords.

Examples

If you want to delete all messages in the administrator mailbox that were received today, use the following code:

```
Search-Mailbox -Identity administrator `
-SearchQuery "Received:today" `
-DeleteContent `
-Force
```

If you want to delete all messages in the administrator mailbox that have been received between March and July, use the following code:

```
Search-Mailbox -Identity administrator `
-SearchQuery "Received:03/01/2011..07/01/2011" `
-DeleteContent `
-Force
```

Using the message type search

The following table outlines the properties that can be used to define an AQS query using a message type restriction:

Property	Example	Description
Kind	Kind:email	Searches all email items
	Kind:meetings	Searches all meeting items
	Kind:tasks	Searches all task items
	Kind:notes	Searches all note items
	Kind:docs	Searches all doc items
	Kind:journals	Searches all journal items
	Kind:contacts	Searches all contact items
	Kind:im	Searches all im items

Examples

If you want to delete all contacts from a mailbox, use the following code:

```
Search-Mailbox -Identity administrator `
-SearchQuery "Kind:Contacts" `
-DeleteContent `
-Force
```

If you want to delete all notes from a mailbox, use the following code:

```
Search-Mailbox -Identity administrator `
-SearchQuery "Kind:Notes" `
-DeleteContent `
-Force
```

Using the logical connector search

The following table outlines the properties that can be used to define an AQS query using a logical connector between two keywords:

Connector	Example	Description
AND	Subject:sales AND Subject: report	Searches for items with both "sales" and "report" in the subject line
OR	Subject:sales OR Subject:report	Searches for items with the word "sales" or "report" in the subject line
NOT	NOT Body:sales Body:(NOT sales)	Searches for items without the word "sales" in the body

Examples

If you want to delete meeting items that have specific content in the body, such as the phrase "Social Security Number", use the following code:

```
Search-Mailbox -Identity administrator `
-SearchQuery 'Body:"Social Security Number" AND Kind:Meeting' `
-DeleteContent `
-Force
```

If you want to perform a discovery search based on keywords used in either the body or subject of the message in a particular mailbox, use the following code:

```
New-MailboxSearch -Name MyTestSearch `
-SourceMailboxes administrator `
-TargetMailbox "Discovery Search Mailbox" `
-SearchQuery 'Body:"Social Security Number" OR Subject:"SSN"' `
-MessageTypes Email `
-IncludeUnsearchableItems `
-LogLevel Full
```

Index

Q

QuotaMessageType parameter 254

R

RBAC
-CustomRecipientWriteScope parameter 315
about 310-312
CustomConfigWriteScope parameter 315
custom RBAC, creating for administrators
   313-315
custom RBAC role, creating for end users
   316-318
for end-users 313
Get-ManagementRoleAssignment cmdlet 315
Mail Recipient Creation role 315
New-ManagementScope cmdlet 315
New-RoleGroup cmdlet 315
RecipientRestrictionFilter parameter 315
Remove-ManagementRoleEntry cmdlet 315
troubleshooting 319
RBAC, troubleshooting
-GetEffectiveUsers parameter 320
-WritableRecipient parameter 320
Default Role Assignment Policy 317
Get-ManagementRoleAssignment cmdlet 320
Get-RoleGroupMember cmdlet 320
RoleAssignmentPolicy cmdlet 318
Set-User cmdlet 316
steps 319, 320
Read-Host cmdlet 68
ReadItems 208
ReceiveConnector cmdlet 242-257
received property 439
recipient
creating in bulk, CSV file used 97-100
email addresses, adding 103-105
email addresses, removing 103-105
filters, working with 100-103
hiding, from address lists 105, 106
moderation, configuring 107-109
recipient e-mail addresses
adding 103-105
removing 103-105
RecipientFilter property 162, 165
recipient filters
working with 100-103

recipient moderation
configuring 107-109
RecipientRestrictionFilter parameter 315
recipient scope
-PreferredGlobalCatalog paramter 66
-RecipientViewRoot 66
-SetPreferredDomainControllers parameter
   66
AdminSessionADSettings global session
   variable 66
Set-AdServerSettings cmdlet 66
used, for managing domains 65, 66
used, for managing forest 65, 66
ViewEntireForest parameter 66
Recipients property 272
RecipientsTo.Add method 397
RecoverableItemsDeletions 403
RecoverableItemsPurges 403
RecoverableItemsRoot 403
RecoverableItemsVersions 403
recovery database
data, restoring from 201, 202
mailbox identity, targeting 203
mailbox restore, request cmdlets 204
parameters 203
RedistributeActiveDatabases.ps1 427
RedistributeActiveDatabases.ps1 script 296
redundancy
reporting on 297-299
Relay connector 257
RemoteIPRanges property 246
remote shell connctions
files, transferring through 61
remote shell connections
-FileData parameter 62
Get-Content cmdlet 62
New-EdgeSubscription cmdlet 62
working 62, 63
Remove-* cmdlets 242
Remove-ADPermission cmdlet 273, 274
Remove-DistributionGroup cmdlet 93
**Remove-DistributionGroupMember cmdlet
   160**
Remove-InboxRule cmdlet 114
Remove-Mailbox cmdlet 89, 356
Remove-MailboxDatabase cmdlet 184, 185
Remove-MailboxItem function 413

Thank you for buying
Microsoft Exchange 2010 PowerShell Cookbook

About Packt Publishing

Packt, pronounced 'packed', published its first book "*Mastering phpMyAdmin for Effective MySQL Management*" in April 2004 and subsequently continued to specialize in publishing highly focused books on specific technologies and solutions.

Our books and publications share the experiences of your fellow IT professionals in adapting and customizing today's systems, applications, and frameworks. Our solution-based books give you the knowledge and power to customize the software and technologies you're using to get the job done. Packt books are more specific and less general than the IT books you have seen in the past. Our unique business model allows us to bring you more focused information, giving you more of what you need to know, and less of what you don't.

Packt is a modern, yet unique publishing company, which focuses on producing quality, cutting-edge books for communities of developers, administrators, and newbies alike. For more information, please visit our website: www.PacktPub.com.

About Packt Enterprise

In 2010, Packt launched two new brands, Packt Enterprise and Packt Open Source, in order to continue its focus on specialization. This book is part of the Packt Enterprise brand, home to books published on enterprise software – software created by major vendors, including (but not limited to) IBM, Microsoft and Oracle, often for use in other corporations. Its titles will offer information relevant to a range of users of this software, including administrators, developers, architects, and end users.

Writing for Packt

We welcome all inquiries from people who are interested in authoring. Book proposals should be sent to author@packtpub.com. If your book idea is still at an early stage and you would like to discuss it first before writing a formal book proposal, contact us; one of our commissioning editors will get in touch with you.

We're not just looking for published authors; if you have strong technical skills but no writing experience, our experienced editors can help you develop a writing career, or simply get some additional reward for your expertise.

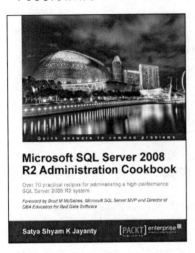

Microsoft SQL Server 2008
R2 Administration Cookbook

Over 70 practical recipes for administering a high-performance
SQL Server 2008 R2 system

Foreword by Brad M McGehee, Microsoft SQL Server MVP and Director of
DBA Education for Red Gate Software

Satya Shyam K Jayanty

Microsoft SQL Server 2008 R2 Administration Cookbook

ISBN: 978-1-84968-144-5   Paperback: 468 pages

Over 70 practical recipes for administering a high-performance SQL Server 2008 R2 system with this book and eBook

1. Provides Advanced Administration techniques for SQL Server 2008 R2 as a book or eBook

2. Covers the essential Manageability, Programmability, and Security features

3. Emphasizes important High Availability features and implementation

4. Explains how to maintain and manage the SQL Server data platform effectively

Microsoft Data Protection
Manager 2010

A practical step-by-step guide to planning deployment,
installation, configuration, and troubleshooting of Data
Protection Manager 2010

Steve Buchanan

Microsoft Data Protection Manager 2010

ISBN: 978-1-84968-202-2   Paperback: 360 pages

A practical step-by-step guide to planning deployment, installation, configuration, and troubleshooting of Data Protection Manager 2010 with this book and eBook

1. A step-by-step guide to backing up your business data using Microsoft Data Protection Manager 2010 in this practical book and eBook

2. Discover how to back up and restore Microsoft applications that are critical in many of today's businesses

3. Understand the various components and features of Data Protection Manager 2010

Please check **www.PacktPub.com** for information on our titles

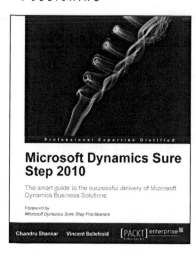

Microsoft Dynamics Sure Step 2010

The smart guide to the successful delivery of Microsoft Dynamics Business Solutions

Foreword by
Microsoft Dynamics Sure Step Practitioners

Chandru Shankar   Vincent Bellefroid   [PACKT] enterprise

Microsoft Dynamics Sure Step 2010

ISBN: 978-1-84968-110-0   Paperback: 360 pages

The smart guide to the successful delivery of Microsoft Dynamics Business Solutions using Microsoft Dynamics Sure Step 2010 with this book and eBook

1. Learn how to effectively use Microsoft Dynamics Sure Step to implement the right Dynamics business solution with quality, on-time and on-budget results

2. Leverage the Decision Accelerator offerings in Microsoft Dynamics Sure Step to create consistent selling motions while helping your customer ascertain the best solution to fit their requirements

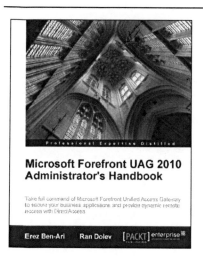

Microsoft Forefront UAG 2010 Administrator's Handbook

Take full command of Microsoft Forefront Unified Access Gateway to secure your business applications and provide dynamic remote access with DirectAccess

Erez Ben-Ari   Ran Dolev   [PACKT] enterprise

Microsoft Forefront UAG 2010 Administrator's Handbook

ISBN: 978-1-84968-162-9   Paperback: 484 pages

Take full command of Microsoft Forefront Unified Access Gateway to secure your business applications and provide dynamic remote access with DirectAccess with this book and eBook

1. Maximize your business results by fully understanding how to plan your UAG integration

2. Consistently be ahead of the game by taking control of your server with backup and advanced monitoring

3. An essential tutorial for new users and a great resource for veterans

Please check **www.PacktPub.com** for information on our titles

Lightning Source UK Ltd.
Milton Keynes UK
UKOW020947190513

210890UK00005B/51/P